AF267424

A Clear Vision to Future Delight

LANDSCAPES and WRITINGS of HAROLD CAPARN FASLA

Second Edition

Oliver Chamberlain

Visit our website at www.StillwaterPress.com for more information.

First Stillwater River Publications Edition

Library of Congress Control Number: 2019920941

ISBN-13: 978-1-950339-74-7

 2 3 4 5 6 7 8 9

Written by Oliver Chamberlain
Cover design by Matthew St. Jean
Published by Stillwater River Publications, Pawtucket, RI, USA.

Publisher's Cataloging-In-Publication Data
(Prepared by The Donohue Group, Inc.)

Names: Chamberlain, Oliver, 1936- author.
Title: A clear vision to future delight : landscapes and writings of Harold Caparn, FASLA, 1890-
    1945 / Oliver Chamberlain.
Description: Second edition. | First Stillwater River Publications edition. | Pawtucket, RI, USA :
    Stillwater River Publications, [2020] | First edition published as: Landscapes and writings of
    Harold Caparn. West Conshohocken, PA : Infinity Publications, 2013, ©2012. | Includes in-
    dex.
Identifiers: ISBN 9781950339747
Subjects: LCSH: Caparn, Harold A. (Harold ap Rhys), 1864-1945--Career in landscape architecture.
    | Landscape architects--United States--Biography. | Landscape architecture--United States--
    History. | LCGFT: Biographies.
Classification: LCC SB470.C36 C53 2020 | DDC 712.092 B--dc23

*The views and opinions expressed in this book are solely those of the author
and do not necessarily reflect the views and opinions of the publisher.*

Preface

Since this book was first published, two of Harold Caparn's important clients for landscape architecture have been identified in Briarcliff Manor, NY, an elite village about thirty miles up the Hudson River from Manhattan. One was an industrialist who built his luxurious estate overlooking the River. The other was a socially active New York City attorney who built a lovely estate and mansion high above the Hudson.

Harold and Clara Caparn lived and worked in Manhattan. Their country retreat, beautifully preserved, has now been found, also in Briarcliff Manor. It will be seen in photos in its original rustic Craftsman style, then with some notable landscape, and finally the home in its more recent lovely extended form.

Also identified, in Westchester County's famed Kensico Cemetery, is the site originally landscaped by Caparn, of a strikingly designed mausoleum commemorating the director of many popular silent films, including that starring *femme fatale* Theda Bara as Cleopatra.

Previously unknown Caparn designs have been discovered for an estate at Onteora Park, NY, in the northern Catskills. For many years tucked away in the attic of the estate cottage, they were discovered by a new owner who carefully preserved them. Details of the garden planting plan and plant list will be illustrated. They give insight to Caparn's vision of what was important to him and to his client.

The garden on another estate at Onteora Park was featured on the cover and in a chapter in the earlier book. It maintains the Caparn garden design but now takes a new approach to the plant material. The new style of garden, featuring native plants, works well with the shingle-style home. The earlier garden and the new planting will both be shown. It is a notable garden evolution often found as garden ageing requires change.

A Web Site in Caparn's name will give links to further information, illustrations, references and sources.

This second edition follows Harold Caparn from his early education as a choirboy and scholar in the English Midlands to further training in London and Paris. He was encouraged by his family to come to America to find employment for his abilities in drawing and horticulture. He quickly found a compatible position with a Pittsburgh nurseryman and garden designer, for whom he created plant lists and drew landscape plans.

After several years of practical experience, he moved to Yonkers, New York, where he established his own office in landscape architecture. From 1902 for four decades, he maintained his Manhattan office and was in the top tier of landscape architects. The high level of Caparn's professional abilities was acknowledged in his election as an early Fellow of the American Society of Landscape Architects (FASLA). He was later elected the Society's eighth President, the first who, though not a founder, was elected by those charter members.

Harold Caparn will be seen in this book, through his leadership in the field, his extensive writing and the variety and quality of his works, as a pioneer landscape artist who shaped some significant American landscapes.

The author's interest in this subject began as a child. My family lived in Jenkintown, PA, where my father was superintendent of growing and grounds for the estate of Lessing J. Rosenwald, former Chairman of Sears Roebuck. Harold's younger brother Arthur T. Caparn and his family lived in Short Hills, NJ, where he was at some time estate superintendent for Stewart Hartshorn, founder of that community. I met Harold several times when he visited from New York City at my grandfather Arthur's home. My father, a florist and grower, my grandfather, a nurseryman and gardener, and my grand-uncle, Harold, had extensive conversations about their work on gardens and in judging flower shows and other's gardens. Their companionable talks introduced me to their passion for the field and attracted my continued interest.

I got to know Harold's daughter, Rhys, as my own family and I traveled to New England for summer vacations. We would stop at her home in Newtown, CT, where we had wonderful conversations about her work in sculpture and mine in music. She gave me some of her father's writing on music in 1980. Her executor had saved and gave me, in 2005, the remaining small archive of Harold's materials that included his client list. My research, beginning with that list, became the basis for this book. As a music historian researching compositional designs, I had interest not only in engaging in the family field of horticulture, but in design considerations that extended beyond gardens to estates, parks and villages. The results I found of Harold Caparn's work rewarded the search.

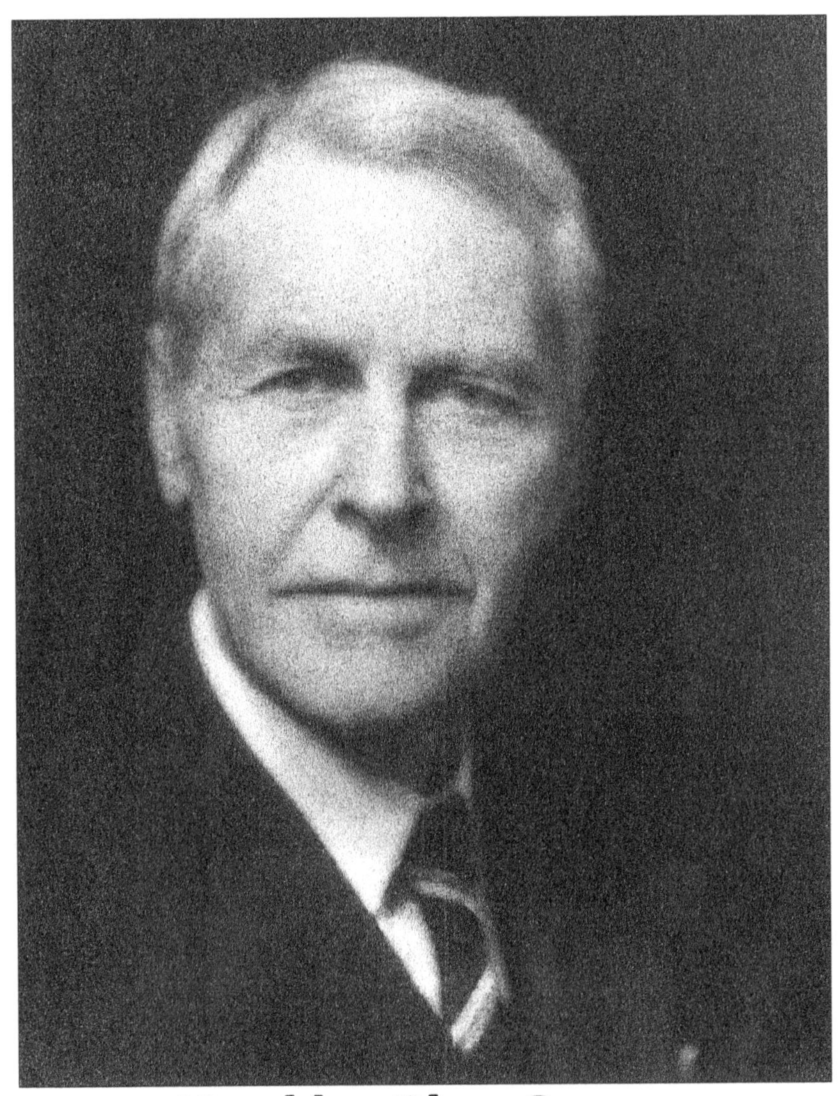

Harold ap Rhys Caparn
(1864-1945)

Fellow, American Society of Landscape Architects, 1905
President, American Society of Landscape Architects, 1911-12

To Kathryn beloved
Umma and guide of our pride
Elizabeth, James, Margaret, Carolyn,
and the grands of great affection
Autumn, Samuel, Ryan, Quinn, Regan.

Delight in friends and family
Develop your clear vision
Persevere with courage,
Accomplish as you can
Tarry not on the rest.

Keep love alive.

A Clear Vision to Future Delight
Landscapes and Writings of Harold Caparn FASLA
Second Edition

Contents

A Clear Vision to Future Delight

Appendices

Prelude

On Monday, January 16th, 1922, *The New York Times* published Harold Caparn's
first salvo against New York's political spoils system. In his article "Park Administration," he stated forcefully that city parks needed to be put under the governance of
a select volunteer Board of Directors that had oversight of a professional Park Superintendent. Such a board was in direct opposition to the spoils system that
awarded the position of Park Superintendent, without competent oversight, to a
crony of the Mayor.

Caparn's goal was to save from blatant neglect the built vision of Central Park's art-
ist-designers, Frederick Law Olmsted and Calvert Vaux. He felt it imperative to save
the swath of green that unfolded informally in lawns, lakes and eye-pleasing vistas,
not only because of its beauty, but because of the necessary and refreshing pleasure
it provided to the many inhabitants and visitors to New York City. Caparn recognized that political favoritism had resulted in the continuing decline over more than
two decades of what he saw as "the greatest park in the world."

Real estate developers and wealthy entrepreneurs, however, saw that valuable land
was being used freely by the vast public without any compensation to the city. They
wanted to construct, in park space, buildings that were practical, commercial and
could return revenue to themselves and, perhaps, the city.

Following Caparn's election in 1911, as President of the American Society of Landscape Architects, he published a number of letters and an article about the plight of
New York's parks. Now, a decade later, he took a hard look at the issue he saw as
the root of park problems. Directly opposed to his approach, of a Park Superintendent overseen by a volunteer Board, was the Landscape Architect of New York City,
Charles Downing Lay, who criticized Caparn's proposal, saying: "Such a scheme is
so foreign to our feelings, and so revolutionary. Why?" Indeed, how did Caparn
arrive at his solution for the parks of New York?

Caparn's action and his writing about Central Park was only one of a number of
public issues that engaged him during his career in New York City. His public leadership put him at the forefront of debates on significant issues. He wrote letters and
articles, participated actively in organizations, spoke out clearly and forcefully and
led the way to influence thinking and find solutions to public problems.

Meanwhile, he earned his living designing a number of private and several significant public landscapes. One of his extant publicly accessible works, designed in 1900, is the New York Zoological Park (Bronx Zoo) and its grand Entrance Concourse and central court. The Entrance and Baird, later Astor Court, with landscape designed by Caparn and buildings designed by Heins and LaFarge, is now a designated New York City Landmark.

Caparn was the town planner and landscape architect of Village 1 in Sheffield, Alabama, built by the Federal government during 1918 to provide essential support to the American effort in the First World War. He laid out the Village lots, streets and parks in a symbolic design that expressed the hope for victory by England and America. It is now on the National Register of Historic Places.

In January 1912, Caparn was appointed consulting landscape architect to the Brooklyn Botanic Garden, a position he held until his retirement in the summer of 1945. He designed, among others, the famed Cranford Rose Garden, the beautiful Magnolia Plaza, the gracious Lily Pool Terrace and the impressive Osborne Garden. He laid out a large portion of the Botanic Garden now known as the Plant Family Collection. Caparn's designs for the Zoo, the Village and the Garden are among his works that can still be seen.

Caparn was also interested in the development of state parks that were representative of their region's flora, fauna, natural resources and history. Two of his earlier influential papers and a talk on state parks were published in *A State Park Anthology* for the National Conference on State Parks held in 1930 at Washington, D.C. His ideas and interest continued to have an impact on the purpose, organization and development of the growing number of state parks across the country.

In 1926, at the invitation of the Superintendent of Yellowstone National Park, he consulted on issues along the Bechler River. Out of that experience came several articles. He stated the important artistic premise that majestic wonder-inspiring scenery could only be fully appreciated, from a distance, when the foreground was uninterrupted by any man-made obstruction. That artistic principle holds true whether the vista is seen over a lawn, a meadow, or a valley.

We will look at Harold Caparn's background in a family of nurserymen, his education in England and France, his experience in creating some lasting landscapes, his leadership in the profession and his thoughtful writing that led to a critical point in the life of Central Park. We will look at Caparn's writings in some detail as they illustrate his battles to save Central Park from the forays against it by general citizenry, business leaders and city politicians. The path he took, after the publication of his article on park administration, would lead toward major advances in Central Park's future as one of New York City's outstanding attractions.

Caparn's remaining office and personal materials do not allow for an exploration of each of his landscapes nor a full biography. This study is based on what remains of his landscape works on the ground, in his and other's descriptive writing, and in plans and photographs. Events in his life have been garnered from the small variety of materials available. The book features some of his work that is extant and can be seen and studied.

Caparn's approach to landscape design benefitted from the successes of Frederick Law Olmsted and the Olmsted firm managed by sons John Charles and Frederick, Jr., and their associates. Caparn, though not a student of Olmsted, nor a member of the firm, espoused the natural, informal approach to design found in many of Olmsted's works. Caparn's landscapes and writings, from 1900 to 1940, place him in the midst of other pioneers who were also developers of this American art form.

1 England to America

Education, family, early employment...1864--1897

Harold ap Rhys Caparn was born on Sunday, December 18, 1864 in the market town of Newark on Trent in Nottinghamshire in the English Midlands.[1] His parents were Ann Elizabeth (Price) Caparn (1830-1912), an intelligent and engaging woman and Thomas John Caparn (1834-1925), a nursery owner, exhibiting painter and award-winning landscape designer.

Harold's middle name, ap Rhys, (pronounced apreece) derived from the Welsh heritage of his mother's male ancestors. It signified that Harold was a "son of Price." His father's forebears can be traced in the region back to the late sixteenth century. Caparn family members were industrious, had been in town service and politics, and although not of a high-born position, were of above-average means. As an adult, Harold capitalized the middle initial "A" for his articles and landscape plans, but wrote out "ap Rhys" when signing official documents.[2]

Harold was educated at the Magnus Grammar School in Newark, founded in the early sixteenth century by Thomas Magnus, emissary of King Henry VIII. When Magnus endowed the Grammar School he also endowed the Song School for training of the choir at the principal town church of St. Mary Magdalene.[3] Harold attended the Magnus School and sang in the choir at St. Mary Magdalene from about age nine through age eighteen.[4]

Harold's uncle, William Horner Caparn, Jr. (1828-1881), was the Music Master at Magnus Grammar School and the organist and choirmaster at Christ Church in Newark. He was also the conductor of the town orchestra and chorus. Harold studied piano and organ with him and performed in his uncle's "house concerts."[5]

Harold's father, Thomas John Caparn, an artist in watercolors and oils and owner of a prosperous nursery, tutored his son in drawing and horticulture. Uncle Thomas also tutored William John Caparn (later Caparne), William Horner, Jr.'s son, in painting and horticulture.[6] William pursued a meaningful life in painting and the development and sale of species of irises from his later home on the Isle of Guernsey.

Harold's family also showed interest in intellectual pursuits, reading Darwin on the evolution of species, Dickens on social conditions of the day and the great seventeenth-century philosopher John Locke on human knowledge, individual liberty and religious tolerance.[7] These interests surfaced later in Harold's life and work.

Harold had done well academically at Magnus Grammar School and was rigorously trained in the choir school at St. Mary Magdalene. Between his schooling and university, Harold spent about four years as a tutor at St. Edmund's School, Canterbury.[8] The School provided education to the young choristers who sang a full week of services at Canterbury Cathedral, seat of the Archbishop of Canterbury, principal primate of the Anglican Church.

Harold was selected for the position of tutor because of his academic accomplishments and as a singer in the Cathedral choir for his musical abilities. This experience led later in life to his critical writing about performances that he attended in New York City. His early musical training and experience was also a factor in meeting Clara Howard (Jones) Royall, a musician and well-known voice teacher in New York City, who became his wife.

Harold's educational progress is seen in a certificate of matriculation from the University of London given in June 1886, when he was age twenty-one. The quality of his previous learning is evident, as he was placed in the First Division.[9]

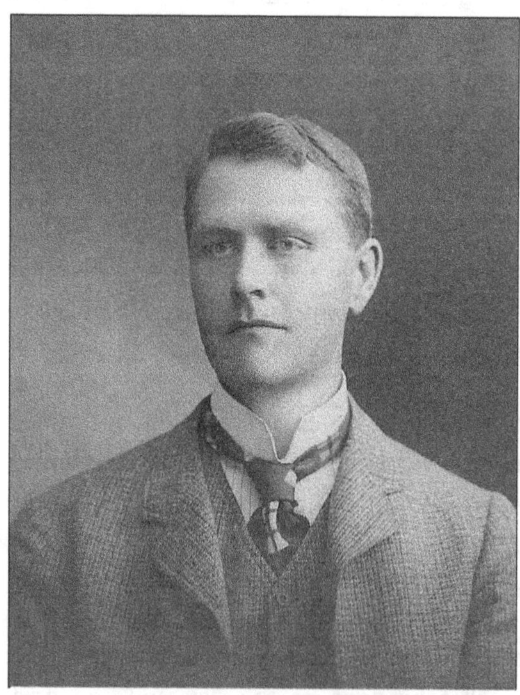

1.1 Harold Caparn, c. 1889, age 25.

He next studied architecture in Paris at the prestigious Ecole des Beaux-Arts. The city and the school were at the center of arts and culture from the early nineteenth century through the early twentieth century. English, European and American students went there to develop and refine their talents. Harold was a student there in the late 1880s before curricula existed in landscape architecture. The study of architecture provided an opportunity for him to consider principles of design in the close relative of landscape architecture.[10]

After his schooling in England and France, Harold immigrated to the United States, arriving on September 23, 1889 (illus. 1.1). In so doing he joined others who had received training at the Ecole des Beaux-Arts. He was to work professionally with several of them in New York City.[11]

Harold's family and their influence

Harold's ancestors in the Caparn family were well-known in Newark on Trent during the eighteenth and nineteenth centuries. The family name, after many variants, settled into the present spelling early in the second half of the eighteenth century.[12]

Harold's grandfather, William Horner Caparn (1804-1872), was influential in the early formation of Harold's life. William was for many years parish clerk of St. Mary Magdalene and was respected in the community as a businessman, Secretary of the local Savings Bank and owner of a large flourishing nursery.[13] Harold learned early from his grandfather and father about plant, shrub and tree identification and growing cycles. It is likely that Harold's grandfather encouraged him to attend the Magnus School in Newark.

By 1854, William Horner's son, Thomas John Caparn, was following in his father's footsteps and was supporting himself with a nursery of his own. In addition, he showed an interest and ability at drawing in his teens.[14] Soon he was exhibiting and selling his paintings. It would become a life-long pastime.

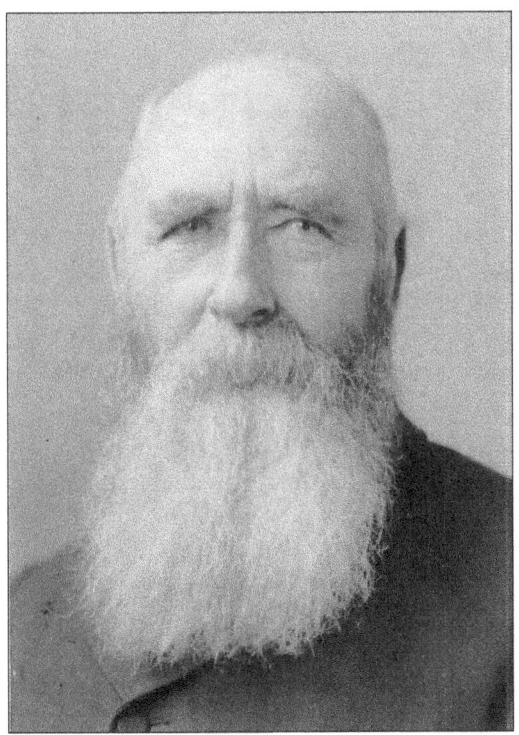

1.2 *Thomas John Caparn, c. 1909,* age 75.

Thomas married Ann Elizabeth Price on August 12, 1863, at the Parish Church of Oundle in the Midlands. As an adult, she aptly managed her husband's wide-ranging interests and also the varied interests of their five children born in Newark on Trent: Harold ap Rhys (1864-1945), Margaret Jane (1866-1940), Arthur Tom (1867-1954), Annie Smith (1869-1952), and Ethel Rose Caroline (1872-1918).[15]

In the year of Harold's birth his father gave first notice of his abilities at garden design. Thomas offered, at Caparn Nursery, flowers, shrubs, fruiting vines and trees and also "designs for every description of ornamental gardening and garden architecture. Plans, elevations and working specifications." Thomas was soon actively engaged in garden and estate design for the landed gentry around Newark on Trent.[16]

By the next year his nursery and design business was large enough to advertise "Furnishing plans for flower and pleasure gardens, ornamental croquet lawns in the most complete style. The only prize in Class 366 (garden design) at the Great International Exhibition, London (1862), was awarded to Thomas John Caparn"[17]

On the death of William Horner Caparn, Sr. in 1872, Thomas combined his own nursery with that of his father, thereby operating one of the largest such enterprises in the Midlands. Like his father, in the previous year he had been named Actuary of the Newark Savings Bank and also later became Secretary of the Bank. In 1873, he opened an office as "Professional Accountant, Estate Agent and Trustee in Bankruptcy." He later expanded that business to three offices. In January 1874, at the same location as the estate business, he opened "Caparn's Seed Shop." With flowers grown in his nursery he won prizes at local and regional flower shows and was a judge at many of them. Throughout his life he showed extraordinary ability at business, although painting seemed his passion.

Landscape Gardening.

THOMAS CAPARN,
Landscape and Marine Artist.

ARTHUR CAPARN,
Professional Landscape Gardner,

CAPARN & SON,

Landscape Gardeners

AND

Horticultural Architects,

are now prepared to receive commands for all classes of Landscape Gardening, including the laying out of Parks, Ornamental Pleasure Grounds, Carriage Drives, Rustic Work.
GREENHOUSES AND CONSERVATORIES AFTER THE MOST IMPROVED EUROPEAN STYLES AND SYSTEM OF HEATING.
The principal prize for Landscape Gardening Design in class 366, at the Royal International Exhibition, London, was awarded to Mr. Thomas Caparn, for beauty and completeness of design.
Ground plans, working drawings and colered elevations in Isometrical Perspective furnished where desired. Special attention given to parcelling out land for building lots and new roads. The systems of Price, Repton, London and Newfield adhered to in all designs for parks and ornamental planting.

Box 31, Milburn, N. J.

1.3 Advertisement, The Budget, June 1886, Millburn, NJ.

Thomas Caparn left England in 1884 at age fifty with his wife and four younger children and settled in Short Hills, New Jersey, where he purchased property.[18] His younger son, Arthur Tom Caparn, developed his own nursery and worked in Short Hills in a supervisory role for the large nursery firm Pitcher and Manda, United States Nurseries. They were an extensive exhibitor at the 1893 Columbian Exposition in Chicago. At some time Arthur also worked as estate gardener for Stewart Hartshorn, founder of Short Hills. He exhibited at flower shows in the name of the Hartshorn estate.

Thomas John, with his son, built a partnership designing and installing gardens. An advertisement in the local newspaper (1.3) indicates that father and son were knowledgeable in some of the most important garden literature of the period including that of Price, London (sic), Newfield and the influential ideas of the renowned English garden writer and designer Humphry Repton.[19] See appendix, illustration 1.3.

Thomas J. Caparn of Summit, New Jersey, is described in an 1894 article in *The New York Times* as a landscape architect. Thomas' long interest in garden design was fully realized in his new homeland when by 1899, at age sixty-five, he had an office at 925 Broad Street, Newark, New Jersey, as a landscape architect.[20] At the same time his son, Harold, had recently opened his office as a landscape architect in Yonkers, New York.

Just as Thomas John outdistanced his father as a nurseryman, turning also to garden design, so Harold ap Rhys would soon outdistance his father in accomplishments as a landscape architect. Thomas lived, however, to see his son elected President of the ASLA, become a published author of many articles and appointed consulting landscape architect to the Brooklyn Botanic Garden. Thomas John Caparn died at Overlook Hospital, Summit, New Jersey, on June 23, 1925, at age ninety-one.[21]

First employment in America

Harold Caparn arrived in America in the early fall of 1889, about three months before his twenty-fifth birthday. Very likely his family communicated with him about opportunities in America. It is assumed that he was employed before the active spring nursery season of 1890 by James Wilkinson Elliott, nurseryman and landscape gardener of Pittsburgh, Pennsylvania.[22] He applied his knowledge of architecture (drawing garden designs) and horticulture (developing plant lists) for the Elliott Nursery until the fall of 1897. At that time he struck out to set up his own office in Yonkers, NY, where we find him in early 1898, writing to *The New York Times*.[23]

While working for the Elliott Nursery he took the opportunity to develop further his own approach to landscape design. It is likely that he had discussions with J. Wilkinson Elliott and possibly also with his father Benjamin A. Elliott, a nurseryman and landscape gardener, about the books and ideas on gardening of

William Robinson, particularly *The Wild Garden* (1870) and *The English Flower Garden* (1883) that influenced the Elliotts. They, with Caparn, agreed on the importance of an informal approach to garden design and the central place in it of hardy plants.[24]

Caparn's work in landscape architecture for J. Wilkinson Elliott is found in a proposed design by Caparn that Elliott selected to include in his book *A Plea for Hardy Plants* (1902). It seems unlikely that Elliott would have included a Caparn design unless he could select from a number of such designs.[25]

Caparn's knowledge of horticulture, learned in his father's nursery, would have been wholly acceptable to Elliott, who learned horticulture in the same way, in the nursery of his father. Additionally, they both viewed landscape design as an art derived from the observation of nature. During his time in Pittsburgh, Caparn could test his own ideas about design and perhaps carry out some directly in commissions for the Elliott Nursery.

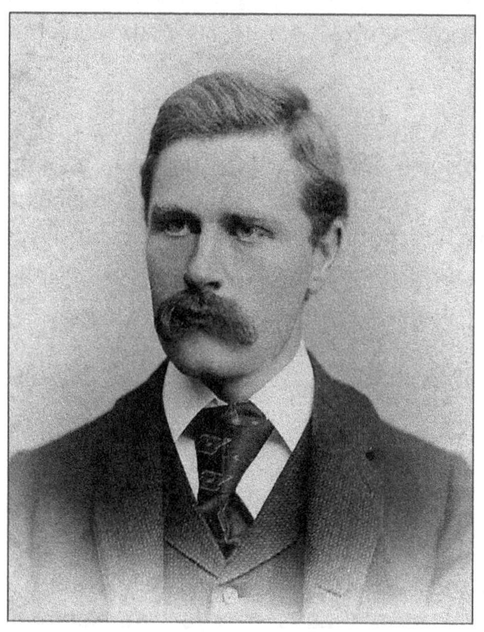

1.4 *Harold Caparn, c. 1897, age 33*

While he worked for Elliott, Caparn contributed five articles to *Garden and Forest*, the leading horticultural journal of the day. His first article, written at age twenty-eight, was published in December 1893. It shows him thinking and writing about the composition of landscape design on the ground and in elevation. Three years later he applied some of those ideas in his suggested improvements to the design of Madison Square Park in New York City. The illustration to that article in *Garden and Forest* in 1896 was his first published landscape ground plan.

J. Wilkinson Elliott had visited, on a trip to England about 1885, with gardener and author William Robinson and later hosted him in Pittsburgh. Elliott, in his book *Adventures of a Horticulturist* (1935) quotes Robinson as saying, "An artistic garden is the rarest thing in the world." No doubt Caparn and Elliott had discussions along those lines; both expressed that idea in their writings. Elliott shows himself to be knowledgeable and discerning as a garden designer.

After several of his own garden plans, Elliott gave space in his book, *A Plea for Hardy Plants,* for a design (illus. 1.5) and plant list by Caparn, of which he says,

"The accompanying plan, designed by Mr. Caparn, I think an especially good one—very original and artistic—and, properly carried out, would make a very charming garden."

Elliott also presented Caparn's explanation of the plan, in part:

> By placing the house in the corner (of the 2 ½ acre lot) the greatest possible extent of unbroken lawn space is secured while the porch fronting the lawn is as private as it could be on a place of this size. The lawn runs up to the house unimpaired by any stripes of arid pavement, and the lines of the house are relieved only by the creepers covering it (Boston ivy on the wall and clematises, wisterias and Hall's Honeysuckles on the porches) and the tall conifers to the south of the house.
>
> The carpet-bedding on each side of the entrance court is justified by the formal lines of building and macadam which it supplements. The shrubbery behind it sets it off and separates it from the main part of the grounds. The interest and value of the vegetable garden (top of plan) could be added to by borders of annuals, herbaceous and tender plants for cut-flowers, grape-vines, and dwarf fruits.

Caparn shows, in an explanation of "picturesqueness," his background with English gardens and writers. His use of "carpet bedding," while here appropriate, was much under discussion at the time. His placement of the house at the corner of the lot in order to achieve a broader lawn and plantings was a theme he continued to develop in later writings and ground plans.

Plant list (cued to plan 1.5)
1. Japan maples
2. Retinispora obtuse
3. Yulan magnolia
4. Magnolia parviflora
5. Shrubbery, with small trees and groups of large herbaceous plants in margins.
6. Oriental spruce
7. Rolllison's arborvitaes, or golden retinisporas
8. Nordmann's fir
9. Scarlet maple
10. Andromeda arborea
11. Balsam fir
12. Norway spruce
13. Colorado blue spruce
14. Purple beech
15. Irish juniper and beds of herbaceous plants
16. Vine-covered summer house (top left)

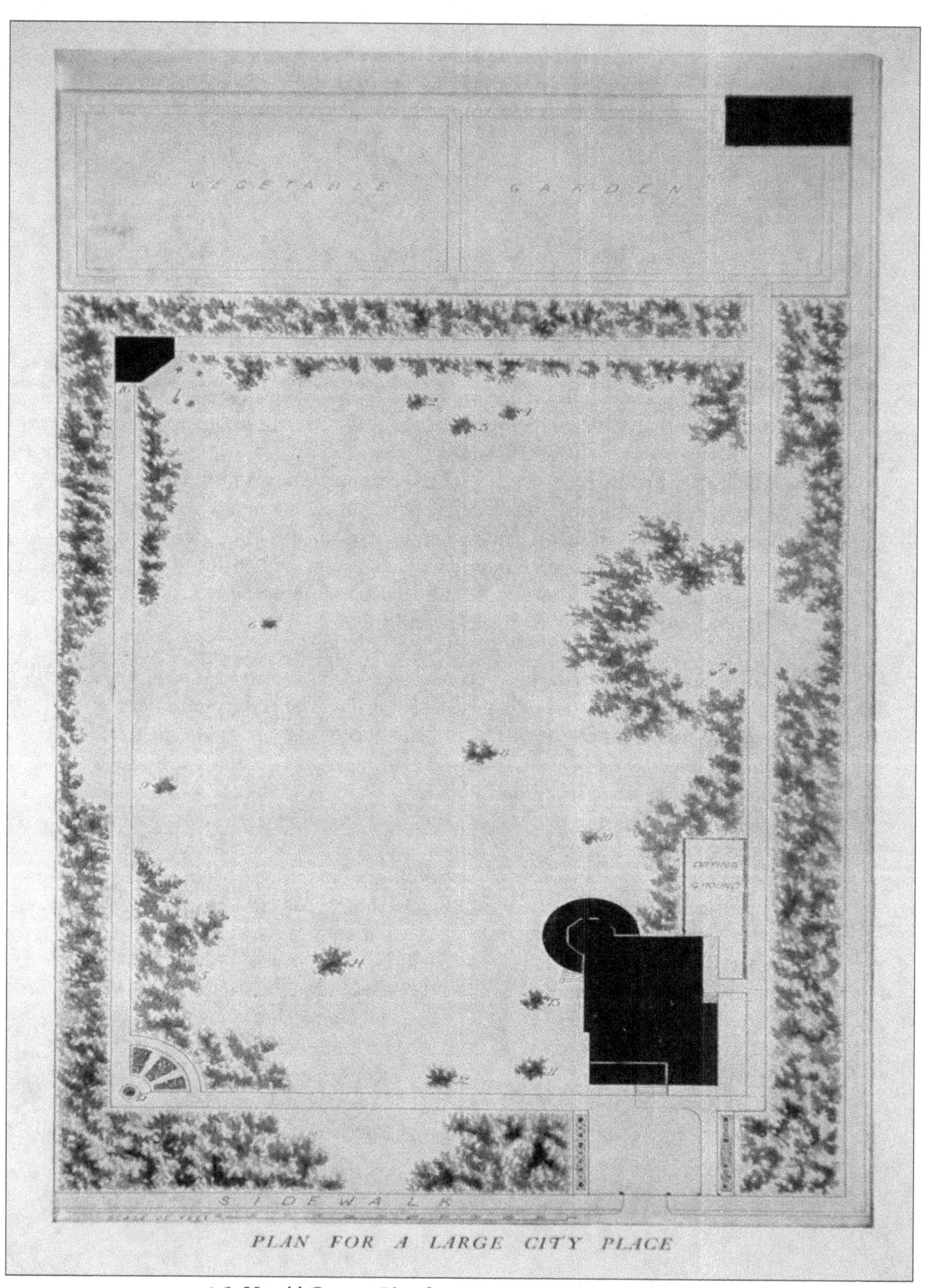

1.5 Harold Caparn, Plan for a Large City Place, published 1902

2 Articles and Letters

An introduction to his writing...1893–1945

In addition to contributing artistic landscapes on the ground, Harold also undertook thoughtful consideration of the subject in his writings. He wrote more than one hundred and twenty articles from 1893 to 1945 that were published in over thirty-five learned journals and popular magazines. Some were concise well-stated remarks of a page or two. Some were instructive as to selecting plant material, growing and maintaining plants, or designing for a garden, home or park. A few were longer with a sweep of history or control of the subject that make them worthy additions to the literature, such as his articles on planning a botanic garden and on the founding of the American Society of Landscape Architects.

His writing carried weight in the contentious debates over issues regarding portions of Yellowstone and Grand Teton National Parks, Niagara Falls State Park and also of Central Park, New York City, as to what should be kept out and what must be preserved.

At the beginning of his career, at age twenty-eight, he arrived at a mature definition and description of the informal approach to garden design. It is seen in his first article, "Composition in Landscape-art," published in *Garden & Forest* (December 1893). The article provides a strong indication of his sensibilities when he compared the landscape artist with those of painting, sculpture and music.

He accepted Beaux-Arts classicism and formal, architecture-based design as a possible approach. His first article, however, and a number of those that followed developed the natural, informal, observation-based approach found in some painters and learned directly from nature.

His later writings reveal his close observation of gardens in France and Italy during his travels there. He was already familiar, through his father and his reading, with the English approach to making natural gardens. This approach was not without principles; they may have been difficult to discern, but he set out to define and explicate them in his writing.

Some of his articles were of enough interest that they were reprinted. Several reprinted during his lifetime included his two articles and a talk on the mission and administration of state parks. They came at a time, well after the national parks development, when state parks were beginning to find acceptance. They were reprinted (1930) for a national conference on state parks in Washington, D.C. He wrote a series of fourteen articles for the journal *Arts and Decoration* (1936-37) on planning various aspects of a yard and garden. The series, less an article on an architectural feature, was reprinted as *A Garden For You* a month after his death.

He wrote letters to editors of two major New York newspapers. He wrote seventy letters to *The New York Times* from 1898 to 1941 on a wide variety of subjects. They will be taken up as they apply in various chapters. He wrote twice to the journal *Landscape Architecture*, at least ten times to the *New York Herald Tribune* on such topics as poor farming practices that produced soil erosion and against coal smoke that produced air pollution, before the introduction of smoke scrubbers.

He provided significant support for maintaining Jackson Hole National Monument as a reserved area. When the debate in Congress threatened to abolish it, he supported its designation in a letter to the *New York Herald Tribune* (written June 23, published July 9, 1944) followed by a number of journal articles. The letter showed his continuing interest in conservation a year before his retirement at age eighty. The letter and articles led to further extension of Jackson Hole and the donation of adjoining lands which continued to grow Grand Teton National Park.

His last letter to the Editor of the *NY Herald Tribune*, in January 1945, "Choking on Smoke" complained, as he had previously, on the deleterious effects of coal smoke on all the neighborhoods and especially to plants in the Brooklyn Botanic Garden.

His last brief article, in *Plants and Gardens*, in July 1945, was on the layout of a small front yard with a plan, a subject he had taken up previously when the Great Depression turned landscape architect's attention from estates to small properties. Following WWII, with many homes constructed and plots to be planted, the consideration as to how to enhance their home was again on the minds of many. Caparn responded.

3 Informal Landscape Design
The central theme...1893–1940

Overarching all his writing was the theme of the informal style of landscape design, which he said, "everyone does, but is little understood." He saw it as a problem to be held up, examined and discussed. His writing on the topic was lucid and insightful, resulting in a rationale for what he considered the general superiority of the informal over the formal manner of design.

Caparn wrote seven articles on landscape composition or design focusing on the informal style. He wrote because he felt the principles of the informal style were more elusive than the formal style and therefore needed greater discussion and support of its principles. They required more effort to obtain understanding in both the practitioner and the viewer.

His earliest article, in 1893, was on this subject and he continued writing on it until 1940. The first article was in *Garden and Forest*, the leading American journal focused on horticulture, landscape design and forestry. The article presented many ideas well-formed that he continued to explain and illustrate over the years. The influence of his father, a painter and garden designer may be understood in his references to "the artist of the brush" and his pictorial imagery.

In his work, Caparn applied either the informal or the formal style of design appropriately in response to the requirements of the site and the client. In his writing, however, he focused on the informal style. Like other visual artists, his concern was how to employ the elements of his art: light that emphasizes and the lack of it, shade, that creates mystery; lines that curve and those that are straight and the relative use and effect of each; the treatment of surface and texture and the proper employment of the range of colors that was being used in gardens of his time.

He gave careful consideration to what should be most important and what subordinate or irrelevant. Everything, he felt, should be in proportion and balance, yet the elements may be irregular in their relationships and not on a controlling axis. Complexity may be found in the overall form that is created by grouping, by the play of differing textures and by repetition and variety. Yet he strove for simplicity and clarity. His aim was to create a place, with the materials available, that would provide exercise for the body and delight for the mind. His further aim was to create an artistic space and a sense of repose, attributes that he found rare in garden design.

In no art more than in landscape-gardening is the sense of repose so necessary to good composition. To this nothing will contribute but the conception of the whole, essentially complete from the first. Each addition must be made with restraint and without uncertainty of purpose, or it will destroy the unity it is intended to create, and so fatally injure any realizing of a consistent and complete design. (*Garden and Forest*, 1893)

The principles of the informal style are primarily those of common sense and repose. It is manifestly inconsistent with common sense that a path should wind for the sake of winding, or that it should take any direction plainly inconvenient. Roads and paths generally do wind to a greater or less extent in the informal style because they are adapted to the contour of the ground and become curved for the sake of a moderate grade and ease of construction, or to avoid defacing a lawn, or to get grace of line, or to lead past objects of interest. To litter an open space with casual and impertinent objects, whether bushes or not, is plainly destructive of repose, and in fact, of artistic effect in general. One of the salient features of the informal style is the unbroken lawn, large or small, interesting and various from its lights and shadows and contours and its setting of foliage. (*Architectural Record*, 1903)

The forms, proportions, and sequence of flowers in a meadow, trees in a forest, the foliage or flower masses and the intervening voids of individual plants, the repetition and irregular yet purposeful groupings of all these may suggest motifs. We may surely rely on them when we arrange our trees, shrubs, and perennials, or lawns and plantations, foliage masses and open spaces. No rules can be formulated for the proportions of subordinate masses or broken-off pieces. Nor can any precise instructions be given for imitating them. But any time spent on copying them with pencil or brush (the only real way to become acquainted with their forms) will be so much pure gain, and will react in originality, vigor, and sureness in one's own compositions. (*Landscape Archtecture*, 1929)

The informal composition lacks the vanishing points (of architectural ocomposition), but it has the seeming diminishing distances of its component features—foliage masses, buildings, etc., so grouped or disposed as to lead the eye from one to the next whether it travels in front of or behind the feature. And it has what is denied to the architectural design: the motion of its curved floor.

This curved floor is perhaps the greatest and most subtle charm of an informal composition. Even though it may not be noticed, it is always felt; and when one can get a rise in the contours silhouetted against a shadow or foliage mass, it is very clearly perceived. The most vital effect of the curved floor appears when the sun is low and the long tree shadows give clear form and emphasis to the modeling of the surface. (*Landscape Architecture*, 1940).

4 Client List

An introduction to his landscape works...1898–1945

Starting in 1898 in Yonkers, New York and for the rest of his life, Harold Caparn worked as a one-man firm, with only secretarial help. In 1902 he moved his office to downtown Manhattan, which brought him into closer contact with those who might employ his services.[1] In the 1920 edition of *Country Life in America*, he is shown among other landscape architects well-known in the field, all in formal poses, while he is shown informally working at his desk (4.1).[2]

Perhaps he meant the photograph to illustrate his approach to his work. He personally provided an assessment of each client's site, heard their desires for treatment, proposed solutions and drew plans; he selected plants, shrubs and trees to fulfill his vision for the site. He convinced the client of his vision and oversaw installation of it to his satisfaction. The breadth of commissions that he accomplished, though not great in number, were uniquely his.

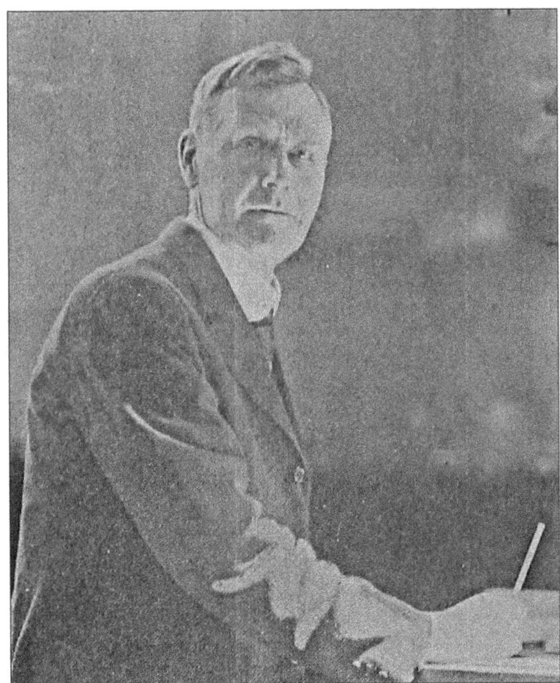

4.1 Harold Caparn (1920) "Landscape Architects Who Have Designed Gardens for Some of Our Great Country Estates."

Caparn's four-page client list, that provides the key to his landscape work, was among the materials kept after his death by his daughter Rhys. It is an important primary source for an attempt to develop a comprehensive view of his work, since the usual office materials no longer exist. Entries on the four pages are numbered starting at 488 and lead consecutively to 667, a total of 179 items. The list begins typewritten, but trails off at the end into a number of handwritten items, seemingly in a last attempt to capture them. The full client list, with his job numbering, by category of work, and with notes about those that are known, can be found in the Appendix.

The client list starts curiously not at number 1 but at 488, giving "New York Zoological Park." That was an early job starting as a consultation in 1899, a year after his move from Pittsburgh to Yonkers. As a large, multi-year job in an impressive public space, he gives pride of place at the beginning of his client list to the Zoological Park, which quickly became popularly known as the Bronx Zoo.

But what happened to the items prior to 488? Perhaps he retrospectively considered that previous work in England--where he may have done some early designs with his father, a nurseryman and garden designer, in Paris--where he likely did designs while studying architecture there, and in Pittsburgh--where he did designs for his employer, a nurseryman and landscape gardener—there were plans that he didn't need to itemize. He may have felt that starting at that point in the list brought him into professional comparison with larger firms or some whose client list indicated more jobs than were completed.

Two items have surfaced other than those enumerated. The earliest is a plan suggested by an article in *Garden and Forest* (1896) for Madison Square Park in New York City. Caparn made the plan in response to a plea in that journal for a better solution to the design of the park from well-known writer on gardens and landscapes Mariana Griswold Van Rensselaer.

The other is a plan for an urban lot, published in J. Wilkinson Elliott's book, *A Plea for Hardy Plants*, after Caparn had left his employ. Both of these were proposed solutions to problems, not plans for direct implementation. In addition, about seven plans have come from other sources, they will be given at the end of client list jobs categorized in the Appendix and noted at the end of this chapter.

Most entries on the client list are not connected to a city and none have dates. Only one entry, for the architect Leon Gillette, has the penciled notation "no plan," so it might reasonably be assumed that other numbered jobs involved one or more plans and that the reference to Gillette was for a significant consultation.

Entries such as those for "Washington" (490) and "Central Park" (627) may not refer to landscape work, but to his considerable research and writing on those subjects about 1901-1903 and 1924-1928 respectively. His article "The Development of Washington," (*American Architect and Building News,* 1903), gives an idealized plan. His list gives the "HR Office Building," (655) for the House of Representatives in Washington, D.C. It appears to be for the design of planting the Cannon Office Building, as seen in a photograph.

There is a general chronological progression of work in his list, but after a little study it does not seem organized in that manner. For example, the entry for the Onteora Garden Club (622), is for work between 1920-1922 as a plan in the Onteora Library records, while that for Maitland F. Griggs' estate at Ardsley on

Hudson (623) was most likely done around 1910 at the time his home was built or shortly thereafter. Several photographs of the Griggs estate exist from the 1920s, however, they show mature plantings.

The last page, repeating some items from the third page, is written on the back of a piece of Brooklyn Botanic Garden stationary announcing that flowers are in bloom; the stationary carries the date 1945 in the summer just before his death in September at age eighty. His daughter Rhys may have assisted him in recalling and writing additional entries.

Many of the clients can be identified, but not the work that was done. Some may remain elusive because no records have been kept, or the work itself has changed over the succeeding years. In an effort to date some of his works, we will at various points in the chapters explore the facts and events surrounding who commissioned the work and the site itself.

From his client list, his articles and other sources, as given in the Appendix, we see that Caparn did designs for twenty-five or more public parks and gardens or related kinds of work—including grounds of two golf clubhouses and the small park-like areas surrounding several public memorials. He did work for two churches, both now on the National Register of Historic Places, St. Philip in the Highlands, at Garrison, N.Y., and Christ Church, at New Brighton on Staten Island. No landscape plans exist at either church.

He did work for several businesses including the H. P. Sinclaire Co. in Corning, N.Y., manufacturer of cut glass at the apex of that form's popularity and for the Thayer chain of hotels, of which one during the period was at West Point on the grounds of the United States Military Academy.

Caparn did about nine real estate projects in which he laid out streets and lots, including part of a residential village at Ithaca, New York; industrial villages in Bridgeport, Connecticut; government housing villages at Tuscumbia, Florence and Sheffield in Alabama and the campus for a biological laboratory on Long Island. He designed two significant health care campuses in New York State at Wilton and Utica and portions of college campuses at Annville, Pennsylvania and Brooklyn, New York.

His client list includes work on the grounds of estates or homes for at least 110 persons. Of Caparn's individual clients that can be identified, many worked in New York City, had homes there or in the tri-state region of New Jersey, New York and Connecticut. There emerges from these a broad picture of the significance of the jobs he undertook and the elevated social, political, professional and economic status of his clientele, often told in *New York Times* articles.

A few works are here added to the client list from other sources.

To Public Parks, can be included Columbus Park in Yonkers, from an article by him; the Treat Memorial in Landing Park, Newark, from a plan in the files of the Olmsted firm; and the grounds surrounding the Club House and Theatre from a plan at the Onteora Park Library.

To Businesses, inferred from a letter from Caparn's attorney, Albert Sprague Bard to F. Donald Coster, the head of McKesson & Robbins, a pharmaceutical company, is work done at his home in Fairfield, CT, and for his business in Bridgeport. No plans survive for either location.

To Colleges and Institutions, can be added work for the Mountain Home for Disabled Volunteer Soldiers in Tennessee, from a plan kept by Caparn. Work for Brooklyn College has surfaced in an official statement engaging him and from later publications by the College.

To Estates and Homes, among his listed works might be added an informal garden of 2 or 3 acres, from an article in May 1904, in *House Beautiful*, which owner has not been identified. The description of this garden appears to differ from the one described above for an urban lot of similar size.

5 City Parks

First public success...1900–1941

Upon his move from Pittsburgh, Caparn opened his office in 1898 as an independent landscape architect at 46 Warburton Avenue, a main thoroughfare of Yonkers.[1] The building housed the Music Hall, where Caparn would have felt comfortable in artistic surroundings. He may also have had a room or apartment in the building since he was given on a census as a "boarder."

Caparn received private commissions in Yonkers for his work. One such resulted in design of the grounds for the estate of Thomas R. Almond. He was the owner of patents and the T. R. Almond Manufacturing Company; the job is identified as number 514 on Caparn's Client List.[2]

Public meetings in Yonkers during 1899 showed that the citizens were very much in favor of city parks. On January 19, 1900, the Park Commission decided to offer prizes for the designs of two parks, to be submitted by March 14. Caparn was awarded the prizes for both Grant Park and Washington Park. They are No. 491 on his client list. A later map shows Washington Park in the center of town. By 1910 a new City Hall replaced the original and a Public Library had been built, donated by Andrew Carnegie.

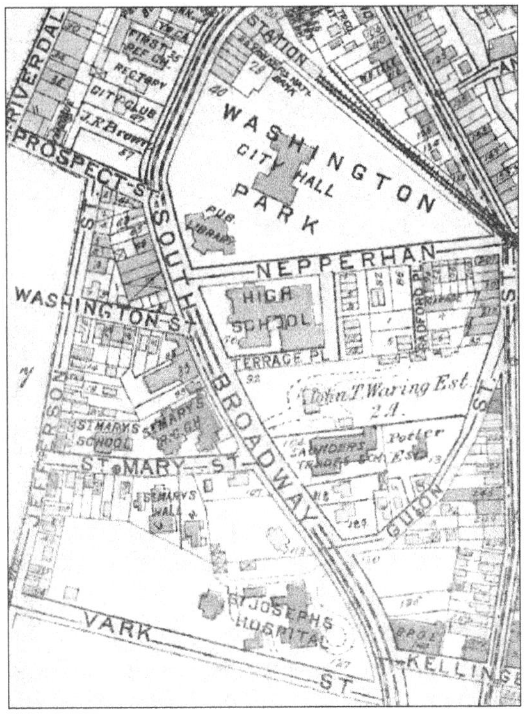

Washington Park was on a steep hill in the center of Yonkers. The descriptions by Caparn of both Washington Park and Grant Park tell what was valued in a city park at the time, how the particular piece of ground was treated and what was not included.

Washington Park covers about five acres. It was chosen as the one piece of land in the heart of the town where the dwellers in dozens of narrow streets and hundreds of confined houses could find within a stone's throw space enough for shady trees to sit under, and green lawns and foliage to rest the eyes and feet, and, yet more important, fresh and cool air to inhale during the summer heats.

In devising a scheme of treatment for Washqton Park the first essential considered was an easy ascent to the high ground in the center, where the trees stand about the old Nesbit House; and the second, to provide for the circulation of a large number of visitors within the Park. Paths of moderate grade in all directions and communicating with a large area for seats under trees were laid out, so as to leave lawn spaces of ample extent and suave contours framed in plantings of trees and shrubbery.

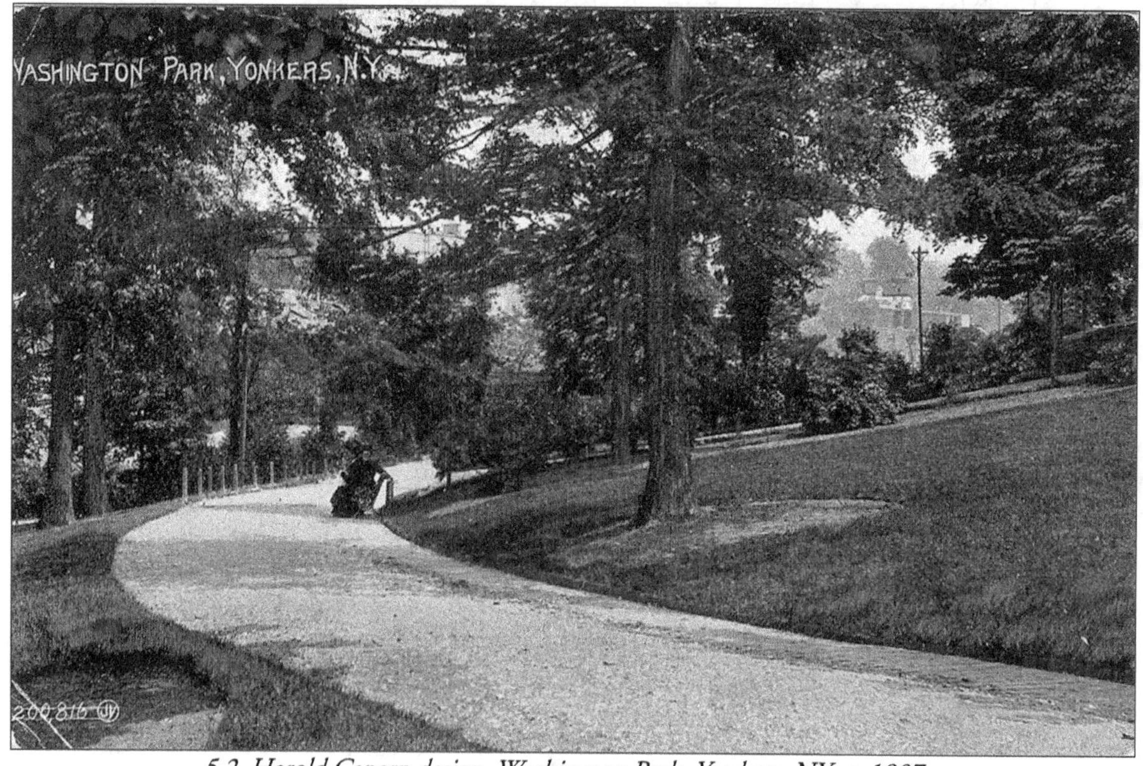

5.2 Harold Caparn design, Washington Park, Yonkers, NY, c. 1907.

A carriage entrance from the highest point of Nepperhan Terrance has been made to and around the house. In the front of the building the ground has been shaped for a garden of the old-fashioned rectangular type [i.e., a garden in the formal style], to harmonize with the house, with box-edged beds to be filled in summer with gay flowers to make a spot of brilliant color contrast with the quiet greens of lawn and foliage.

The description was written shortly after the founding of the American Society of Landscape Architects; Caparn uses the new terminology for his work. The stationary for his office, not far from the Park, gives his title as Landscape Architect.
Nisbet House, at the center of Washington Park, was replaced by City Hall designed by the active local architectural firm Edwin A. Quick & Son in 1907 and the land around it was again landscaped. What had been in the first years of the

century a beautiful, reposeful park was now a built-over and busy place. All that now remains of the turn-of-the-century park are a few old trees on the slope towards Broadway.

Of Grant Park, the second park for which a prize was offered, Caparn said:

> The site of Grant Park was chosen as almost the only one with large trees left in thickly settled parts of the city, as well as for its high and excellent situation. The people [in the neighborhood] now have a pleasure ground and breathing space close to their doors which cannot be diverted to private purposes or encroached upon by the buildings of a growing population.

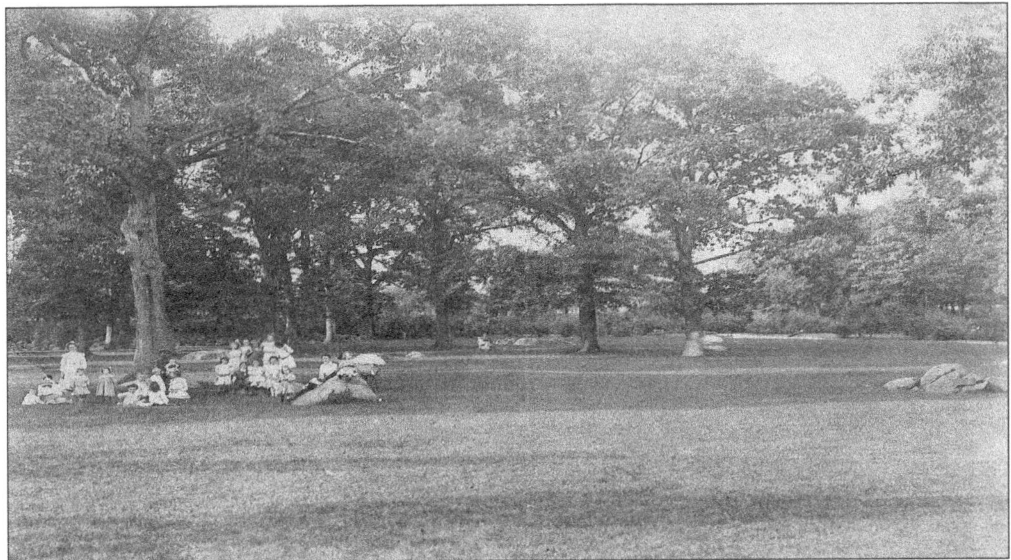

5.3 Harold Caparn design, Grant Park, Yonkers, NY. Central lawn, grove and boulders, c. 1905

> A broad path leads round the Park for those who wish to saunter or rest in, not merely to cross it, and communicates with entrances at four points where it has been found that entrances are needed. The whole is so arranged that the routes across the Park in all necessary directions are nearly as short as possible, so that there will be little temptation to wear tracks across the grass in order to pass from one point to another.

The perimeter planting described by Caparn and in the early photo, is no longer seen. The central lawn with boulders remains, as do old trees, together with paths. There are benches scattered about for rest in shade; however, one corner of the park is now dedicated to various devices for the play of young children. It is a modern adaptation of the park for neighborhood needs. Some planting of perimeter shrubs today, as shown in the photographs of the original, would help to restore the park and create an island of repose and green in the midst of a busy neighborhood. Grant Park was laid out in the informal style that Caparn was already writing about at the time.

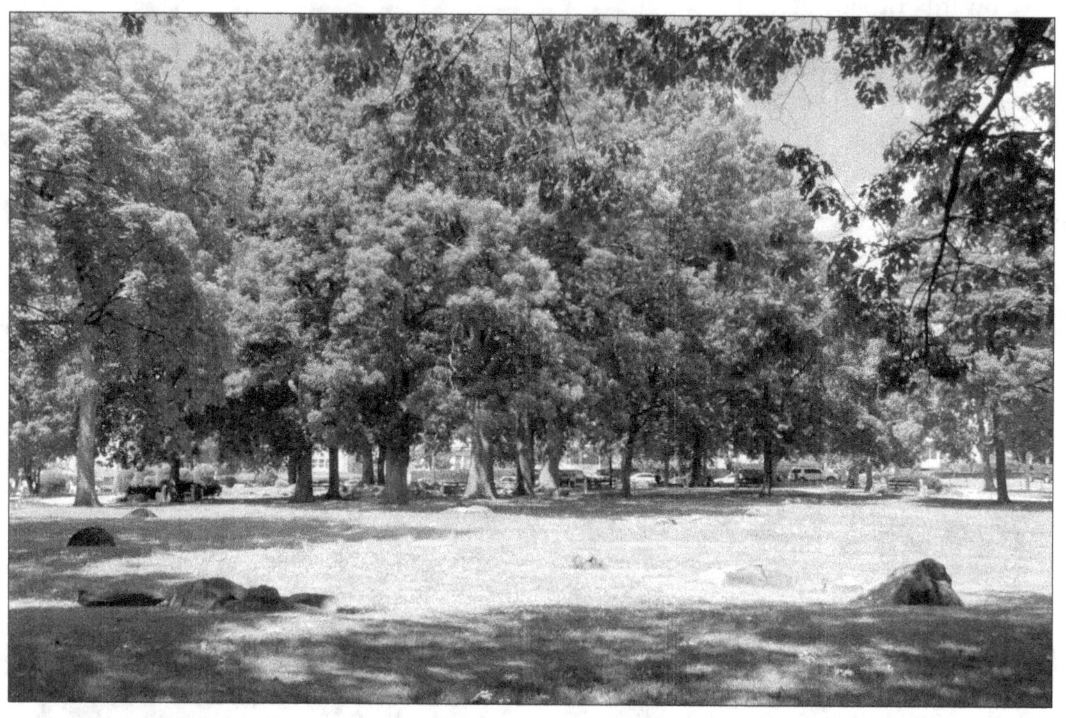

5.4 Harold Caparn design, Grant Park central lawn, grove and boulders, 2007

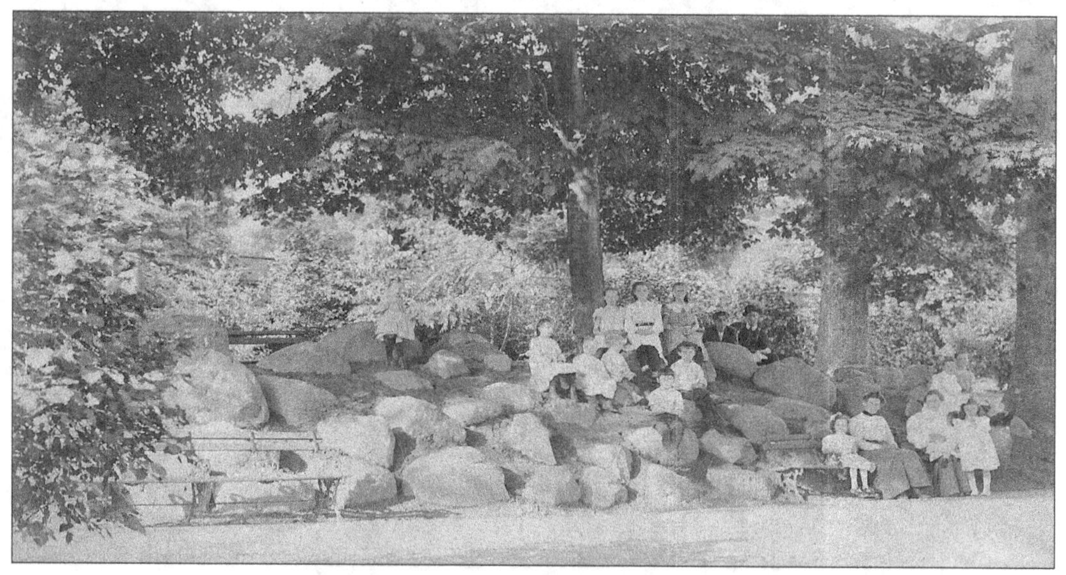

5.5 Harold Caparn design, Grant Park, area of rock garden, c. 1905.

Caparn continues: It has fortunately been possible to satisfy all conditions and yet preserve the large central lawn entire; for on large expanses of turf, undisfigured by roads or superfluous objects of any kind, depends the dignified and reposeful effect of park scenery. Various large stones have been spared as being of special geological interest and decorative in themselves, and where they tend to appear scattered they are united by plantations of rhododendrons.

In constructing Grant Park the aim of the Commissioners has been, not to make costly and elaborate work which might be more for display than use, but to make the Park of the greatest use to the greatest number without sacrificing its beauty. For without being beautiful a park cannot be useful; nor, indeed, can it be beautiful without being useful.

In an article in *Parks & Recreation* 12, 1928, Caparn says of Columbus Park in Yonkers:

This park is interesting as a treatment of a very steep piece of ground, one of those sites that are costly and inconvenient to build on and which, when built on, are likely to produce plentiful crops of bill

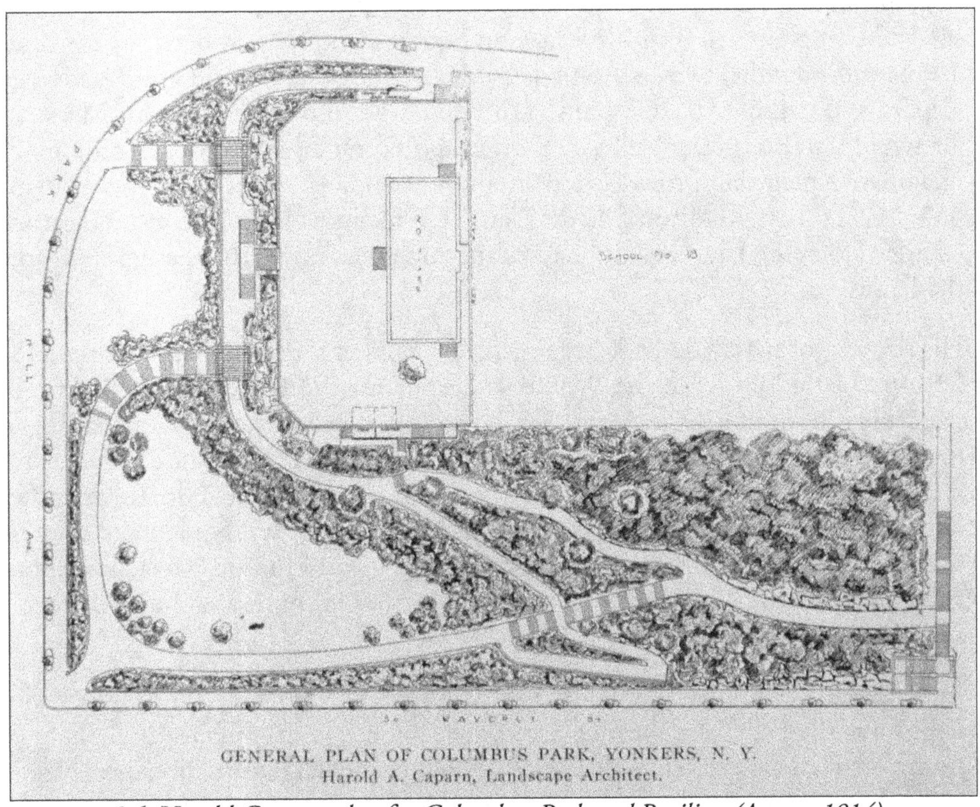

5.6 Harold Caparn, plan for Columbus Park and Pavilion (August 1914)

boards. The best use for such a left-over piece of ground under city conditions is to make it into a park. As a park it can always be made beautiful and probably useful also. By useful is meant useful for physical recreation as well as mental.

Nothing resembling a level surface was in the original site and as it is surrounded by a rather dense population, it seemed desirable to make one. From this elevated plateau thus created there is a fine view of the Hudson River (seen over a mile or two of house tops), and a large shelter pavilion (concrete with green tile roof) was erected on it so designed that the view of the river would be interrupted as little as possible. This structure is for rest, lectures, dances or other social gatherings, and would be an excellent place for meetings. It was his thoughtful architectural contribution to this park design in Yonkers.

New York City Parks
Madison Square, Riverside, City Hall, Inwood Hill, Battery

In addition to his design of parks in Yonkers, Caparn wrote on Manhattan parks. He had suggestions to improve Madison Square Park, located between 23rd and 26th Streets bounded by Madison and Fifth Avenues and a portion of Broadway. Caparn's "Madison Square Again" (1896) was written in response to Mariana Griswold Van Rensselaer's plea in *Garden and Forest* for a better balanced, more imaginative plan. He provided a plan and later noted on his client list as item 584, "C. D. Lay, Madison Square Plan." He likely worked in consultation to Charles Downing Lay, the City Landscape Architect, on further design ideas for the Park.

His support of Riverside Park began with his talk, as a representative of the NY Chapter of the ASLA, to the Women's League for the Protection of Riverside Park. He is noticed in *The New York Times* (1916) as was activist Amelia Bingham, NY actress and producer, whose mansion was at 103 Riverside Drive, who said: "I have lived on the Thames, on the Seine, on the Rhine, but always come home to the glory of Riverside Park." Caparn fought with city planners to preserve beauty for this important park overlooking the Hudson River. Planning and debates leading eventually to construction carried on for several more decades. (see online history)

In an article, "The New York Post Office Blight" (1921), Caparn proposes the removal of the Federal post office, which he critiques as an "architectural blight," from City Hall Park. Eventually City Hall Park was enlarged and became a pleasant foil to the surrounding tall buildings. The result was not directly Caparn's plan, but certainly his vision.

Caparn wrote a letter to *The New York Times* (1931) in which he supported keeping the northern tip of Manhattan in its natural state as Inwood Park. He said:

> This tract of 150 acres forms the furthest north end of Manhattan Island. Its tip is a wooded promontory which, in past ages, parted from the promontory of Spuyten Duyvil opposite, to let the Harlem River through. The whole park is a high rocky bluff, covered for the most part with fertile soil, on which grow some of the finest trees in the State. This park site has natural or natural appearing forest, pot holes, Indian remains and a valley. This and more is actually on Manhattan Island and has been acquired by the city for a park.

Caparn's recommendation for a park kept close to its natural state was heard. The Park is now described as being of 136 acres. The site where Native Americans "sold" Manhattan to the Dutch is marked now by a large rock and plaque. The area of the park along the Harlem River includes Manhattan's last remaining natural salt marsh, which attracts large numbers of waterbirds. Across the Hudson River one can see the imposing Palisades, left by the Wisconsin ice sheet. The glacier moved boulders from the Palisades to Central Park, plowed up topsoil, leveled the earth, and filled in depressed areas with glacial till. The glacial activity sculpted the characteristic terrain of Inwood Hill Park, with its dramatic caves, valleys and ridges.[3]

Caparn wrote a short piece, "Adding to Battery Park," in *The New York Times* (1939):

> Most of us would sympathize with the desire of Charles Downing Lay, to preserve Battery Park as a unit and without encroachment by the proposed bridge to Brooklyn. Caparn proposed filling in the bay along the Battery seawall, where there is a shoal. It would add several acres to the park just where they would be most impressive, both to those within the park and to those viewing it from the bay. It seems that whatever may be practicable should be done to preserve and enhance the unity and the quality of this unique and too-little-remembered spot, which should be a fit entry to the most surprising city in the world.

The bridge to Brooklyn was changed by President Franklin D. Roosevelt to a tunnel under the East River. When it was finally completed in 1950, it was the longest continuous underwater vehicular tunnel in North America. Meanwhile Battery Park survived and prospered.

Caparn wrote again two years later "Battery Park Plan Proposed; Remodeling Suggested to Make Area Into Desirable Residential Section," *The New York Times* (1941).

Now that we can look forward with some confidence to the time when Battery Park will be cleared, one may speculate as to the future, not only of the park but of the neighborhood also. (He brings here the same argument he used for Bechler Meadows.)

Probably New Yorkers have always been aware of the rare character of the park acres as the foreground to the tall buildings of the greatest business district of this great city. It seems that it is not only Battery Park that should be remodeled, but also its immediate hinterland, by which is meant the spaces covered by non-public buildings, valuable neither historically nor commercially, for some distance north and east of the park.

This neighborhood could well become one of New York's finest residence sites. Its views over the harbor and the two rivers are superb, and its air better than in other large areas of Manhattan. Its convenience to the business district of lower Manhattan is obvious. Many thousands would find it within easy walking distance of their daily occupations.

If the ancient, uninteresting buildings could be replaced by tall apartment houses, designed and placed in harmony with a far-seeing general plan and with open green spaces, the whole could be planned to give an impression of an extension of Battery Park. An enterprise such as this could hardly be carried out without a master plan, to the general principles of which private enterprise would conform.

Caparn was proposing extensive city planning, perhaps extending to and beyond Wall Street. From the 1960s into the first decade of the twenty-first century planning and construction brought about the vision that Caparn had enunciated decades earlier. To the north and west of the area are now residences and apartments in Battery Park City as suggested by Caparn. Battery Park remains an area well-used by inhabitants of lower Manhattan and visitors to the shores of New York. What came about was not his design, but certainly his vision for the area.[4]

It may be noted that Caparn also designed other city parks, not included in the present discussion: Denison Park in Corning, NY; Rorick's Glen Park in Elmira, NY; Lincoln Park and Milford Park in Newark, NJ for the Newark Park Board; the Treat Memorial, Landing Park, in Newark was likely done as a subcontract for the Olmsted Brothers, for which a plan is in the Olmsted NHS files in Brookline.

6 New York Zoological Park

Spaces natural and beautiful...1899–1904

The New York Zoological Park was chartered in 1895. Dr. William T. Hornaday (1854-1937) was selected as the Director and Chief Curator in the following year. He had worked, a handful of years earlier, with landscape architect Frederick Law Olmsted at the Smithsonian National Zoological Park in Washington, D.C. Director Hornaday selected the site in The Bronx for the Zoological Park and determined its general landscape lines and its building style.

In the autumn of 1899, upon the recommendation of John De Wolf, landscape architect of the New York Park Department, landscape architect Harold Caparn was engaged by the Zoological Society Executive Committee to present a detailed study of the entrance concourse and the approach to Baird Court around which were to be animal houses. The Park, still under construction, officially opened to the public on November 8, 1899.[1]

The work of Caparn, in consultation with De Wolf and Board of Managers Chairman Henry F. Osborn, as noted in the *Fourth Annual Report* for 1899, (published May, 1900) "resulted in the production of an attractive and satisfactory approach to the Court [from the north], providing amply for access for carriages to the restaurant and to the south side of Lake Agassiz, and bringing about a treatment quite in sympathy with the beautiful natural features of this portion of the Park. Mr. Caparn is now engaged upon the details of Baird Court and its connections on the south."[2]

As seen in the plan (6.1) approved by Hornaday and Osborn, Caparn designed the entrance concourse from the north (right) around an oval garden, up steps past another garden to a bandstand (circle), flanked by the Bird House (top) and a planned Tropical Mammal House (bottom), followed in the center by the water feature of a sea lion pool (kidney-shape) and a monument in the center of the green on which faced the Lion House and the Monkey House.

The *Sixth Annual Report* for 1901 (pub. April 1902), notes: "The general design of Baird Court and its approaches, as submitted by Mr. Caparn, was approved last year (1900). The design of the details will be undertaken at once by Messrs. Heins & LaFarge; in the meantime extensive excavations have been made for tree-planting to shade the Court."

A letter from Henry Osborn to Heins and LaFarge of June 1, 1900, directs that a clay model be made of Baird Court and another letter several weeks later indicates that Caparn's plans for the area are complete and the model is in progress. Heins and LaFarge could then work on the details of the buildings for the lions and the monkeys.

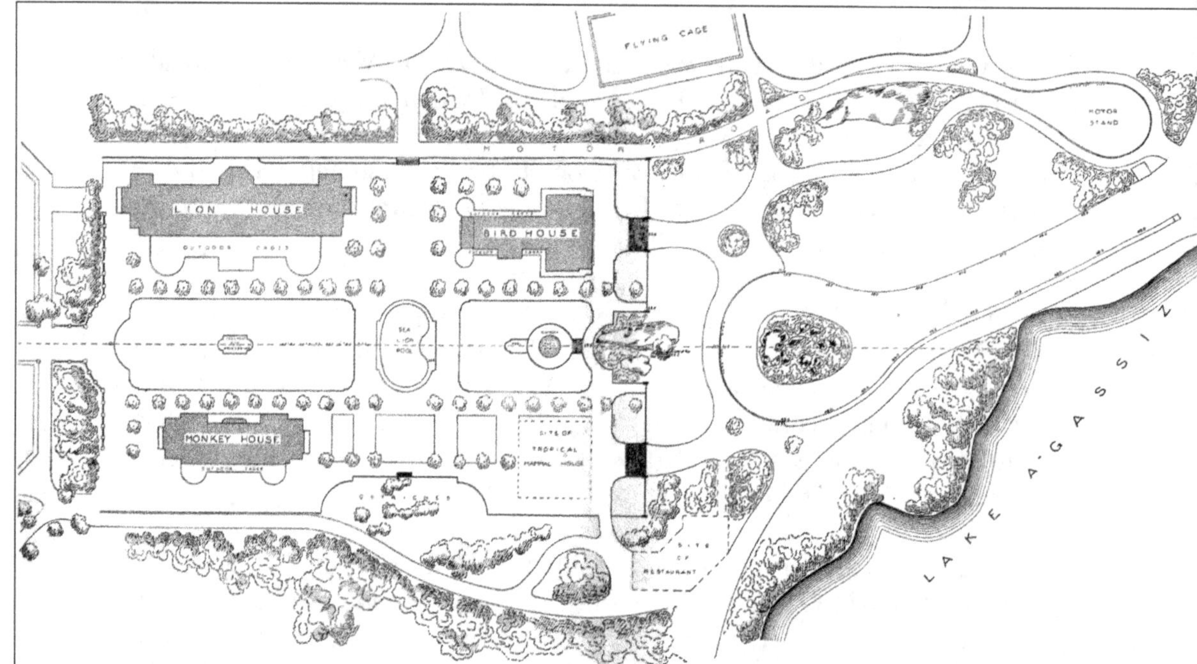

6.1 Harold Caparn, Plan for the entrance concourse and Baird Court, New York Zoological Park. 1900.

Sometimes full credit for general layout is given to the architects, with only a nod for "landscaping," but such is not indicated here. The central position of Caparn in the overall landscape design of Baird Court, the North Steps and West Steps can be seen. Some aspects of the Baird Court landscape plan and its requisite considerations of grading, walkways, water, and drainage clearly appear to be agreed in conjunction with the design of the buildings among the principals from September through December, 1900.[3]

"During the past year the work of erecting the large buildings located on Baird Court was begun (that is, in 1901). This Court, when finished, will be characterized by a classic formality, in contrast to the remainder of the Park, which will be left, as far as possible, in a natural state."

The uninterrupted formality of the long green of Baird Court, with its water feature of sea-lion pool and the attractive Beaux-Arts style animal buildings, remains from the turn of the century as a fine example of the City Beautiful movement. It brought beauty and classic restraint to a populous area of New York City. It promised an oasis in which to escape the bustle of the streets. It offered a reposeful setting from which to view exotic animal exhibits.

Over the five years from 1900 through 1904, during his engagement with the Zoo, Caparn further developed his plan. While the Steps and the Court were formal in design as an entrance to the Zoo, the grounds, designed as animal-friendly open landscapes, followed the Committee's desires and Caparn's dictum "keep it natural."

Regarding an additional feature, the 1902 *Report* states: "The City is indebted to Mr. William Rockefeller for the gift of a magnificent antique Italian fountain from Como, Italy. After long consideration and the best advice, it was decided to place this fountain directly opposite the Sea Lion Pool and nearly north of the Primate House in order to give the lines of the fountain the background of the trees on the east side of the court. The grading and planting of this section of the court will complete the setting for this beautiful monument."[4]

It is unclear just when Caparn recommended to the committee, and Mr. Rockefeller, not to place the fountain in the Court, where its exuberance stood at odds with the restraint of the court buildings. He no doubt recommended that it be moved to the Entrance Concourse, his design that had already been approved, and placed in the middle of an enlarged and circular grass frame, around which carriages and cars would enter to deposit passengers. It would then be the focal point for patrons arriving through that grand entrance to the Zoo.

He proposed, in complementary Italianate style to the fountain, great steps and gardens to serve as appropriate backdrop to the fountain while grandly leading to the central Baird Court. The work for his plan of the entrance concourse likely took place after Caparn had left the Zoo's employ. Such complex plans often took years to implement.

The 1902 *Report* comments on the administration of the Park, and states: "We are indebted to our architects, Messrs. Heins & LaFarge, for the successful completion of the designs of the newer buildings. Also to Mr. H. A. Caparn, our landscape architect, for his valued advice on many difficult questions of park treatment." The statement likely conveys kudos for success regarding the final placement and complementary design in which to set the fountain.

Caparn laid out a walkway throughout the whole length of the Park along the eastern bank of the Bronx River and Lake. In addition to the construction of 4,500 linear feet of Telford macadam walk ten feet wide, following the coutour of the ground, two bridges were constructed—one 30 feet in length, the other 50 feet. For very nearly its entire length, this walk follows steep hillsides. The difficult character of the surface involved a great deal of costly rock blasting and filling. The curves of the river bank were followed as closely as practicable, and the contour of the ground was adhered to as nearly as was consistent with the construction of easy grades.

Caparn's vision for the Zoo was for much more than pleasant landscapes to attract visitors to the animal exhibits. He recognized the need for the Zoo to preserve species before they became extinct. His vision has proven appropriate for various species, which now, though dying in the wild, are reproducing in the care of conservationists.

In a letter to *The New York Times* (April 24, 1904, p. 6), Caparn defended the Zoo against criticism and recognized the need for zoos to provide a future for certain species. His letter brought additional letters, some critical of zoos and menageries, but also some in support of the Zoo. Caparn was concerned not only with the landscape, but also with the conservation of animal wild life for the edification of humanity.[5]

The Bronx Zoo, laid out on 265 acres enhanced by the Bronx River, remains one of the largest metropolitan zoos in the United States, providing a habitat for many endangered animals. The New York Zoological Park was Caparn's first large success. It would prove to be an auspicious work for a young landscape architect at the beginning of his career. Baird Court (later Astor Court) and its stairways is now a designated New York City Landmark.

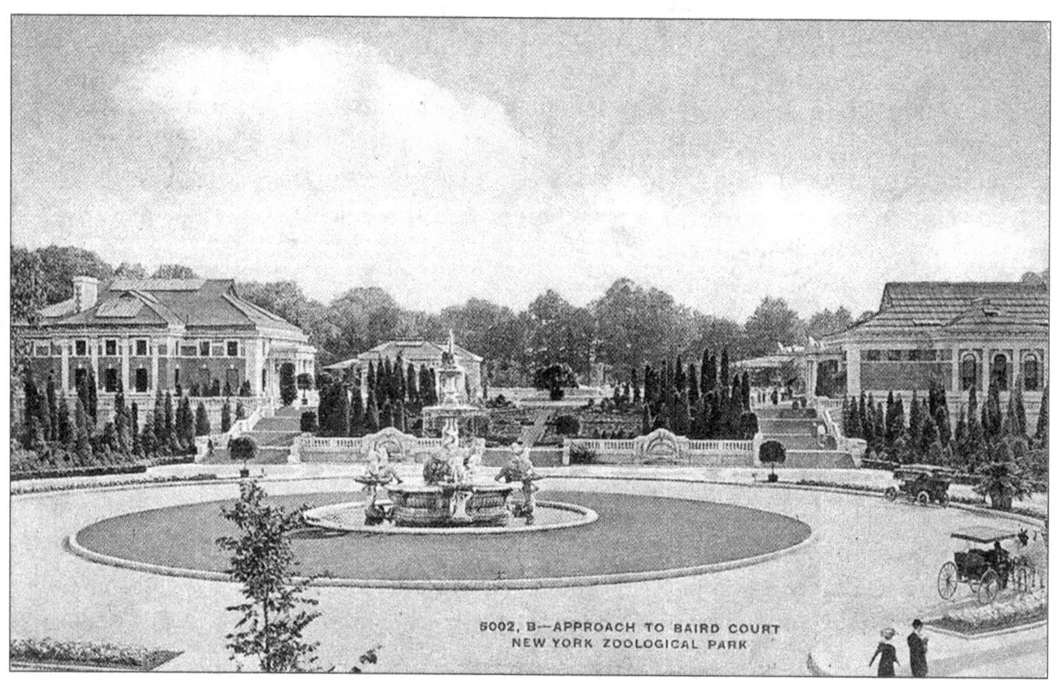

6.2 Harold Caparn design, New York Zoological Park, Rockefeller Fountain, Great Steps with Italianate gardens, leading to Baird Court. Right, Bird House, left, Administration Building.

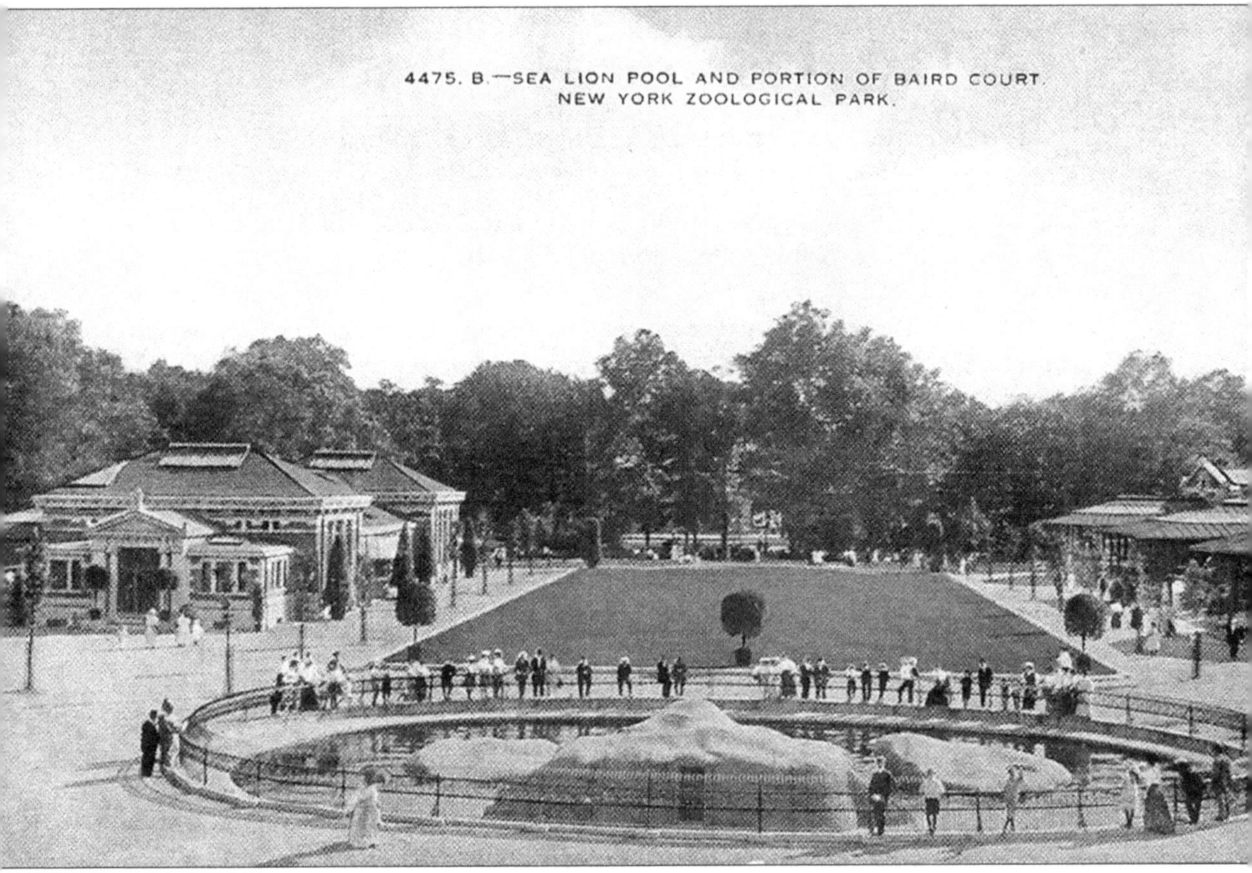

6.3 Harold Caparn design, New York Zoological Park, the Sea Lion Pool in Baird Court framing the long green with the Primate House left and Lion House right. The Elephant House at the far end of the green is hidden by trees. Note young trees planted within the walkways, planned by Caparn to shade the Court.

7 Estates and Homes
Designs for some significant clients....1903–1928

Caparn designed landscapes for homes and estates of about 110 individual clients. The following plans and photographs show twenty-five years, 1903-1928, of Caparn's work. With the effects of the Great Depresseion, Caparn and others turned their attention to smaller places. He was among the earliest to carefully consider the challenge of designing for a home with lesser frontage. Such was his last published design, in July 1945, of the "Layout of an American front yard." What he saved in plans and illustrations, shown in the following, however, represent work for elite clients.

Attention is usually given to the main focus of a landscape design in lawns and gardens. But Caparn also designed entrances understanding that by thoughtful design the introduction could determine how the viewer would respond to what followed. Worth noting are the many ways to create the entrance to a private estate. The following can be viewed as illustrations: At Larchmont, NY, for the property of A. H. W. Johnson, Caparn designed the main entrance gate and plantings to disguise the off-set angle of the house, which is not parallel to the close-by street, but rather to a body of water in front of the house. The effect produced for the visitor, entering from the street, is informal and seems quite in balance and inviting (see description, photos and plan). At Ardsley on Hudson, for the Maitland Griggs property, the stone-work entrance and wall welcome the visitor in a semi-formal manner directly to the front door of the home (see photos). Both are simple in the effect produced. Several others are more complex.

At Schuylerville, NY, for the estate of D. A. Bullard, the entrance drive, from Broadway (bottom center), includes a view over a large lawn to a glimpse of the rear of the home and the flower gardens attached to it. The front of the home with porte cochere (porch) is approached by the winding drive and looks off toward broad meadows shaped by shrubs. The entrance is designed to provide a brief view to the full effect of both sides of the house and grounds (see plan). At Briarcliff Manor, for the Mairs and Hungerford estates, the entrances are clearly defined by stone gateposts carrying the estate name and wrought-iron fences giving a glimpse of the home and grounds. The effect produced is of a formal approach. The grounds within, however, show informal, but carefully constructed delights to mind and eye (see photos).

The trees along the entry drive to the Willard estate (7.1) keep the focus on the home. Formal gardens to the right of the home can be enjoyed later. Kitchen gardens are conveniently set off behind the home and greenhouse.

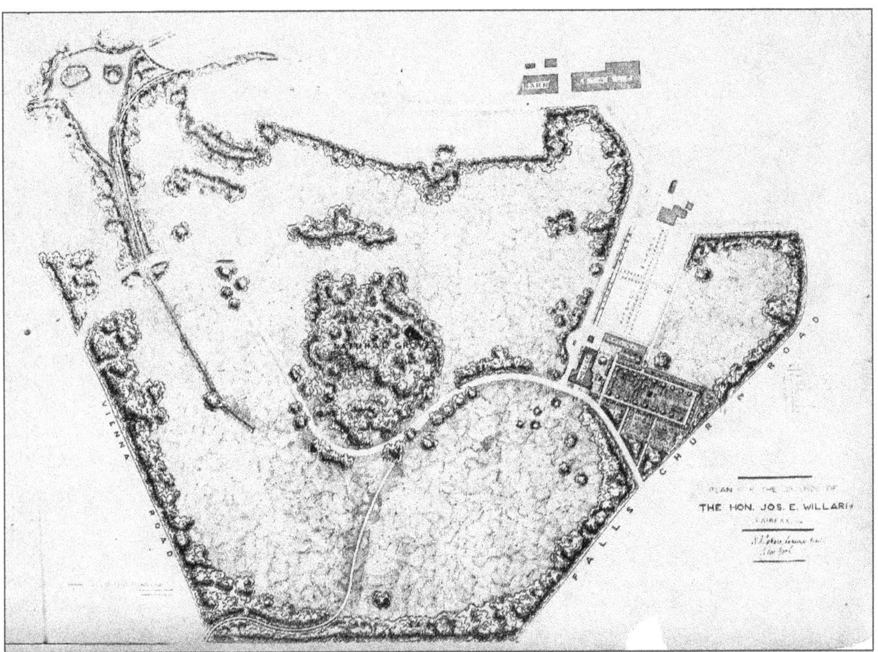

7.1 *Harold Caparn plan, estate of The Hon. Joseph Edward Willard, Fairfax, VA. The plan, number 493 on his client list, is the Caparn entry, number 65, for "Gardens and Lawns at Fairfax, VA" in the Chicago Architectural Club exhibit at the Art Institute of Chicago, 1903.*

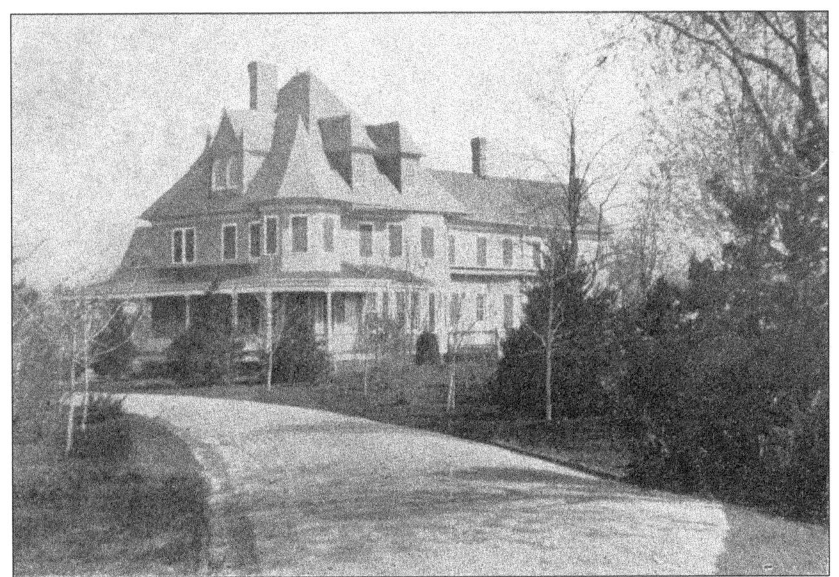

7. 2 *Harold Caparn design, portion of drive, lawn, plantings, estate of J. E. Willard. Willard was Lieutenant Governor of Virginia, later ambassador to Spain.*

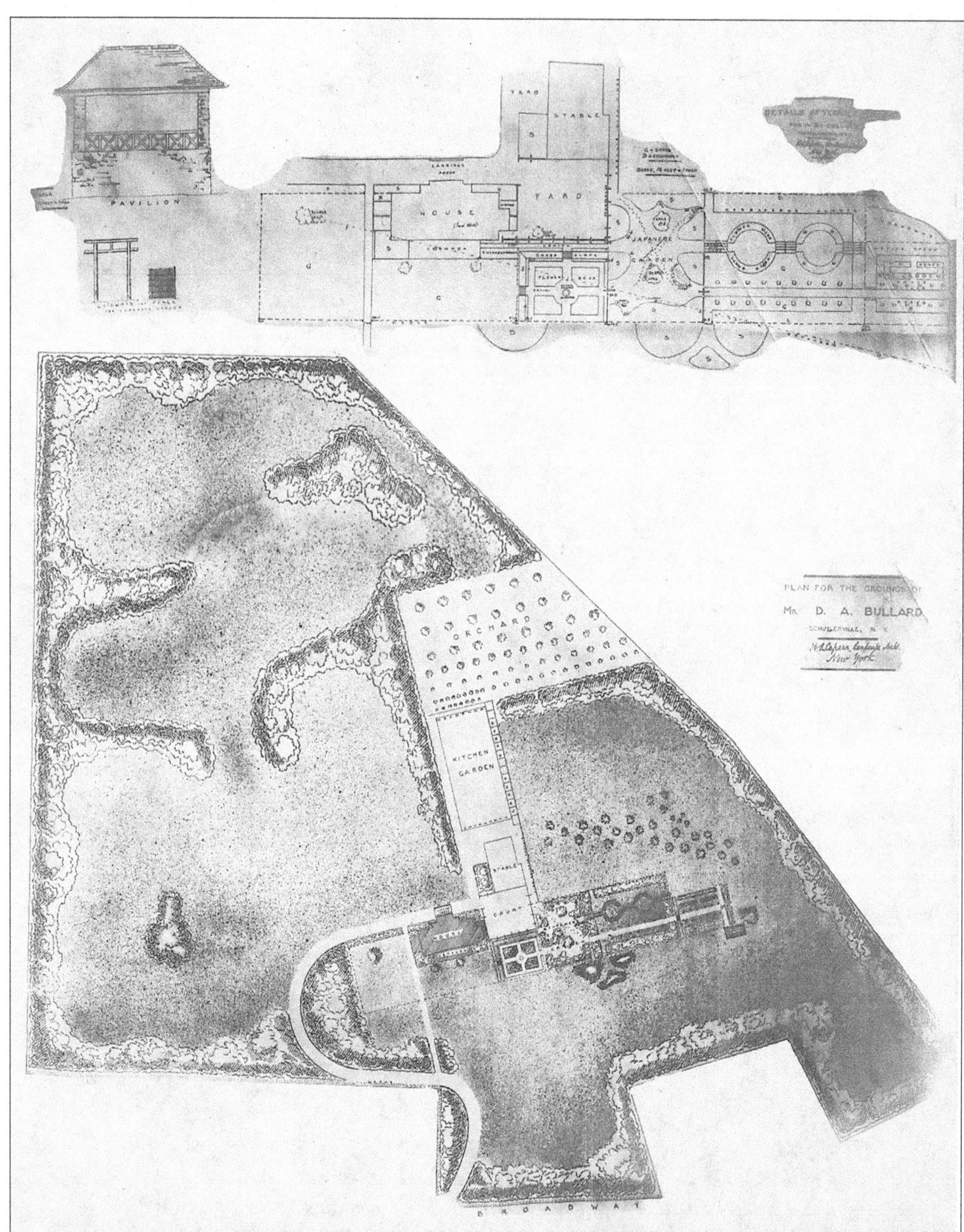

7.3 *Harold Caparn, plan for the grounds, estate of D. A. Bullard, Schuylerville, NY, number 492 on Caparn's client list. Daniel Alpheus Bullard (1869-1911), was President of Schuylerville National Bank. The Bank Board included John Alden Dix, Governor of the State of New York, whose estate landscaping plan was also executed by Harold Caparn*

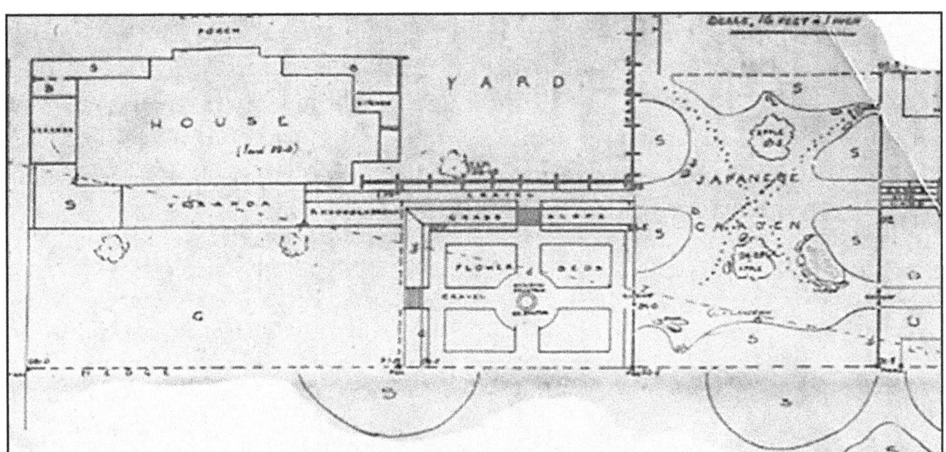

7.4 *Detail of 7.3. Harold Caparn plan, estate of D. A. Bullard. [key: G = grass, S = shrubbery] Plan shows house with veranda looking over a wide lawn to a sunken set of four flower beds surrounding a sundial. A gravel walk leads to a Japanese Garden with lantern, and raked sand around rocks.*

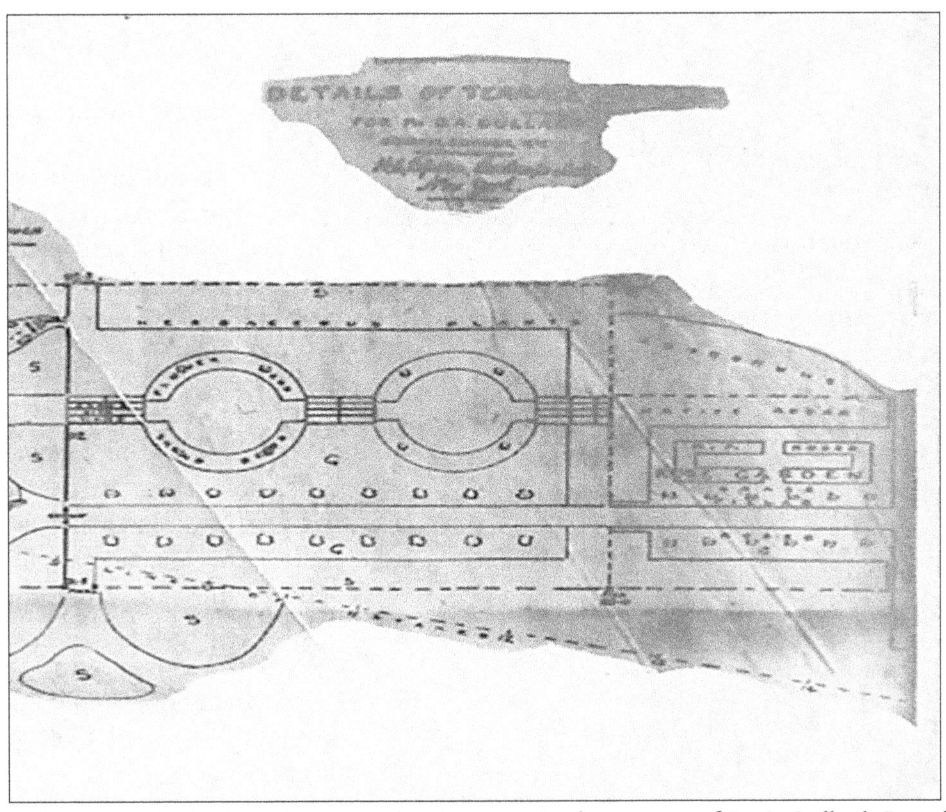

7.5 *Detail of 7.3. Harold Caparn plan, Terrace Gardens, estate of D. A. Bullard. Pergolas and walk bordered by herbaceous plants lead from Japanese Garden to the Rose Garden (right) with native roses and hybrid perpetuals in beds, a precursor to his later rose garden designs. Caparn entered the estate design in the exhibit of the Chicago Architectural Club, shown at the Art Institute of Chicago, 1906.*

The residence of Webb Horton in Middletown, New York, is seen in an early photograph. The construction was begun in 1902 and finished in 1906 on a design by Frank J. Lindsey. Webb's son Eugene, whom Caparn gives as number 524 on his client list, later built a church and hospital to honor his father. After his father's death in 1908, Eugene Horton occupied his father's forty-room mansion, now on the National Register of Historic Places (1990).

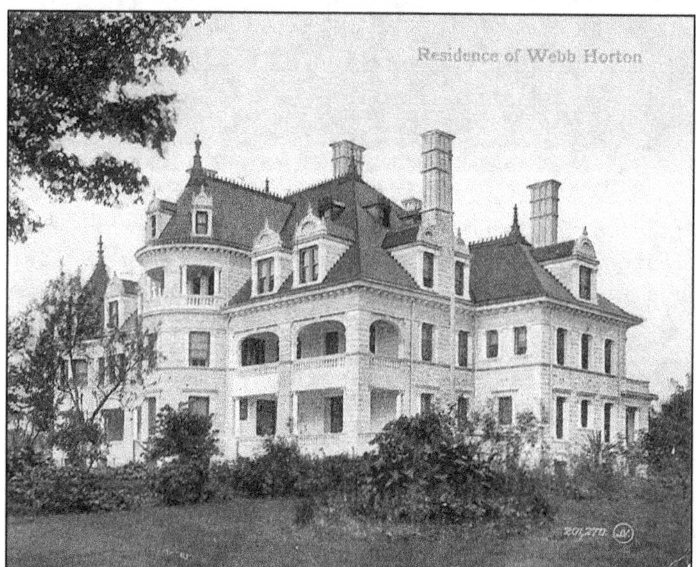

7.6 Harold Caparn. The Horton Residence, Middletown, NY. Portion of landscape shows an informal arrangement of trees and shrubs. The Horton Residence, later, Morrison Hall became part of SUNY Orange, surrounded on the campus by curvilinear drives and walks, designed in the informal Caparn style.

Edward and Catherine Lyman in 1866 bought the former Whitmarsh Estate with large home and grounds in Northampton, Massachusetts. Their son Frank Lyman, after the turn of the century, built a summer home on the estate. Around 1910 Harold Caparn designed the landscape and gardens for the newer home, which is number 567 on his client list. Lyman later made it his permanent home.

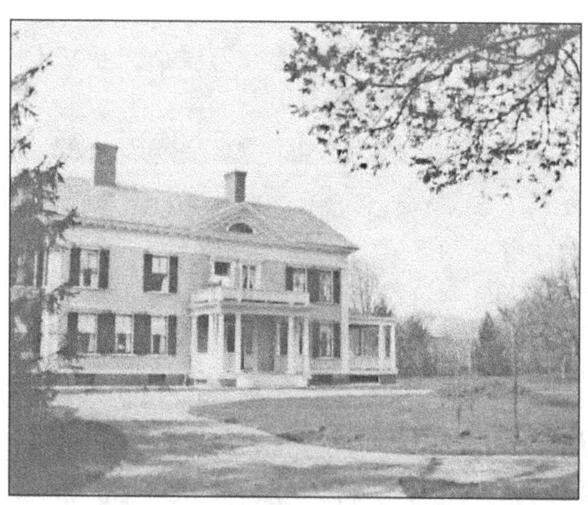

In 1946, Smith College purchased the estate, making it first a graduate center and using the estate greenhouse for genetics studies. In 1962 the Elisabeth Morrow Morgan Nursery School moved into the former Lyman home and it became part of the Smith College Campus School.

7.7 Home of Frank Lyman, later a part of Smith College. Photo, c.1907. Harold Caparn landscaping plan still under construction.

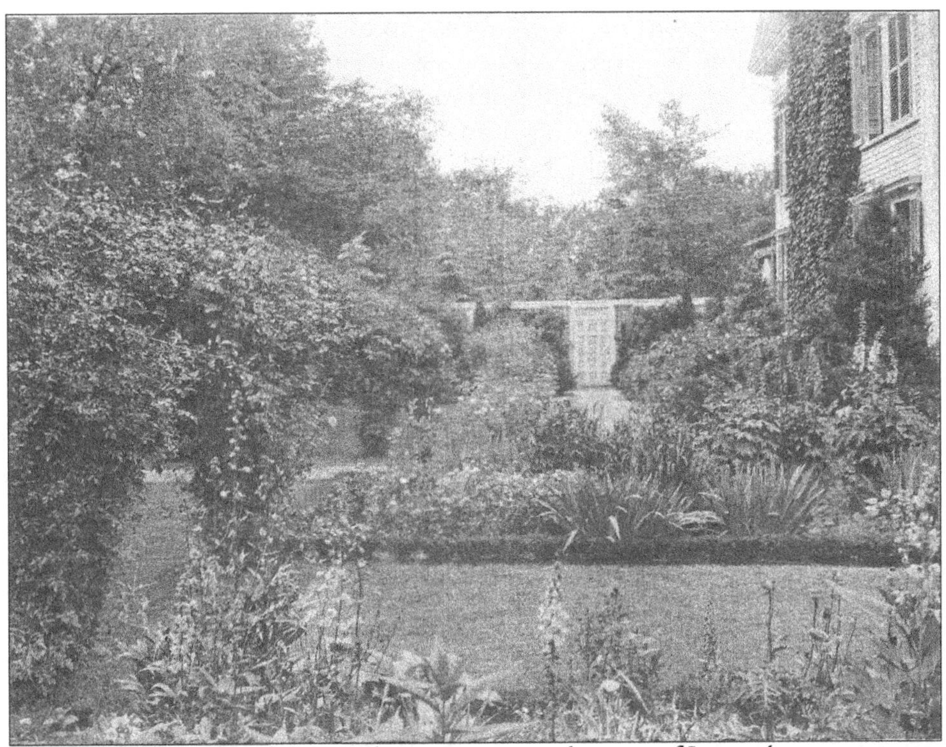

7.8 Harold Caparn design, mature garden, rear of Lyman house.

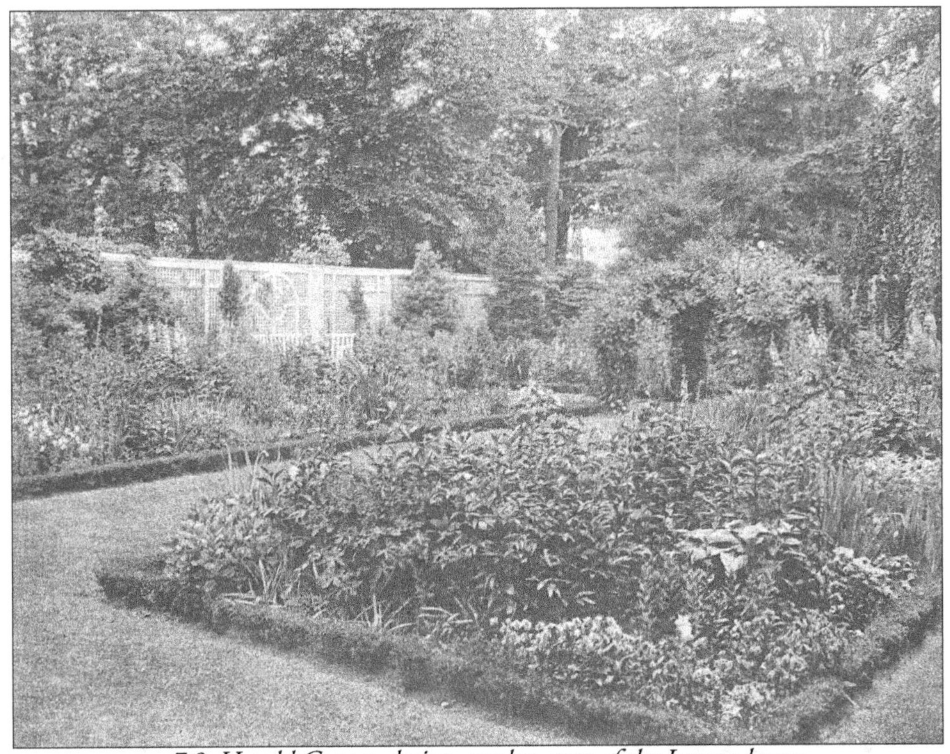

7.9 Harold Caparn design, garden, rear of the Lyman house.

Caparn designed the estate of J. C. Willever, in Millburn, New Jersey, number 507 on his client list. Willever was vice president of Western Union for which he developed the "singing telegram" and many other event-specific ready-made telegrams. He was a witness for Caparn's naturalization in 1900. He was a member of St. Stephen's Episcopal Church, Millburn, as were several of Harold's family. The photographs, 7.10, 7.11, 7.12, likely taken by Caparn, c. 1910, were part of his archive.[1]

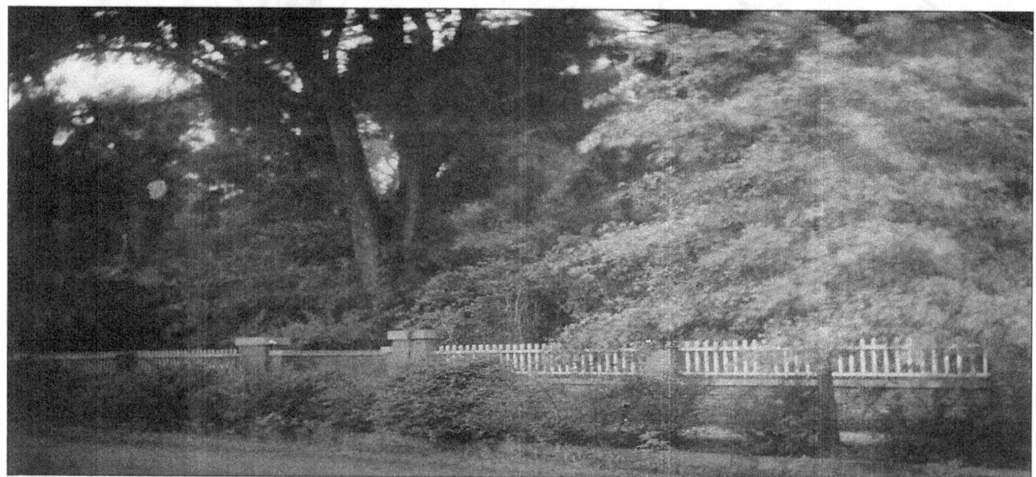

7.10 Harold Caparn landscape, wall/fence with seat, left center; estate of J. C. Willever.

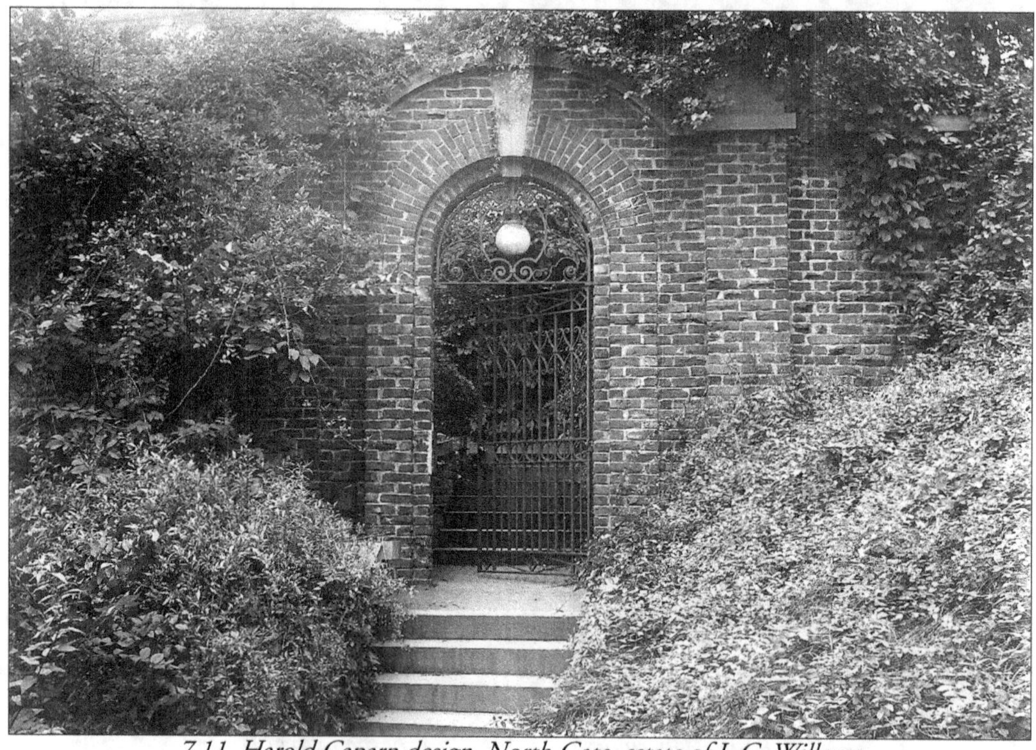

7.11 Harold Caparn design, North Gate, estate of J. C. Willever

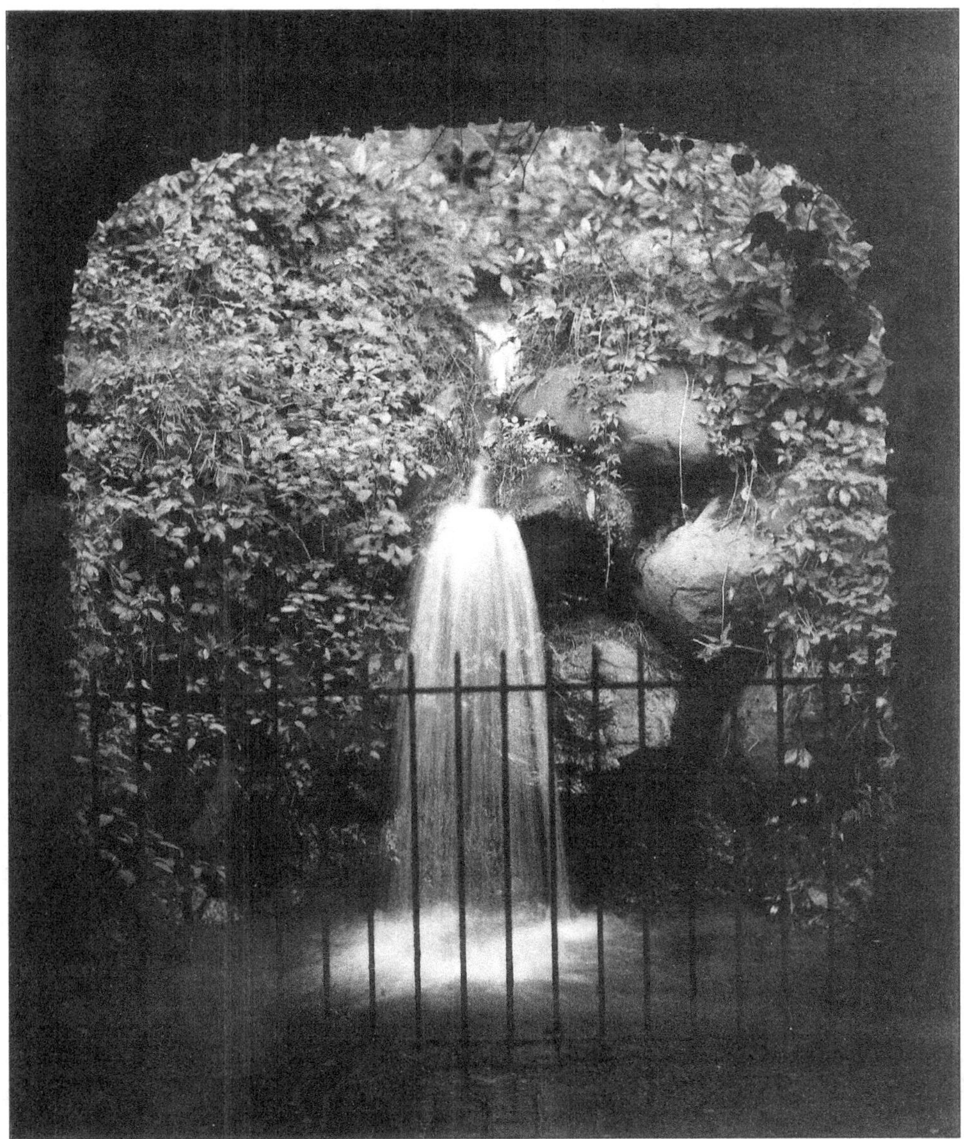

7.12 Harold Caparn design, East Gate, with waterfall, estate of J. C. Willever, Extant on Glen Avenue, Millburn, NJ.

The home of Maitland F. Griggs, Ardsley on Hudson, NY, was built around 1910. He is number 623 on Caparn's client list. The home was of special interest at the time as it was constructed entirely of steel and concrete, designed by architect Robert W. Gardner. Such construction helped to protect Griggs' art collection. Part of the entrance court to the estate can be seen in photographs, from the Caparn archive (7.14, 7.15); the photos were included in *The Work of Roman Landscape Contracting Company*, a portfolio published by the Company, c. 1925, and also in the book *Illustrations of Work of Members* of the ASLA published in 1931.

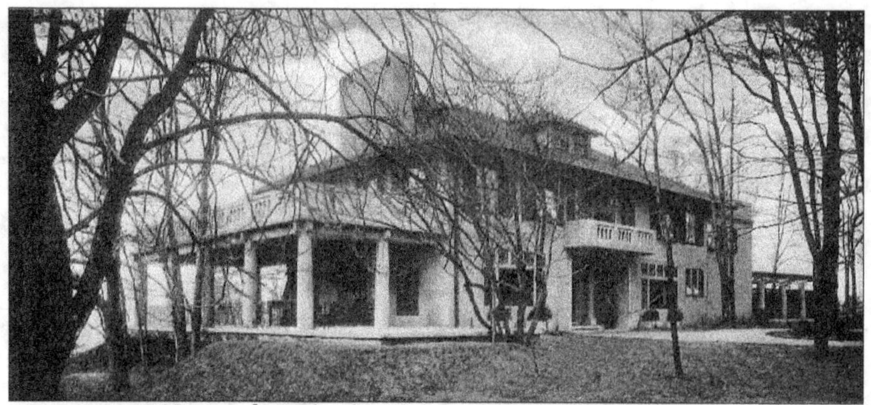

7.13 *Home of Maitland F. Griggs, Robert W. Gardner, architect,*
Harold Caparn, landscape architect.

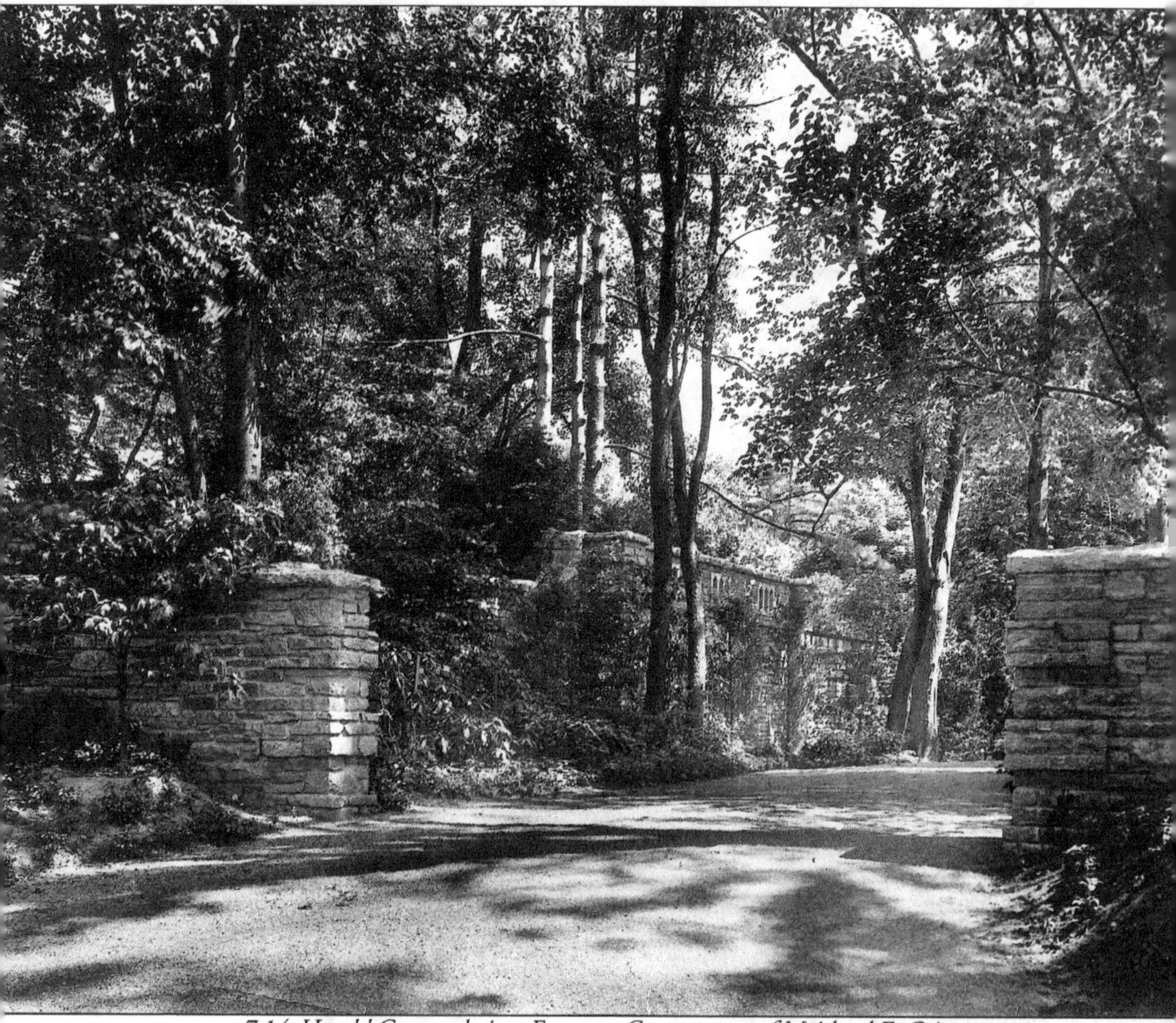

7.14 *Harold Caparn design, Entrance Court, estate of Maitland F. Griggs.*

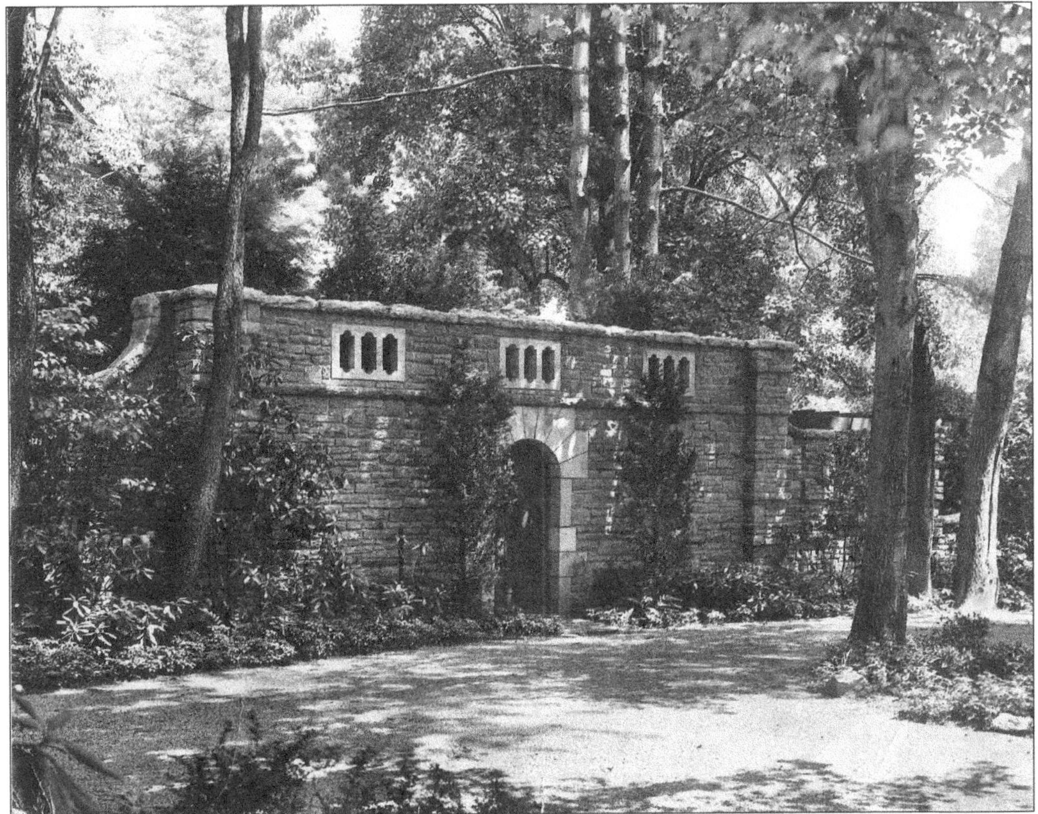

7.15 *Harold Caparn design, Entrance Court, wall and door,*
estate of Maitland F. Griggs. Extant.

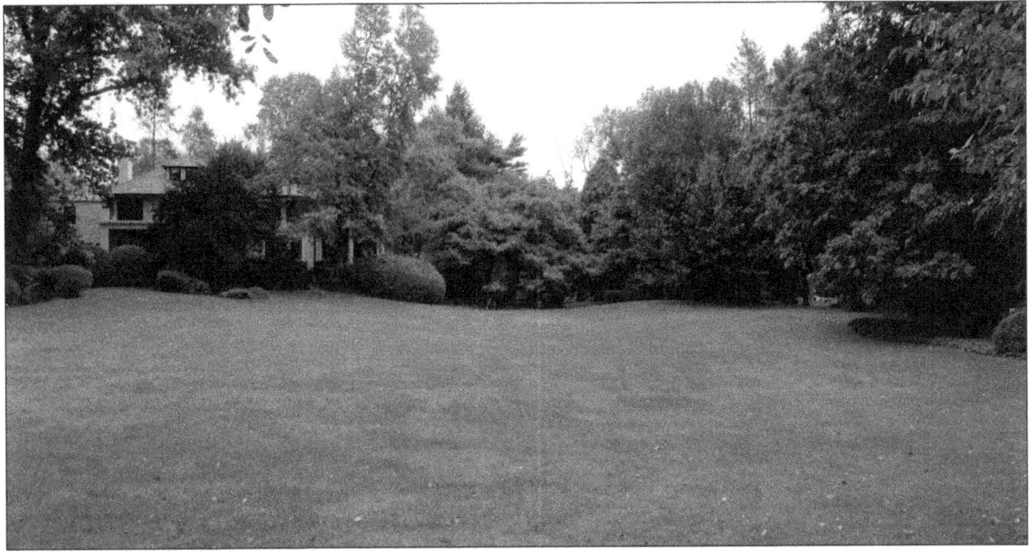

7.16 *Harold Caparn, landscape, Griggs estate, view on opposite side from entry, looking over broad sweeping lawn surrounded by older and newer trees and shrubs, still in the informal style laid out by Caparn. The lawn provides a peaceful view from the columned porch on the right side of the house.*

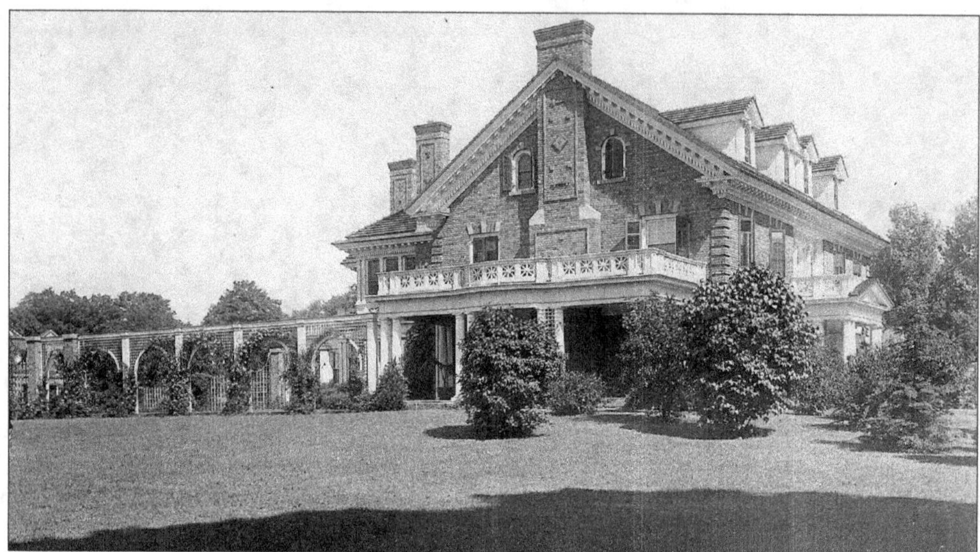

7.17 Harold Caparn landscape, residence of Robert D. and Maria Smith Eaton, Norwich, NY. Designed by Gaggin and Gaggin Architects, Syracuse, 1914. Number 568 on Caparn's client list. Fence, left, with arches, encloses a sunken garden leading from the rear of the home to the owner's business.

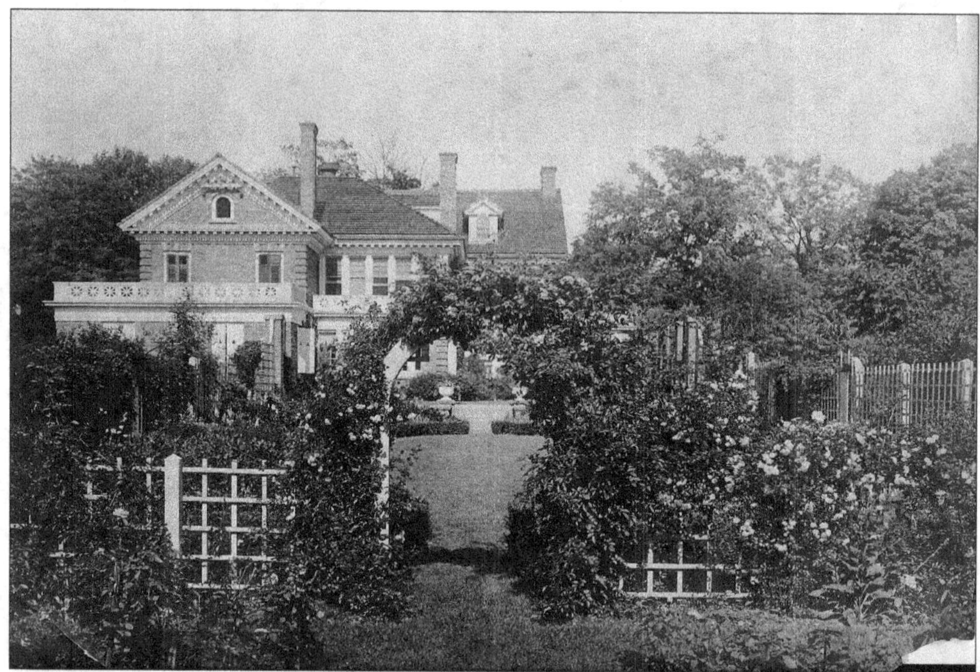

7.18 Harold Caparn design, looking into sunken garden, Eaton estate. The garden was laid out between the home of Eaton, president and chairman of Norwich Pharmacal Co., and the company office building to the rear, providing a lovely view and walkway. When the last of Eaton's sons retired from the company in 1957 it became the Jewish Center of Norwich. A terrace behind the home can be seen, but the garden no longer exists. The home is on the National and State Registers of Historic Places.

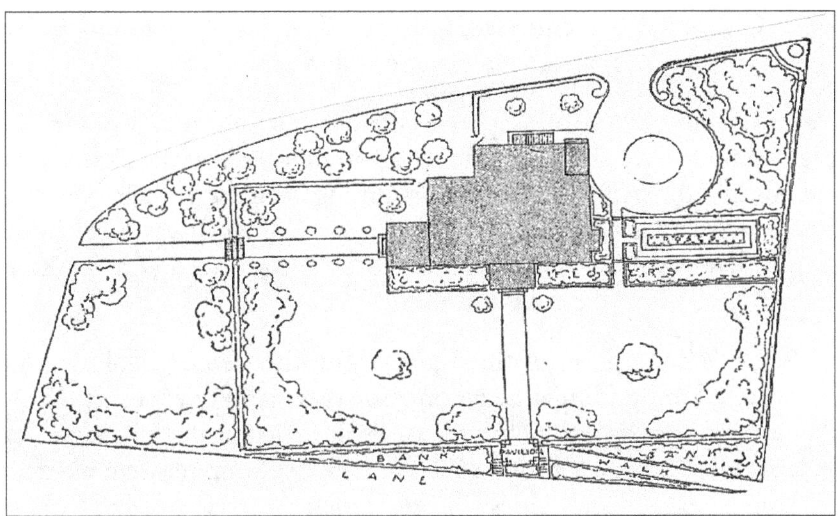

7.19 *Harold Caparn plan for the home of J. H. Tanner, Cayuga Heights, Ithaca, NY. The house faces left; the walkway from the side of the house, bottom, gives a path, through a pavilion, to a lane. The circular drive, top, gives service access to the rear, the kitchen and the kitchen garden. The garage is located across from the circular drive, on Tanner property. Number 574 on Caparn's client list.*

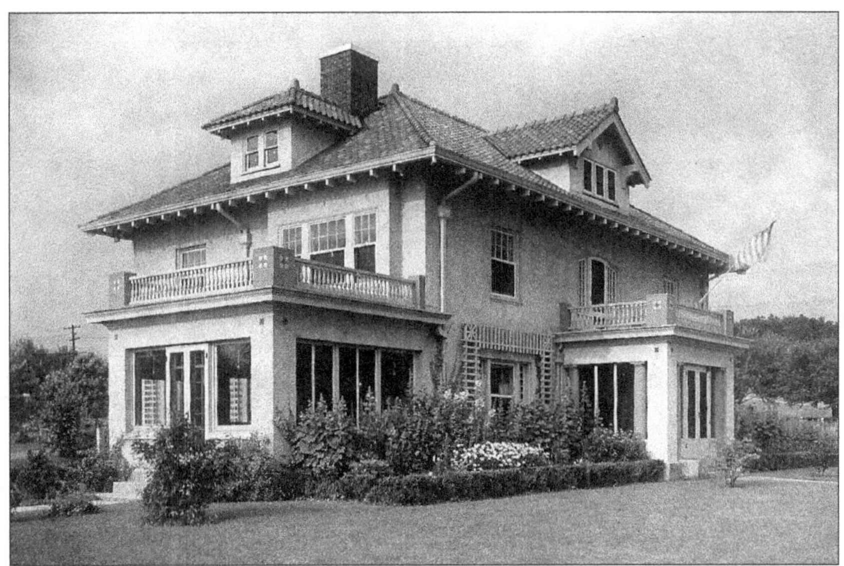

7.20 *Harold Caparn, landscape c. 1916, for home of J. H. Tanner, professor of mathematics, Cornell University, as seen in the plan (7.19). The home is first on The Parkway, Caparn's design of a major access road through the Village of Cayuga Heights. Tanner was the son-in-law of Jared Newman, trustee of Cornell and developer of Cayuga Heights, whose home was across the lane from that of Tanner. The home still exists although large trees have changed the setting from Caparn's plan.*

Jerome B. Pound was the developer and owner of a series of southern hotels. His seventeen-acre estate, Stonedge, was on the east brow of Lookout Mountain, outside of Chattanooga, Tennessee. Clarence T. Jones of Chattanooga, was the architect, Harold A. Caparn the landscape architect.

J. B. Pound is number 630 on Caparn's client list. Jo Cormier, widow of Richard Cormier, conductor of the Chattanooga Symphony, knew the Pounds and had a home on the property. She recalled swimming at night in their pool. Her recollection was that there were many more trees and that it was more beautifully landscaped than is shown in the partial view on the postcard (7.21). Stonedge is now a development of fine condominiums.

Pound's description of the estate, from his *Memoirs*, follows: We had dreamed of building a new home for years, and after securing this location [on Lookout Mountain] we decided to begin building as early as possible.[2] While on a trip to Europe the next Summer we looked at many homes in European cities. When we left America, we had intended to build a large home on the English style of architecture with a white exterior. During a trip through Italy my wife was especially charmed with the Italian-Spanish architecture, and decided to change her mind and build a home of this type.

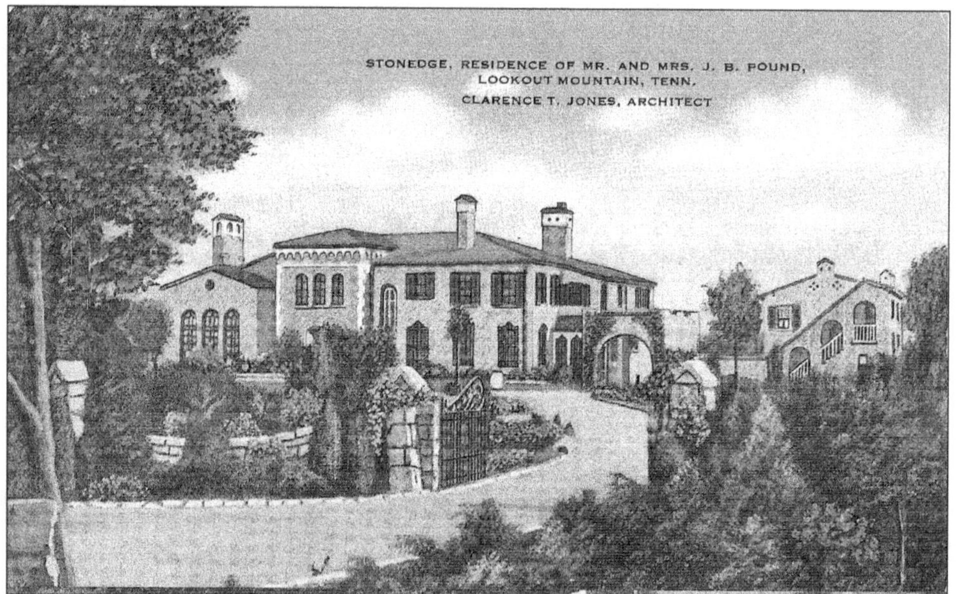

7.21 *"Stonedge," the residence of Mr. and Mrs. J. B. Pound on Lookout Mt., TN. Tract purchased, January 1924. Grounds and house completed 1928. landscape by Harold Caparn.*

When we returned from this trip, we employed Mr. Clarence T. Jones, well-known architect, and started building this home. It was when finished, and is now, one of the most imposing residence properties and homes to be found on Lookout Mountain or elsewhere in the South.

The grounds have been beautifully landscaped. We have a very lovely swimming pool equipped with flood lights for night swimming. In addition to the many beautiful shrubs and flowers which we have on the place, we maintain two greenhouses so that we may have cut flowers the year round, and also furnish cut flowers for the Hotel Patten, Chattanooga, Tennessee. [400 rooms, owned by Pound]

One of the most beautiful parts of our garden is the Rock Garden and "The Dogwood Ravine." In the Dogwood Ravine we have one hundred dogwood trees, one-half white and the other pink. I had a stone bridge built across this ravine and during the season, when the dogwood trees are in bloom, a view from this bridge is a sight seldom seen anywhere. Standing on this bridge, you are above the trees and you can look down into the blossoms and see their real beauty.

The examples seen in this part of the chapter display some of Caparn's representative home and estate landscape work. Caprn also did designs for two owners and consulted for another in Tuxedo Park, New York, which work can no longer be seen.[3] What is now available, in existing sites or in plans and photographs, illustrates only about twenty percent of his work for individuals. His client list included a number of well-known and well-to-do clientele, as seen in (F) 226ff.

The following part of the chapter centers on a home with an outstanding garden in Onteora Park, but also includes a Wild Garden behind the Library, a plan for the Club House and Theatre, and a detailed blueprint for an estate garden. Caparn work in that elite community extends from about 1914 to 1927.

His work at Onteora Park

Onteora Park was founded in 1887 as an artist's colony near Tannersville, New York, in the beautiful northern Catskill Mountains. It was developed by the pioneer interior decorator and textile designer Candace Wheeler (1827-1923) with her brother Francis Thurber. Eventually a small community of about seventy owners of Stick and Shingle cottages, they built a church, a library, the Onteora Club and Theatre, which provided community gathering places. In 2003 Onteora Park Historic District was placed on the National Register of Historic Places.

As Mrs. Wheeler says in *The Annals of Onteora 1887-1914*, "Mrs. (General George) Custer came permanently and built "The Flags," and a ledge was found for a low cottage built for Mrs. Schuyler Van Rensselaer which took the name of "The Twigs."[1] Mariana Griswold Van Rensselaer (1851-1934) writer on art, architecture, history and garden design, wielded great influence on the development of American landscape design through the publication of many articles and especially her *Art Out-of-Doors: Hints on Good Taste in Gardening* (1893). She became an active member of the Onteora community. Half a dozen years after founding Onteora Mrs. Wheeler built a home there herself.

Wheeler sets the scene that no doubt inspired Caparn in his design work at Onteora. In her *Annals of Onteora*, she says: "In the growth of Onteora, artists and authors did not cease, for the tradition of peace and beauty still remained with it. Perhaps its very existence was owing to the painters who first loved and haunted the mountains." Among the painters was Thomas Cole, famous for his Hudson Valley scenes, including Kaaterskill Falls in the area, and among the writers, Mr. and Mrs. Samuel Clemens—Mark Twain—and family.

Harold and Clara Caparn were vacationing at Onteora Park in the summer of 1909, when their daughter Rhys was born; she would later make her own mark as a graphic artist and sculptor. The Caparns asked their friend, Mrs. (Lee Wood) Ben Ali Haggin, Jr., (1856-1934) a leader in the community, to be Rhys' godmother.[4] Caparn later designed the estate landscape for Mrs. Haggin, no. 585 on his client list.

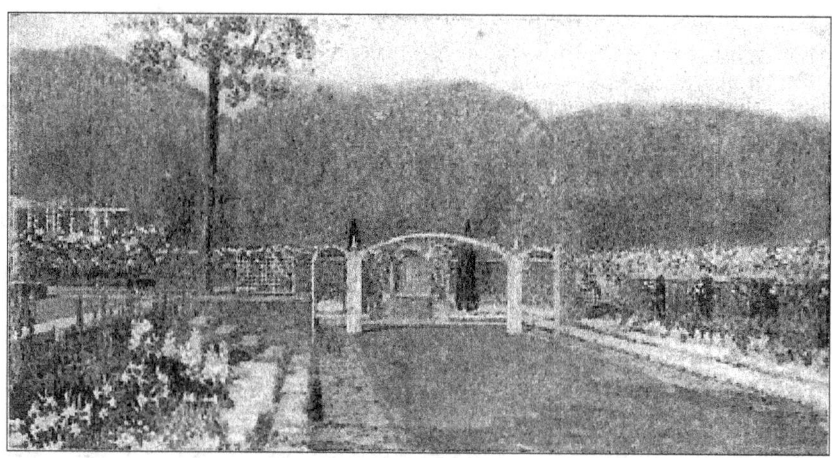

7.22 Harold Caparn drawing of the Cloister Garden for the estate of Mrs. Ben Ali Haggin, Jr. The arches, in front of the devotional wall niche, are reminiscent of a church rood screen; they are not seen in later images of the garden.

The Cloister Garden

As part of his design of the estate grounds in the informal style about which he often wrote, Caparn also designed what was called in the influential journal *The Craftsman* (1914), a "cloister garden," in a more formal style. About the cloister garden the journal says: "Although the garden as it flourishes today is not an exact reproduction of this sketch, still the beauty of this mountain garden is here delightfully suggested in the long stretch of green leading up to the shrine, in the pergola, vine-draped at the side, in the beds of white lilies and blue larkspur, in the masses of green at the back, and the wide arching blue overhead. This closed-in gentle garden is one of such peace and beauty that it is difficult to speak of it with sufficient restraint."

The central block of the Wheeler-Haggin home still exists. It has additions in the same Craftsman style as the original home, made by later owners. In his solution to designing on a steep slope, Caparn surrounded the shingle home on three sides with a retaining wall of native limestone. The home faces in a southerly direction looking toward High Peak and Round Top mountains. To the west side of the home there are steps leading to paths on gentle inclines off into the woods and delightful vistas, all designed by Caparn in the informal style.

The Cloister Garden, given a more formal setting, is on axis running east from the front of the home. A terrace, above the stepped-down garden, frames the north side of the garden (left side, photos 7.22, 7.23) where one could sit and view the distant mountains. A wall defines the east end of the garden. The wall has an arched niche set into it (center), that provides a focal point at the end of a long green. On the south side, another step down, a pergola (right, 7.23), enclosing a walkway, is supported on its outer, south, side by a high wall. On the west side, the home and a gate set in the wall complete the garden enclosure. The design of the garden will be seen to reflect the interests of its commissioner.

Mrs. Haggin was interested in the arts, revealed in her membership and activity in the MacDowell Club of New York City. The Club was named after the composer Edward MacDowell (1860-1908), still known for his second piano concerto and especially his piano suites. MacDowell was greatly interested in relationships among the arts, as was Mrs. Haggin.

She is described in an article, "MacDowell Club to Give New Christmas Masque," as an officer of the Club. John White Alexander, the painter and muralist, a friend of Haggin and of Caparn, was President of the Club, where his wife designed the costumes for the Masque and Ben Ali Haggin, III, was in the cast. The Masque illustrates the interest of the well-to-do, together with artists of their acquaintance, in creative pursuits in semi-dramatic events.

A regular visitor in the later years of her residency, was Mrs. Ben Ali Haggin's son, (James) Ben Ali Haggin III, recognized as a portrait painter and known also for his stage designs, including those in New York for the Metropolitan Opera, Beaux Arts Balls and the Zeigfield Follies. As entertainment for the Onteora community, he staged tableaux vivants at the home of his mother, using the niche and the garden wall for a backdrop. A *New York Times* article (August 3, 1930) tells of one such entertainment, where he "authored the pageant 'In a Convent Garden' that was produced in London several years ago." The director of the Metropolitan Ballet and members of the Kosloff Ballet were among performers. Haggin had likely known them through his work on designs for their companies. The pergola with steps giving out before the niche (7.24) provided for entrances and exits to such theatrical entertainments.

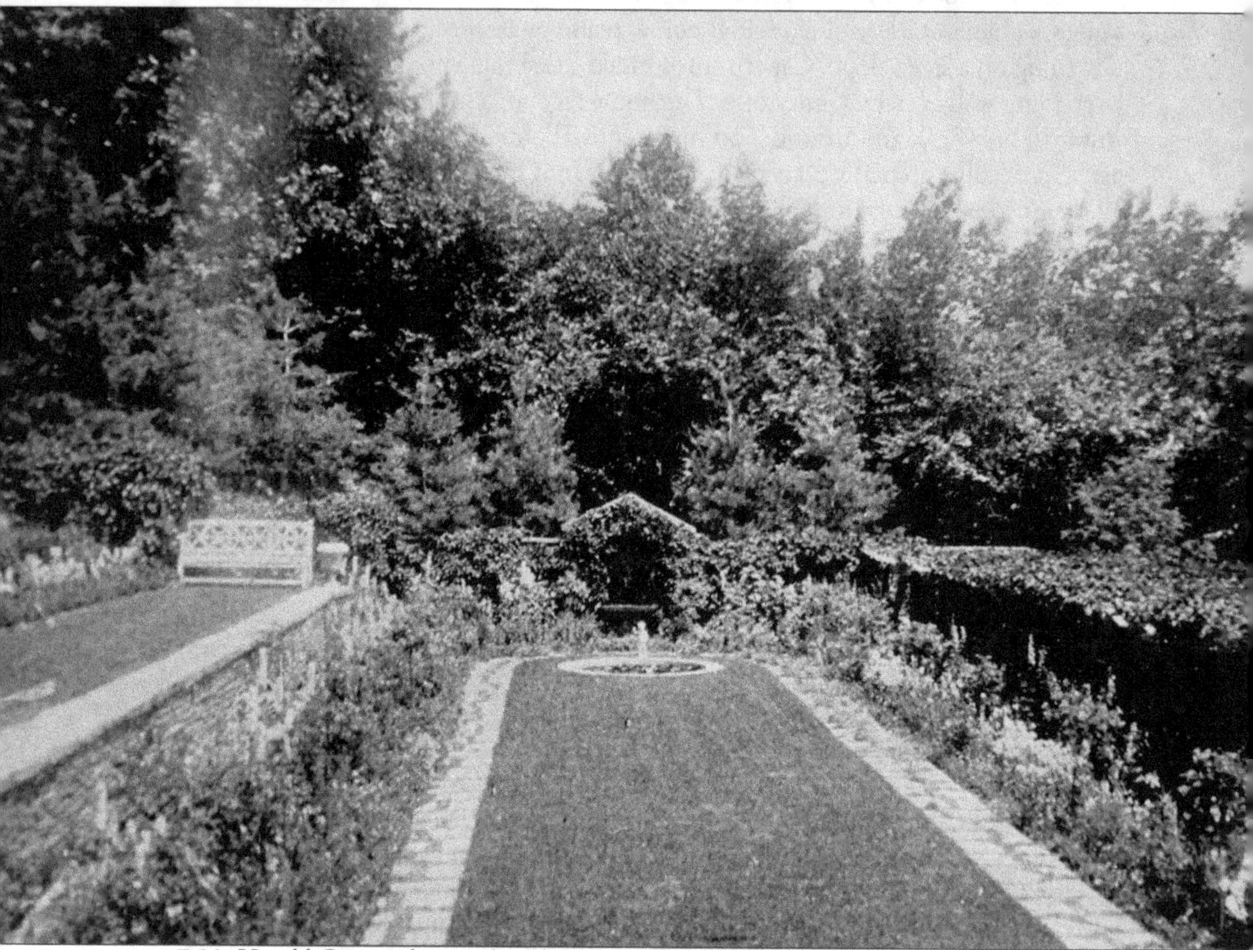

7.23 Harold Caparn design, the Cloister Garden of Mrs. Ben Ali Haggin. photo c.1930.

The Onteora Club House, in its reception and dining area displays photographs of such outdoor entertainments from the time of the Haggins. They illustrate an era when such pastime engaged the members of the community. Caparn, as a member of the Architectural League of New York, would have known directly of outdoor garden entertainments from a Fête des Fous presented by the League on February 26, 1917, in costume, as a medieval Masque.

Caparn had also written an article, "Design for an Outdoor Theatre" in the *Journal of the International Garden Club* (June 1918), that shows openings in walls on either side of the playing area from which to make entrances and exits. His article gives examples of plays and playing spaces that he recommended for outdoor performance. Ben Ali Haggin III found the space and pergola in Caparn's design apt for the presentation of his theatricals.

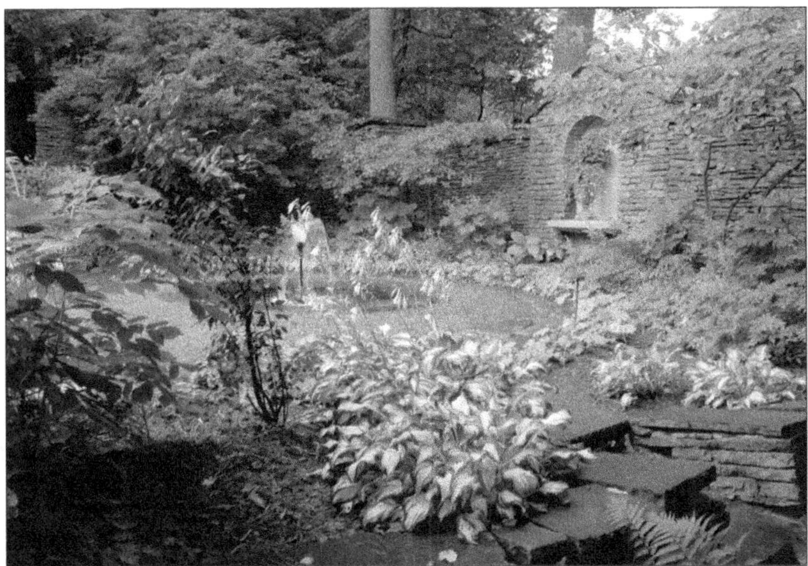

7.24 Harold Caparn design, area leading from the pergola to the space before the niche in the wall of the Cloister Garden where Ben Ali Haggin, III, presented entertainments for members of Onteora Park.

The arched niche in the Cloister Garden wall, at the far end of the lawn, was originally designed as a shrine. Harold Caparn, in his design of the garden no doubt collaborated with the artist William Laurel Harris (1870-1924) who designed the devotional inset of the shrine. Caparn knew Harris as a fellow student of the Ecole des Beaux-Arts; later as a religious muralist. Both were members in New York of the Municipal Art Society and especially the Architectural League, where Harris was president in 1912, while Caparn was president of the American Society of Landscape Architects.

Caparn's design of the niche in the wall fit perfectly with the intent of Harris to make a mural in the arched niche as a shrine to St. Rose of Lima.[5] The shrine shows the figure of St. Rose, (Lima, Peru, 1586 – 1617) surrounded by long-stemmed roses, where she is crowned with a halo, a symbol of sainthood, all in a color scheme in purple, green and rose on a background of gold.

A comment in the article in *The Craftsman* implies that the garden had changed from its original state to that as seen in Caparn's drawing. That original was a rose-garden. The original rose-garden was planted to enhance the shrine, however, it had not survived a harsh winter at Onteora. It was then replaced by a garden of larkspur and lilies as in Caparn's drawing in *The Craftsman.*

The naming of the garden and its enclosed character becomes clear. It was an offering, by way of the arts of mural design and garden design to St. Rose of Lima, who lived in a garden grotto and whose head was crowned with roses. She was the first saint of the Americas and a patron of gardeners.

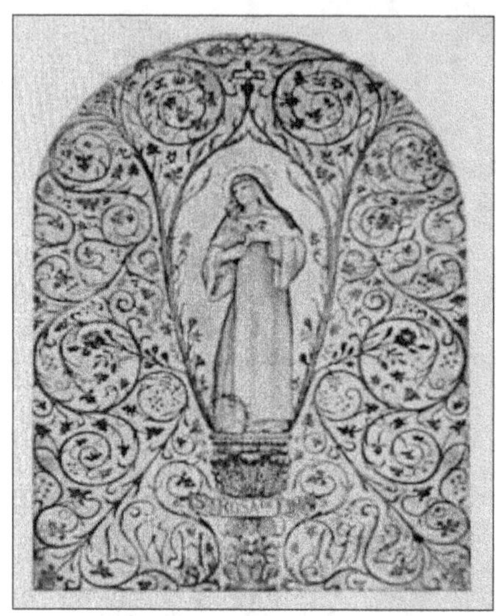

7.25 William Laurel Harris, St. Rose of Lima, wall inset.
Initials of the commissioner of the shrine, Lee Wood Haggin, are lower left.
Initials on lower right may be her dedication to her late husband, James Ben Ali Haggin, Jr.

Mrs. Haggin shows her depth of interest in the interrelatedness of the arts with the shrine in her Cloister Garden. As a member of the MacDowell club she likely would have known composer Edward MacDowell's lyric piano piece, "To a Wild Rose." It would have completed her idea of the interconnected arts of music, theatre, mural and garden design.

After years of disuse of the Cloister Garden by other owners, the owner of Wildmuir reconstructed the Garden with the help of his research, images at the Onteora Club and those such as 7.23. His result was a successful garden, 7.26, in the style of Caparn's English model.

Over a number of years as a traveler and observer of world garden styles, and his interest at home in native plants as an active member and Chairman of the Mountain Top Arboretum, he wanted a new design for the cloister garden. It should require less maintenance but show his interest in native plants and European garden design.[6]

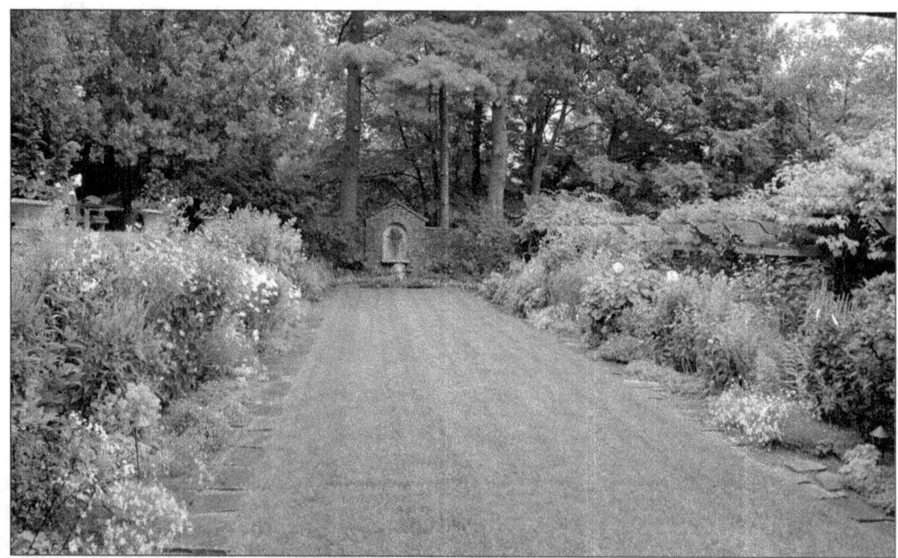

7.26 Harold Caparn design, the Cloister Garden at the private estate Wildmuir, Onteora Park, NY. Planted in the English tradition of flowering perennials as borders to the lawn. Photo 2008

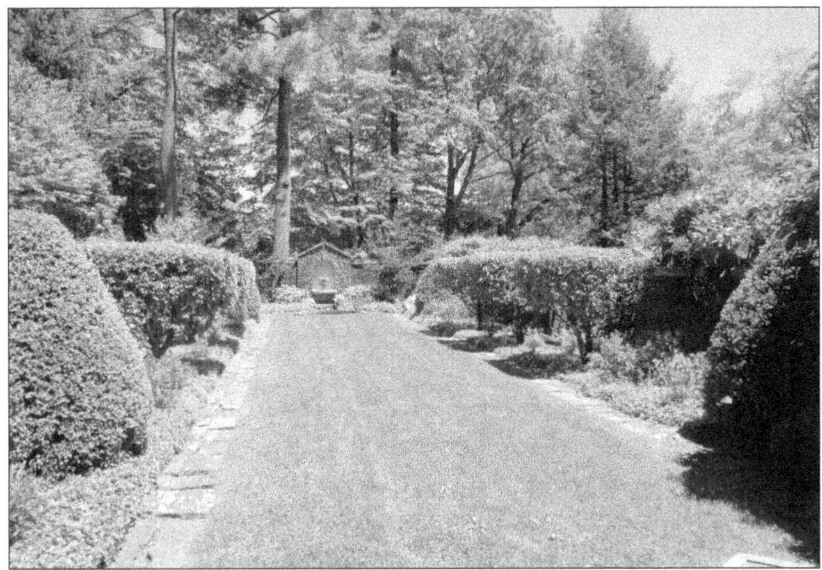

7.27 The replanted Cloister Garden, with prominent shaped dwarf birches. Planting design by Jamie Purinton, RLA. Photo 2019.

The outcome in the new planting design is less painterly, with colorful perennials, but more sculptural, with shaped deciduous and evergreen plantings. It suits the restrained Craftsman style of the home.

The garden illustrates what Caparn had said (*The House Beautiful,* 1905): "In whatever style it is laid out, the general design of a garden is more important than the details of planting. The flowers can be moved or replaced every year; but the scheme they express and decorate should be good and permanent."

At the end of the garden next to the house, the owners have made a stone patio for informal conversation or meals, ideal to view the garden and to enhance "the house outdoors," that Caparn wrote about in a series of seven articles of that title in *Countryside* (January-July, 1917), where he concludes: "One's outdoor home may, and usually should, be generously furnished with foliage and flowers, but always with a certain soberness and reserve."

The gate to the enclosed garden is seen in the wall, the entrance to the walkway beneath the pergola can be found to the left of the gate. The relation of the garden to the house flows naturally with steps coming down from the interior making easy access to the eating area and the garden.

The owner has extended the ability both to cook and eat in view of the Cloister Garden. He built a Rumford fireplace that would efficiently provide heat for cooking and warmth to the surrounding area for a cozy evening in the upper patio surrounded with a frame of plantings. Such extension of the garden design would have delighted Caparn in the artistry with which it was accomplished.

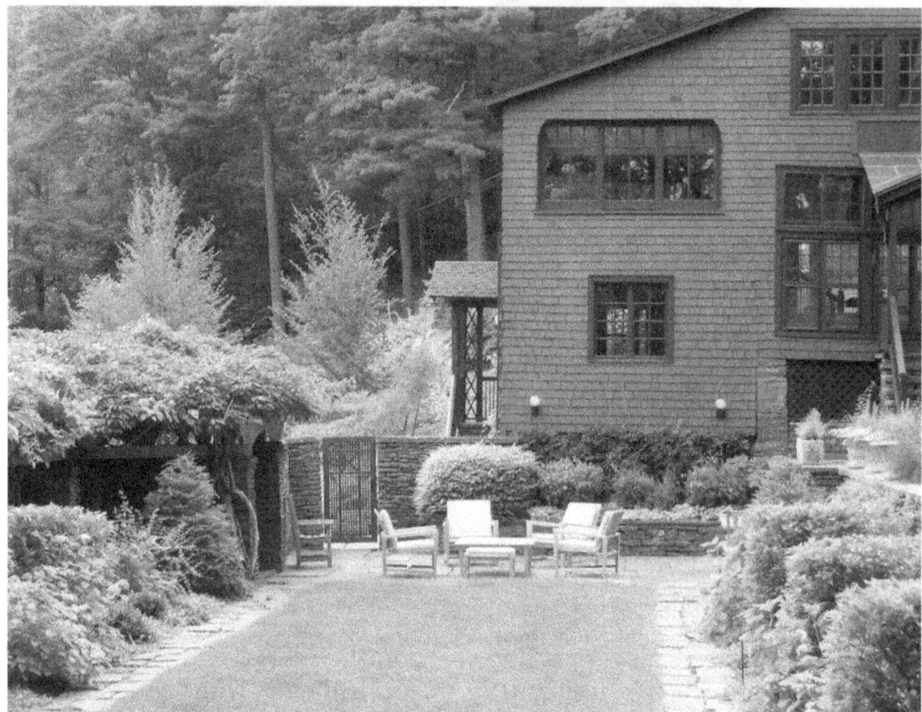

7.28 Cloister Garden, looking toward the home. Design by Jamie Purinton. Photo 2015

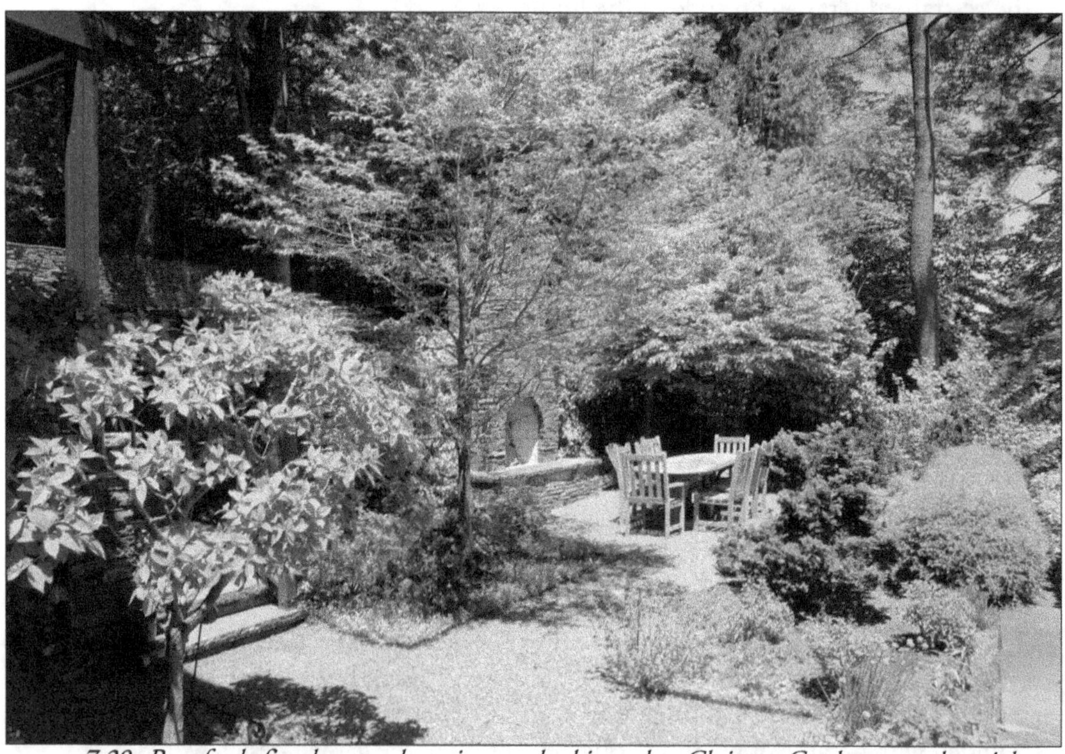

7.29 Rumford fireplace and patio overlooking the Cloister Garden, to the right. Design by Jamie Purinton. Photo 2019

The Candace Wheeler Wild Garden

The Onteora Garden Club, on September 21, 1920, made the decision to honor Onteora's founder Candace Wheeler with a garden at the Onteora Library. Mrs. Ben Ali Haggin, Jr. kept a journal beginning on that date that recorded the event and also identified Caparn as the designer of the Wild Garden; it is number 622 on his client list. Her journal continued to detail the many plants and other gifts given to the garden over the next decade by the residents of Onteora Park.

The Program of the "Dedication of Ground for the Candace Wheeler Wild Garden," on September 7, 1921, identified Mrs. Haggin as president of the Onteora Garden Club. At the Library on that date, the board of the Onteora Club in a resolution presented by president George Barron, deeded the land on the slope behind the Library to the Garden Club for the purpose of creating the garden. A ceremony to honor Mrs. Wheeler at the garden began with the entrance of children representing flowers for the new garden. There followed songs, poems and speeches by relatives and friends of Mrs. Wheeler.

A plaque honoring Candace Wheeler was affixed to the largest boulder in the garden. Mrs. Haggin, as chair of the executive committee of the Garden Club, and with personal enthusiasm, took an active part in developing the garden. She was described in the *Craftsman* as the "head gardener" at her home. Here she supervised the planting and gave generously to the building of the garden, as recorded in her journal.

Also making donations to the garden were Mrs. John White Alexander, widow of the painter, who contributed toward the development of the garden and gave *Ampelopsis Englemanii* (peppervine*)*; Mariana Griswold Van Rensselaer, who gave toward the development of the garden and *Hydrangea arborescens*; Dr. Cornelius Rybner, pianist and faculty member of Columbia University, who presented a recital at the home of Mrs. George Barron to raise funds towards the Library terrace.

Mr. Harold A. Caparn, who "throughout the development of the Garden, gave professional services including plans and personal supervision." In July 1921, he had given a lecture at the Library on "Wild Gardening." His talk no doubt described how a wild garden would be laid out, plants would be selected, planted and maintained, what blooms, fruit and colors would grace the garden and what other features it would contain as the proper form and approach by which to honor Mrs. Wheeler.

The problem for Caparn in designing the garden at the Library was that it would be planted and maintained by volunteers from the Garden Club who were mostly summer residents in the small community. He made therefore a Wild Garden, understanding that flowers, shrubs and trees that were native or could be naturalized to the area would not require a great deal in the way of maintenance. His planting plan is seen below. It gave simple, yet specific directions to Garden Club members as to where and what was to be planted.

Wild Garden for the Library, Onteora Park, N.Y. Made for the Onteora Garden Club, Nov. 25, 1922 F. N. 622. D2. Harold A. Caparn, Landscape Architect, New York
Scale 1in. = 8ft.

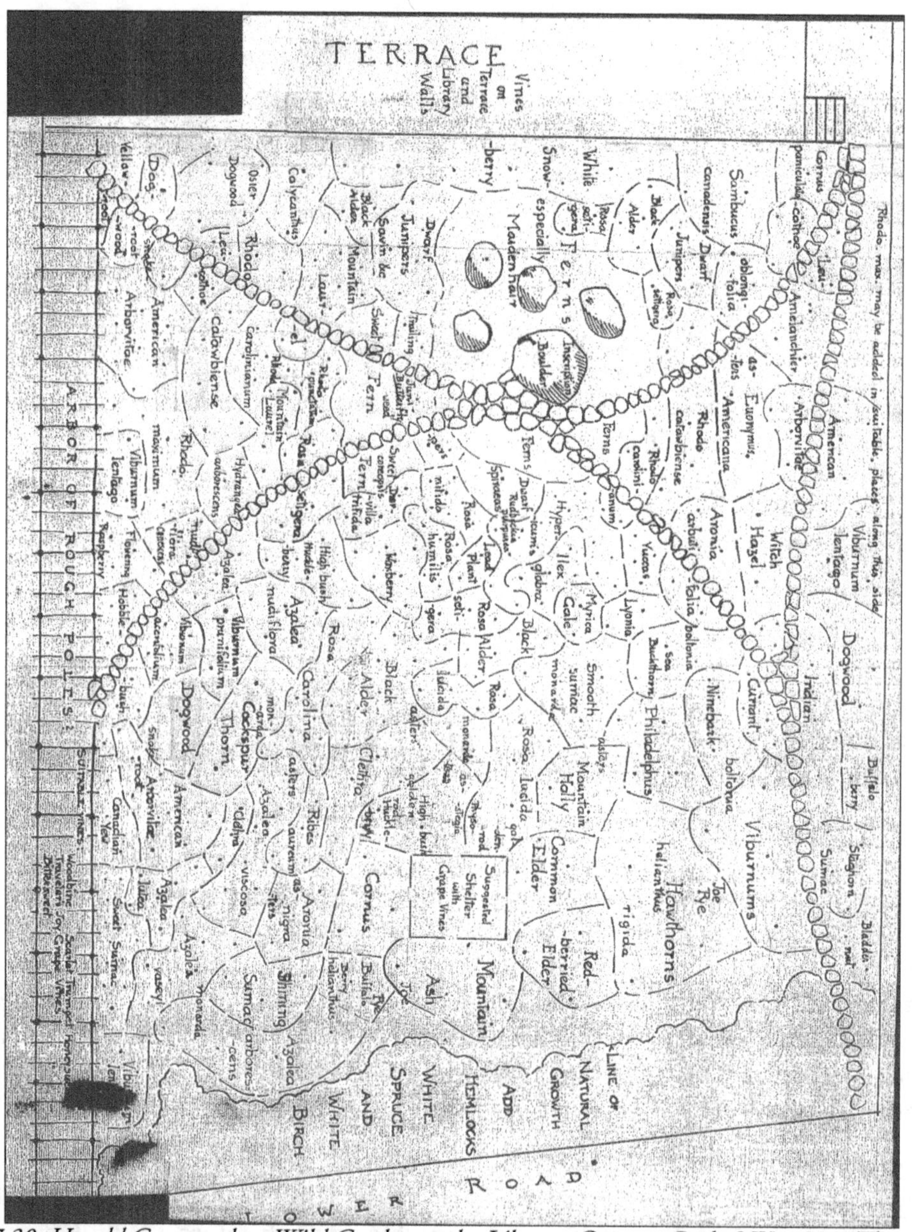

7.30 Harold Caparn plan, Wild Garden at the Library, Onteora Park, NY, 1922. The rear of the Library faces the Terrace and the Garden. Lower Road is at the bottom of the hill. The Arbor, left, was meant to cover a walkway from Lower Road up to the Terrace that led to stone steps then into the Library. The walkway still exists.

On November 25, 1922, Caparn presented his plan for the Wild Garden. His ground plan shows the boulders, with the "inscription rock" that is still seen in the garden. The central "shelter," meant as a secluded place for reading, contemplation and conversation, with a grapevine-covered pergola, is now only an open space. It was probably never built by the volunteer gardeners. Nor was the arbor of rough poles, seen at the bottom of the plan, covered with various vines over the walkway from the Lower Road up the hill to the Terrace at the rear of the Library.

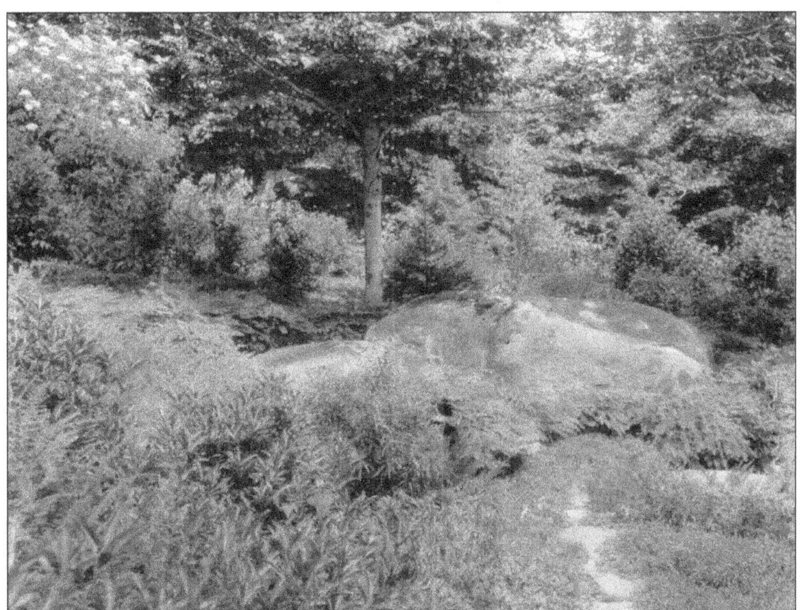

7.31 Harold Caparn design, portion of Wild Garden with Inscription Boulder, c. 1930.

A bronze plaque on the largest boulder in the Garden, right above, is inscribed:

This Wild Garden is dedicated to Candace Wheeler
One of the founders of Onteora
One of its most gracious spirits
The maker of its first garden
September 1921

On November 3, 1922, Mrs. Wheeler, then age 95, wrote from her home at 33 West 67th Street, New York City, to Mrs. Haggin: "If anything could be finer than the inscription you had put upon that great stone, I have not seen it. I feel as if I were the most fortunate woman in the world to have such dear, thoughtful, gifted friends."[7]

The Caparn's daughter, Rhys, said about Onteora Park in the book by Robert Beverly Hale, *Rhys Caparn* (1972): "John Alexander, the talented painter and muralist, summered there, as well as Ben Ali Haggin, the attractive and popular theatrical designer. The John Alexanders and the Ben Ali Haggins became great friends of the Caparns." Both Mrs. Alexander and Mrs. Ben Ali Haggin, Jr. contributed to Rhys' sculpture studies in Paris through finding teachers, residences and other support. On her career in sculpture, Mrs. Alexander provided to Rhys much kind and wise advice.

Harold, an amateur pianist and organist, no doubt felt very much at home with such friends. He designed the two gardens for Mrs. Ben Ali Haggin but with a sense also of interaction and social responsibility to the community for the Wheeler garden.

He considered landscape architecture an artistic endeavor and wrote and lectured about it as such. He took that approach to his lecture in New York on "Garden Architecture and Sculpture," given at the Metropolitan Museum of Art in 1918, published in *Architecture* (February 1919). Of Mrs. Haggin's Cloister Garden, Rhys, a prize-winning sculptor trained in Paris and New York, said that "it was among her father's best pieces of work."

The Cloister Garden and the Wild Garden in Onteora Park reveal on a small scale the art of Harold Caparn, who was highly regarded as a professional colleague and as a designer of parks and gardens by many of the founders and pioneers of American landscape design.

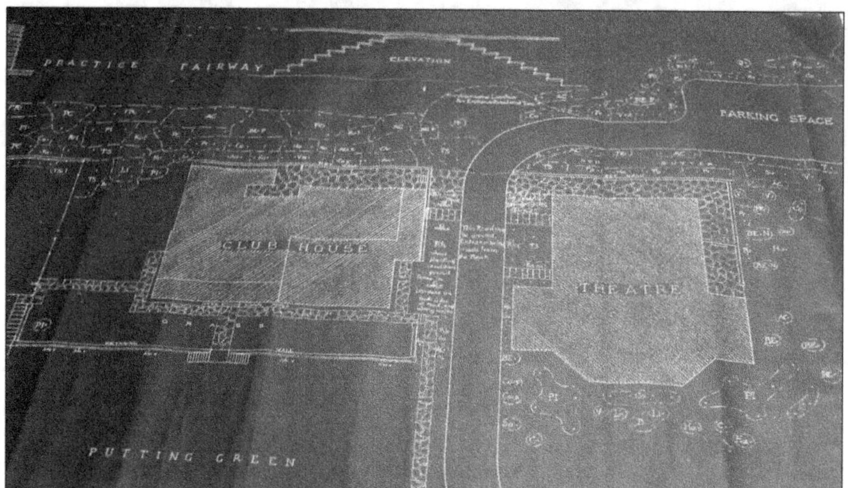

7.32 Harold Caparn plan, blueprint detail, Onteora Club House and Theatre, 1926.

Caparn presented, on September 25, 1926, a landscape plan for the area surrounding the Onteora Club House, a recreation and dining facility, and the Theatre, a 250-seat venue for plays, readings, lectures and other events. The Onteora Library holds sketches and a blueprint plan for the area. The plan, 7.32, seen in part shows extensive plantings as well as street access and parking. On the plan and in his client list it is number 622. The Wild Garden is also given as 622, for the Onteora Garden Club; both may have been done at the behest of Mrs. Ben Ali Haggin. The plan was not implemented, perhaps because by the time it had passed through the approval process, the Stock Market Crash occurred, and it was put on hold. It is a fine addition to the plans that are extant of Caparn's work.[8]

Caparn's Client List gives Eliz. D. Dwight as job number 638. Elizabeth Davis Monod, widow of George Monod of Paris, married Frederick A. Dwight of New York, widower of Elizabeth King (Wakeman) Dwight. Frederick and Elizabeth D. Dwight resided on Park Avenue in New York City. He was a Yale graduate and an attorney.[9]

At the cottage they shared in Onteora Park, she made changes to the interior to suit her taste. For the exterior, she hired Harold Caparn, already known for his work at Onteora, to completely redesign the grounds and gardens. When the work was done the Caparn plans were safely tucked away in the attic. Through following owners they went undisturbed. When a new owner acquired the property, history was discovered in the attic.

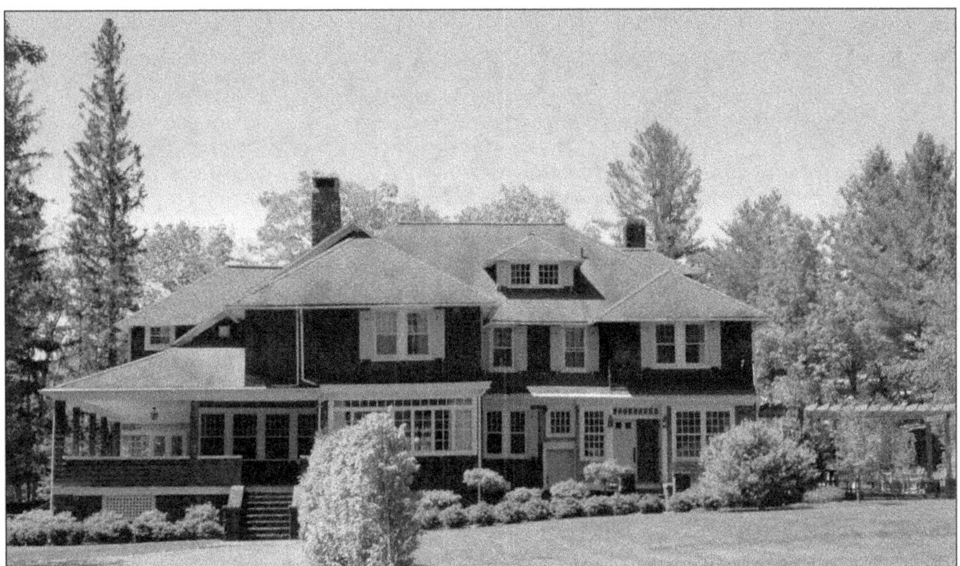

7.33 Cottage "Sans souci," Onteora Park. photo 2019.

The plans found and preserved represent a most complete view of Caparn's presentation of his vision for a private property. His work on the landscape is given in a blueprint in great detail, including a plant list cued to the plan. The Lily Pool no longer exists. The garage has been remodeled into work and relaxation space. The plan extends Caparn's work at Onteora to another home, presented in the year after his plan for the Onteora Club House and Theatre.

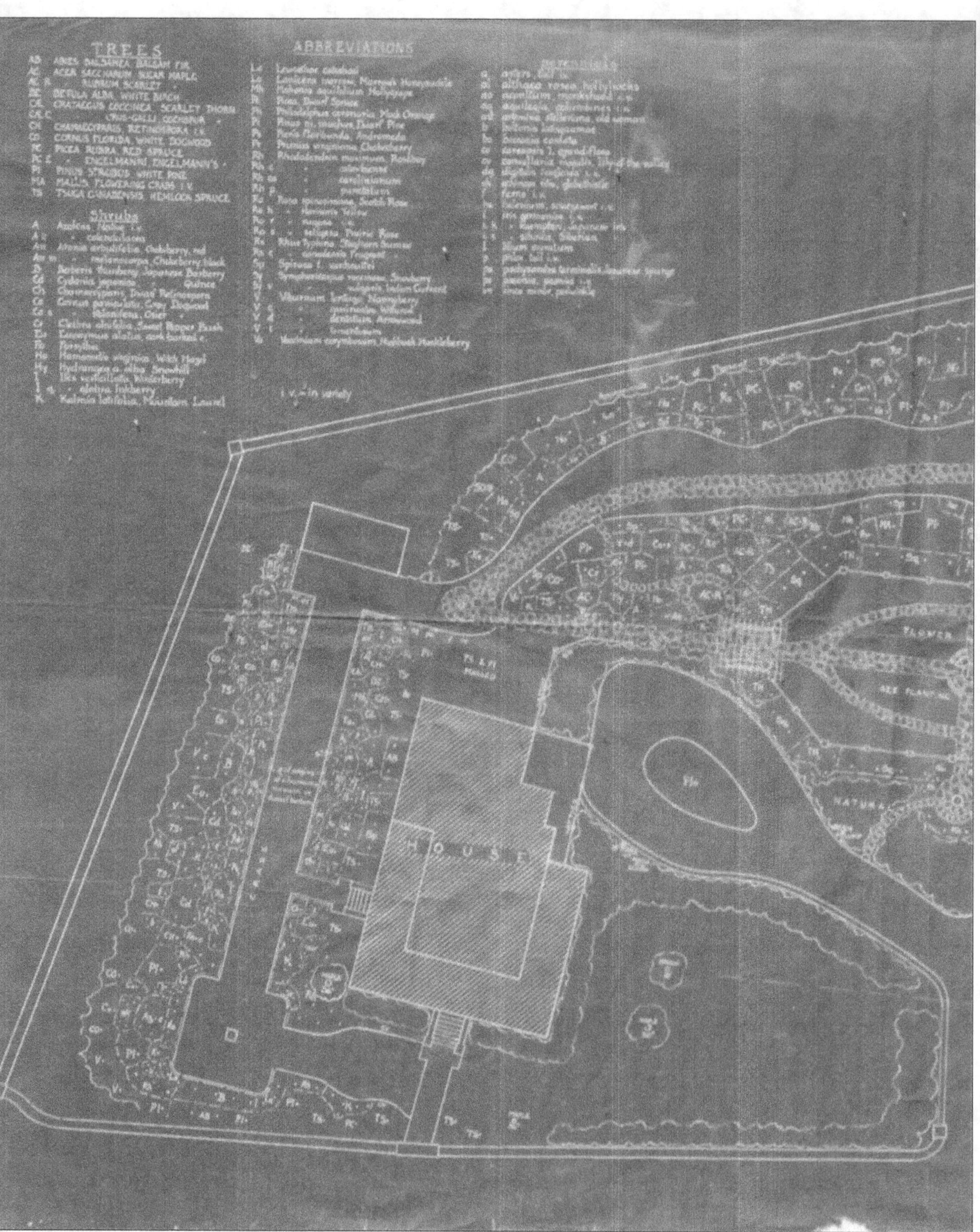

7.34 Caparn blueprint plan for the remodeling of the estate grounds, 1927.

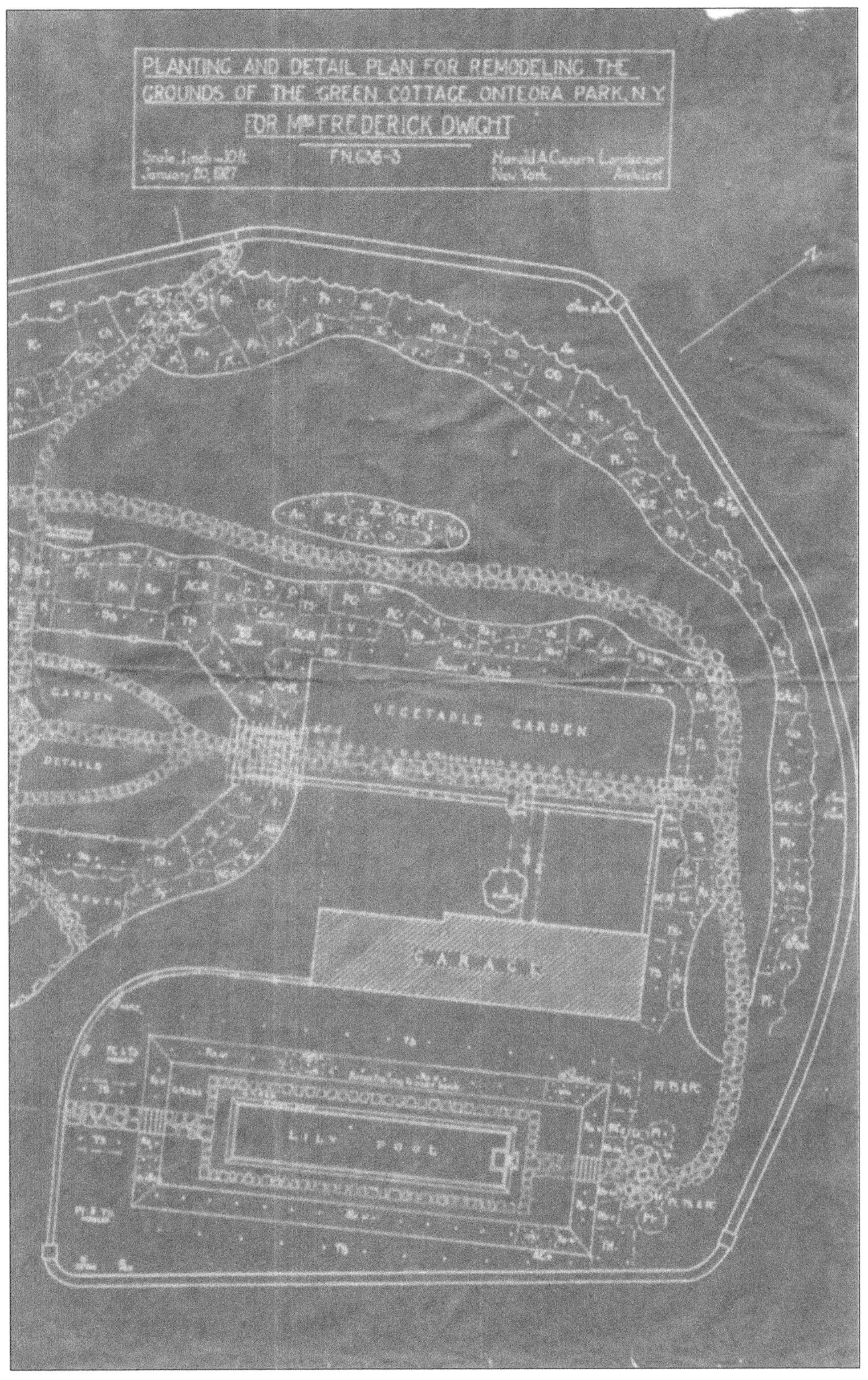
PLANTING AND DETAIL PLAN FOR REMODELING THE
GROUNDS OF THE GREEN COTTAGE, ONTEORA PARK, N.Y.
FOR Mrs FREDERICK DWIGHT
Scale 1 inch = 10 ft.
January 30 1927
F.N. 606-3
Harold A Caparn Landscape
New York
Architect
VEGETABLE GARDEN
GARAGE
LILY POOL

8 Country Place

Marriage, family and country retreat...1906–1925

Harold married Clara Howard (Jones) Royall (1866-1970) on October 12, 1906 in New York City. She was at the time a successful teacher of singing in the City. Clara had married George Claiborne Royall in North Carolina earlier and sought divorce. In New York she found employ for her considerable training and talents in music. She and Harold met through that mutual interest and enjoyed attending many concerts together.

Harold and Clara were vacationing in 1909 at Onteora Park in the northern Catskills when their second daughter, Rhys, was born. The Caparns now sought more than just a place for respite. They needed a country retreat, closer to their Manhattan home, where they could spend longer periods away from the city for themselves and their daughters.

To meet their desire for a retreat, in June 1911, Harold bought five acres in the elite village of Briarcliff Manor, about thirty miles up the Hudson River from Manhattan. In following years they were noticed in entries in the New York Social Register at their summer retreat, "Fernie Farm." [1]

Caparn M&M"Harold ap Rhys (Royall–Clara H Jones) LtKennethCRoyall–USA–atFtJacksonSC Lt Geo C Royall–USA–at Chickamauga Pk Tenn	Phone No 116 "Fernie Farm" Briarcliff Manor N Y

8.1 Social Register, New York

The additions to the Caparn listing are for Clara's sons from her previous marriage. George Jr. (1896-1967), was a career Army officer. Kenneth Claiborne Royal (1894-1971), was a graduate of the University of North Carolina, where he was inducted into Phi Beta Kappa. He then went to Harvard Law School, earning an LLB, and was named an editor of the *Harvard Law Review*. He was commissioned an army lieutenant in 1918. In June 1942 he rejoined the army as a lawyer and with a colonel's commission. He was promoted to brigadier general in November, 1943. Under President Harry S Truman he rose in July 1947 to become the Secretary of War and two months later to occupy a Cabinet post as the first Secretary of the Army. In April 1949 he resigned to become senior partner in a NYC law firm of which he became head in 1958, remaining until his retirement in 1967.

Harold and Clara's daughters and their half-siblings were very likely visitors to the retreat at Briarcliff Manor. Anne Howard (1907-1971), was a writer, and Rhys (1909-1997), a sculptor. They each attended the Brearley School in New York City. After graduation, Anne lived in France and studied at Le Cordon Bleu. Rhys first attended Bryn Mawr College, but withdrew in her second year and joined her sister in France to study sculpture. They each married, Rhys to Herbert Johannes Steel in September 1935, Anne to Robert MacDonald Moore, Jr., in July 1938. Rhys had been close to her father and as a child learned "her father's enthusiasm for designed space--the positive shape of a tree, the negative shape of the sky, the precise angle of a slope."[2] Rhys also was influenced by the natural surroundings of the country retreat. As she grew older they formed a background to her life's work in sculpting animals and drawing landscapes.

Harold and Clara were active in many professional organizations. Clara earned a better than average yearly income for the time as a voice teacher in New York City and was professionally active. She founded "An Hour of Music," their first meeting held at Fernie Farm; it gave scholarships to promising young musicians. Harold kept a landscaping office in Manhattan and they had an apartment there at different addresses at different times.[3] Over the next several decades, they and their daughters appeared as the subject of articles or notices in *The New York Times*. They can be found in the *New York Social Register*, 1918 to 1938, a recognition of their continuing economic and social status.

A map of Briarcliff Manor from the 1930s shows the retreat located on South State Road, registered in the name of Clara Caparn. The location off a country road was an idyllic setting for a retreat. Unlike some who built showplaces during the Country Place Era (c.1890-c.1930), the Caparns wanted a natural, reposeful place in which to relax from their busy New York schedules. Harold proceeded to landscape the property and purpose-designed the building as a music studio for his wife.[4]

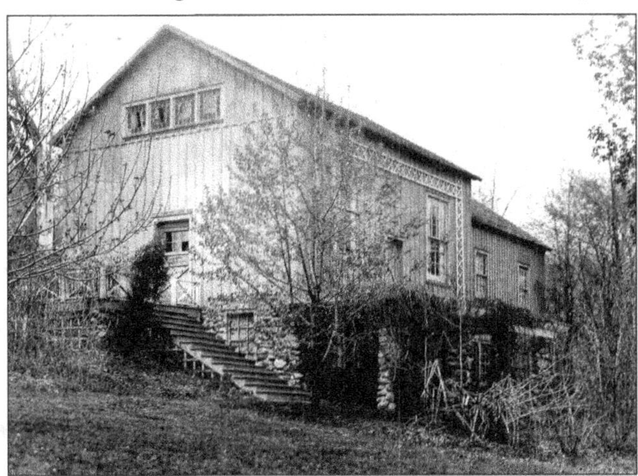

8.2 Caparn country retreat, "Fernie Farm," Briarcliff Manor, NY, c. 1912, seen in early photo.

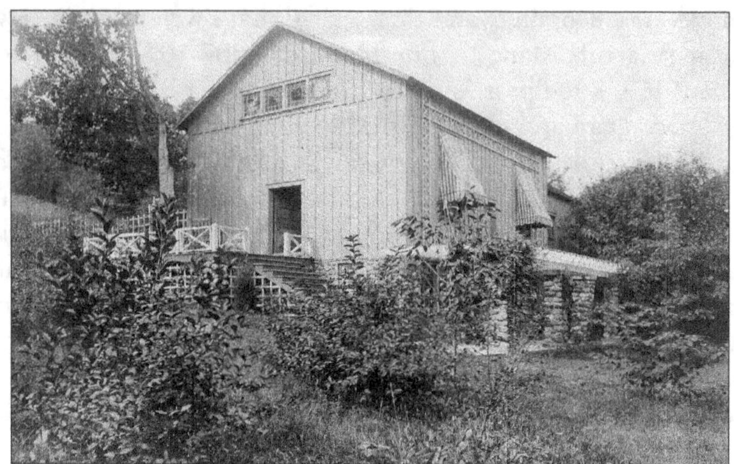

8.3 *Fernie Farm, c. 1915. After work by Caparn on the Craftsman-style building and the informally designed landscape.*

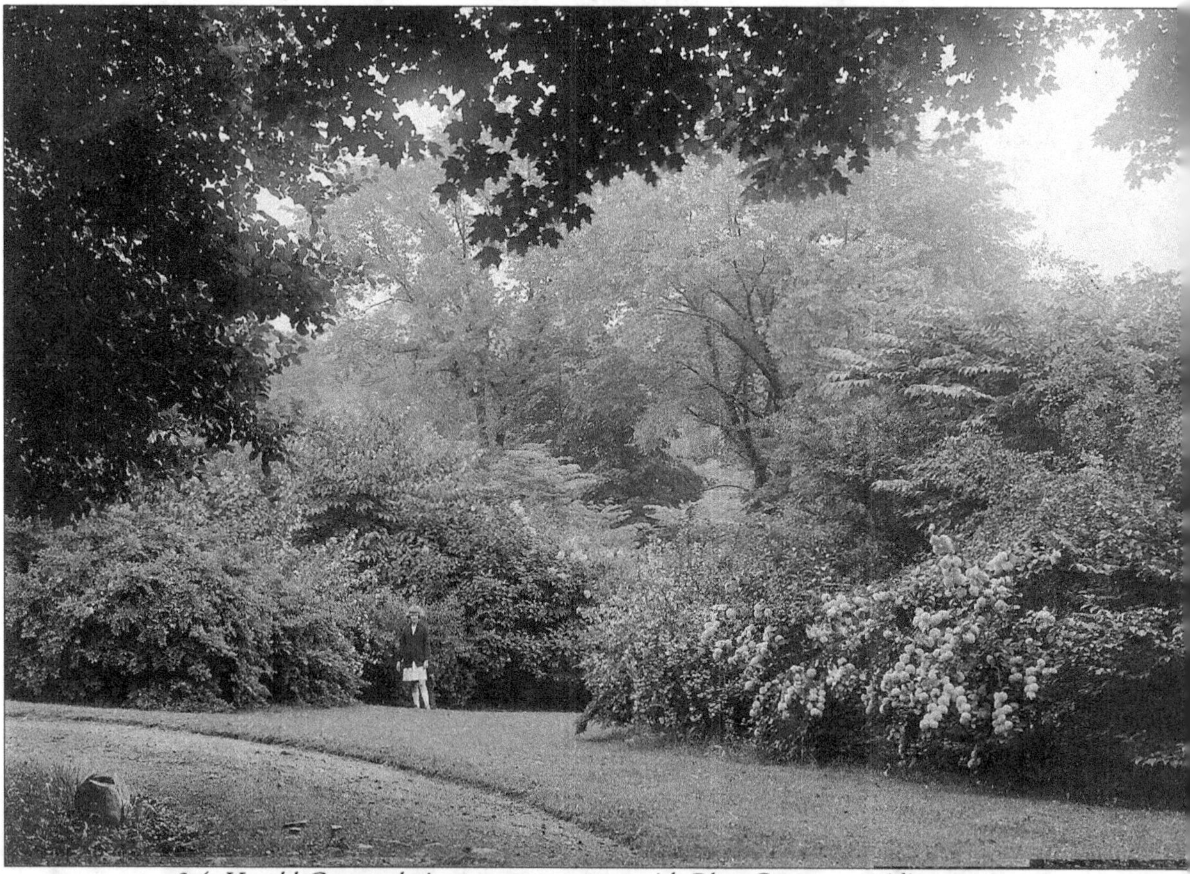

8.4 *Harold Caparn design, country retreat with Rhys Caparn providing perspective to his landscape plantings, c. 1921. This photograph can be found in the Library of Congress collection "American Memory," and in the Frances Loeb Library, Harvard University.*

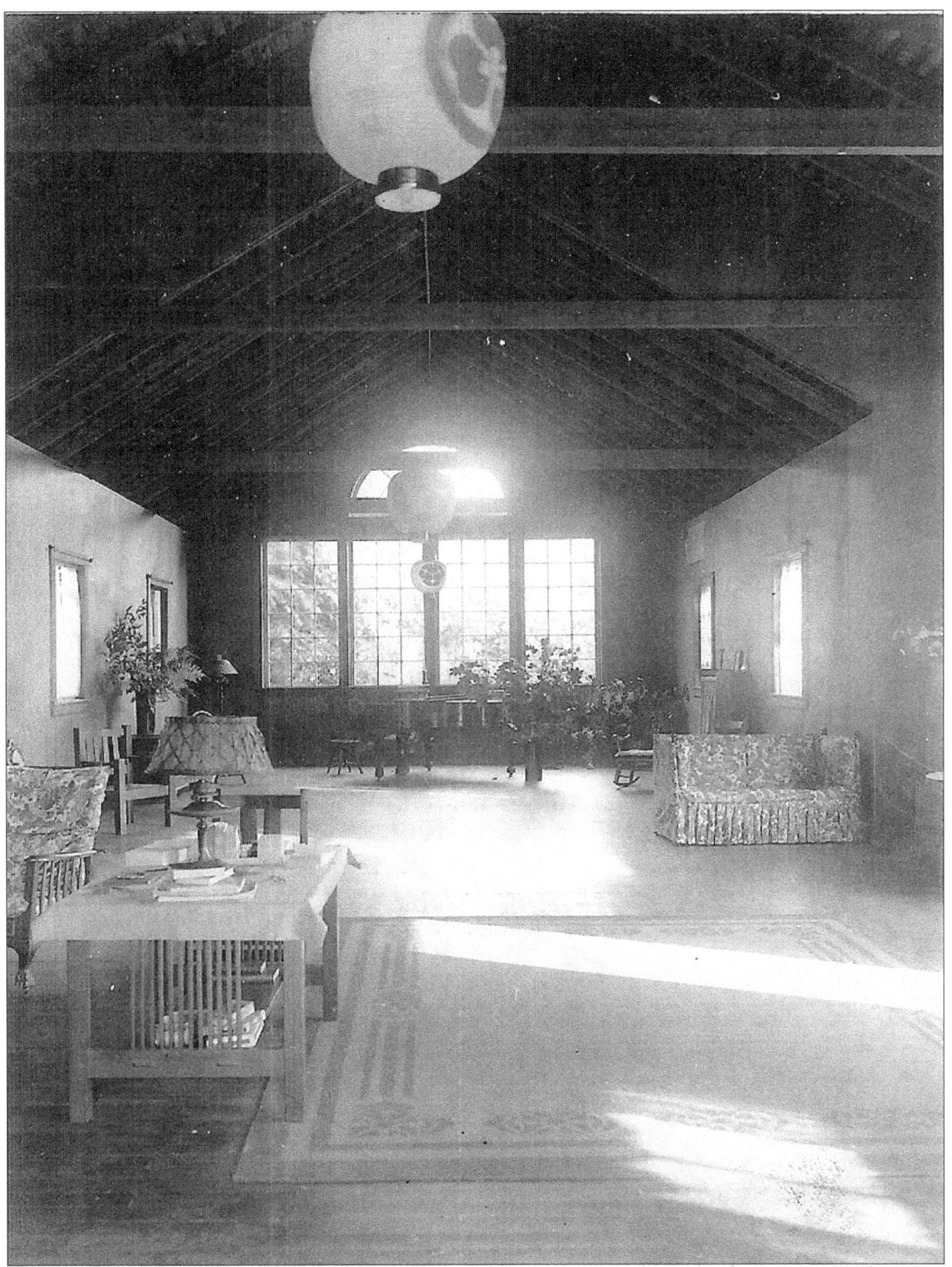

8.5 *Harold Caparn design, music studio, with grand piano and Stickley furniture, second floor, Caparn retreat. photo, c. 1915.*

Later photographs of the Briarcliff Manor property show a profusion of trees and shrubs planted in informal style, without a central lawn, but giving the sense of entering a restful environment.

The illustration, 8.5, shows the interior of the Caparn retreat, second floor, that was a music studio for Clara. Harold also from time to time enjoyed playing the grand piano in the studio, a pastime at which he was quite competent. The length and height of the room, with walls of hard surface and open rafters to the interior of the roof, would have provided an acoustically responsive chamber for voice and piano. That would be ideal for its later use, when the Caparns invited community members and friends in for musicales.

The large windows make it a light, airy place in which to read or perform and to view the outside landscape. This room is simply decorated with Stickley furniture, a hanging set of graduated Oriental bells and lanterns and with fresh flowers that bring harmony between outside and inside. The ground floor, with a vine-covered veranda, leads to interior living spaces that would be cool in summer. The style of the dwelling fits with the style of the surrounding landscape by Caparn. Craftsman influence of the house and studio by Caparn can be seen in the large open multi-function room with exposed beams and ceiling, windows through which one can interact with the environs, the stained glass windows in the gallery of the studio, and the stone pillars supporting a vine-covered pergola over the veranda. It shows the simplicity, clean lines and visible construction that were the hallmarks of the American Craftsman style.

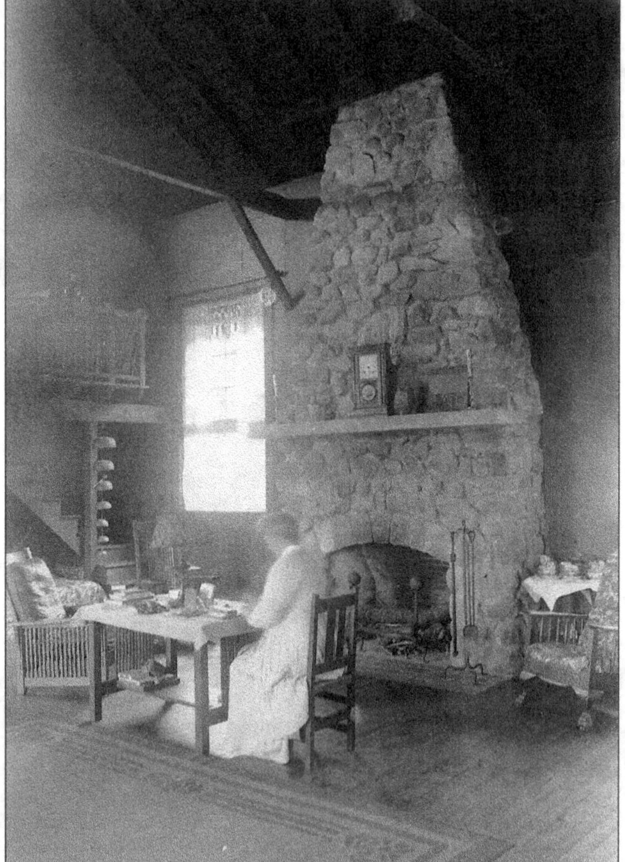

8.6 Clara Caparn in her music studio, at opposite end of room of 8.5; note fireplace and loft, both still exist in the modern revision of this room. photo, c. 1915.

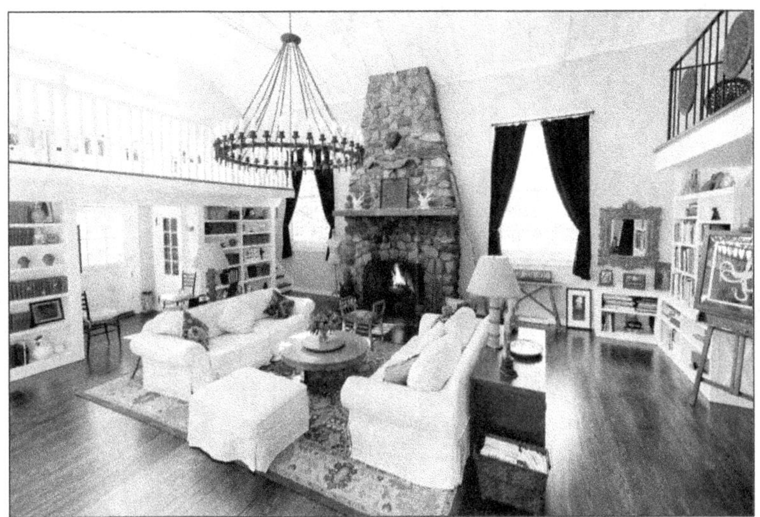

8.7 End of music room, now living room, with original fireplace, loft. Photo 2018

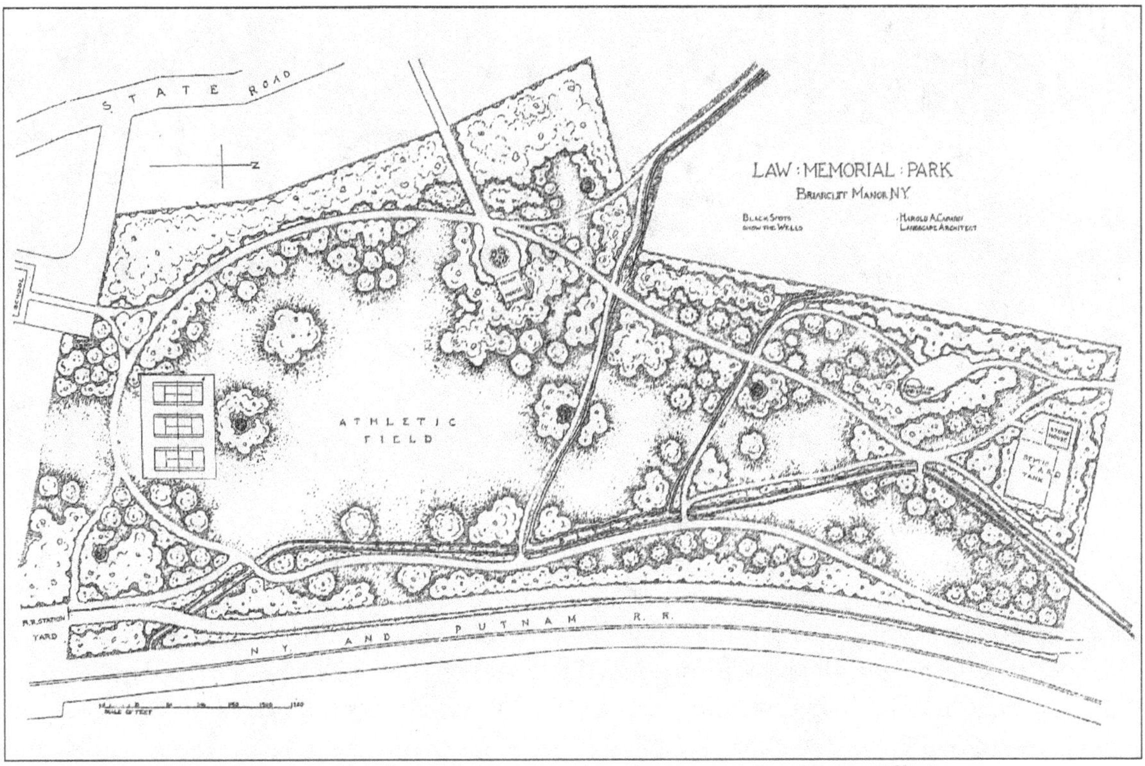

8.8 Harold Caparn plan for park incorporating the town wells of Briarcliff Manor.

Caparn designed a park for Briarcliff Manor that is still extant, although it has undergone renovation and development. Law Memorial Park, in the center of Briarcliff Manor, was designed by Caparn, c. 1925. It still has some lovely old trees that were likely planted during the period. A small pond with a curvilinear wall and a fountain shows signs of Caparn design.

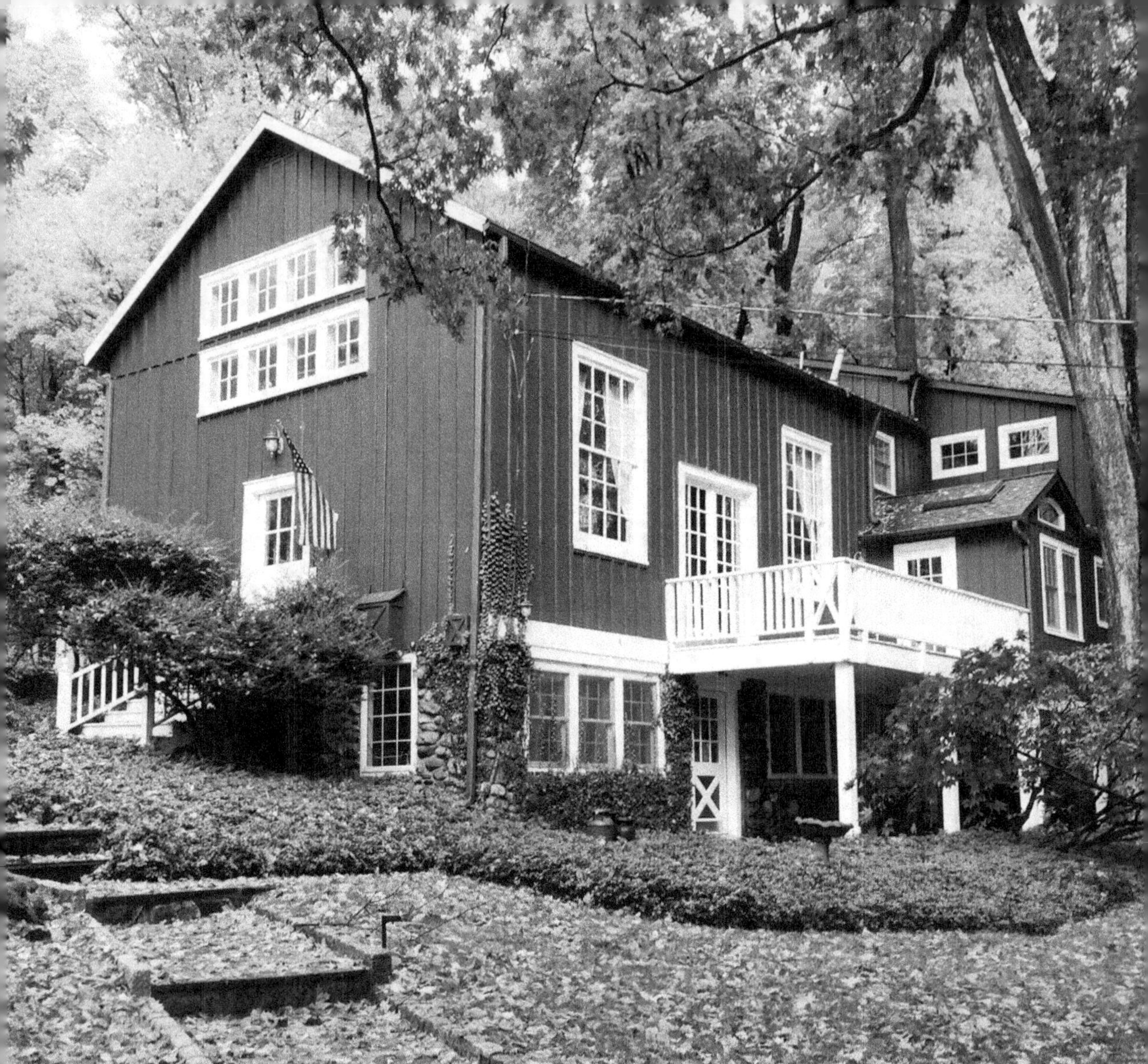

8.9 Harold and Clara Caparn's former retreat, extended, updated, Briarcliff Manor. Photo 2018

On an adjacent site he laid out a plan (labeled as Law Memorial Park) for a park surrounding the water supply for the village. The town wells provided a challenge for landscape design, described in a Caparn article on the problem. Beside tennis courts, left, and a pavilion that could be used as a bandstand for summer concerts, upper right, the park incorporated the coverings of the five wells-the dark centers-into the design, seen in the plan, 8.8. The plan was not carried out and the site is now overgrown.

Caparn's interest in music can be seen in his incorporation of bandstands in several of his park designs, as in the original plan for Baird Court at The New York Zoological Park, Riis Park on Jamaica Bay, at Denison Park in Corning, as well as this plan in Briarcliff Manor (small circle at end of open space, upper right). He believed that a community band, like an amateur chorus, brought the community benefits and enhanced the lives of the participants. His early training in music can be seen in his designing into several landscapes the space in which to present concerts. He speaks of these benefits again in his letters concerning the 1939 World's Fair and its concert hall.

Country Place Estates in Briarcliff Manor

Caparn designed two estates high above and overlooking the Hudson River. Client List No. 633 was for Olney B. Mairs (1876-1943). A NYC attorney with the significant firm White and Case, he was a graduate of Williams College and Columbia University in law. He and his wife had a residence in New York City on Fifth Avenue, a summer residence in East Hampton, L.I., his office was at 55 Broadway. The 1918 *New York Summer Social Register* gives: Mairs Mr&Mrs Olney B (Eva E. Ward) at their home called "Greylock" in Briarcliff Manor.

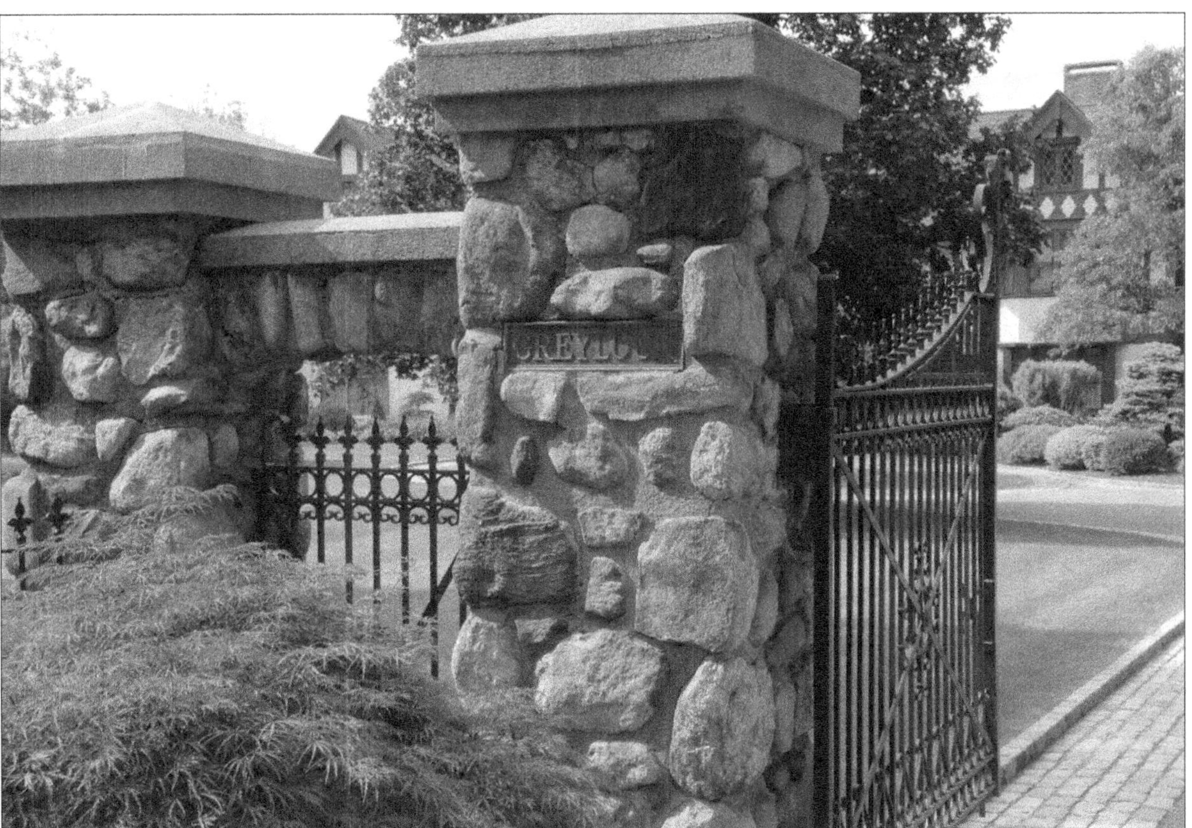

8.10 Gateway, "Greylock," plaque on the gatepost. Briarcliff Manor. Photo, 2019

While the house is original, c. 1905, the grounds show Caparn influence in curvileanar designs of architectural ground features.

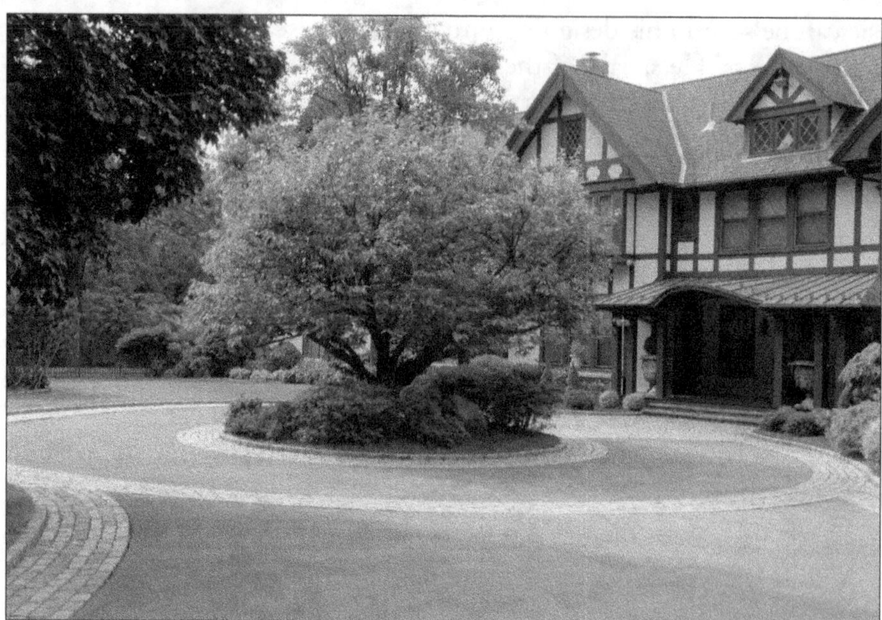

8.11 Greylock, with circular drive in front of entrance to home, found in other Caparn plans. Photo, 2019

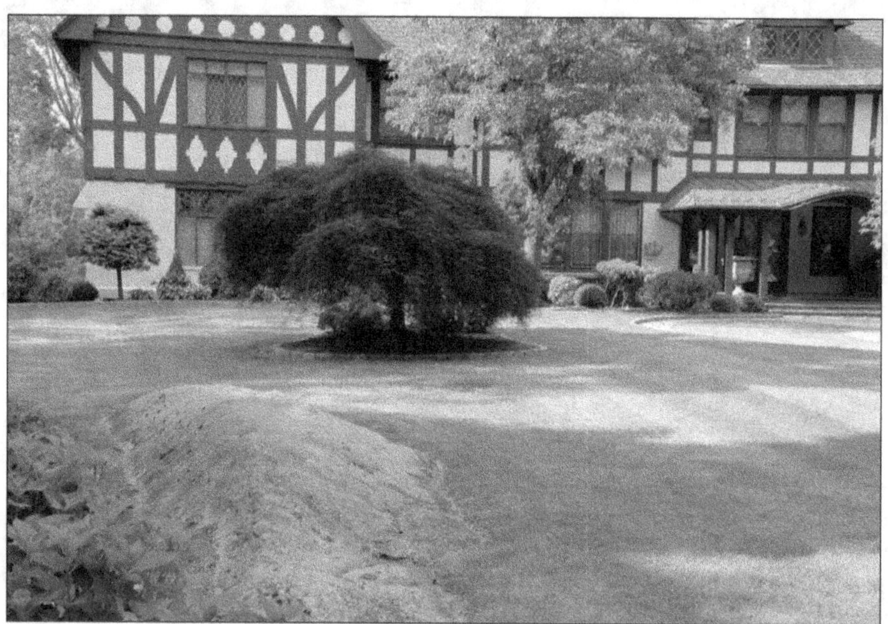

8.12 Greylock, shows a rock ledge, foreground, which, as Caparn recommended addressing a problem, has been incorporated into the design of the landscape. Photo, 2019

Caparn Client List No. 531 was for U(ri) T(aylor) Hungerford (1843-1926). He was the owner and President of Hungerford Brass and Copper Co. Their offices were on Pearl St., NYC, and also in Philadelphia and San Francisco. He was the founder, in 1916, of the Charlotte Hungerford Hospital in Torrington, CT, in honor of his mother, born in Torrington, where he also grew up. His home, "Hohensichtlich" built in the 1890s, was a prime location overlooking the Hudson River from a high point of the hill.

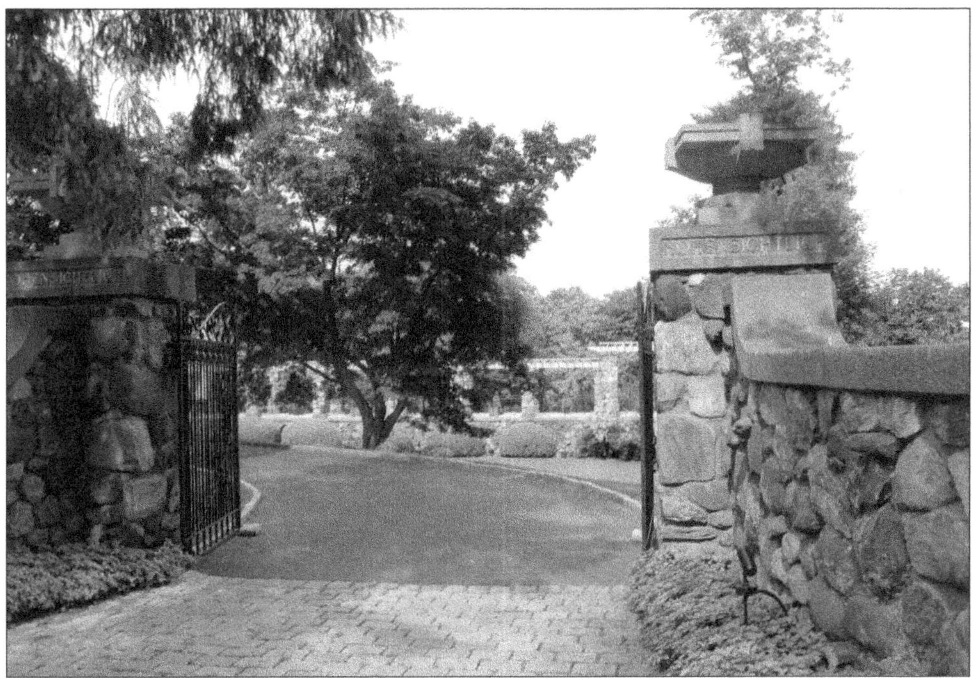

8.13 Gateway, "Hohensichtlich," inscribed, gateposts, Briarcliff Manor. Photos, 2019

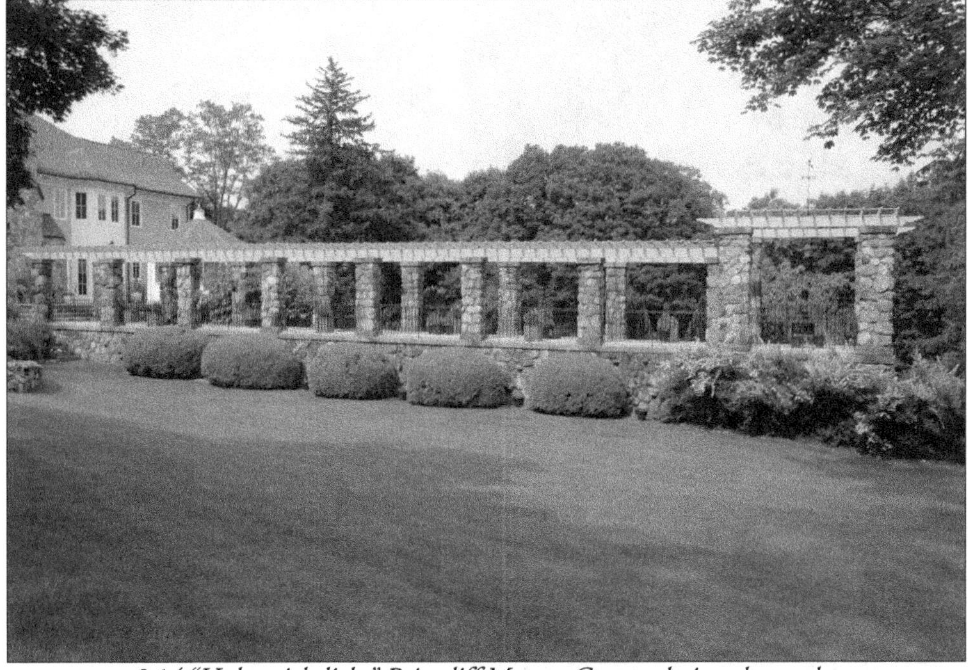

8.14 "Hohensichtlich," Briarcliff Manor. Caparn designed pergola.

The Caparn design of a pergola exists at the top of the hill, below it a swimming pool and below that a terrace, illustrative of Caparn's designs on a steep hill.

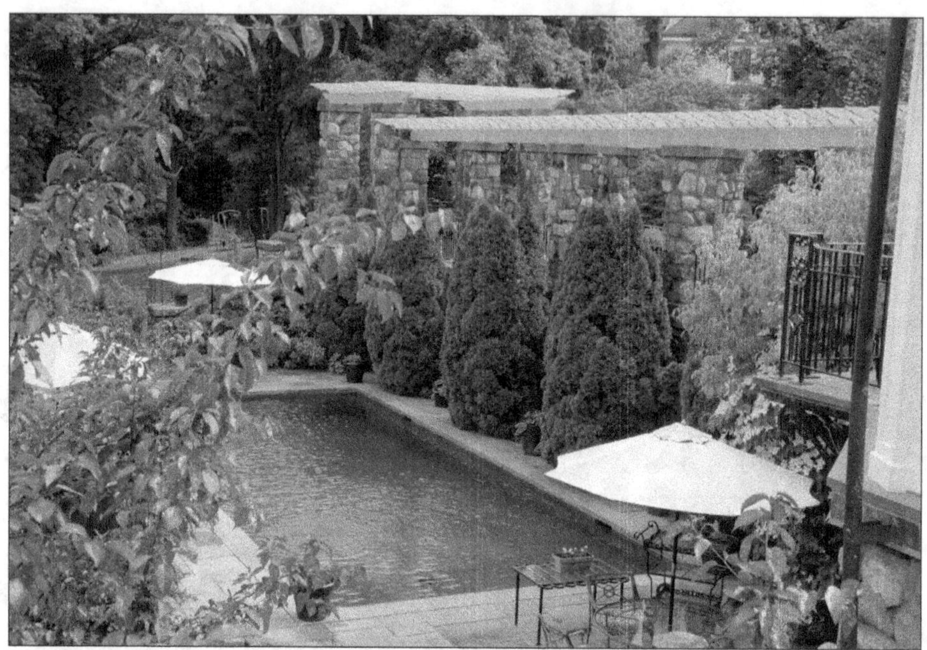

8.15 Swimming pool is screened by the pergola, 8.14. It is above the terrace, 8.16.

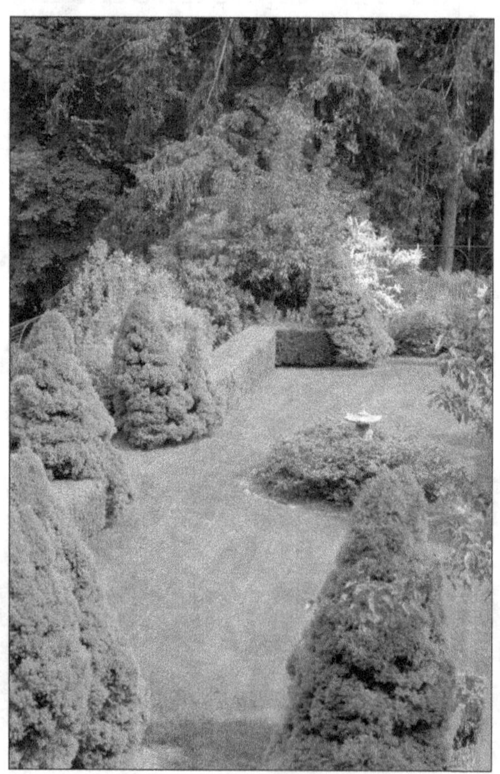

8.16 The property, on a hill, was given a terrance on the lowest designed level.

Caparn's affection for Briarcliff Manor was expressed in his design of an outdoor theatre for the community. It would be flexible in design, capable of presenting a wide range of styles of plays. He no doubt felt that the intellectual and artistic interest of the residents would support such a project. He wrote an article about the theatre, the plays that it could accommodate and how that should be accomplished. His interest in other arts, is seen in his consideration of other outdoor theatres of which he was aware. His article on the outdoor theatre ranged over the problems that needed to be solved to build it. He said that, in view of the mental training, the mutual help and community spirit that outdoor theatricals elicit and foster, it would be hard to find a form of recreation more pleasant and profitable than can be had in the outdoor theatre; his article appeared in the *Journal of the International Garden Club* in 1918. The article is a review of Frank Waugh, *Outdoor Theatres*, Boston: R. G. Badger, 1917.

Caparn's interest in landscape architecture as an art, is also found in his interest in the visual arts of drawing, painting and photography. His passion for music was expressed in the performance areas for music incorporated into several designs, such as Jacob Riis Park and his plan for the park in Briarcliff Manor. He felt that both instrumental and choral music provided opportunities for expression and beneficial interaction among residents of several cities and villages.

Now to his proposed theatre, he continues:
> Let us consider the essential differences between the outdoor and indoor theatre. The indoor theatre has not only an enclosed stage, but an enclosed auditorium. Furthermore, the stage is illuminated and the auditorium darkened, causing the greatest possible concentration by the audience on the stage-picture and action.

> On the other hand, the outdoor theatre, though enclosed at the sides, has no roof, and the auditorium is as light as the stage excepting for night performances. The result is less concentration of attention and more diffusion of thought and impression among the audience. This may be expected to call for more simple and definite dramatic design and speech and action on the stage. It makes no difference that the stage may be of grass, the wings and backdrop of trees, bushes, hedges or pergola columns, for any of these, or rather, imitations of them, might be used for similar purposes indoors. The only basic difference between the outdoor and the indoor theatre is that the latter shuts out the sky.

> Again, we must not forget the radical difference between the outdoor theatre by day and night. At night, when the auditorium is dark and the stage in artificial light, the conditions do not differ greatly from those of the indoor theatre. There is almost as much concentration on the stage as indoors. There is the added mystery of the night, the sense of being in the limitless open, the pure air, all aiding to key one up to a greater sensibility, a more romantic expectation. In such conditions, the only kind of drama that cannot be appropriately presented will be that which depends on stage management or machinery or setting, or is trifling, banal, ephemeral, local, too thin in design and construction, too dependent on facial expression, byplay or stage business, lack of carrying power, or any kind of small scale, petty or ignoble quality unfitting it for the canopy of the sky.

His familiarity with plays is revealed in his further specific consideration:

> Why should not "The Servant in the House" [modern morality by Charles Rann Kennedy] or "Paid in Full" [modern 'reality' by Eugene Walter] be given in the open air? Such a piece as "The Seven Keys to Baldpate" [mystery farce--play within a play--adapted to the stage by George M. Cohan from the story by Earl Derr Biggers] could not but lose some of its fun, its snap and point if played out of doors, simple though its stage setting may be. Why should not "The Rivals" [Sheridan's comedy of manners] or "She Stoops to Conquer" [Goldsmith's 18th-century comedy of manners] be played out of doors? Comedy is not inconsistent with fresh air, or we should have to exclude "As You Like It" [Shakespeare's comedy]; nor even farce, for then Aristophanes would have to seek cover, a thing he never thought of. Neither is complexity of plot and change of scene necessary hindrances to outdoor presentation, for both these are characteristic of Shakespeare, and the changes of scene can be handled in the simple ways of his own time.

In short, it would be difficult to find any real play, that is, one depending for its interest on the interplay of human emotion that could not properly be presented out of doors. Of course, the play and the presentation must be adjusted to the theatre, the audience and the available resources in funds and actors.

All this is not saying that any good play could be produced in any outdoor theatre. Some plays would fit one theatre, some another. One could even imagine a [Sir Arthur Wing] Pinero drawing room play in some small and sophisticated outdoor theatre. What kind of plays were produced two or three centuries ago in the small Italian garden theatres? Recalling the precedents for many kinds of drama out of doors, farce comedy and deep tragedy of the ancient and modern classics, it is plainly unsafe to dogmatize on what could not be well presented out of doors, given the right conditions.

As for stage effects, properties and setting, it is astonishing how few are needed to produce an illusion. The writer has seen a very enjoyable version of [Shakespeare's] "Midsummer Night's Dream" played in an open grass court, and recalls the deep impression made by a really excellent performance of [Edmund John Millington] Synge's play "The Shadow of the Glen" on a grass stage with sides and background of foliage and two or three pieces of furniture to represent the interior of an Irish farmer's cottage in which the action takes place. No one seemed to miss the walls and roof or to require any further aid to the imagination.

Stone seats can be used not only in stadia and Greek theatres, but in very much smaller and simpler ones as in the very attractive little garden theatre of Mr. Charles Gould at Tarrytown, N. Y. where the stage is enclosed by cement columns. With a stage in keeping, the tiers of stone seats are very handsome.

Finally, in the same journal in June 1918, Caparn presents his design for an outdoor theatre that he says was made for a syndicate in Westchester County, then laid on the shelf, like so many other projects, because of WWI. A note on one of the illustrations indicates that he had in mind Briarcliff Manor as the place for his outdoor theatre. He has researched the form his design might take.

As far as the writer knows, this scheme differs from any yet constructed in providing a theatre usable not only for any play that can properly be given out of doors, but for complete presentation of the classical Greek drama. When they are given, not merely the scenery, but the stage and orchestra have to be constructed. [In Greek drama] the Chorus went through rhythmic movements round an altar on a circular space in front of the stage and five or six feet below it, intoning at intervals their comments to explain the action on the stage and fill in the pauses. This circular space was the orchestra.

In the scheme here illustrated, a grass stage of an extreme width of sixty feet [the stage width equivalent to many modern indoor theatres] is enclosed by walls or wings with side entrances and curtains at the back which could be kept as a background, covered by a backdrop, or drawn so that the landscape beyond would take the place of a backdrop. It would be easy to put a temporary background across any part of the stage so as to make it as deep or shallow as might be desired.

When a Greek play is to be staged, a mat of the desired pattern and forty-five feet in diameter is laid over the grass stage which becomes the orchestra. The tall columns and open wood pediment with the curtains are movable, and for the presentation of a Greek play would give place to a movable stage with the necessary scenery. All this apparatus could be constructed so as to be easy to move or install and could be kept in a convenient place of storage when not in use, under the seats or elsewhere. Six dressing rooms are provided. The seats are intended to be built into the side of a hill, and as shown on the plan, would accommodate an audience of twelve hundred. They are intended to be built of concrete, but could be of wood, or camp chairs on grass terraces.

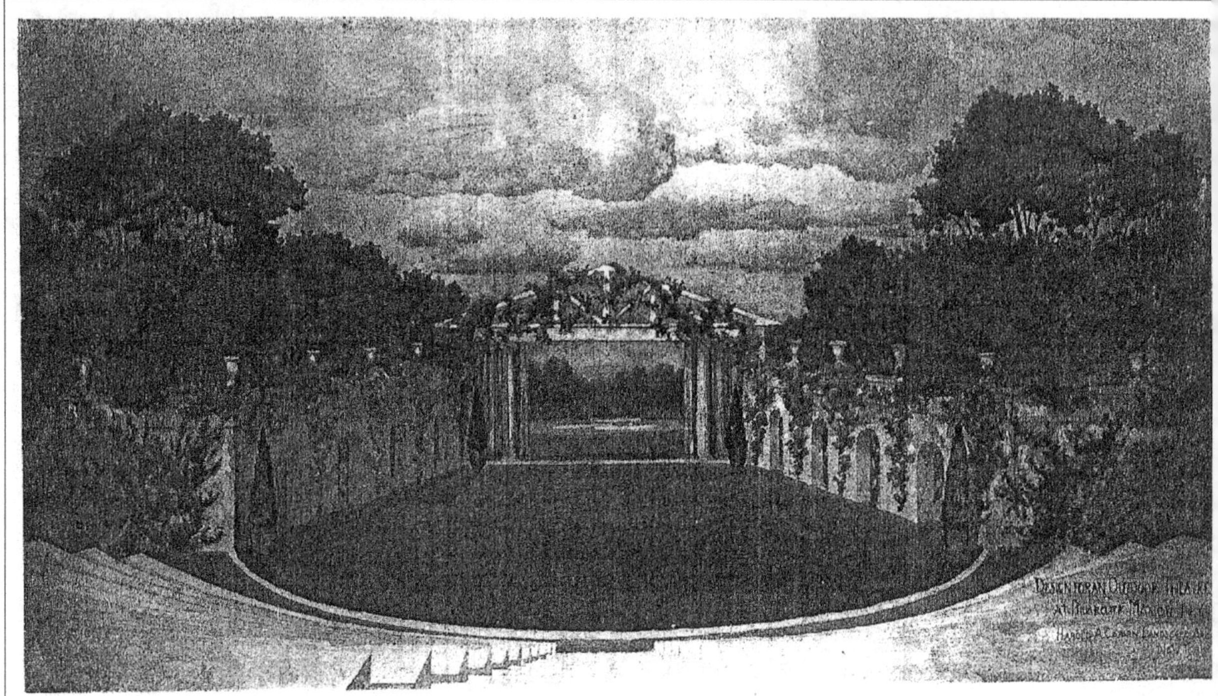

8.17 Harold A. Caparn, elevation of Outdoor Theatre.

The highly patterned area in 8.18 is covered by a mat. That area, as shown, is for the chorus in an ancient Greek drama, the principal actors playing on the raised, movable stage (to the right in the illustration). For modern drama, the mat could be removed and the actors play in that area. The proscenium, connected to the dressing room structures on either side, could provide curtain, backdrop or be left open. Entrances by the actors could be made from arches on either side of the central stage, shown in the first illustration above. Altogether it is a simple, effective, flexible and ingenious design for an outdoor theatre.

The construction of Caparn's projected outdoor theatre, number 602 on his client list, was interrupted because of World War I that limited projects other than those directed toward the war. In his writing and in his theatre design Caparn shows his sensitivity, understanding and the complementary relationship of a sister performing art to his primarily visual landscape art.

In addition to his great interest in another performing art, music, he here shows his depth of knowledge and understanding of theatre. He had also given a lecture on Greek dance at the Metropolitan Museum. He has shown his interest in the visual arts in his comments on painting and especially on landscape painters and his understanding of sculpture in his lecture and articles on that art form. Beside creating an armillary sphere, his landscape designs are often sculptural in effect. He made his own photographs, several of which rose to artistic claim, to illustrate some of his articles. His breadth of artistic interest and sensitivity to other forms of artistic expression is often found in his articles and his landscape design.

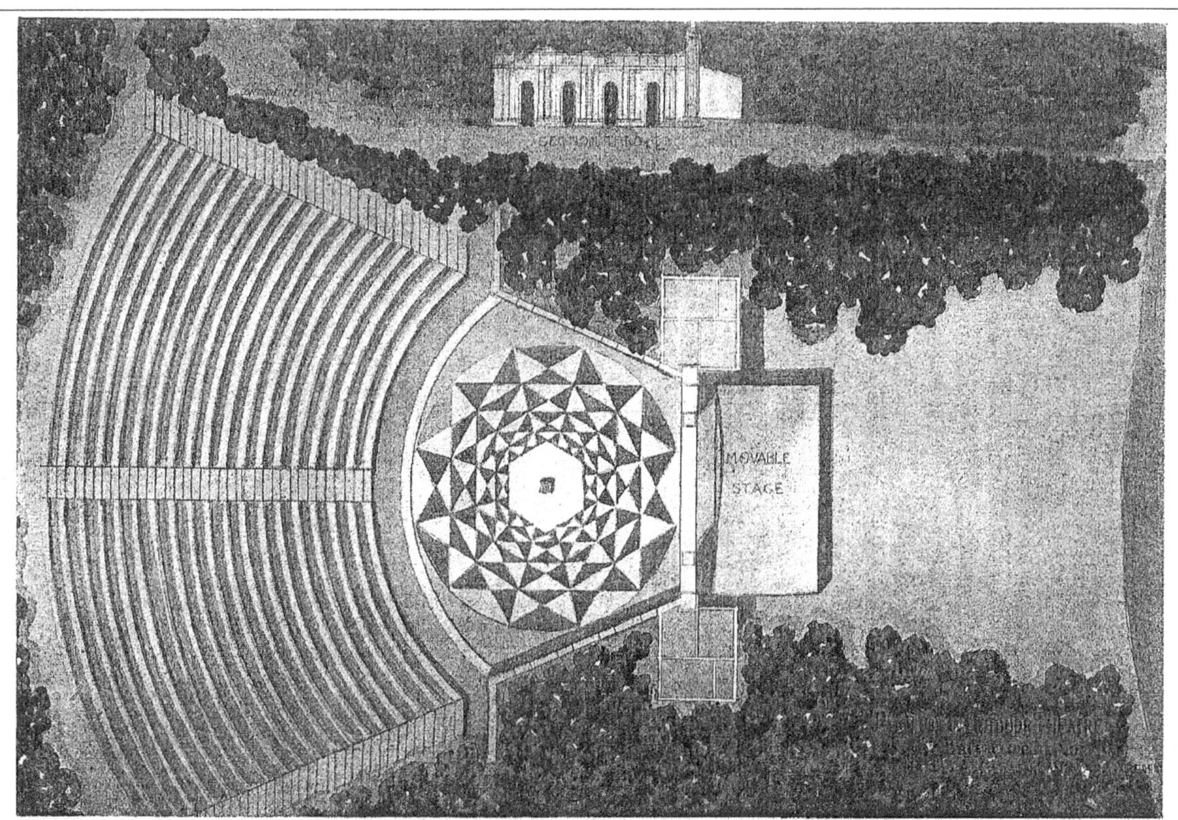

PLAN OF OUTDOOR THEATRE WITH SECTION THROUGH CENTER, SHOWING STAGE USED AS ORCHESTRA AND MOVABLE STAGE FOR GREEK PLAYS

8.18 Harold A. Caparn, Plan of Outdoor Theatre.

9 A Great Waterpark

Recreational space for a metropolis....1906–1931

Caparn made his proposal for a great water park first as a talk at a 1906 meeting in New York of the ASLA. He then wrote an article, (ASLA *Transactions* I), proposing to create a park in the whole of Jamaica Bay, portions of which belonged to the boroughs of Brooklyn and Queens (article, map, below). He followed up later with letters to the editor of *The New York Times* in the 1930s, proposing a new plan that included a golf course.

His article, "A Great Water Park in Jamaica Bay, New York" (1907) concerns a water area with islands of just over 16, 000 acres, or a little over 25 square miles. The marsh surrounding it is 8,500 acres, and in the bay are 4,200 acres of marsh. With so great an extent of surface at or near water-level it will be plain that the general character is one of low skyline and great expanse, with the monotony always produced by the absence of any definite boundaries of the middle distance.

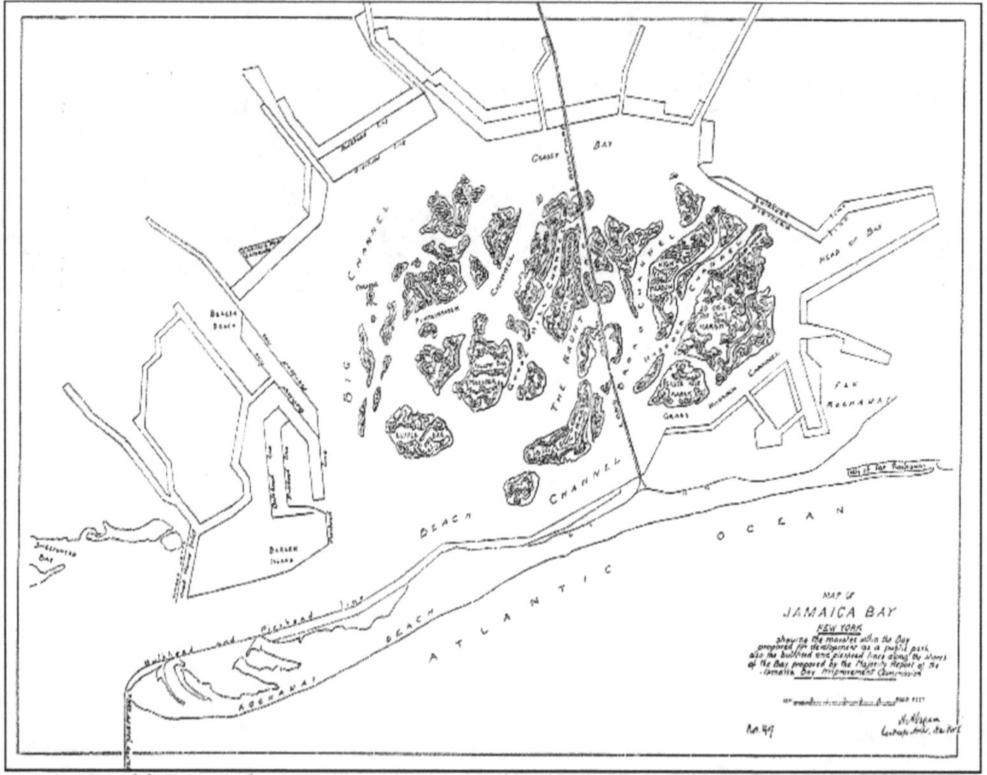

9.1 Harold Caparn drawing, Jamaica Bay Park. The site he proposed for a great water park, 1907

Since taking up the subject of a park in Jamaica Bay, which had been proposed several years ago in a general way by the City Improvement Commission, amongst others I have learned that a Commission of Engineers has been appointed to report on Jamaica Bay as a site for a harbor for ocean-going vessels with docks and wharfage. To provide for this the Commission has advised the dredging of Jamaica Bay, the filling in of the marsh-land and the construction of an immense system of docks along the shores and on the land to be filled in the bay. The line of docks proposed along the shores of the bay is about twenty-five miles long.

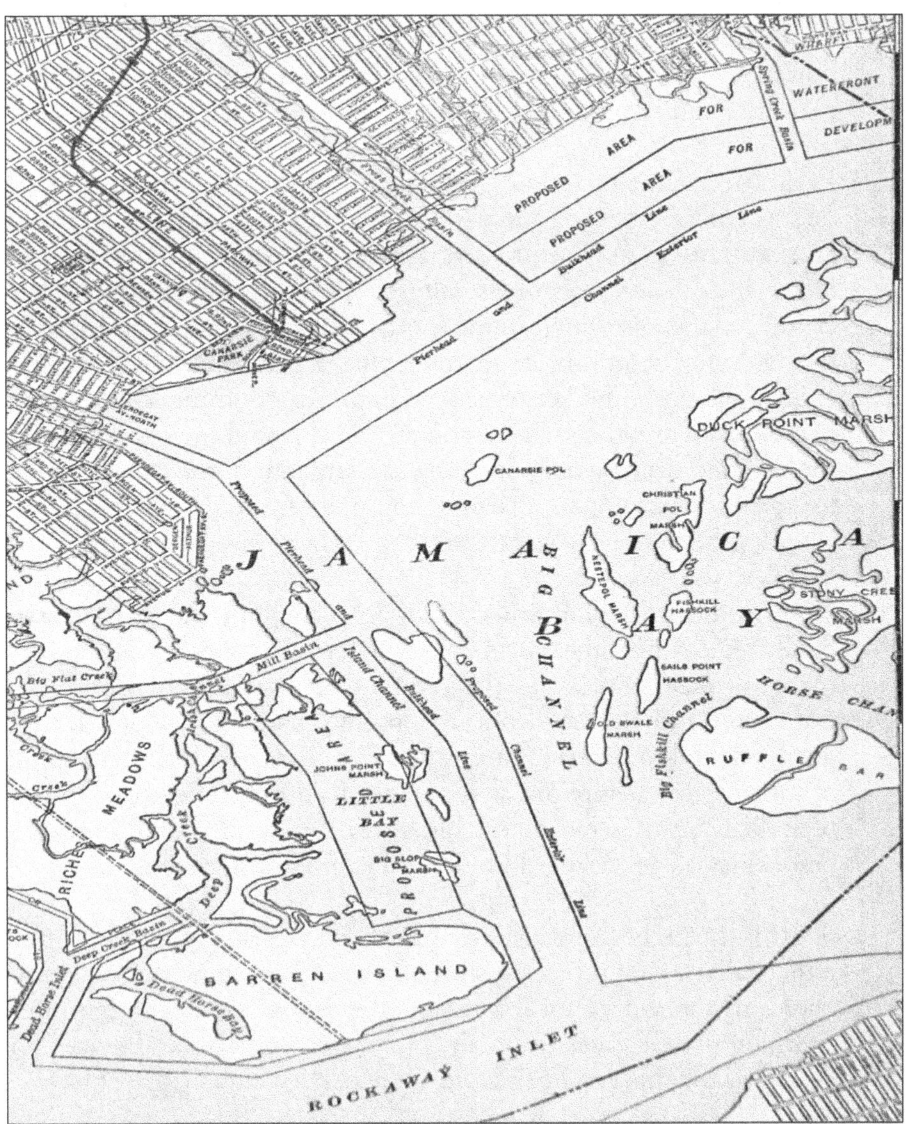

9.2 Map, 1917. Proposed Area for Waterfront Development in Jamaica Bay showing pier-heads, bulkheads and channels (long lines in the Bay).

Caparn argues against the proposed usage of the bay: it might keep pace with the commercial needs of New York for thirty or forty years only; that Newark Bay and its tributary rivers and kills are as yet practically undeveloped, that the Hackensack Meadows could be dredged and filled for the same purpose, and that all these places are on the mainland and in direct communication with all the lines of railroad excepting those leaving the Grand Central Station.

There being so much other water-front along which wharf and harbor facilities may be expected to develop [on Staten Island, Brooklyn, Queens and The Bronx], it seems not unreasonable to suppose that the interior of Jamaica Bay may not be required for seventy-five or one hundred years; perhaps not at all, for unforeseen commercial conditions may arise and the increase of New York's trade may not go on forever.

In the meantime, I would suggest the use of the interior flats and channels of the bay for a public park. Not a conventional park with lawns and exotic trees and shrubs and asphalt walks, but a water-park with many and intricate channels intersecting the great level areas of reclaimed marsh, on which all the sports of smooth water, rowing, sailing, fishing, and swimming in all their phases may find ample space and endless variety. The scenery is widespread, soothing and eminently paint-able in broad and dun or broad and splendid tints borrowed from the sky; and everywhere pervading is a large monotony that is perhaps its greatest charm—the charm of the prairie, the desert, a still sea, or cloudless heaven, or whatever one can imagine vast and simple.

Now, as the sentiment of a work of art is the only thing that makes it finally worthwhile, the sentiment of Jamaica Bay, not its extent, is what makes it most valuable to the people of New York. It is different in expression and in uses from any public park with which I am acquainted, and in park-making as in other kinds of art, the true solution of the problem before one is surely not to try to impose one's ideas or prejudices on the conditions, but to find how the conditions can be best expressed or idealized in the terms of one's command.

How is this to be done so as to make such a park, practically as well as esthetically, as useful as possible? The land, or much of it, must be raised high and dry, not less than three feet above mean high tide, by dredging the channels to obtain filling for the islands. (he goes on to describe how this can be done in some detail)

It is not worthwhile at this stage to propose any definite layout for this archipelago, this larger Venice without the buildings. It would be difficult and very tedious to devise a better division of land and water than now exists. It would be merely necessary to widen some of the channels, perhaps close some few others, and dredge as much filling from the water area as might be necessary to raise the land to the requisite height.

The principal means of access to, and circulation in, the park would be by means of excursion steamboats starting from convenient points along the shore of the bay, and touching at the principal islands. There should be no elaborate and costly road system, but I would propose one wide boulevard running across the bay alongside the Long Island Railroad so as to make one set of drawbridges serve for both steam and other traffic. There might be one or two branches traversing some of the larger islands, but all should be arranged to use as few bridges as possible as they would clearly be a hindrance to sailing and other floating traffic for which the park would mainly exist.

This would be a truly wild park, kept wild and uninjured by proper regulations. Place might be found for thousands of summer campers who would pay a small rent for their privileges…augmented by the receipts from fishing privileges, rent of boats, etc.

The land area proposed for park purposes is about 3,660 acres. That this is not excessive for a city such as New York, which will soon be the most populous in the world, is proved by the examples of Paris, London, and Boston which have found it to their advantage to set apart such great territories for park purposes, much of it even beyond their own boundaries. It seems clear that its acquisition by the city would be easy and economical, and that New York has an opportunity of acquiring, perhaps for fifty, perhaps for one hundred years, perhaps for all time, a public recreation ground quite unique in character and whose value it is not possible to estimate.

Caparn has stated his case for a great water park. In the year following Caparn's proposal, *Architectural Record* (June 1908), in its Notes & Comments columns, devoted space in support headed "A Great Water Park in Jamaica Bay."

After defining the problem of docks and shipping facilities for Manhattan, it notes that in March 1906, Mayor McClellan had appointed a commission of three engineers to consider the possibilities of Jamaica Bay as a solution. They issued a majority and a minority report. Both proposed to dredge material from the bottom of the bay to raise the swamps and lowlands and to deepen the channel through Rockaway Inlet to the ocean. The column then picks up Caparn's theme that New Jersey, with excellent facilities in Newark Bay and the Hackensack Meadows, will expect to keep pace in the race for business.

It continues, "Harold A. Caparn, a New York landscape architect, proposes utilizing the flats within the bay as depositories for the material making them navigable, and using them as a great water park for all kinds of aquatic sports, sailing, rowing, motor boating, steamboat excursions, swimming, fishing, and even summer camping." It continues, "There are about 4,200 acres of these flats, mostly submerged at high tide and already belonging to the city, so that little more than the expense of raising them a few feet above high water is needed to secure for Greater New York a pleasure ground quite unique in character and usefulness."

It concludes, "We are thus left to imagine a vast circle of commerce, an apparently endless chain of great docks and wharves served by a waterway three-quarters of a mile wide dotted with all kinds of shipping from ocean liners downward, and all enfolding numbers of spreading green islands with pleasure craft of a great city riding on the ample and tortuous channels. This surely is a picture of a superb civic possession, a scene unparalleled among the municipal parks of the world, and having the advantage of costing so little that the city would not feel the expense."

But action, after much discussion, was slow in coming. Caparn in the meantime broadened his appeal by including a golf course as part of the recreational attraction of the water park.

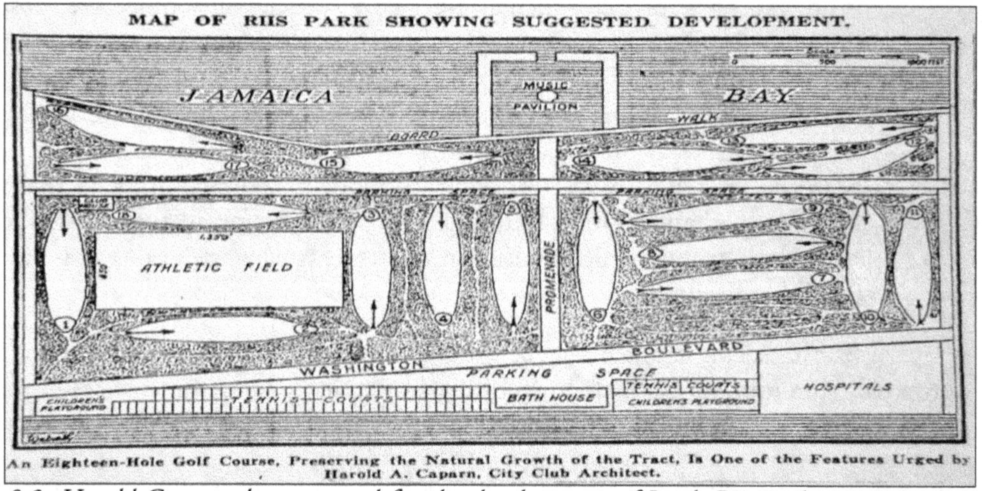

9.3 Harold Caparn plan, proposal for the development of Jacob Riis Park, Jamaica Bay, 1931.

A Report on "The Future of Jamaica Bay" was issued on July 18, 1938, to Mayor Fiorello H. LaGuardia by Robert Moses, Commissioner of The City of New York Department of Parks. It takes us back to the time of Caparn's talk and article (1906-07) and then discusses developments during the meantime. The report states that thirty years prior the first plan was made to transform Jamaica Bay's acres of water, marsh and meadowland into a vast industrial port and ship terminal. In 1938, the plan, according to the Report was not perceptibly different than it was thirty years before. Industrial and commercial activity, however, had been confined to a small area and the pier idea was aborted.

The Report continues, that since about 1935 the recreational and residential development of the bay and its environs had proceeded apace with a reconstructed Jacob Riis Park, a new Marine Parkway Bridge, Rockaway Beach rehabilitation scheduled for completion in the next year, the development of Marine Park, the removal of the old dilapidated Canarsie amusement area and the making of a new Canarsie Beach Park. Progress was slowly being made towards Caparn's vision of a public park.

Finally the report says, "the new program, presented by the Park Department, calls for the complete rezoning of the bay and its surrounding area; transferring all islands to the Park Department for recreational use, including protection of scenery and water; encouragement of swimming, fishing, boating and preservation of wild life." City officials finally had heard the needs of the people. They were headed, now with political support, in the direction Caparn had envisioned more than twenty years before, toward a park for public recreation and wildlife preservation.

The final chapter can be found in a 2002 document of the National Park Service. "When the United States Congress created Gateway in 1972, it marked the culmination of decades of hard work by local governments, citizen groups, the National Park Service, and members of Congress to create one of the first urban national parks in the United States. The recreation area brings the national park experience to residents of the nation's most densely populated city. It protects portions of the coastal ecosystem of one of the world's most highly developed commercial and industrial regions, and it provides a model for how degraded resources can be rehabilitated."

A connection might be made from Caparn's 1907 article on Jamaica Bay to the following developments. His idea formed a basis and reference point to succeeding proposals. He no doubt followed them with great interest and where possible encouraged their progress. He would be pleased with the outcome in Congress sixty-five years later designating Jamaica Bay, its islands and environs as a park and the use of the bay today as a public recreation area and wildlife refuge. His vision for a great water park for the people of New York City had been fulfilled to the delight of the people.

10 Brooklyn Botanic Garden

A place for education and enjoyment...1911–1935

The Olmsted Brothers firm of Boston began work on the site of the Brooklyn Botanic Garden in 1910. The general plan, location of the structures and site preparation was done by that firm from 1910 through 1919. Together with Dr. Charles Stuart Gager, the first director of the Garden and the architectural firm McKim Mead and White, they sited the principal structure, the Laboratory, now Administration Building. In 2007 it was named a New York City Landmark.[1]

Harold Caparn was known to the Olmsted brothers as they began work on the Botanic Garden. In 1905 he had presented a paper at a New York meeting of the ASLA upon his election as a Fellow of the Society. The meeting and following discussion were attended by John Charles Olmsted, first president of the Society. Caparn was known through regular ASLA meetings, his work as a Trustee beginning in 1907, when Frederick Law Olmsted, Jr. was president, as an editor of the first volume of *Transactions* and as Treasurer of the Society beginning in 1909.

Rhys Caparn's notes on her father for the ASLA Council of Fellows states that he started work on the Brooklyn Botanic Garden in 1911. The brief descriptive paragraph with his photo in *Country Life in America* (1920) also gives 1911 as the beginning of his work at the Garden. He consulted during that year on the Native Flora Garden with the first curator of plants, Norman Taylor. He was elected President of the ASLA for the year 1911-12.

As of January 1, 1912. he was formally appointed as the consulting landscape architect to the Brooklyn Botanic Garden. At the same time he also held an appointment as faculty in landscape architecture at Columbia University.[2] The Olmsted brothers greeted his appointment with "hearty approval," having known his abilities for a number of years. Caparn worked cooperatively, but independently, with the Olmsted firm until 1919 when they had completed their work on preparation of the land.[3] Caparn's charge was to design the variety of gardens within the Garden.

Caparn began shortly after his appointment to lay out a section on the development of plant life, to be a central educational and research feature of the Garden. Over the next decades he proceeded to design, as resources permitted, a rock garden, a garden of irises, a rose garden and rose arc, a horticultural section, pools for a collection of water lilies and a plaza featuring magnolias. We will look briefly at these outstanding gardens.

Caparn's article, "Planting a Botanic Garden" (1915), is about a portion of the design of the Brooklyn Botanic Garden written, with Norman Taylor, one year after the planning for the Systematic Section was completed and published three and a half years after Caparn was appointed consulting landscape architect. The basis of plant development in related families and its layout on the ground was a bold move, not well known at the time, but its educational value fit well with the mission of the Garden.[4]

He explained: This would not have been difficult where there was plenty of space but, even as it is (about 48 acres at the time), the visitor will be able to find, in obvious propinquity to any perennial, its most nearly related shrubs, if it has any, and a little further on its related trees.

The layman or semi-layman, the gardener, landscape architect, or plant-lover of any kind, who judges and values plants according to their outward appearance and qualities only, will be mildly surprised to see that alders, witch-hazel, and snowballs, though they may produce similar mass effects in planting, are no way akin; while the elm and the stinging nettle have almost everything in common except the trifling difference that one grows a hundred feet high, weights a few tons, and lives for 150 years, while the other is a mere weed.

The man of science, on the contrary, will disregard all these superficial and elementary matters; but he will be soothed and gratified by the discovery of plants growing here of which there are only one or two in captivity, and the knowledge that the orders are arranged in the general sequence laid down by Engler and Prantl in their *Die natürlichen pflanzenfamilien* (1887-1915), a scheme of practically universal adoption in herbaria, but rarely laid on the ground itself, at any rate in this country.

He goes on to describe the plantings, but cannot leave without a nod and explanation in the artistic direction: Park-like scenery is, to a great extent, produced by the interdependence of open and closed spaces, of lawn and foliage; but here, where lawns of respectable extent as open spaces, could not be obtained, the grass strips (walks) and beds together are treated as open spaces, and surrounded and separated by such foliage masses as the shrubs and trees most nearly related to the herbs in the beds would afford.

During the time he was laying out the Systematic Section, he had occasion to also develop an Iris Garden. In 1913 and again in 1919, Harold's cousin William John Caparne, then living on the English Channel Island of Guernsey and known widely for his propagation and sale of irises, sent him bulbs, plants, and seeds for the Brooklyn Garden. In 1918 Harold Caparn laid out an Iris Garden and soon had 90 varieties of irises collected for the Brooklyn Botanic Garden.[5]

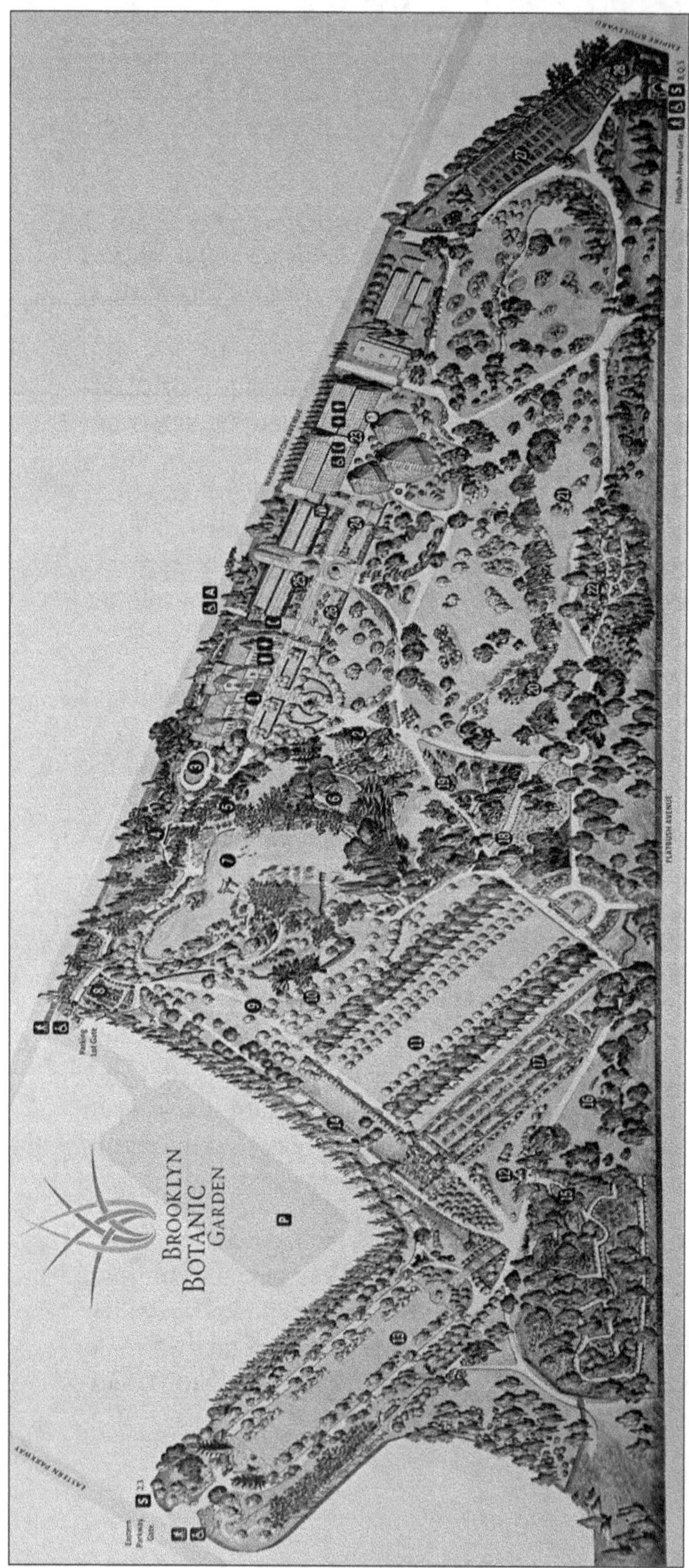

The illustration (10.1) gives an overall view of the Brooklyn Botanic Garden as it appeared in the second decade of the twentieth-first century. The original 48 acres were expanded by the North Addition (Osborne Garden), bringing the Botanic Garden to about fifty-two acres, its current size.

10. 1 Artist's rendering of a map of the Brooklyn Botanic Garden, c. 2010.[6]

Areas of interest, regarding Caparn's work include:

1. Magnolia Plaza with compass and armillary sphere (center left)
8. Herb Garden
11. The Cherry Esplanade terminating in the Rose Arc
13. Osborne Garden with columns, benches and fountains
15. Native Flora Garden with plants growing within 100 miles of New York City
17. The Cranford Rose Garden with pavilion
18, 19, 20 and 21. (pass the semi-circular Rose Arc ending the Cherry Esplanade) and enter the Plant Family Collection, presenting plants in order of their evolutional complexity
24. Lily Pool Terrace with fountain

Magnolia Plaza

During the early 1930s Caparn designed a compass on the ground of stones from various parts of the world. Centered in the compass, he designed an armillary sphere as a focal point for his layout of the Magnolia Plaza in front of the Laboratory Building. His daughter Rhys at age 24 was about to have her first solo show of sculptures at the Delphic Studios in New York. He invited her to make sculptural models of the zodiac signs that surround the ring of the sphere as do the constellations that ring the path of the sun over the year. The armillary sphere, produced in bronze, was erected in 1933 and stands at the center of the beautifully renovated Magnolia Plaza in front of the Administration Building.

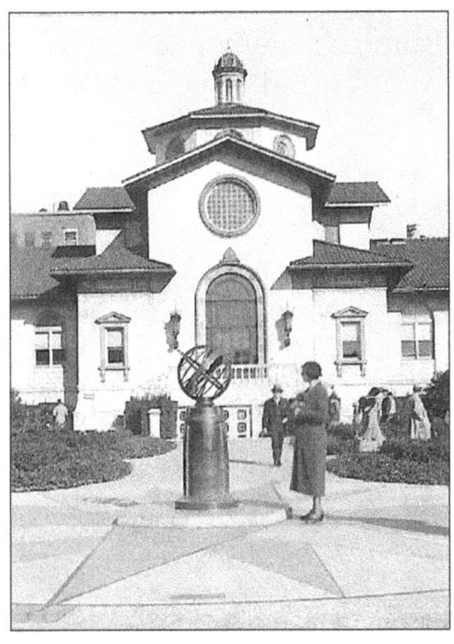

In 1980 Rhys Caparn gave her bronze sculpture "Moonrise" (1968) to the Garden in memory of her father.[7] These two sculptural contributions to the Garden by father and daughter may be seen as symbols of sun and moon to represent the passage of days and evenings in the pleasures of the Garden.

10.2 Harold Caparn design, Armillary Sphere, with compass on the ground. Brooklyn Botanic Garden. Located in the plaza before the Laboratory Building, c. 1935
10.3 Harold Caparn design, Compass and Armillary Sphere, Magnolia Plaza, Administration Building, 2006.

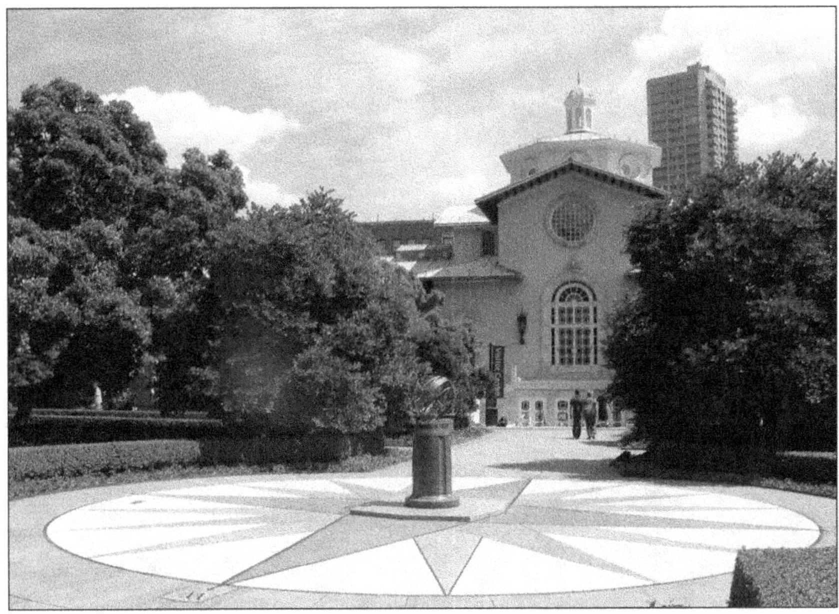

Lily Pool Terrace

In 1919 Caparn designed the Water Gardens and Fountain, now the Lily Pool Terrace. The water gardens were donated by Alfred Treadway White, a major Garden supporter. They were included in Olmsted Brothers plans and were set as two balanced rectangles with a large fountain between. The fountain was funded by Albert Jenkins and designed by Caparn. The Lily Pool Terrace is a collection of aquatic plants, with borders of annuals and perennials. Balustrade and Steps set it off from the Magnolia Plaza. The Terrace is one of the Caparn-designed architectural features of the Garden.

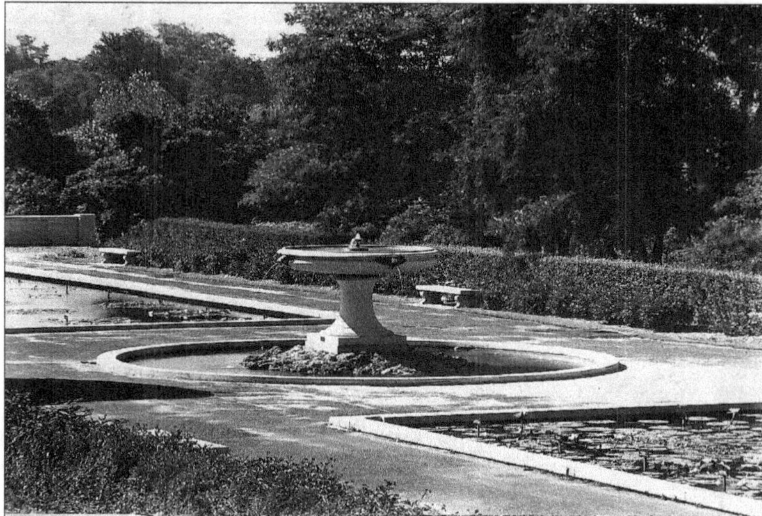

10.4 Harold Caparn design, Jenkins fountain, between the water gardens, photo, c. 1925.

10.5 Harold Caparn design, Lily Pool Terrace with Jenkins fountain. photo 2006.

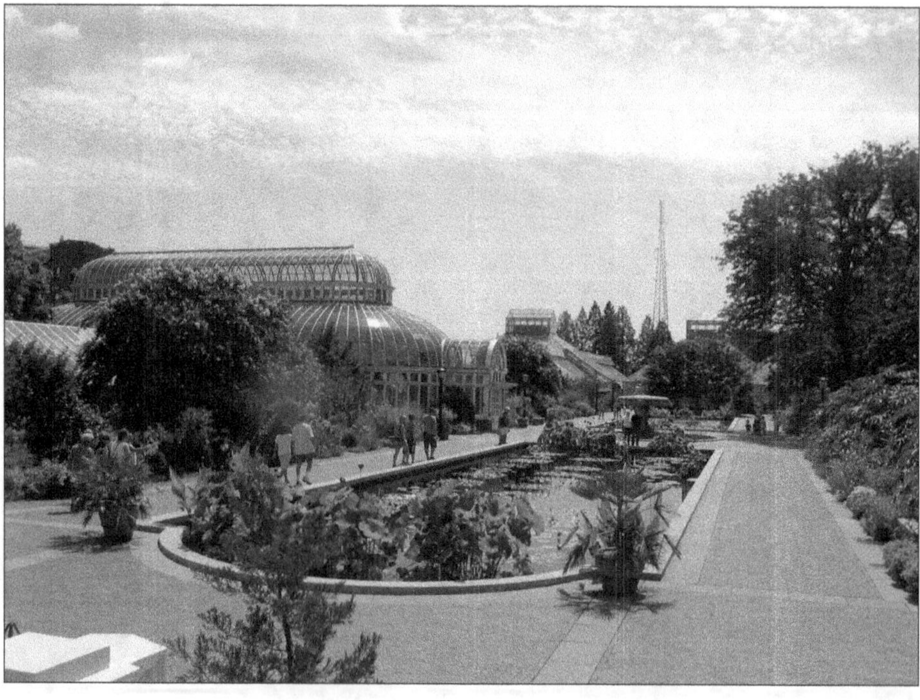

The Plant Family Collection
Laid out through a large portion of the Garden

Caparn wrote four articles about the need in the design of botanic gardens for the intertwining considerations of botany, gardening and horticulture, the difference between a public garden and a private one and the educational value of presenting on the ground the theory of plant evolution. His last such article, on "The Planning of a Botanic Garden" (July 1932), is mostly about the Systematic Section as it evolved from its planning in the first years of the Garden to how it turned out on the land. The article is illustrated by a diagram of the Systematic Section as it looked in 1928, with notes and detail. This plan is now an historic document, since the section, now known as the Plant Family Collection, has continued to evolve in the Garden.

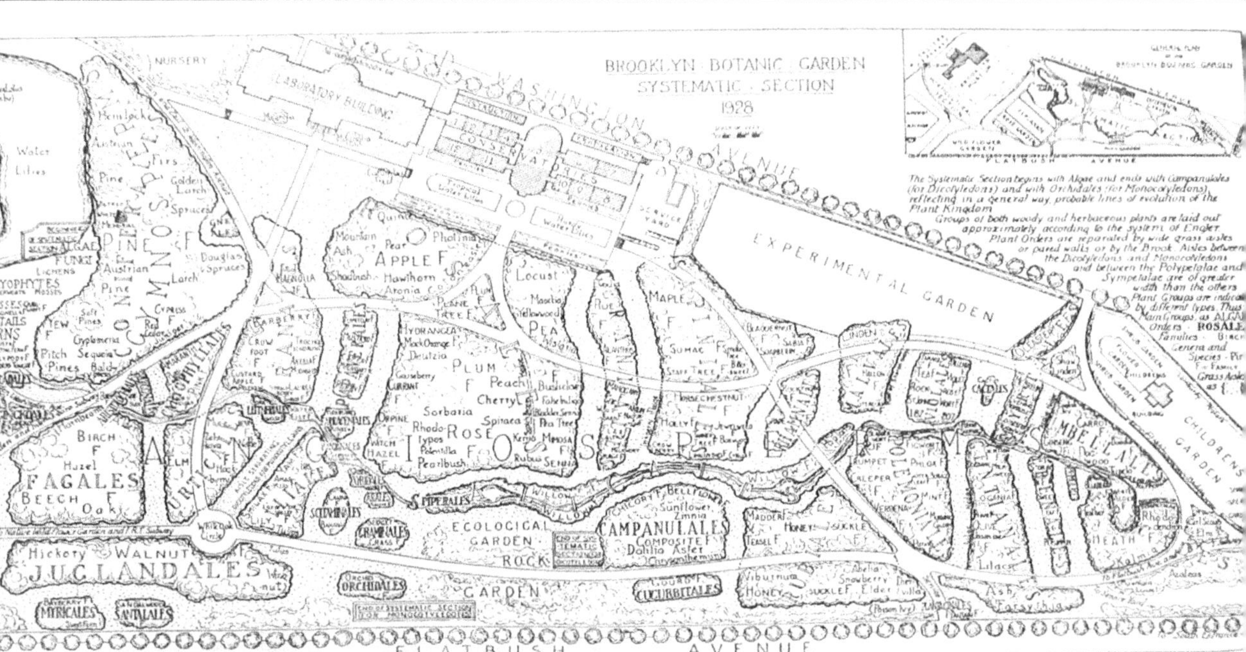

10.6 Harold Caparn Plan, 1928, Systematic Section (later Plant Family Collection). Shows the empty plaza before the Laboratory Building prior to his design for that area as center of the magnolia collection, including compass and armillary sphere.

Caparn's Additional Note at the end of the article is forward looking: The Systematic Section, though originally proposed by the writer, has of course been made possible only by the united efforts of the officials of the Brooklyn Botanic Garden through many years and all have cooperated in necessary remodeling. A project such as the Systematic Section can never be considered finished for the reason that the knowledge of the subject is not complete. In the light of new discoveries of facts, new conclusions are reached, so that the Systematic Section of any botanic garden can, with minor exceptions, represent only the status of the science at the time when it was laid out and planted.

The Brooklyn Botanic Garden's renewal and reconsideration of the Plant Family Collection brings this aspect of the Garden into greater access enhancing its educational mission. Through part of the Plant Family Collection, a water conservation project now takes water from the Japanese Hill-and-Pond Garden into a brook that existed, now renovated and newly planted, as Belle's Brook, into a Water Garden. The Water Garden features a pool that, during heavy rain, acts as a catch basin. The water is recirculated to the Japanese Garden, reducing significantly the use of water by the Brooklyn Botanic Garden.

Osborne Garden

Completed in 1935, the North Addition as it was known, was designed by Caparn to display ornamental plants. (map 13) It had a large central lawn surrounded by plant beds framed by evergreens, the whole encased within walkways featuring ten pergolas covered with wisteria. In 1938 Sade Elizabeth Osborne provided funding to build the paired columns, benches and fountains at either end of the garden in memory of her husband. These elements were designed also by Caparn and were presented after various approvals, on the Osborne's wedding anniversary in April 1939, when the Garden was dedicated and named the Osborne Garden. The extensive central lawn is now framed by azaleas, rhododendrons and flowering trees backed with Hinoki false cypress.

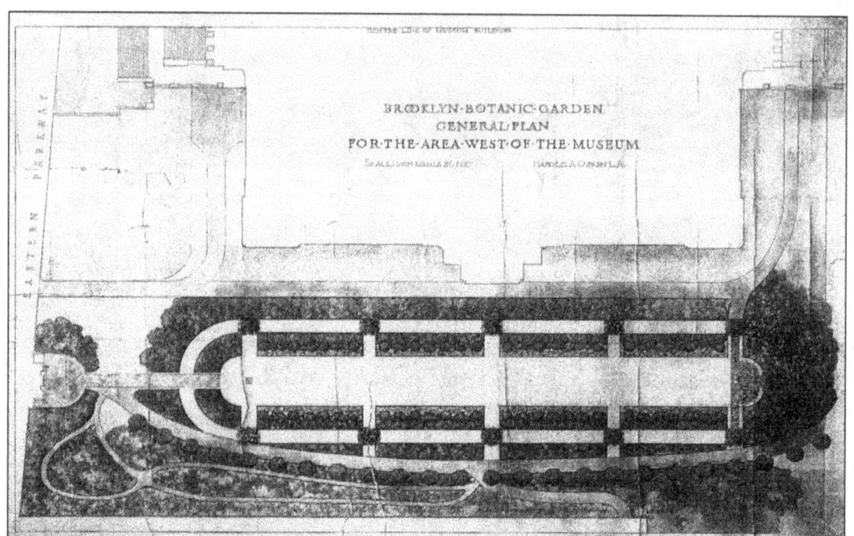

10.7 Harold Caparn General Plan, North Addition, November 1929. It shows beds for ornamental plantings around The Long Green and walkways surrounding the whole with pergolas on either side of the garden.

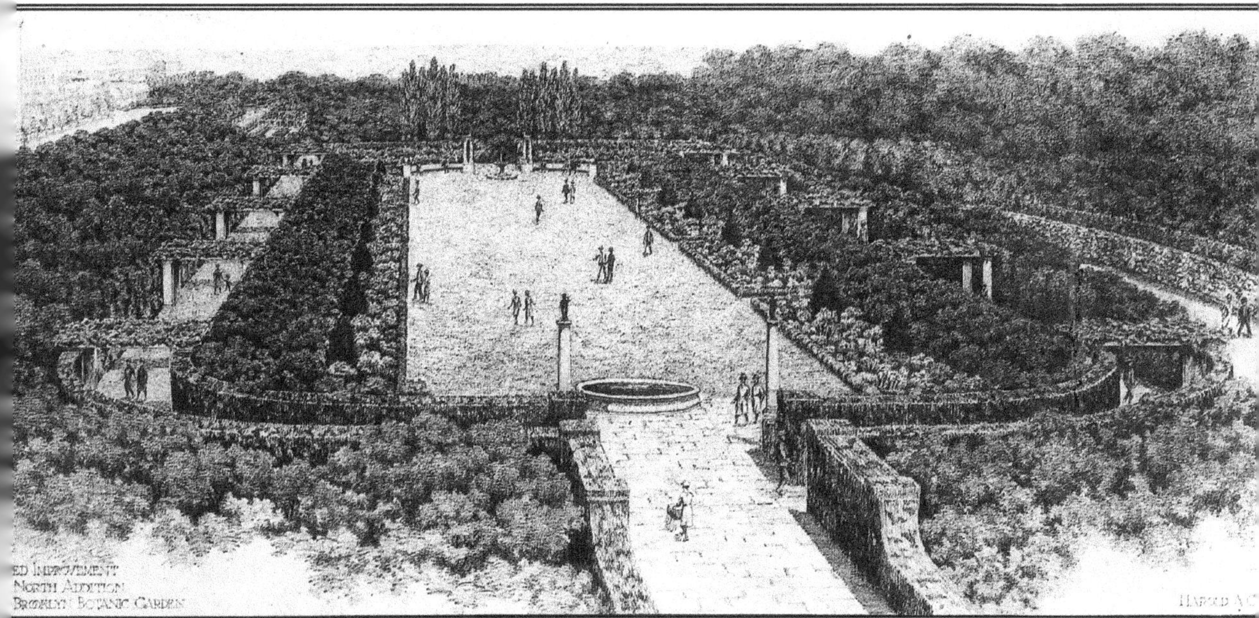

10.8 Harold Caparn Proposed Improvement of the North Addition, elevation, 1935.

North Entrance from Eastern Parkway, foreground, leading to a water basin/fountain, later a planter for annuals. Osborne memorial columns, foreground, do not now have statuary. This Italian-style garden has architectural features modeled after the Boboli Gardens behind the Pitti Palace of the Medici in Florence; design of columns, seats and fountain for the south entrance, seen in illustration 10.9.

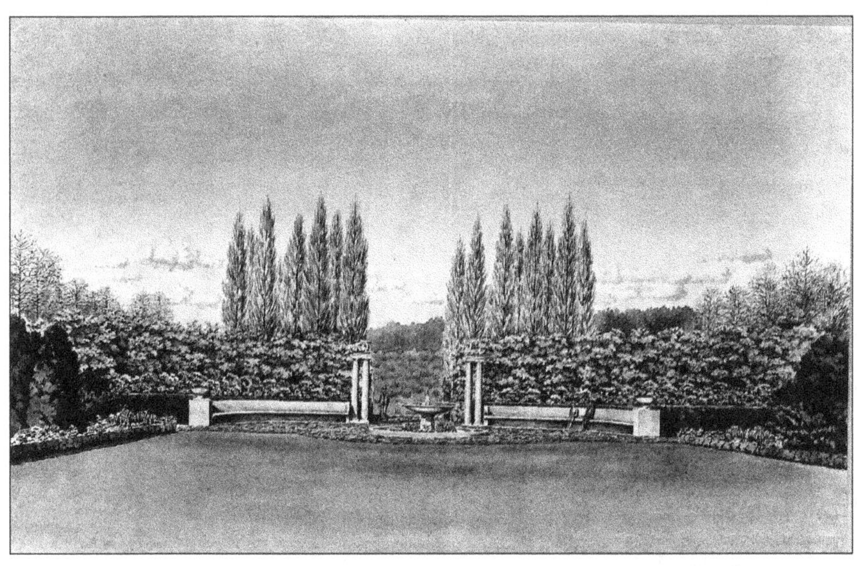

10.9 Harold Caparn design, south entrance to North Addition; coupled columns, seats, fountain, 1936.

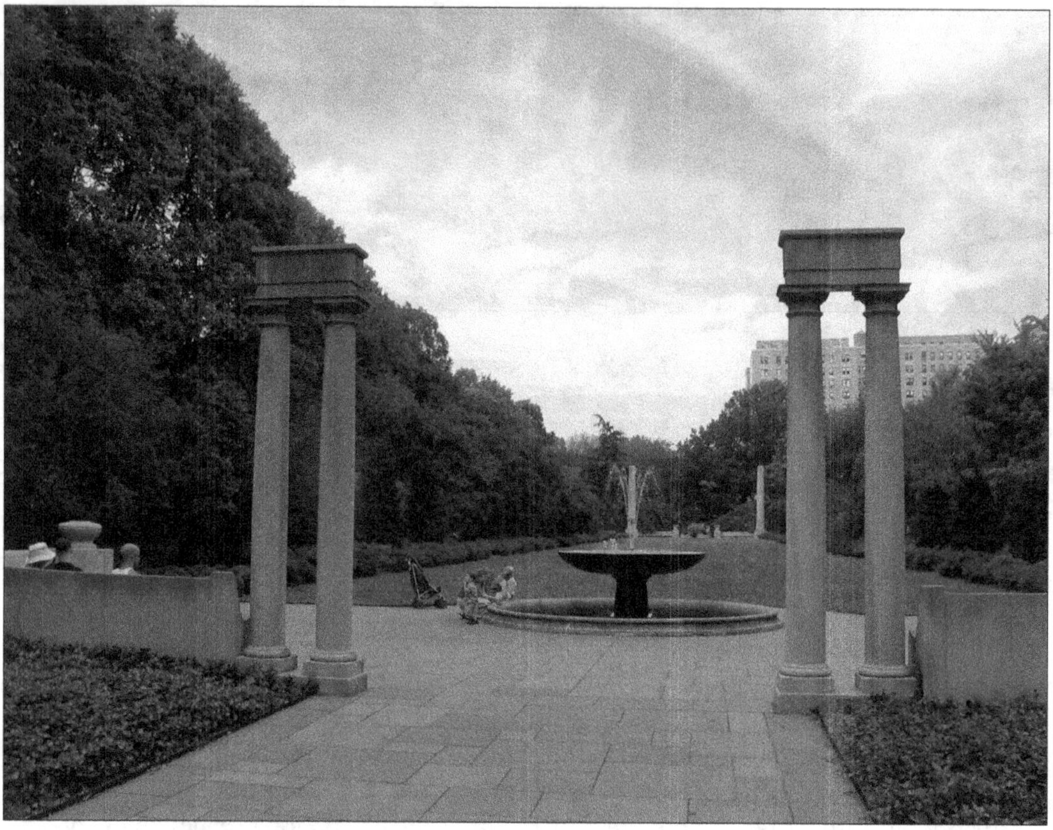

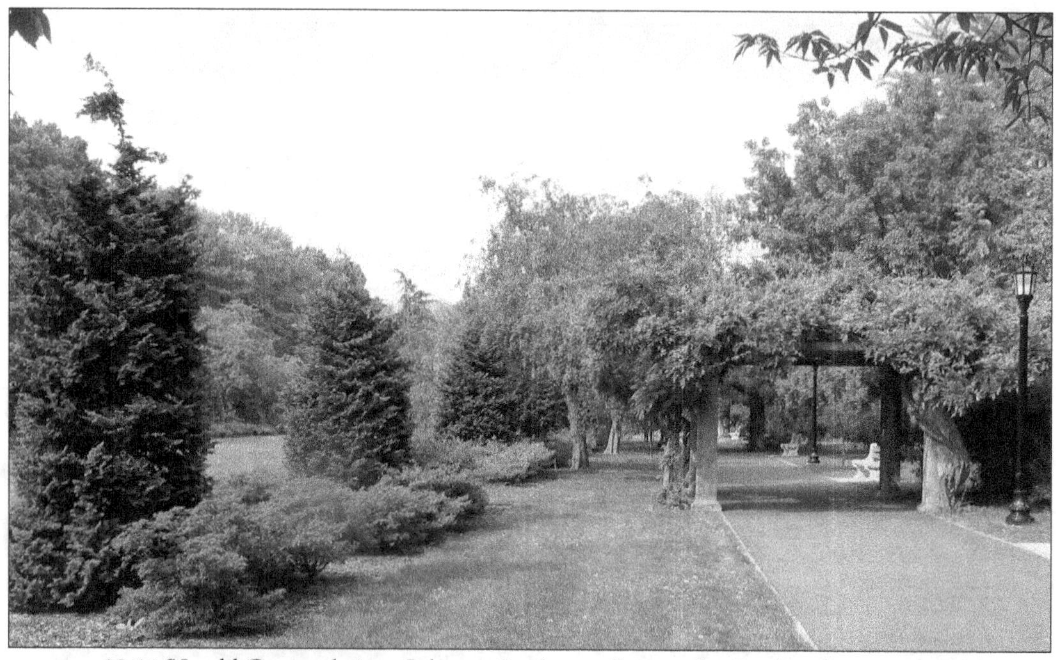

10.10 Harold Caparn design, Osborne Garden, south entrance; columns, seats, fountain; 2006.

10.11 Harold Caparn design, Osborne Garden, walk, pergola, Garden plantings. 2006.

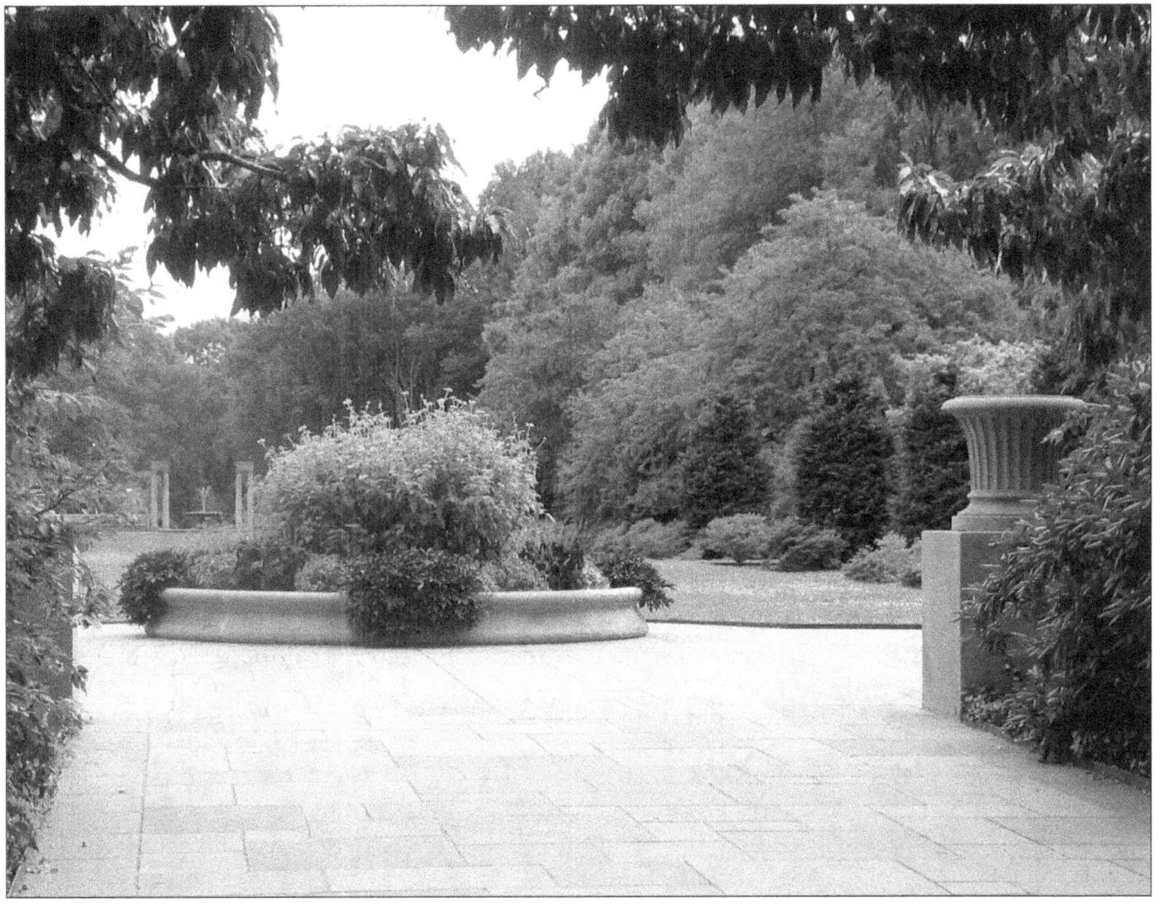

10.12 *Harold Caparn design, Osborne Garden, north entrance; water basin planter, one of pair of urns, right, fountain, paired columns at far end. 2006.*

Summing up the creation of the North Addition (Osborne Garden), the *Brooklyn Botanic Garden Record* (v. 28, 1939, 22), states:

It is the purpose of a botanic garden to promote education in botany, and one of the branches of botany is ornamental horticulture, and, in particular, that aspect of it which concerns the utilization of plants to make a beautiful garden, or, to change the order of words, to make a garden beautiful.

The Horticultural Section (Osborne Garden) was planned to exhibit only horticultural varieties, and species which have value in landscaping. One may be an excellent botanist, but a very poor landscape architect. The Brooklyn Botanic Garden, at its very beginning decided that the planning of its grounds should be done by the close association of landscape architect and botanist. No wiser decision concerning the Garden was ever made, and the appointment of Mr. Caparn took place in 1912.

Cranford Rose Garden
Its model and evolution

Caparn wrote nine articles on roses and rose gardens, in *American Rose Annual* (1918, 1921, twice in 1925, 1939, twice in 1941, and 1942) and in *Arts and Decoration* (1937). He admired the beautiful blooms of Hybrid Tea and Hybrid Perpetual roses but found the foliage to be "weedy," and thought the more bush-like foliage of older varieties better to group in landscape design for artistic effect.

He designed a rose garden, in 1917, for an estate on the north shore "Gold Coast" of Long Island. The rose garden for the estate turned out to be significant not only for the estate owner, but also as a proving ground for Caparn's ideas of how to make, to the satisfaction of his landscape architect's mind, a successful garden only of roses. He had a reason for designing it and observing its growth and measuring the reaction to it of those who might succumb to its charms.

He sought to solve questions arising from using only roses for a garden and what the impact on the viewer would be when the hybrid varieties were not in bloom. To test these questions, he placed the hybrid varieties in compact, easy-to-view central beds, about four to six plants wide, with paths on either side. He surrounded the central beds with older varieties as a substantial border, enhanced by climbing roses on arches over the paths and on garden-enclosing fences.

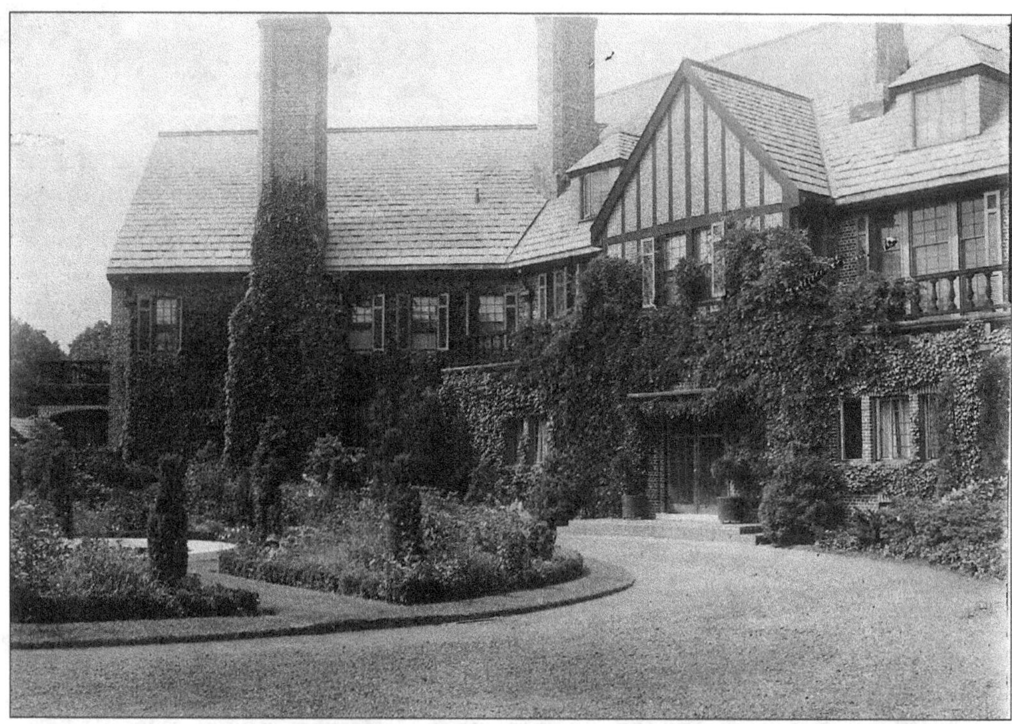

10.13 *Harold Caparn, landscape design, c. 1917, home of William J. Tully, 1920s.*

This design provided aspects of unity and variety and areas of highlight and shadow desirable to the landscape artist, but not available only from beds of the hybrids. He tried out the design on the estate of W. J. Tully and then wrote two articles about the experience. William J. Tully was number 587 on Caparn's client list. Caparn did the design for the estate at Locust Valley in addition to the rose garden. A photograph of the home shows a beautifully designed entrance landscape that had matured over that of an earlier photograph.

Caparn planted his rose garden design in 1917, in a rectangular plot of about 230 x 80 feet. In his design, the beautiful blooms could be seen and savored up close in beds, while the bushier varieties provided a satisfactory landscape frame in a garden featuring only roses.

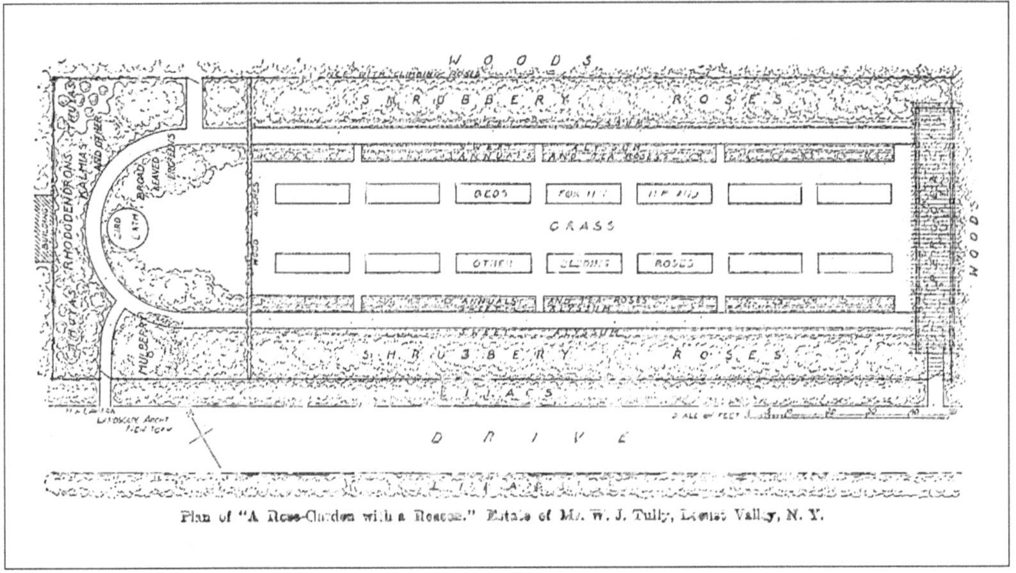

10.14 *Harold Caparn plan of rose garden, estate of W. J. Tully*

Caparn described the Tully garden in articles in *American Rose Annual.* The first article, with plan, "A Rose-Garden with A Reason," (1918) was just after he had it planted. The other article, "The Working Out of a Real Rose-Garden," (1921) was three years into its maturity.

He summed up in the "Reason" of his approach to balance older and newer rose varieties: So this rose-garden came into being, a simple scheme with wood fences supporting climbing roses for boundaries, along them twelve-foot borders of single or wild roses; then long beds of Hybrid Perpetuals and Hybrid Teas. The reader must be the judge of the success of this scheme…to judge what kind of contribution the rose can make toward garden scenery. If the gentle reader should visit this garden when rose-time is over, or not yet begun, he will probably find that the rose can be attractive and pictorial.

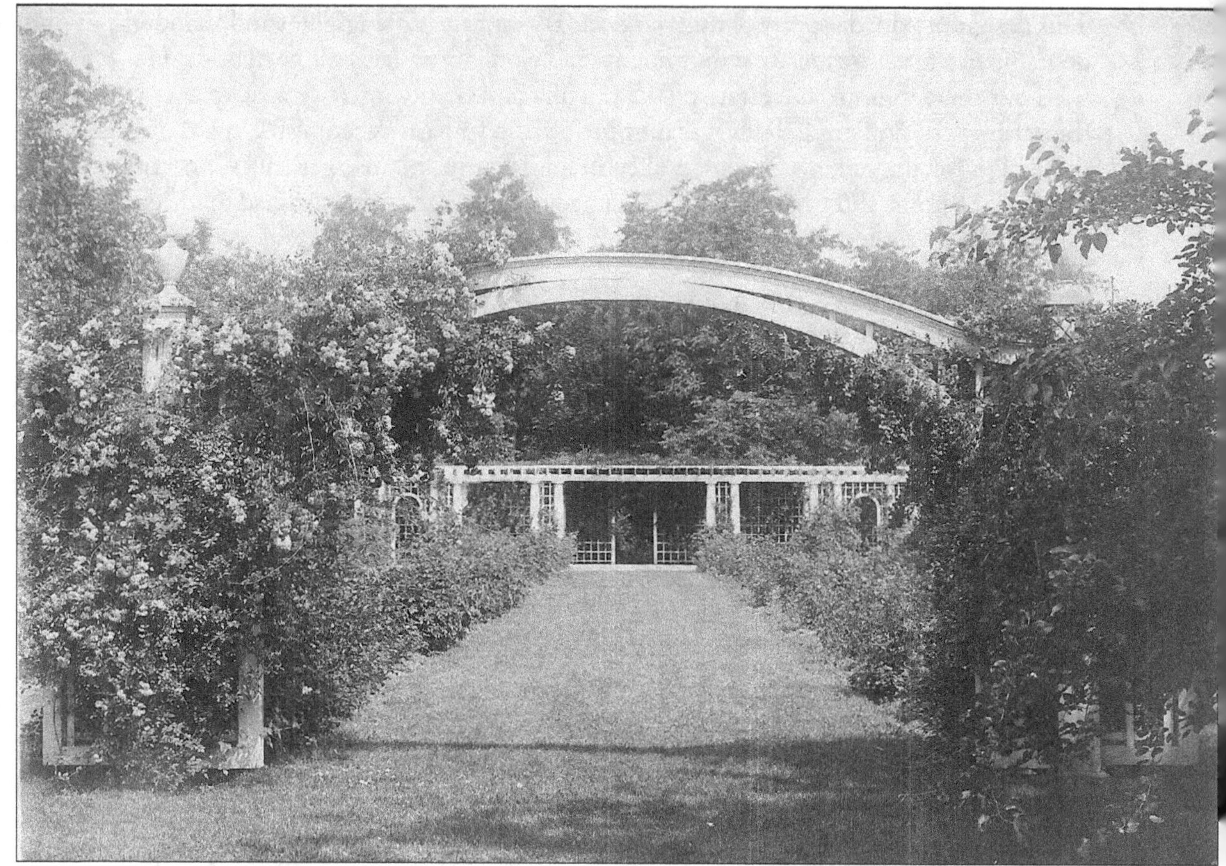

10.15 *Harold Caparn design, Tully rose garden, arches, c. 1921. Looking L. to R. in the plan, 10.14, towards the arbor at the far end.*

Caparn's 1921 article, "The Working Out of a Real Rose-Garden," gives his rationale for the design of the Tully rose-garden and the basis of his objection to the hybrid varieties as a landscape object:

> No rose enthusiast, and few other flower-lovers, will deny that the rose is the most fascinating of all flowers. But when they speak of the rose they mean the double rose, the Hybrid Perpetuals, Hybrid Teas, Teas, Noisettes, and so on. They seem to forget that if these are the most lovely of all double flowers, the single roses have a quality all their own, only approached by their near relation, the apple blossom. But the plants that produce these imperial double garden roses are almost unmanageable in a garden scheme. Scrawny, gawky, ill-clothed, they seem to care nothing for their looks and for getting on harmoniously with their neighbors. Nevertheless, though they refuse to mass, an occasional Hybrid Perpetual may be used in mixed shrubbery if its neighbors are selected with due judgment.

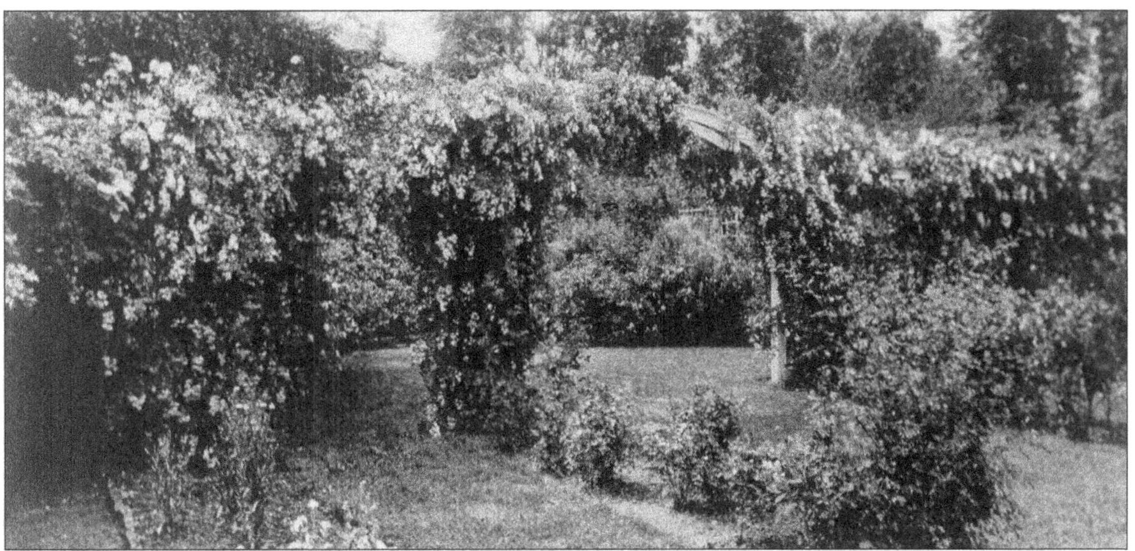

10.16 Harold Caparn design, Tully rose garden, looking R. to L., in the plan. Reverse of photo indicates that it was taken in 1928.

But single roses, the wild species of the temperate zones, on the other hand, all form good bushes, or, at least, bushes that can be used effectively in one conjunction or another. One of them, *Rosa rugosa*, has such fine qualities of form and foliage that it is to be found in most mixed shrubberies. Among the climbing roses, too, with the blood of Wichuraiana, are now a considerable number of varieties, not merely with decorative flower-masses, but with rich and glossy foliage.

> *The least sentimental of mortals feels himself slipping when the rose reigns in June—who, for instance, could resist the allure of the loveliness pictured above? The garden of W. J. Tully, Esq., Locust Valley, Long Island.*
> *H. Caparn, landscape architect*

10.17 Plaque accompanying the photo, 10.16

Most designers of rose-gardens who attempt to make them more than mere rows of beds introduce shrubs, trees, and vines of other species to make their creation look like a garden instead of a nursery. What they are really trying to do is to distract attention from the roses, and to satisfy the eye with a grouping of conifers, architecture, lily-ponds, or whatever the means may be. This may be very meritorious as design, but it hardly seems correct to call it a "rose" garden."

Caparn saw the success of the garden only of roses on the Tully estate. In 1919 Dr. C. Stuart Gager, invited Caparn to design a Rose Garden for the Brooklyn Botanic Garden. He later issued a challenge in an article and in the *Brooklyn Botanic Garden Report* to find a generous patron to fund the Rose Garden.

The original, smaller rose garden was moved to accommodate larger, more complete features. Caparn then designed a rose garden framed by a viewing pavilion at one end and a pergola at the other. This rose garden had historical and scientific reasoning, in that the layout of the central beds was planned to be a chronological and educational exhibit of the many varieties of roses under cultivation at the time.

Finally, in 1927 Walter Cranford, an engineer, stepped forward with a $10,000 donation and later with another $5,000 to complete the project. Construction began in June and a year later, in 1928, the larger rose garden (10.18), opened to great approval.

Coming next along the path from the large Osborne Garden, the breadth. length and complexity of the Cranford Rose Garden (map 17), requires the viewer to explore to full extent the individual varieties and beauty of the many types of roses on display.

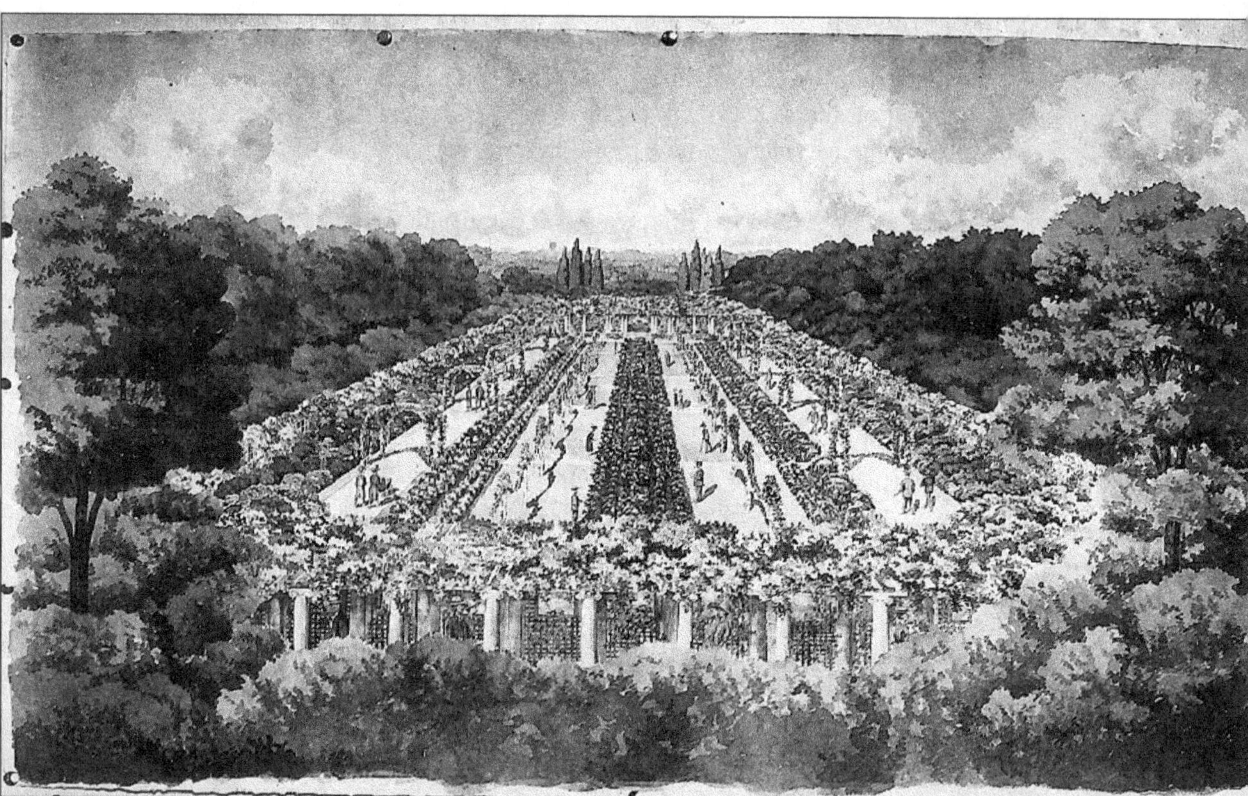

10.18 Harold Caparn proposed plan, watercolor, for the Brooklyn Botanic Garden Rose Garden, c.1925.

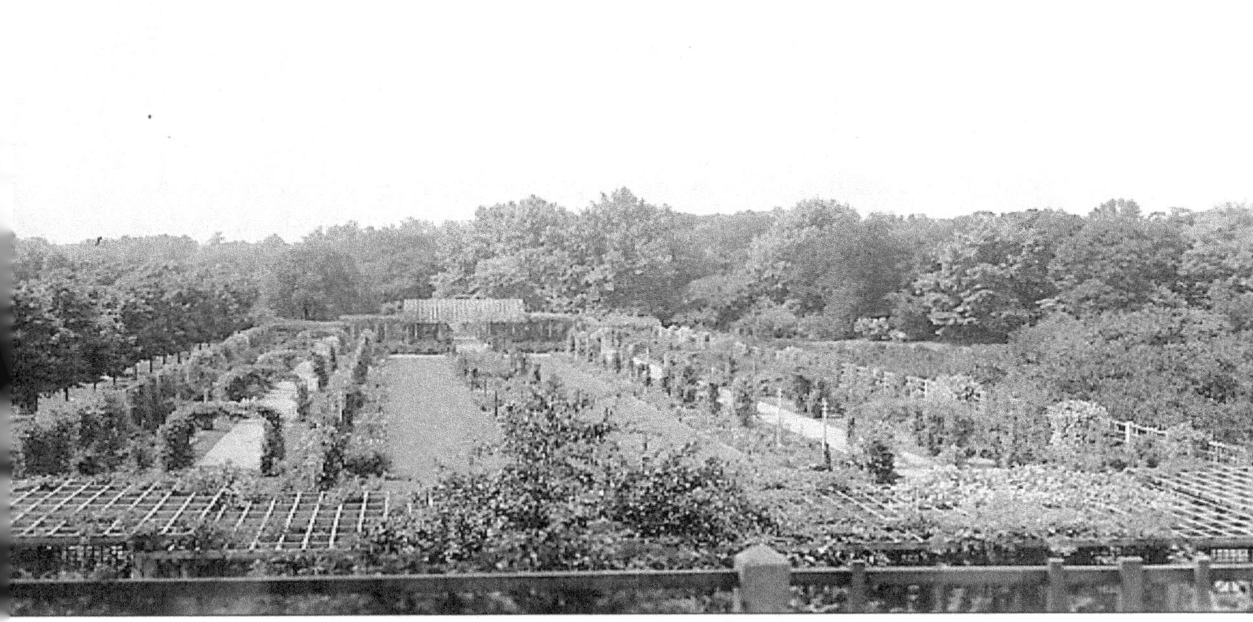

10.19 Harold Caparn design, Cranford Rose Garden from Overlook area. photo 1930s.

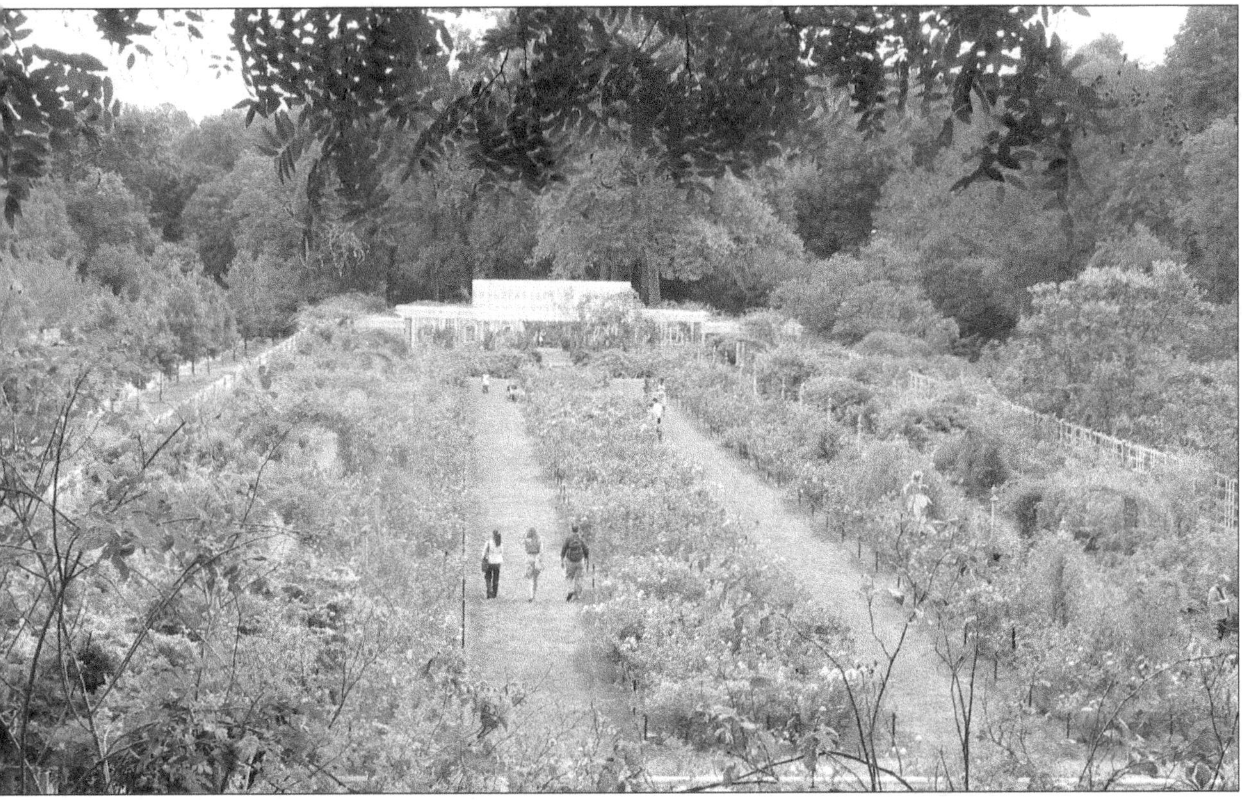

10.20 Harold Caparn design, Cranford Rose Garden, from Overlook area. photo 2006.

When, in 2005, rose rosette disease was found in some plants in the Cranford Rose Garden, action was taken. Some plants were removed, some replaced and remedial efforts were taken with the soil. The Garden continues to provide care against the disease. While the resulting collection of roses has changed somewhat, Caparn's design of the Garden remains.

After Cranford's death in 1935, his widow provided the funds to build a Rose Arc with semi-circular pool, designed by Caparn, located across a walkway from the Rose Garden. The Rose Arc also provided a terminus for the Cherry Esplanade, planned by Olmsted Brothers and laid out by Caparn. The Esplanade runs from the adjacent Brooklyn Museum of Art and thereby connects the Museum with the Garden, both of which were formed under the aegis of the Brooklyn Institute of Arts and Sciences. Also under Institute sponsorship were the Brooklyn Children's Museum and a Biology Laboratory, later named the Cold Spring Harbor Laboratory; added later was the Brooklyn Academy of Music.

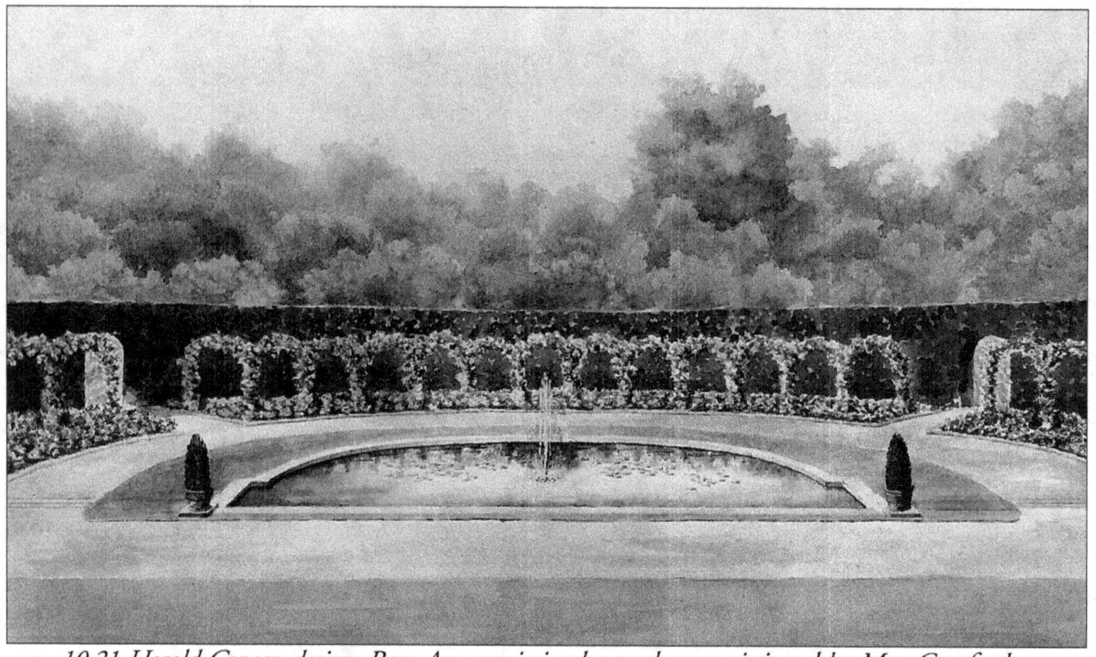

10.21 Harold Caparn design, Rose Arc, semi-circular pool, commissioned by Mrs. Cranford, 1936.

The beauty of these rose garden designs places them today among the best known and most often visited of rose gardens in America.

The Brooklyn Botanic Garden is to the visitor not only a wonderful collection of trees and shrubs and flowers, it is also a kaleidoscope of ever-unfolding plant views, anchored by the architectural focal points set by Caparn, such as the differing fountains and columns at either end of the Osborne Garden, the viewing pavilion overlooking the Cranford Rose Garden, the pool and fountain of the Rose Arc, the armillary sphere and compass in the Magnolia Plaza and the balustrade, steps, pools and fountain in the Lily Pool Terrace. No doubt the restriction of space—finally about 52 acres—provided impetus to make artistically the most of the available canvas.

The Brooklyn Botanic Garden is, like the layout of a fine art museum, such that the visitor finds both educational and artistic interest throughout. The designed as well as the planted beauty still attracts yearly many visitors and supporters to the Brooklyn Botanic Garden. As Caparn said in several articles, "aside from the beauty of the plants themselves, a garden cannot be beautiful if it is not also useful, and cannot be useful if it is not also beautiful."

Harold Caparn's landscape and architectural design at the Brooklyn Botanic Garden over thirty-two years remains his most enduring achievement in works on the land.

11 Central Park
A passionate advocate...1898–1933

Caparn's support of the artistically outstanding vision of Frederick Law Olmsted and Calvert Vaux in designing Central Park in Manhattan, NY, caused him to write a number of letters to the editor of *The New York Times* and to several journals between 1898 and 1933. By his public actions and through his writing he spearheaded the drive to save Central Park from neglect and destruction. For thirty-five years his voice was often heard and respected. He felt there could be no more important task than to preserve the greatest of city parks.

Caparn's *New York Times* letters (1912-3, 1912-6,) seek broad public support leading to his first larger article on the subject, "Central Park, New York, a Work of Art" in *Landscape Architecture* (1912-7). That was followed by more letters in the *Times* and by a letter to the editor of *Parks and Recreation* (1924), "Defends Central Park." He wrote a review in *Landscape Architecture* (1928) on the book by Frederick Law Olmsted, Jr. and Theodora Kimball focused on Central Park. His article on "The restoration of Central Park" was published in *American Civic Annual* (1929).

Finally, in 1933, he wrote twice in *Parks and Recreation* on park damage and the policing needed; in the same year he wrote his last letters to the *Times* regarding the park. City administration and its attitude toward the parks changed with the inauguration in 1934 of Mayor Fiorello LaGuardia who directed more money to the parks. Caparn then turned his attention to another problem, pollution from coal smoke that damaged all the parks as well as the Brooklyn Botanic Garden.

Caparn's letter to *The New York Times* (August 2, 1904) is worth viewing for the scope of assaults that had to be repulsed, starting at the second paragraph:

> This proposal [an ambitious scheme to turn Central Park into a parkway and building lots] appears to have two objects: the opening of an artery of traffic through Central Park, and the substitution of a rectangular boulevard for the informal park. It is argued that Central Park was all very well as a piece of "rural" scenery until the skyscrapers destroyed the illusion, but now it is an absurdity, because it no longer deceives.

But if we really must go direct why not make a tunnel like the new one under the Quirinal Gardens at Rome? But the assumption that a straight parkway is better artistically than a "rural" park is another matter. Why must everything within the city be straight?

Many of the attractive cities of the world—Vienna, Florence, Nuremberg, Rome—have more important curved lines than straight. New York is so ugly because of the endless monotony of its right angles, the vain repetition that perhaps has a good deal to do with the bold deadness of most of its individual buildings and the grossness of some of the newer ones.

The fact is, Central Park is a revolt and a relief from the general rectangularity. It is like taking a weight off one to get away from the streets into the curves and irregular surfaces of the great park, and even the smaller ones, badly as some of them are designed, are a grateful change from the crude formality all about them.

He next took two public actions. First, he aligned himself and the New York Chapter of the ASLA in *The New York Times* (April 7, 1909) against a grab for Central Park land; second, he wrote a letter about the general problem of encroachments on park land. The National Academy of Design wanted to build an Art Gallery in the Park. An important objection was that once any building that might house any kind of commercial interests was permitted, the park would be open to all such buildings and cease to be a park.

Caparn, on behalf of the ASLA, presented to The West End Association, representing over 500 residents of the upper west side, a resolution condemning the Academy's plan. The campaign, in which he had a leading role, was successful in rebuffing this attempt to build in the Park.

Caparn followed with a letter in *The New York Times* (April 28, 1909), stating his general view: We seem to be having an epidemic of raids on the parks—first Central Park, then Macomb's Dam, now Crotona Park. Their danger has usually been in their purposes being good in themselves, and bad only in the endeavor to encroach on public property set apart for other uses.

He continues: The modern city is divided into two classes of areas—the blocks, to be built on, and the streets and parks, to be kept open. The need for parks or open spaces for ventilation is understood so well that no one nowadays would think of making a city plan without ample allowance for them. If they are essential, is it not perfectly plain that any encroachment upon them is bad and dangerous in principle? Is it not especially bad in New York, where the park area is quite inadequate to the population? There ought to be a permanent Park Protective Association, to promote, through public opinion and legislation, the principle that park lands are for park purposes and for nothing else.

Again Caparn felt compelled to write to *The New York Times* (March 14, 1911) on another encroachment, under the heading "The Parks in Spring," and subheading "Landscape Architect Deplores Threat to Convert Them into Coney Island Exhibits."

> He begins: Spring is nigh, and the green buds will soon be swelling, even the green buds in the parks of Manhattan, where they are more costly, more valuable, and apparently less valued than any other green buds that are raised for profit or pleasure.

> In Central and other parks the trees and bushes will be broken, the flowers despoiled, and the lawns effaced; for the temporary pleasure of a few the inheritance and permanent benefit and pleasure of the many will be destroyed; and, in short, works of art that have cost great sums of money and half a century to produce will be pillaged with no great benefit to any and incalculable loss to all.

> Furthermore, the parks are threatened from a new direction; well-meaning city officials, who plainly do not understand the best uses of parks, are preparing to cumber them with things better suited to gymnasiums, playgrounds, and pleasure resorts of the kinds that depend on crowds, novelty, and excitement.

> Next, Caparn writes "New Central Park Lawns" in *The New York Times* (March 14, 1912), on the conversion of the sites of the reservoirs into lawns and park scenery: Not only is such treatment in harmony with the intent of the designers of the park, but nothing would be more useful or more popular. Central Park is the most popular thing in New York, and one of the most useful, and its popularity and usefulness are largely due to the grateful relief its indefinite lines and surfaces afford from the endless rectangularity of the street plan.

On April 4, 1912, Caparn wrote from his office at 156 Fifth Avenue in his capacity as President of the ASLA, to John Muir in care of Professor Henry Fairfield Osborn at 650 Madison Avenue. Osborn had been chairman of the Management Committee, with whom Caparn worked in his designing of The Bronx Zoo. Caparn hoped that Muir, the naturalist and conservationist, founder of the Sierra Club, might be able to help in the fight against intrusions on Central Park.[1]

Caparn says: The American Society of Landscape Architects is planning a movement to arouse public interest in and appreciation of the layout and purpose of Central Park. We wish to bring people to understand that it is a work of art of inestimable practical value as a recreation ground to an immense population. Some such steps seem necessary because of the continual attacks on the integrity of the Park made from many sides and the prevalent lack of organization and argument for its defense among a majority of those who value it as highly. We wish to arrange one or more public meetings at which speakers with different points of view should present the subject from many sides all tending to a similar conclusion, that of the preservation of the Park according to the general intent of the original designers. Caparn issues to Muir an invitation to speak: Your reputation and personality would be of very great advantage to a cause which we consider to be really inseparable from those to which your lifework has been devoted.

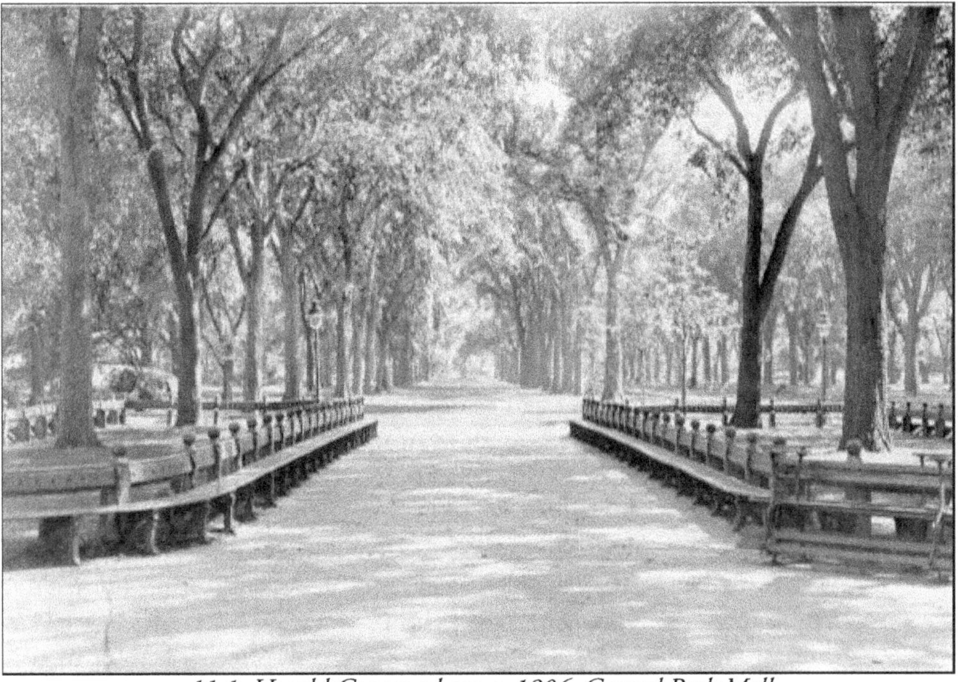

11.1 Harold Caparn photo c. 1906, Central Park Mall

Caparn's next letter, in the same year, to *The New York Times* (May 31, 1912) says: It is refreshing to see so much opposition to the project of placing Mr. Frick's generous gift of the Lenox Library Building in Central Park. Admirable as it may seem to many at first glance, it would be but another precedent for using Central Park for building sites. If Mr. Frick wishes his gift to be really popular he would do well to consider its location outside of but adjoining the Park, say, for instance, at 110th Street, where buildings and presumably land are comparatively inexpensive. Here in America we do not look upon parks as settings for buildings, however beautiful, and in Manhattan, in Central Park in particular, we wish to get away from buildings as far as possible.

In another letter he says: The park scene for its own sake is so much an American outgrowth that it has some claims to be an American invention, perhaps our greatest art invention. Central Park was the first notable instance of it, and it is so sympathetic with our National temperament that as soon as anyone tries to inject unnecessary architecture into our favorite parks there is a loud and widespread outcry.

Now, to his important article: "Central Park, New York: A Work of Art" in *Landscape Architecture* (July 1912), he begins:
The designers of Central Park decided that the best expression they could bestow on it, that which would be of the greatest value to the greatest number, was one which would recall the feeling of the woods and meadow, rocks and water, of rural scenery. This would give the relief of suave surfaces of ground and mobile masses of foliage to minds and bodies wearied with the endless rectangularity of the streets.

So they laid out a scheme, simple in its main structure, though looking complicated enough on the map, consisting of a road running all around the park, with certain cross-roads to provide for the east and west traffic. Four of these are the famous sunken roads which are said to have been the means of Olmsted and Vaux gaining the prize, and which they so skillfully treated that you can seldom see them unless close upon them, and often cannot see them at all even when crossing them. The reason for concealing them was that they were intended for business traffic, which should be kept out of the park.

On this road plan is superposed a system of walks crossing the park in many directions, leading to and helping to create an endless variety of scenes of grass and trees, lakes and rocks. Several sheets of water of considerable extent occupy the sites of former swamps, the muck of which was used to enrich the lawns and woods. These walks penetrate and enclose pieces of ground of the most varied shape, size and expression. Yet all are connected so admirably that one passes insensibly from one to another. Everywhere is displayed the utmost resource of the artist and variety of treatment, as consistently as though the true solution of the problem of each part had been found without effort.

When conditions are at their best, after rainy weather or in the early morning or evening, there is a wonderful air of calm beauty pervading it all, so that one marvels more and more that such a thing with such a sentiment should exist in New York City. Now, if you travel in any rural district, you will find in all directions the raw material or the motive from which Central Park is made. There will be trees and bushes, meadows and rolling ground, buildings and bridges, rocks and water, each in its way more or less beautiful because of the beauty of many or most of the details, the cheerfulness and vitality of it all: in short, because it is the country, as big and free as all out-of-doors.

But, though there is much pictorial beauty, it will be seldom that you find a scene, small or large, that composes well. By composing well I mean not only showing orderly arrangement, just proportion, good lines, and so on, but conveying the impression of a complete picture, 'carrying through' as it is called. This is the quality that conveys an impression of unity to the mind, that gives the effect of simplicity to the most complex design, and may be seen in a book cover, a Corinthian column or a church façade.

This is what is done in Central Park; each successive part into which the uneven surface naturally resolves itself is treated according to its own suggestion, with thoroughness and reserve. Buildings and other subordinate objects are carefully set where they will do least harm to the general composition. The ragged countryside planting is arranged in groups or masses or borders with due regard to the habit of the trees, texture, and color of foliage, sky-line and so on. For the rough or divided surface of land is substituted the smooth and continuous lawn, displaying the best contours of the ground, and preserving them unbroken to their logical end. In fact, an informal park is mostly constructed of endless variants of these two features of lawn and planting, of open spaces surrounded by covered ones.

Yet the general impression conveyed by a well-designed, large city park is that of being in the country. The city park is not an imitation of the country, it is a paraphrase of it; and, if you want to create in the city the country feeling you must reproduce not its accidents and incidents, its roughness and casualness and disorder; you must reproduce its essentials, its openness, its vitality and its verdure, its contrast of the surfaces of the ground and the masses of woods, of the light greens of the grass and the dark of the trees, their freedom and grace and benignity.

Central Park, in view of its extent, its cost, its location, is perhaps the most important and interesting thing of its kind in the world. It is one of the best-loved and one of the worst-hated public recreation grounds in the world. It is admired without reserve by vast numbers of people of all kinds, and it is condemned with as little reserve by some others.

Artists say that, being a long and relatively narrow rectangle set in a system of parallel lines, its layout should also be rectangular, that we ought to have something like the Champs Elysées or the avenues at Versailles. They say that it should have a scheme in scale with its size, that you should be able to see through it from end to end and, in fact, that there ought to be something grand and vast, instead of the rural prettiness they see in it at present. They decry the meandering lines, the indefinite surfaces and vistas, that everywhere abound. In short, they find in it little but irresolution and aimlessness, and an expression which excites in them only the contemptuous verdict that there is no 'design' in Central Park.

We need not concern ourselves with the naïve utterances of the 'practical men' or the real estate operators, but the views of some of the others touch us very closely, for among them are some of the men in our own world of artists whom we most respect, and in whose class we all hope to be [contemporary landscape architects]. But, if you examine their criticisms of Central Park, you will find them all merely expressions of personal opinion, not of natural laws or canons of art. You will find that they may have been misled by prejudice for or against one style of design, or by an imperfect understanding of one style of design—the informal. They may assert that a rectangular piece of ground should of necessity have a rectangular plan, which seems about as reasonable as that a rectangular frame should of necessity enclose a picture of rectangular pattern; or that the veining in a marble panel must properly be perfectly symmetrical, like a piece of floor cloth.

The boundary lines of Central Park were laid down, not by nature or the conditions of the problem, but by the city engineer. Why should they necessarily control the design? As a matter of fact, once inside Central Park, it is as a rule hardly possible to tell what or where the boundaries are; and when you can see a boundary it is a row of high buildings so far away that they seem to be in no conflict with the park scenery; and probably from no point within is it possible to discern the entire size and shape of the park. In short, once within, you lose all sense of the boundaries, and are affected only by the park itself.

It seems to me that there could be no such grateful relief from the rigid rectangularity of the New York streets, nothing in so pleasant contrast with the eternal parallelism of the city plan, as the indefinite lines and surfaces of the park; its undulating lawns with foliage, the contrasted verdure of its grass and trees and bushes. When we get into a large park, we surely want to escape straight lines, not to discover new ones; to find vegetation in its natural freedom, not shorn into the forms of stone and wood. Probably nothing could be more fortunate than that its principal park in the heart of Manhattan Island should be composed of lines and forms and textures that recall the best of the country scenes of pasture and wood and water, and provide continual refreshment and solace for those wearied with the ruthless lines and angles and bricks and mortar of the surrounding streets.

I admit, at once, that the plan of Central Park on paper looks about as vague and shapeless a thing as I know, but then so does a study in anatomy; and, whatever one may think about the park plan, one will certainly not deny that the anatomical plan represents a thing quite perfect in design from beginning to end with complete connection and coherence between all its parts and with all of them mutually interdependent. The structure of the human brain shows no regard for its appearance on a medical chart, yet its design surely shows as comprehensive adjustment of parts to a complete whole as we can conceive. So it is with an informal landscape design; so long as it is logically conceived and consistently maintained, so long as it 'carries through' not only in feeling but in actual structure, and so long as it serves the purposes, practical and esthetic, for which it is intended, it matters little what it looks like on paper.

This brings me to another charge against Central Park: that it is a succession of separate features pretty enough in themselves, but not sequential nor connected by any big scheme worthy in scale of the size of the tract, not such as need the serious attention of an artist to compose. If for the abusive word 'pretty' you substitute 'beautiful,' half the sting is taken from this severe arraignment. Again we have an adjective which is a matter of personal opinion. To me the scenes of Central Park seem as beautiful as any I know of their kind. Their relation to each other is so well managed that you cannot find where the line of separation occurs, but pass imperceptible from one to the next. It may serve more and better purposes by being a succession of scenes adjusted to the natural contours, aptly united and rationally separated, than by being constructed on a single motive apparent at a glance.

They who find a lack of simplicity and dignity in Central Park forget that it was made not only for those in it, but for those over it, who can look down on it from the surrounding buildings, the upper stories on Fifth and Eighth Avenues and Fifty-ninth and 110th Streets. Before them opens a prospect of massed foliage, with openings of green turf, and from some parts of shining water, perhaps as superbly simple as any formal scheme that could be imagined. I think that the design of Central Park is, all things considered, and allowing for certain imperfections, very good; but I cannot demonstrate its excellence except in the same way that I can demonstrate the excellence of design of Michelangelo's Last Judgment, or a landscape of Corot.

Inasmuch as most artists nowadays are educated in schools of art, and emerge therefrom supported by the confidence and authority of their school, it is usually assumed that such training is necessary to produce an artist. But in all arts there have been men of eminence without conventional training, and notably so in landscape design. No more striking instances of the self-evolution of natural gifts can be found than in the designers of Central Park, Frederick Law Olmsted and Calvert Vaux.

Vaux was an Englishman who had turned to landscape design through natural preference, and the extent and value of whose work was never popularly known, and perhaps never will be. As for Olmsted himself, it is often assumed that he entered on the construction of Central Park as an inexperienced amateur, and succeeded by a miracle. But he had a strong natural inclination for such work. He had traveled through Europe, and studied its scenery natural and artificial. He had traveled 5,000 miles on foot and horseback, to observe the scenery of his own country; and, in fact, for fifteen years he had steeped himself in the works of nature, and of art as applied to nature, and was so full of her precedents and suggestions that he could discover and explain the sentiment inherent in any piece of ground, and propose a fitting method of treatment.

It is worth while to linger a little on this man who, by his career and his achievements, was one of the very greatest of American artists. His personality, his career, and even his writings, bear many striking resemblances to those of Humphry Repton in England, in the previous century, whose books are probably the most valuable contribution to the literature of landscape design in existence, at least in the English language.

The fact remains that few people can enter Central Park without becoming sensibly happier, that it produces to a greater or less extent in those who enter it such sensations as its designers wished. And, surely, for a man to be able by his creation to arouse in innumerable others who come after some such sense of beautiful in nature as has inspired himself, to instill into them something of his own spirit, is a great achievement; and the means by which he does it is entitled to be termed in a very high degree a Work of Art.

Caparn here summarizes the pros and cons of contemporary thought about Central Park. He is disappointed that some landscape architects have found the need to criticize it because it is not formal, but informal in its design. In the year when he is President of the ASLA, he puts the weight of his opinion clearly in support of the Park.

Caparn was elected President of the New York Chapter of the ASLA in 1920; he campaigned from that office to support Central Park and the other parks in Manhattan. Beginning in 1922, for the next eight years he wrote at least once a year to *The Times* about the parks. In 1922 he is found four times in the paper, starting with his proposal to put city parks under a board of directors. "Park Administration," in *The New York Times* (January 16, 1922), takes a position in opposition to Charles Downing Lay, the City Landscape Architect: "In Thursday's Times is an article on the city park question by Mr. C. D. Lay, in which he criticizes adversely the idea of putting the city park system under the control of an unpaid board. Such a scheme is said to be "so foreign to our feelings, and so revolutionary. Why?"

> Caparn: The plan of a board of trustees or directors controlling paid and skilled executives is the best known and longest tried of all democratic systems of administration. By it are managed all kinds of organizations, public and private, business, social, civic, religious and philanthropic. It is the most usual and successful form of park administration, as, for instance, of the Palisades Interstate Park and of the Hartford parks. The former is controlled by a board of twenty (ten from New York and ten from New Jersey), the latter by a board of ten. The City Botanical Gardens, the museums, the Zoological Park and other institutions are administered in a similar way.

> The city park executives need a court of resort and appeal to establish a policy of management (guided by the experience of the executives), to advise and instruct them in cases of doubt and to take responsibilities which an executive ought not to be expected to bear. This need is probably more vital in New York than in any other city. In New York such a court of control and appeal (or park board) should be unpaid, because, owing to the prestige of such an office, it would be easy to get the best administrative talent in the city to serve without pay; because the appointive power would be embarrassed by office seekers, and because there would not be another set of salaries unnecessarily added to the city budget.

> The unsatisfactory conditions of the city parks are not the fault of any commissioner. They are mainly due to a system which renders it impracticable for a commissioner to make good as he should. A citizen,

no doubt of ability, is put in charge of a complex park organization with very little established policy and tradition. He combines administrative and executive functions as is done in no other park system with which the writer is acquainted. He has to run his department much as a corner grocery store is run, but without the grocer's experience. He has his own business in mind, at least part of the time, and the wonder is that, under the circumstances, the average Park Commissioner does as well as he does.

The park ought to be the charge of executives who make the parks their real business and stay on it during business hours, as they do in other cities. To aid, counsel, direct, relieve and be responsible for those technical men there should be an impersonal controlling authority, a board of the best administrative talent New York has to offer, and this the city can have for the asking. This form of governance, unpaid board overseeing paid executive and staff, is the form found for all sorts of non-profit entities today. Now, as then, it has proven effective.

On June 24, 1922, *The New York Times* chronicled in a lengthy article, the proposal received by the Board of Estimate from Rodman Wanamaker, Chairman of the Mayor's Committee on a Permanent War Memorial. It detailed the need for $600,000 in appropriation for the thirty-four acres covered by the reservoir and three additional acres, to be used for "a memorial arch, the largest swimming pool in the country, a lagoon set in the centre of approaches to the Metropolitan Museum of Art and the American Museum of Natural History, a wading pool, sand-pits, playgrounds and running tracks."

Caparn wrote to complain and to submit that additions should take the park into consideration. "Sees Central Park A Dumping Ground--Proposed Memorial Plan built Around Reservoir, Not Park, Says Architect" in *The New York Times* (June 29, 1922). It begins: "Further opposition developed yesterday to the proposed invasion of Central Park by a swimming pool, a wading pool, a stadium, a cinder track, an arch and other features which have been included by the Mayor's Committee in plans for a memorial to the New York boys who died in the war. The plan was denounced yesterday by Harold A. Caparn, an official of the New York Chapter of the American Society of Landscape Architects."

Further, "A protest against making the park 'a dumping ground' for things which could not find a home elsewhere, was voiced by Harold A. Caparn, who said: 'The scheme as described seems to be based not on the park itself, but on the lower reservoir, as thought the lower reservoir were the controlling feature. It is an accident, an arbitrary thing made for economic needs which no longer exist. It seems to the writer that if the park is to be considered as the site for a war memorial, the conception and design of the memorial should be based on the park itself, not on its accretions, the reservoirs.'"

In July 1922 he wrote: What is the Park itself? It is ideally and potentially, the site bounded by Fifty-ninth Street, Fifth Avenue, 110th Street and Eight Avenue, treated as a whole, as one consistent scheme of which every part is a real part, not a casual addition. It should be a park, a self-contained entity, not a great space which might be a convenient dumping ground for all kinds of structures which cannot find a home elsewhere. To have made Central Park on a consistent plan throughout Olmsted and Vaux must have had a clean slate to work on; that is, they should have had the whole tract as Nature made and left it, or, at least, without immovable impediments. They did not have such conditions, so the Park has never been completed.

Now that the time is in sight when one or both reservoirs can be removed, is it not reasonable to consider the completion of the Park in such a spirit as would have inspired the designers themselves? Plans for any great development within the Park should be based not on the reservoirs, but on the assumption that the reservoirs are not there, that a really great and spacious composition in scale with the size and importance of the Park can be created.

Central Park's largest lawn contains nineteen acres, while the Long Meadow in Prospect Park, Brooklyn, is three or four times its size, and the Open Lawn in Franklin Park, Boston, has 160 acres. Such a great space on the site of the two reservoirs might be a fitting foreground to an architectural monument, a work of art worthy of its dedication and of the city. This movement for a war memorial may be the city's great opportunity, not only for the creation of a war memorial, but for the completion of the greatest of its parks. But whether the memorial is placed in Central Park or not, it should be no less in imagination than the Lincoln Memorial with which comparison has been suggested. Like Lincoln, the dead soldiers were martyrs in the cause of liberty and their monument should not be an excuse for public utilities that would be more useful elsewhere.

If there is to be a memorial, let not the reservoirs impede and control it as they have impeded and controlled the Park. In conclusion, let me suggest that it is not of very great importance that the work should be finished by a certain date. This will soon be forgotten, except by the historians. What is important is that such a work should be undertaken without haste and with due breadth of vision, so that those who come after may have no cause to regret that the city's most ambitious memorial was ever put up.

His grand plan was never worked out; only a few WWI memorial trees and statuary can be found in the Park.

Finally, came a proposal he could support. In *The New York Times* (July 3, 1922), he says:

> This is a line of endorsement of Mr. [Samuel] Parson's proposal to plant 40 large elms in the Mall in Central Park so that the present generation may be able to see what the Mall looked like in the nineteenth century. There is little doubt that 40 public-spirited citizens can be found to subscribe $1,000 apiece for a tree, and this should be an object lesson leading to an organized campaign for the rehabilitation of the Park.

> Most of the $1,000 will be spent on digging and planting the tree, and this is right, for even in these days of increasing tree lovers the impression is all too prevalent that a tree can be bought and handled like a fence post and set in much the same way, and yet grow cheerfully. No greater mistake could be made. If a tree is to succeed it must have air and water both to roots and top and good soil to grow in so far as its roots can reach. The moving and planting operations should be watched from beginning to end by an expert tree mover, much as a surgeon watches a surgical operation. Both the tree planter and the surgeon desire a quick recovery and a vigorous life for the patient after the operation.

> Some years ago Boston Common, dotted with sickly trees, worn and packed down by centuries of intensive use, was cultivated by an elaborate and expensive process, and many who did not understand trees jeered. But the elms took on a new lease of life, and today any one who doubts the use of treating a tree well is advised to go and look at Boston Common.

But in the next year he had to write again, this time to stay a major disruption to Central Park. He wrote to *The New York Times* (November 5, 1923), under the heading "Cost of a Park Subway—Fifty Years Required to Restore the Trees and Grounds." He says:

> The Transit Commission proposes that a four-track subway should be built along the western edge of Central Park, most of it by the cut and cover process. They require fifteen feet width for each track, making with space for walls say about 65 feet. Also the privilege of making

sidings (width not specified) not exceeding half a mile in length for each mile of roadway. How much additional space would be excavated is uncertain, depending on the contours of the ground, which are very irregular for the entire distance.

This would mean the destruction of many of the best trees in the park, growing where they are most valuable to the general park scenery. They form the outer foliage frame of the park, and are of great value in giving to it that sense of seclusion which is so important a part of its charm. The foliage frame, in fact, is essential to its being a park at all, not merely an open space. If any one will go to any part from which the buildings of Eighth Avenue can be seen, he will be able to see how great a void would be left if this screen of foliage were removed.

It is not only the trees included in this 65-foot strip that would be lost, but many others, whose root systems would be deprived of soil and moisture by the excavation, and yet others which would be filled around or left standing above the general level, as the case might be.

The modeling of the ground and the entire scenic composition along this side of the park was very carefully studied, and the alterations in grade would necessitate a readjustment of most of the ground in question, with the permanent loss of much of its attraction.

We are told that the soil and trees would be restored 'as far as possible' to the satisfaction of the Park Department. But the only way to put back trees as good as those now standing is to make the soil conditions right, then plant young trees and wait fifty years or so for them to grow.

Probably the Transit Commission is no more anxious than any one else to injure the park, but considers it to be its duty to put the issue squarely up to the citizens. They calculate that it will cost about $2,000,000 less to make a subway by this cut and cover process than by tunneling deep enough to leave the park uninjured. In other words, it will cost the people of New York about $2,000,000 to avoid the loss of this two miles of park scenery for fifty years or so. Included in the mass of a subway bond issue and spread over a term of years, this would seem a small price to pay for preserving the integrity of the park for a half century. Cannot the city afford to foot the bill?

In a brief letter to *The New York Times* (June 10, 1924), Caparn finds some solution to the problems that have vexed him:

My attention has been drawn to the proposal of Commissioner En-right to build a combined war memorial and art centre north of Central Park. This grandiose idea is especially interesting as showing that there are members of the City Administration who can think of these subjects without the desire to invade the parks.

This site has been suggested by many people. It is accessible by both elevated and subway, and while it would have all the advantage of the park scenery as a foreground, it would provide a paved open space round the memorial sufficient to accommodate very large crowds. These conditions are not to be found in the middle of Central Park.

"Defends Central Park" (July 1924) is a letter to the editor of *Parks and Recreation*:

With regard to Mr. Olmsted's [F. L. Olmsted, Jr.] interesting paper on Metropolitan Parks, in which he speaks of the advantages of the originally proposed East River site for a great park on Manhattan Island, instead of the present Central Park. If the park had been located along the East River, it would have had the advantages of river front scenery, but corresponding difficulty of accessibility. Furthermore, although the additional spaciousness, that important quality on which Mr. Olmsted dwells, would have been considerable, the river prospect would have been not towards a boundary of woods and rocks, but to the shore front of Long Island City and Brooklyn, which is like the typical shore front of which no more need be said than that it would be difficult to find any scenery less suggestive of escape from the sights and sounds of the city.

Then it should be remembered that, though Central Park has no river front, it has not only its very picturesque lakes, but also the two reservoirs of about 137 acres. The promenade round the upper and larger one is very popular, and at least it is not bounded by docks and factories. Taken altogether, Central Park has an unusual proportion of water area, and probably much more varied than would have been that of the riverside park.

Considering its history, its situation, the number of people it serves and its value as real estate, Central Park is the most remarkable and interesting city park in the world, and perhaps the most valuable civic possession of any city.

Caparn is the center of an article in *The New York Times* (January 4, 1925), "Suggests Changes For Central Park." "A number of suggestions for the improvement of Central Park were offered yesterday by Harold A. Caparn, landscape architect at 18 East Forty-first Street, based on a study of the park covering several years."

The fact that Central Park at the time it was made should have found two young men capable of producing such a piece of work, which was to be the prototype of all the American parks that have been made since, that has worn so well and proved so adaptable to the unimagined changes in city conditions, is little less than a miracle. But, being after all only human, these two young men made, as I see it, two mistakes. They did not provide adequately for short cuts across it for pedestrians, and they accepted its rectangular shape, apparently, without attempting to modify it.

If the park had been pointed at both ends, so that its north and south boundaries were diagonal streets instead of members of the gridiron plan, the north and south traffic would have flowed easily by instead of butting into it, and the impediment to north and south traffic would have been far less noticeable, and perhaps would never have become serious. In the late 1850's and early 1860's it would not have been difficult to remodel the street layout north and south of the park so as to provide for all of this.

The first of these errors, the lack of short cuts, is not serious, for it would not be difficult to rectify it without materially changing the plan of the park. The second is far more difficult to correct, but even now it may not be impossible to find ways and means of meeting the needs of traffic without vital injury to the park. Nothing seems to me more fortunate than the general spirit and style of treatment of this park, which preserved, developed, displayed and utilized all the natural scenic qualities, destroying hardly any of them, so as to be a perpetual contrast to and relief from the eternal rigidity of the plan of Manhattan.

Then what I would like to do that seems practicable or may become practicable, is study the soil conditions in every part of the park. They vary considerably, as one can easily see from the varying conditions of growth in different parts. Atmospheric conditions are, unhappily, beyond remedy, so long as the community is willing to inhale smoke, dust, gases and gasoline fumes; but even as it is there seems to be no room for doubt that most of the ordinary kinds of deciduous and broad leaf evergreen trees and shrubs can be grown with fair success in Central Park, so long as the proper soil conditions are produced and maintained.

Dead trees and bushes are being removed with disheartening rapidity. These, of course, should be replaced, and much new planting has been done. But not only should the dead growth be restored, but young trees and bushes should be added to plantations that have reached maturity, and where the expert eye can see that they are likely to stand still or deteriorate before the new plantings may be ready to take their place.

Something ought to be done about some of the buildings, more especially those on the shores of the lakes. But I hesitate to suggest that these be replaced with new ones, for we should be very likely to get smart new structures, well designed, perhaps, but which would stick up in the park landscape like sore thumbs.

None of this would be of much avail unless the park could be properly protected. For the preservation of the park itself, for the greatest good of the greatest number, the public should be excluded from certain parts of it, such as many plantations, which are not intended for traffic and which traffic injures or destroys.

Lastly, Central Park ought to be completed, and this cannot be done so long as the reservoirs are there. The lower reservoir of about thirty-seven acres has already past its usefulness, and is due for removal. Engineers of the Water Department will not listen to any idea of dispensing with the upper reservoir, and it may be many years before this will be seriously considered. But it seems plain that another reservoir could be built to take its place in some outlying part of the city or outside of it (as the old Forty-second Street reservoir gave way to the library).

None of these reforms, however, can be effectively initiated and carried through and perpetuated until the system of park administration itself is reformed, until park executives are given real authority and responsibility; until, in short, the Park Department is taken out of politics and run on principles such as those of any other large business concern.

Four months later, Caparn is again the center of an article in *The New York Times* (May 27, 1925), "Would Take Parks Out of Politics." "The second public hearing before the Committee on Municipal Administration appointed by Mayor Hylan took place yesterday in the office of Commissioner of Accounts David Hirshfield. Representatives of civic organizations recommended revisions of the City Charter, which they argued would result in greater economy and efficiency. The consolidation of the tenement house, building, and fire departments, for inspection and administration, and a re-organization of public park management were among the reforms advocated."

Harold A. Caparn, representing the New York Chapter of the American Society of Landscape Architects, discussed in detail the plan which he has advocated for some years to place the parks under the control of a body of trustees and executives who are experts in park management, and whose tenure of office would not be affected by changes in the City Administration. At present, he said, the park commissioners only begin to know their jobs when they are replaced by others, who in turn must familiarize themselves with their duties at the expense of the parks and the taxpayers.

Mr. Caparn suggested that an unpaid board of trustees be appointed by the Mayor from a list of eligible persons submitted by technical, civic, and commercial bodies, this board in turn to choose competent executives and specialists to maintain and improve the parks. Such a system, Mr. Caparn declared, would permit a continuity of policy not possible now. It would be comparable, he pointed out, to the manner in which the museums, botanical gardens and public libraries are managed.

Asked by Commissioner Hirshfield for specific recommendations for park improvement, Mr. Caparn said he would decide on a policy as to what areas should be used as playgrounds, and what parts kept as lawns, and provide an ample police force to protect the restricted portions. He denied the system he recommended would, as the Commissioner suggested, remove the control of the parks from the public. If the people were not satisfied, he declared, a way would be found to change the system. J. R. Brinley, a trustee of the Landscape Architects' Association, and Miss Mabel Parsons, daughter of Samuel Parsons, known as the "Father of Central Park," spoke in favor of Mr. Caparn's plan.

In the next year, Caparn is heard three times in articles and letters. "One-Man Control For Parks Urged," *The New York Times* (March 22, 1926), picks up the subject of the previous years. "A radical change in the form of administration of the parks was urged yesterday by the New York Chapter of the American Society of Landscape Architects. The attitude of the chapter was made known through Harold A. Caparn of 18 East Forty-first Street."

The chapter would have the control of all city parks placed in the hands of a park board composed of nine trustees to be recruited among representative men and women. The board members in turn, according to the ideas of the landscape architects, should then hire a park executive to have city-wide charge, with five other experts in charge of the boroughs.

Mr. Caparn made public a letter from George McAneny, Chairman of the Transit Commission, endorsing the idea and a letter from former Attorney General George W. Wickersham to the New York State Chamber of Commerce approving the legal aspects of the suggested change. Mr. Caparn also gave out copies of a letter the chapter sent to Henry de Forest Baldwin, Chairman of the Charter Revision Commission which, in part, follows: 'We are convinced that the efficiency of such an organization as we have proposed is almost entirely dependent on the character of the Park Board. Our scheme of a board of directors or trustees (commissioners) controlling the paid executives is, in one form or another, the method of administration of park systems throughout the country as at Hartford, Philadelphia and the South Park system of Chicago. It is found to function well in this city in many institutions, as for instance, the Public Library; also in the Palisades Interstate Park and the Essex and Hudson County park systems of New Jersey.

In the next year, Caparn brings another organization to lobby for the scheme. In "Wants City Parks Under New Control," *The New York Times* (February 2, 1927), the article begins:

A complete change in the administration of the city parks, to take them out of politics and put their maintenance and management on a business basis, is suggested by the City Gardens Club in the forthcoming issue of its publication, *The Bulletin*, through Harold A. Caparn, Chairman of the organization's Committee on Parks.

After restating the scheme, he continues: Many individuals and organizations have labored during the past year to bring about an improvement in the condition of the city parks. But in spite of all this effort there is little encouragement in the park situation for the New Year except for the reports of the willingness of certain wealthy citizens to make large contributions toward the renovation of Central Park. Let us hope that the City Administration will not get the habit of expecting continuous outside aid, so that each year the hat will have to be sent round to keep life in the parks of a pauperized city.

Park Commissioner Gallatin, when his attention was called yesterday to the suggestion of Mr. Caparn, said he could not see material advantage in change such as Mr. Caparn proposed. 'Worthwhile men who might serve on such unpaid boards, would scarcely be able to devote sufficient time to park matters and the result would be that the superintendent, or whatever he might be called, would, in fact, manage the whole thing. That is usually the history of such unpaid bodies. I presume that what is meant is something like the Chicago system, where they have a large number of such boards. But the point is that Chicago spends a vast amount more on her parks than New York does. While unquestionably the condition of the parks here might be better, I think the people are really getting what they pay for. The time may come when the public will be willing to spend more money on parks and I hope it will come.'" In the face of such opposition from the City Hall down, Caparn did not give up. It would still be several years before his pleas were answered.

In the meantime, during the next year there appeared the book on Central Park of great authority that gave Caparn yet another opportunity to bring the subject to the fore. He reviewed in *Landscape Architecture* (1928) the book "Central Park, as a Work of Art and as a Great Municipal Enterprise" that was volume II of *Forty Years of Landscape Architecture, Professional Papers of Frederick Law Olmsted, Sr.* Edited by Frederick Law Olmsted, Jr. and Theodora Kimball (New York: G. P. Putnam's Sons, 1928). It was of 575 pages, with illustrations.

> Caparn says: The design and execution of this work are based on documents and other records relating to Central Park from 1853 to 1895. It is divided into two parts: (I) The History and Evolution of Central Park, and (II) Selected Papers of Olmsted and Vaux. As might be expected, in Part I the writings of Olmsted and Vaux are incidental, while in Part II they are the substance of the book.

> The value of both Parts I and II lies in their tracing the development, not only of Central Park, but also of the character and artistic power of the designers, and especially of Frederick Law Olmsted. As the story unfolds, Olmsted gradually emerges from the trials of his experiences with the equipment of a remarkable gift for organizing and managing men and things, a rare power of analysis, and those qualities of tact, patience, and persistence that combined to give him his unique position among American artists, perhaps the greatest of all in influence and accomplishment.

> No better summary of the thought pervading the book could be written than the following passage from The Landscape Architect's Review of Recent Changes, written in 1872:

> *'The park throughout is a single work of art, and as such, subject to the primary law of every work of art, namely, that it shall be framed upon a single, noble motive, to which the design of all its parts, in some more or less subtle way, shall be confluent and helpful.'"*

Two quotations from it will serve as illustration: A spokesman of a delegation desiring to have a speeding track in the Park appeared at a meeting of the Park Board. Mr. Olmsted was deputed to explain some of the objections to his project, and was unable to do so without referring to 'landscape considerations.' The comment of the spokesman was 'Oh, damn your landscape! We came here as practical men to discuss a simple practical common-sense question. We don't know what the landscape has to do with the matter before us.' In another place, Olmsted, after describing the persecutions to which he had been subjected to induce him to misuse his opportunities of patronage, says: 'Let it be understood what this meant to me—the frustration of purposes to which I had for years given all my heart, to which I had devoted my life; the degradation of works in which my pride was centered; the breaking of promises to the future which had been to me as churchly vows.' This was preliminary to a serious nervous breakdown.

The "Restoration of Central Park" (1929) in *American Civic Annual* begins with an Editor's Note: 'The Olmsted volume on Central Park has revealed the early struggles to create a park in the face of politics, graft, and stupidity. The present-day neglect of Central Park has become a well-known disgrace. Its restoration has begun, as outlined by Mr. Caparn. Let us hope that the new park-consciousness of our people will operate in New York to protect this famous old park.'

> Caparn follows: In the heart of the richest city in the world, of a value as real estate almost fantastic, it is yet in notoriously bad condition, starved of funds for maintenance, and with inadequate and unsystematic protection. Of late years, out of the vague immensity of grumbling, the popular discontent has taken shape enough to induce the Board of Estimate to appropriate $1,000,000 for doing work that should have been done thirty years ago, and continued as part of the regular routine of park management ever since. This result, though admirable as far as it goes, was not achieved without great expenditures of time, effort, and money by a handful of civic-minded people, by much newspaper notoriety and a general stirring up of dust and noise that looks like lost motion, that was probably inevitable, but that never ought to have been necessary. The underlying cause of the need for all this fuss was what is known as POLITICS. (his capitalization)

> The parks lack the three conditions without which proper upkeep is impracticable. These conditions are: (1) continuity of policy of management; (2) security in office of the officials; (3) protection.

This movement may be said to have received its first impulse from the Parks and Playgrounds Association which, for many years, under George Gordon Battle and Miss Lulu Morton, exercised a quiet and unassuming protective influence over the New York parks. Its work was later supplemented more aggressively by the Central Park Association under the leadership of William Bradford Roulstone who was active in the litigation which kept the American Museum of Safety from occupying the Arsenal Building in Central Park, thus establishing the principle of the immunity of parks from invasion by private interests. This latter association procured a report on the condition of Central Park from Olmsted Brothers of Brookline, Mass. Other organizations, among which were the Fifth Avenue Association, whose General Manager is Captain W. J. Pedrick, the New York Chapter, American Society of Landscape Architects which, since 1921 [under Caparn's presidency, expressly extended to fight for the parks] has endeavored to awaken public interest in reforming the city parks administration and taking it out of politics, and the City Gardens Club [where Caparn was vice president and chair of its parks committee] contributed their share to the general cause.

A well-known tree-doctoring firm drew much public attention to the subject of park restoration by digging round and fertilizing a number of large trees in Central Park at its own expense. All these have had their part in arousing public interest in the renovation of the parks, which resulted in the appointment of a subcommittee of the Mayor's large Citizens' Committee, and in the appropriation of funds above referred to by the Board of Estimate. When this fund became available, the plans for spending it were put into the hands of Mr. Herman Merkel [known to Caparn as formerly an Assistant Superintendent at United States Nurseries, Short Hills, NJ, where Caparn's younger brother Arthur had worked, and as Chief Forester for the Bronx Zoo, where Caparn himself had worked], who drew up a report which supplemented that of Olmsted Brothers. These two reports dwelt on the common-sense view of the situation, which might be summarized by saying that the well-understood principles of farming must be applied to raising crops of trees, bushes, and grass.

So far, the results of this long and discouraging campaign appear in a revivified appearance of many parts of the park, and especially in the cultivation and fertilizing, not merely of new plantations, but also of many of the priceless old trees and bushes. This does not sound like a great accomplishment, and its results may finally be lost for want of a proper follow-up through a series of years of the work already done. But they may well prove to be the saving of the life of Central Park, for a park without trees and bushes is hardly a park at all, but merely an expanse of vacant lots.

Having gotten the restoration started, Caparn two years later must again fend off another ill-considered proposal. "Central Park Plans" in *The New York Times* (March 24, 1931) is his letter to the editor on the subject: So much correspondence in support of the plan for a formal avenue across Central Park connecting the two museums has appeared in the newspapers that it becomes necessary to consider the subject from other points of view.

No good citizen could wish to disparage the organization, the management, the great achievement and the popularity of the two museums. Whatever else New Yorkers may have to apologize for, they can always point with pride to these two superb institutions. But this does not justify the damage to another great public utility, the Central Park, in order to glorify the others.

The desire for a wide concourse across the park between the two museums could only be justified by the expectation of great throngs passing to and fro between them. But what reason is there for any such expectation? How many visitors desire to take in both museums in the same afternoon, or even in the same day? Both are so full of treasures, so interesting, that a mere attentive walk through one of them is likely to bring on an attack of museum fag, so that the last place that most people leaving one of them would seek would be another and quite different museum.

It is probably desirable that there should be an easier approach to the Museum of Natural History across the park for visitors from the east side, and to the Museum of Art from the west side. But this can be arranged without detriment to the structure of the park plan, and so amply provided for in the plan for the lower reservoir site of the Society of Landscape Architects. An additional footway could be made south of the transverse road if necessary by no great extension of existing walks.

So much for the traffic consideration. As for the esthetic side of the question, the plan proposed for a formal avenue only shows the impossibility of arranging such a connection between the two museums satisfactorily, or, in fact, at all. Under this plan the avenue starts from the south end of the Metropolitan Museum, running past it instead of at right angles to the main entrance, as one would expect of a formal approach. It runs straight for about two-thirds of the way across the park, then turns sharply into a curve to reach the entrance of the Museum of Natural History. The straight part of this avenue neither begins nor ends anywhere in particular. But in the journey it would succeed in destroying, or greatly marring, the greatest opportunity in the history of the park for the creation of a large and stately composition, an open lawn scene as proposed in the plan of the Society of Landscape Architects, in size and quality worthy of the park.

Such a lawn because of its extent, would not only be far more beautiful when its frame of trees was grown, but far more useful than the two lawns that have been destroyed by intensive use and lack of protection, the ball ground and the North Meadow. And the lake at the south end impounded by the long and frowning rock ridge which would provide the light in this park picture and give a quality to the whole so rare and so characteristic of the topography, would be lost to a straight strip of asphalt with row of trees quite out of keeping with the general composition, and with no compensating advantage to the two great buildings it is intended to serve, nor to the park or the public.

Two years later Caparn wrote on another, often considered, issue: how to accommodate playgrounds and children, older youth and young adults in their need for space in which to pursue more vigorous games.

He wrote to the editor, *The New York Times* (May 16, 1933), "Those Who Need the Park." He says: In regard to the controversy over the old reservoir site in Central Park, none of us will quarrel with the idea of doing more and better for the "kids" than has hitherto been done. They ought to have been thought of two or three generations ago when Harlem was a village and vacant lots were cheap and plentiful.

But the champions of the "kids" appear to forget, for the most part, the needs and claims of everyone else. For parks are needed and used, at one time or another, by everybody, and this includes the kids themselves. A large park is one of the most democratic things we have. It can be and is used simultaneously by all classes, from boys and girls who romp in it, from those who sit or lie on "keep off" lawns and leave litter, to those who ride through it in taxicabs or limousines or on horseback. The weakness of this majority, however, is that it has no organization and few to press its claims against those of an organized, vociferous and energetic minority.

The class described as "the kids," on the other hand, is limited in age (say from 10 to 25) and consequently in numbers. For its play it requires special indestructible and consequently largely barren areas not consistent with general park purposes, which require not only beautiful scenery but freedom from undue noise and danger from flying balls.

Also they forget that when they and the players and the audience are gone, the playground may be empty, partially or wholly, until next week. But many observers don't appear to notice the emptiness of empty playgrounds, but only the fullness of full ones. Anyone interested in this subject is advised to watch any of the numerous small parks in Manhattan that have both playgrounds and seats with trees to note the number of those in the seats. Taking all hours of the day and all days of the week, it will be found, in most cases, that the seat-holders greatly outnumber the players.

It is for this great but mostly silent majority that a large lawn such as that proposed for the site of the old reservoir in Central Park is so valuable. Properly made and administered, it may be not merely the scenic centre of the park but, counting the number of daylight hours of its use, it may, and should be, the chief centre of the park's activities. Many kinds of games not annoying or dangerous to bystanders may be played on it. Everyone knows how people like to sit or lie on the grass, especially where there are trees, and form family or social gatherings, and watch the children play or help them play.

Those who use the lawns for such purposes are very likely to scatter papers, and worse, still, broken glass, but that is largely due to lack of well-studied and systematic control. The common defect in park protection is not merely that it is inadequate but that it is unsystematic; visitors do not know just what to expect and so do not learn to feel sure just what they may or may not do. Necessary park rules should not only be enforced; they should be enforced consistently. And the park guardians should not only have the power to enforce them; they should have the ability to explain the reasons for them.

In a large lawn occasional bare patches do not show up conspicuously and are easy to repair. Those who are critical of bare patches worn by use would do well to look less at the patches and more at the whole lawn. If parts of it are unduly worn, they should be fenced off until they have time to recover, and once in so many years the whole lawn should be plowed up and remade. This should be done in sections in successive years.

We might remind the playground advocates that already three of the finest lawns in Central Park have been given up to ball games—the ball ground, the North Meadow and the lawn on the west side from Ninety-fourth to Ninety-sixth Street, now converted into tennis courts.

This is written in entire sympathy with and understanding of the crying need for playgrounds and athletic fields. But many of those best qualified to express opinion believe that playgrounds and athletic fields should be excluded from parks (excepting playgrounds for small children). They should be provided generously, but outside of the park boundaries. The rights of the small minority of players of rough games should be fully and gladly recognized, but not at the expense of ignoring the rights of the great majority in their parks.

Some of these days when these principles are understood and means of providing for athletics outside of the parks discovered and adopted, we may perhaps hope to see the barren wastes of Central Park restored to the people and again become what is more needed than ever before: places of refuge from the sights and sounds of the city.

An article appeared in *The New York Times* on the same day as Caparn's above letter. "Central Park Fight Carried to Mayor" (May 16, 1933) showed the extent to which a proposal could garner advocates and opponents. Park Commissioner John E. Sheehy had presented a plan to make athletic fields: a running track, five baseball diamonds, pits for pole vaults, broad and high jumps, a playground and a wading pool on the Central Park reservoir site. Mayor O'Brien held a hearing at City Hall to hear both sides. The president of the Municipal Art Society had requested the hearing, which brought forty organizations that were represented directly or indirectly at the hearing. Speaking in favor of the plan were, among others, the Community Councils of the City, the Public Schools Athletic League, the Amateur Athletic Union, members of the city school system and several clergy.

Speaking for the Sheehy plan, G. T. Kirby, president of the Public Schools Athletic League, "demanded playgrounds and athletic fields in the reservoir site as a protection for children who risk traffic dangers when they play in the streets, or tend to develop criminal tendencies. I'm not saying we should turn Central Park over to a great athletic field. I am asking shall we turn the boys loose on the streets and to crime." The priest of the Church of St. Gregory on West Ninetieth Street described "the absence of playgrounds in his neighborhood, and asserted that there should be nothing incongruous in a child playing in the park. What is beauty? You may have it in a tree or in a child." The Rev. Joseph J. Murray, speaking for the Metropolitan Association of the Amateur Athletic Union, read that organization's resolutions endorsing the Sheehy plan, "We are looked upon as advocating a destructive policy; we are advocating a constructive policy of the greatest good for the greatest number." Rabbi Schachter of the West End Synagogue, asked "Shall we have a recreational centre which will make for the maximum physical, mental and spiritual development or shall we not?" Beside William J. Lee, a former park superintendent, also speaking for was G. W. Smalley of the Phoenix Civic Association, who "confessed that he had cut grass and trimmed shrubbery around the Metropolitan Museum of Art for five years as a park employee without ever having felt the urge to go into the museum to gaze at the art treasures. He discounted the claims of the opponents of the project on the ground that twelve of the societies were 'art' groups."

Speaking against, The Municipal Art Society, through its representative, said: "The Municipal Art Society was organized for the purpose of making and keeping New York an attractive place in which to live. It believes that the people crave beauty as well as bread. We believe we are standing on a firm foundation when we point out to you that if all, or even part, of this great tract of thirty-five acres is allowed to remain a sandy waste instead of being made, as the landscape architects have proposed, a great meadow framed with appropriate planting of trees and shrubs, the park will suffer esthetically in a great degree." He quoted from *The Daily Mirror* (May 9): 'Beauty is as necessary to the health and happiness of a city's population as recreation. There can be no real recreation without some chance of enjoying nature. There are too few beauty spots in New York. Too many areas whose beauty should have been preserved have been made sacrifice to commerce and utility. Central Park, small enough as it is, should be beautified to its fullest extent. Baseball diamonds are useful and wholesome things. But Central Park is not the place for them.'" In addition he named all the newspapers as opposed to the Commissioner's plan for athletic fields.

Speaking against also were: the vice president and secretary of the Park Association, the Fifth Avenue Association, the New York Building Congress, whose representative cited the experience of the planners of the Bronx River Parkway, and suggested that while there was much to be said on both sides, playgrounds could not consistently be placed in public parks. Others represented the Garden Club of America, Arthur F. Brinckerhoff, chairman of the parks committee of the New York Chapter of the ASLA, who said: "We as landscape architects have come to have great regard for consistency in landscape design, and as this controversy has continued we have realized the gravity of the situation as a result of a failure to follow consistency. The failure has been on the part of the city in not providing adequate playgrounds."

Others who spoke were from the City Club, the Woman's City Club, the Citizen's Union, the Horticultural Society of New York, Charles N.

Lowrie of the Fine Arts Federation [charter member and past president of the ASLA immediately before Caparn] who said "the athletic fields and playgrounds were inconsistent with park design." William Bradford Roulstone, founder of the Central Park Association and veteran in many successful legal fights on park encroachments, who said that "the elevated railway in Battery Park and the Brooklyn Bridge elevated entrance in City Hall Park originally had been winked at as 'temporary' encroachments." Harold Caparn "asked the Mayor not to forget that behind every boy who might play on a baseball diamond in Central Park there would be a family group excluded from that site." Playgrounds and baseball eventually won over lawns.

But from the time, in 1933, when Robert Moses became Park Commissioner, Caparn and others were fighting a rear-guard action. They looked back wistfully toward the vision of Olmsted and Vaux, of a pastoral, rural parkland, planned for the beauty of its natural pleasures and meant for walking, horseback riding or horse carriages. The post-World War I generation and the Roaring Twenties wanted active rather than passive entertainment as their form of escape from the rigors of work and the boredom of the rectilinear streets and buildings. Beside keeping out some undesirable elements, especially buildings, from the Park, Caparn and others, who heard and responded to his pleas, did accomplish the beginning work of restoration of the great urban park. It changed like other parks and recreation areas to meet the new desires and ideas of the times. The Park, after all, proved resilient and accommodating to change. That, more than anything else proved the strength of the designers' vision and the worth of the supporters' fight for the grand old Greensward.

12 Real Estate Projects

Gracious spaces for living and learning...1914–1926

Caparn was involved with two real estate projects, where he laid out streets and lots, and, if we can judge from his client list, probably also several more such projects. The ones described here involved a developer's dream that grew into a village and a plan for the campus of a biological laboratory, its streets and spaces laid out for scientific labs and homes for resident scientists. Another such project, in which he laid out streets, lots and parks, is treated separately in the chapter on Village 1 in Sheffield, Alabama.

"White Park," Ithaca, New York (c. 1914).

The project was advertised in an Alumni Bulletin of Cornell University at Ithaca, New York, by Jared Treman Newman, sometime mayor, developer and Cornell trustee, who stated that the new development would be the very best in the area. Newman, an attorney, had Judge Charles Hazen Blood as his partner in the venture. They purchased more than 250 acres of land in the very early twentieth century. In a letter from Caparn to Newman, it appears that Caparn was involved as early as 1901 with the development of Newman's real estate plans. Newman said later in his advertisement that they had gotten Warren H. Manning of Boston to do the layout and Harold A. Caparn of New York to do the landscape plan. After several purchases of land and announcement of the development, about 1914, World War I intervened. It appears that Newman put his development plans on hold. Nothing more is mentioned by Newman of work by Manning. We will limit our discussion to those aspects that involve Caparn.[1]

From Newman's later writings it is clear that Caparn did the general plan for the area mostly between Triphammer Road on the east and Highland Road to the west (map 12.2). Between those existing roads Caparn laid out a straight central avenue, broader than other streets, called The Parkway. At the time, the term "parkway" would have had special meaning for Caparn. He was closely following the development of an early public parkway. The Bronx Parkway followed the Bronx River, starting near the Bronx Zoo, where Caparn was engaged in design from 1899 to 1904. The Bronx Parkway had an adjoining stretch of attractive landscaped greenway. Caparn no doubt had in mind also the landscape bordering his Parkway at White Park. As Carol Sisler described in her book, "The beautiful white pines which border The Parkway were planted according to Caparn's plan."

Connecting to The Parkway he laid out Oak Hill Road, White Park Road, Iroquois Road, Upland Road, Northway Road, several smaller roads, and Midway

Road intersecting Klinewoods Road to the north. Beside the layout of the streets, Caparn also laid out the lots, perhaps with the planned extension of Ithaca City water lines and a planting plan for the area. In all, he laid out about 100 lots. This area was incorporated as the Village of Cayuga Heights in 1915. It was several hundred feet above Cayuga Lake and many of the lots had a clear view of the lake. Based on Caparn's general plan, Carl Crandall, a local civil engineer, staked out the lots and made a map of the area in February 1921. After Caparn had laid out the development, a local architect was engaged by Newman to do further design details on the lots as Newman negotiated the final sales contracts.

Newman had presented in 1914 some display ads in the Cornell Alumni Bulletin. In 1921, however, he took a different approach, placing a series of advertisements in *The Ithaca Journal-News* under the heading "White Park Notes." These ran weekly, sometimes daily and were conversational in tone and subject matter, promoting the advantages of buying a home lot in the area, describing the features of each of a number of the lots, and offering deals by combining two lots or portions of lots, or at a wholesale price in the month of June for purchase of several lots at the same time.

It seems, from Newman's pricing of the lots, from \$1,200 to \$8,000 [in 21st century dollars for an average wage earner about \$80,00 to \$540,000 for the lots], he was thinking of professors and professionals as buyers. In fact, he mentions in his "White Park Notes" several professors who had bought lots, among them Porter and Spring (lot 216), and a physician, Dr. MacGachen (lots 223 and 224).

The Ithaca Chamber of Commerce in 1933 said of the development, "Cayuga Heights has become the residential showplace of the City." After the initial push to sell lots in the most southerly section, White Park, Newman began opening up further sections for sale. In a March 1936 *Ithaca Journal-News* article that included a map he states: "You will recall that 'Midway' is the third of perhaps a dozen sections. The first is White Park [bounded by Triphammer and Highland, by Kline Road/the grounds of the Country Club of Ithaca and by Iroquois Road]. It seems appropriate that the second section which for want of a suitable name we called 'Intermediate' should be named after Mr. Caparn of New York City, a very capable landscape architect whom Mr. Blood and the writer first employed. He not only planned the roads in White Park, but also laid out The Parkway as far north as Klinewoods. Midway is next, lying between 'Caparn' and Klinewoods. This is the only known instance of a developed area named for Caparn.

Cayuga Heights became the site for stately homes with beautiful surroundings. The area still exists and is still thought to be among the most desirable residence locations in Ithaca. J. T. Newman is given as number 573 on Caparn's client list.

Newman retained one of the largest lots for himself, no. 240. Cornell Professor J. H. Tanner is given on Caparn's client list as No. 574. Tanner appears to have purchased lot 238 in White Park; a description, plan and photograph of his home lot is given in the chapter on Estates and Homes.

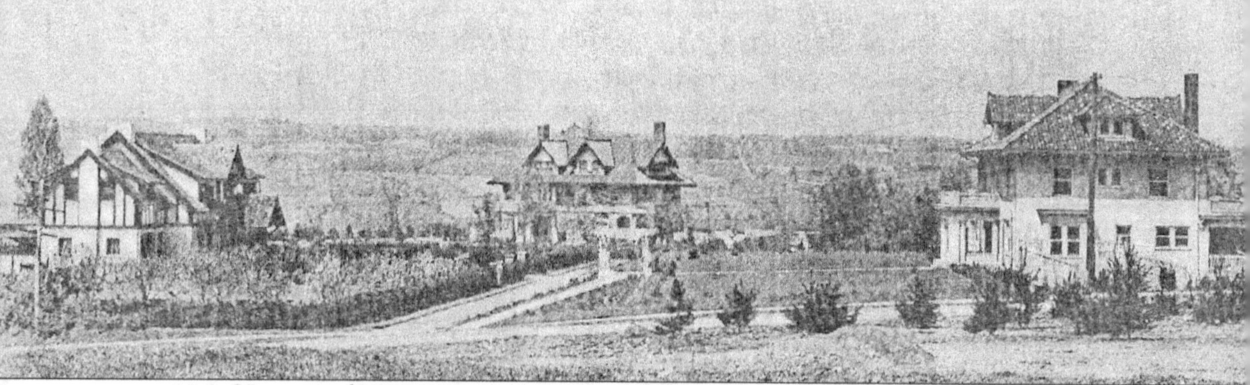

12.1 Homes at the entrance to Cayuga Heights, Ithaca. Left, Peer home, center, home of Jared T. Newman, developer of the Heights, right, home of Cornell Professor John Tanner. More on the Tanner home, including a photograph and ground plan in the chapter on Estates and Homes.

At the junction of Highland Road, The Parkway and White Park Road, shown on the map, can be found the lot owned by Peer, behind that the lot of Jared Newman and across a lane from Peer the property of Professor Tanner, seen at the right in the above photo. The home of J. H. Tanner will illustrate Caparn's treatment of a modest property, although a substantial home, which still exists at Cayuga Heights. About 1916 the homes looked as in the photograph. The entry pergola from the street to the left side of the Tanner home can been seen in the center of the photo, 12.1, before the Newman home; it is as given in the landscape plan. The good size of the homes shows something of the grand plan that Newman had for the development of Cayuga Heights that was shortly to be incorporated as Cayuga Heights Village.

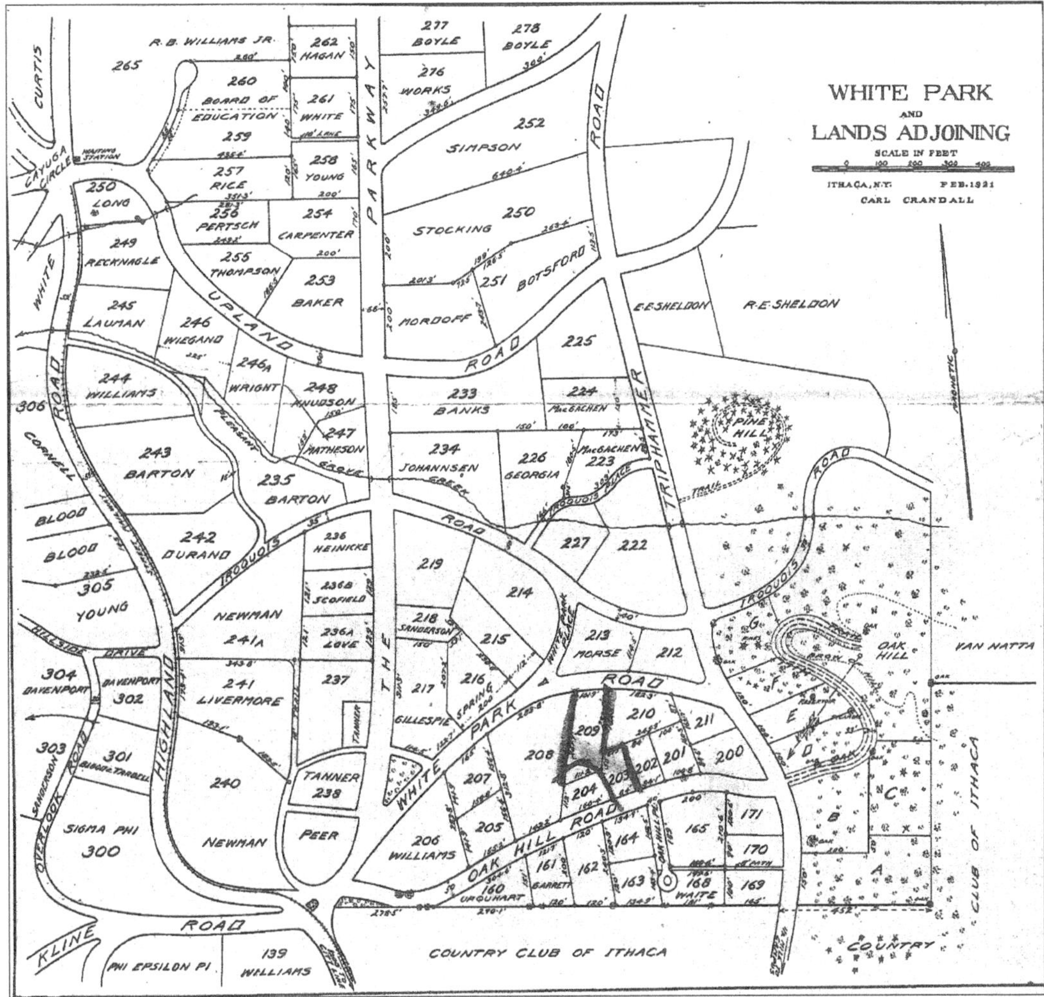

12.2 *Harold Caparn design, Cayuga Heights sections, 1921. Carl Crandalll map, showing "White Park" and "Caparn," based on the general plan for the area by Harold Caparn, c. 1914. The added lines seem to indicate that lots 209 and 203 were to be joined for sale.*

Long Island Biological Association
Cold Springs Harbor, Long Island, NY

Three research laboratories that still flourish came out of the nineteenth-century interest in discoveries in the natural sciences. Each started as a school for the study of biology. Each was located seaside. The earliest, started in 1888, was the Marine Biological Laboratory at Woods Hole, Massachusetts; later, in 1930 it was incorporated as the Woods Hole Oceanographic Institution. The last, begun in 1898, was the Harpswell Laboratory in Maine for students at Tufts College; incorporated in 1913, it moved to Salisbury Cove, Maine in 1921, and the name was changed to The Mount Desert Island Biological Laboratory.

It is the second of the three laboratories, founded in 1890 as the Biological Laboratory of the Brooklyn Institute of Arts and Sciences, which is of interest here. It was the Brooklyn Institute that later, in 1910, also founded the Brooklyn Botanic Garden. Some connections between the two will be found in this chapter.

The Biological Laboratory, originally a summer school for biology teachers, was joined in 1904 by the Carnegie Institution of Washington that established a Station for Experimental Evolution, set up to prove Darwinian theories. It was located next to the Laboratory on land fronting on the inner portion of Cold Spring Harbor. In 1923 the Brooklyn Institute transferred ownership of its facilities to a local entity, incorporated in 1924 as the Long Island Biological Association (LIBA). Still later, in 1963, the Biological Laboratory was joined by the Carnegie Station and the combined entity was named the Cold Spring Harbor Laboratory of Quantitative Biology, changed in 1970 to the name it now owns, Cold Spring Harbor Biological Laboratory. It has been the site of major research on DNA and discoveries that have garnered prestigious awards.

The main campus of the Cold Spring Harbor Biological Laboratory occupies a 118-acre site on the northern coast of Long Island, along the western shore of Cold Spring Harbor. It is principally along Bungtown Road in the Village of Laurel Hollow, an area rich in the history of Long Island families Tiffany, Jones and de Forest. Like its neighbor in Massachusetts, Woods Hole, it has grown beyond its original campus. The main campus was accepted to the National Register of Historic Places in 1994. Elizabeth L. Watson, wife of James D. Watson, former director, president and chancellor of Cold Spring Harbor Laboratory, affectionately described in her two books on architectural aspects of the campus buildings, identification of the trees in its arboretum and notes on its outdoor art collection.[2]

Caparn's work began in 1926 not long after the transfer of the facilities to LIBA under its new young director, Dr. Reginald G. Harris. Caparn records the job, number 653 on his client list, as "L. I. Biol. Assn." (LIBA). Director Harris was the son-in-law of Charles B. Davenport, the previous director of the Biological Laboratory from 1898 to 1924. In 1904 Davenport had become director also of the Station for Experimental Evolution, founded in that year. The Carnegie Station's financial resources and facilities grew more quickly and well beyond those of the Biological Laboratory. Davenport wanted, however, to expand the Biological Laboratory facilities and housing in order to conduct year-round research.

When Harris became director in 1924, it was natural that he should see his predecessor and father-in-law's goal as his own. To that end he convinced the board in the next year to raise the funds to acquire the property from the estate of Townsend Jones adjacent to the Station property. The site would be ideal since it stood next to the land the Biological Laboratory leased from the Wawepex Society, with that Society's early buildings used for research and teaching. Harris then engaged Harold

Caparn to develop a landscape design for the whole of the then 32-acre property. Caparn responded by laying out road access, lots for additional buildings and for houses for researchers and staff. His plan was to provide for expansion of the Biological Laboratory's facilities well into the future.

The planning project was initiated by Timothy S. Williams, President of the Brooklyn Rapid Transit Company, a member of the Boards of both the Brooklyn Institute of Arts and Sciences and the Long Island Biological Association. Williams retired in 1923 from the Transit System. He then turned his attention to developing the board of LIBA. The board included many prominent local residents of the Long Island north shore "Gold Coast," among them investment banker Marshall Field, publisher and businessman Arthur Hines Page, John H. Jones Stewart, nephew of the Biological Laboratory's founder John D. Jones, William K. Vanderbilt, financier and yachtsman, Childs Frick, naturalist and board member of the Museum of Natural History in New York, and Henry W. de Forest, attorney and president of the Brooklyn Institute of Arts and Sciences, among others. In 1925 Williams, together with director Harris, began the fund drive with the board to raise the money needed to purchase the Jones property. They were successful with the purchase in 1926.

Caparn had done personal landscape design work for T. S. Williams about 1905, indicated as an early item, number 500, on Caparn's client list. Williams, knowing Caparn's work for himself and since 1911 for the Brooklyn Botanic Garden, no doubt highly recommended Caparn to the LIBA director. Dr. Harris wrote Caparn on July 2, 1926: "At the request of Mr. T. S. Williams I am sending you the surveyor's blue print of the property of the Long Island Biological Association at Cold Spring Harbor."

In a letter to Dr. Harris of August 25, 1926, Caparn, after several visits to the site, proposed to lay out the property, showing his considerations in doing so:

> The principle entrance from the Shore Road [now Bungtown Road] is made where the grade is highest and near the centre of the property line. This point is about twenty feet higher than the frontage further north, making it practicable to reach the [still] higher levels of the property [well behind the entrance] by grades that are not too steep for frequent use.

> The sizes of lots run from about a quarter of an acre to an acre. I would consider that variety in the size of lots is a definite advantage. The larger lots are on steeper ground [those behind the entrance]. The more level sites [to the western side of the property] are mostly cleared and would be likely to require and receive more intensive upkeep, which is another reason for making them smaller. Also, the greater accessibility and less cost of construction on these level lots should make them more valuable in proportion to area than the steeper lots [i.e., for individual houses for staff].

The local road towards the northwest corner has the advantages of seclusion and shortness. It would tend to give individuality of treatment and create a local community spirit of several families [around a cul de sac], and would dispense with a second entrance on the Oyster Bay Road.

Caparn's "Road and Subdivision Plan," (12.3), for LIBA, Cold Spring Harbor, was dated October 27, 1926; it was revised slightly at the request of Dr. Harris, as noted on the plan, on December 28, 1926, in preparation for printing in the 1926 Annual Report of the Association. Elizabeth Watson, in her earlier book on the Biological Laboratory homes, reproduces the plan, to which identifying notes are added here.[3]

Caparn's plan shows the topography of the site. The land fronting on Cold Spring Harbor belonged to the Wewepex Society. Caparn includes it in his map. He would have walked the whole site and made notes and plans based on the topography, as he recommended in several of his articles. His intimate familiarity with the site as it existed is reflected in several letters to Dr. Harris.

More recent street names—Bungtown Road, Moore's Hill Road and Stewart Lane—are added in parentheses to Caparn's plan, below. Five of the six buildings original to the site are indicated as full black rectangles in illustration 12.3.

Caparn's plan for additional Biological Laboratory buildings along Bungtown Road would add to the ones already there (see map). His plan shows the main entrance (indicated by an arrow) from Bungtown Road on high ground between Osterhout Cottage and Hooper House on the east side of the road, then skirting to the rear of Williams House on the west side of the road.

His plan shows roads in the parcel winding up over the ridge with sites on either side for Laboratory buildings and then down to a more level portion to the west with area for playing fields at the center of a section of housing for staff. In all, he lays out forty-eight lots for buildings.

> Continuing Caparn's letter: The most difficult part of the problem is the treatment of the two rows of lots along the Shore Road north of the main entrance. I assume a succession of Institution buildings along the Shore Road. Back of these would be the private dwellings. My idea is that the Institution buildings would be on the lower level with a comparatively level yard behind them with a high bank formed by connecting the two present excavations and on the top the road as shown. It would be possible to dispense with this road by making the lots along it accessible by steps up the bank and building the garages or a common garage into the bank.

It might be noted that although Caparn had written several times previously against the placement of ball fields within Central Park, he was not against such playgrounds. He wrote also suggesting that playgrounds for athletic activities be included in city planning. As seen in his plan for the Biological Laboratory grounds, he incorporated space for athletic activities in the area near the housing for faculty and staff. He was well aware that those personnel and their families would need recreation areas for relief from their work.

While this planning for the future use of the property was under way, however, reality intervened. In the year of the purchase of the Jones property, an old whaling era warehouse on the Wawepex property, used for research and teaching, was destroyed by fire. It needed to be immediately replaced. Arthur Page, board member and son of Walter Page, founder of Doubleday, Page & Co, turned to a former colleague at that company, Henry H. Saylor, to design three new laboratories for LIBA. The first, completed in 1926, was the building for teaching botany later called Davenport Laboratory in honor of the earlier director of the Biological Laboratory. Next, completed in 1928, was an administration and research facility planned to support a year-round program called the Nichols Building. After that, during that same year, the LI Biological Association purchased the building known as Williams House that required extensive renovations before it could be used for housing. In the next year, 1929, the James Laboratory for biophysics was completed, named to honor the second chair of LIBA, a gift of his widow. All these additions generally follow the plan as set by Caparn. Then the Stock Market Crash of 1929 fell upon the well-to-do supporters of LIBA and progress was slowed significantly.

While Harris had been successful in building LIBA in response to immediate needs, the visionary plan of Caparn for the whole of the property had been bypassed by those needs. His plan, however, was correct for the property in several respects. It dealt with the topography in a sensible and useful way. The placement of the entrance accessing the major laboratory buildings and their location on the steep inclines at the east of the property proved best in the long term. The use of the western side of the property for housing on the more level areas of the site also proved to be the best solution for that need, although not implemented until about twenty-five years later. In all, the campus turned out in some ways as Caparn envisioned it. The later selection and nurturing of trees as an arboretum would have delighted him, together with the placement of an outdoor collection of sculpture.

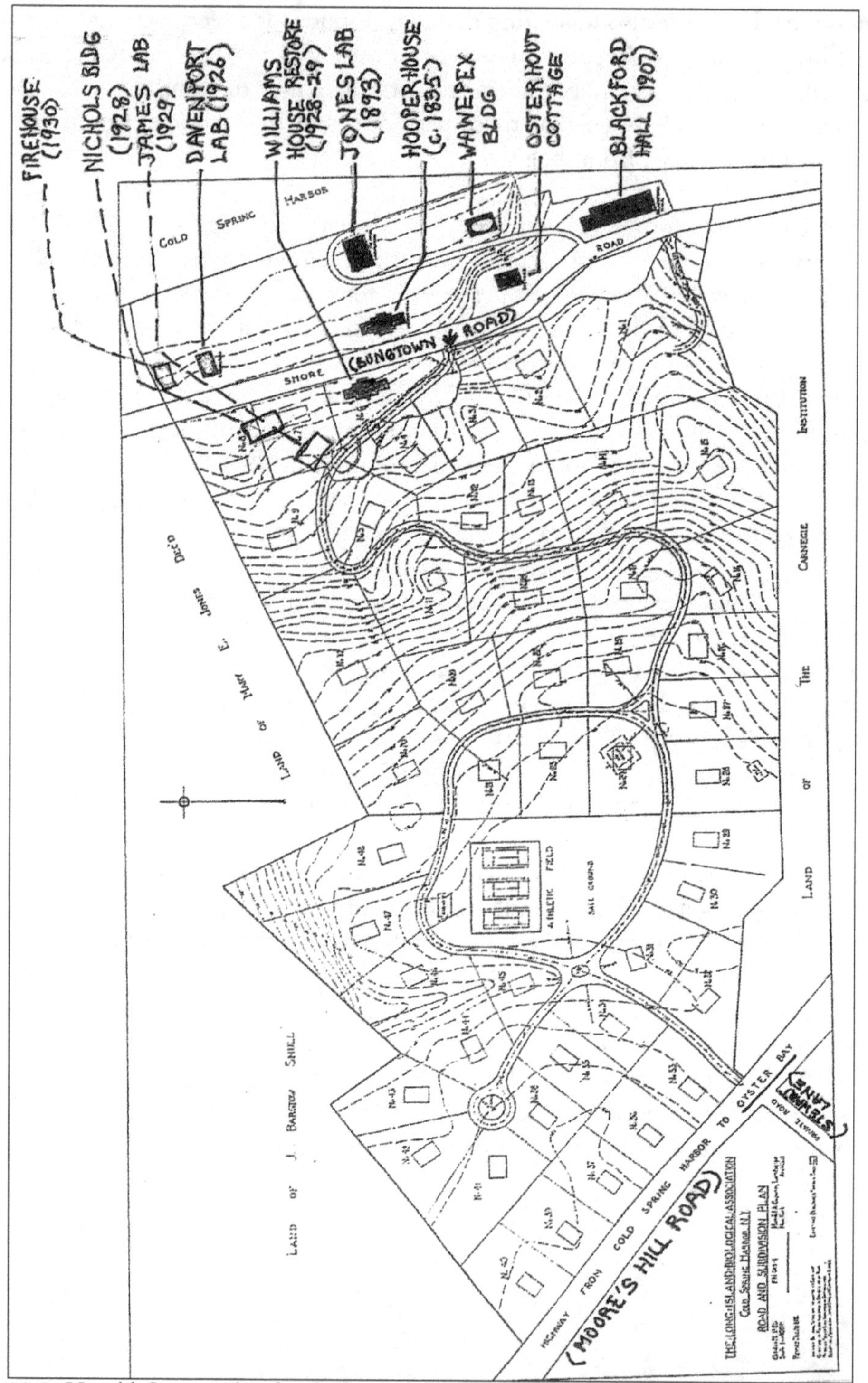

12.3 *Harold Caparn plan for the layout of lots and streets for the Long Island Biological Association. the scale of the original plan is 1" = 1000 ft. Identification of buildings by the author.*

13 State Parks

Their development, organization and purpose...1917–1924

City parks were a natural outgrowth of plots of land left over after streets were laid out, where a town needed to put memorial statuary, or centrally located like the New England village green that originally served as a place for sheep to graze or voluntary militia to train. The desire to create such space and the administrative ability to do so were in close connection. After the 1860s, the building of Central Park in New York influenced the purposeful construction of other city parks. In the next decade the national park as an interest of the federal government began to find acceptance with the establishment of legislation to reserve large areas of wilderness and scenic beauty like Yellowstone. But state parks presented special problems in that states developed different approaches to acquiring the land, designating who was to administer it once acquired and what kind of use, maintenance and public information would be provided.

> Caparn wrote first about the topic in "Some Reasons For A General System of State Parks" (1917). It was a passionate article aimed at promoting the idea: state parks are made neither to make scenery nor to protect it as it is. A state park is made, perhaps, because some generous person has presented it to the state, or because the state has acquired it for some specific purpose, other than public recreation, and it would probably not be there at all but that the land is of small value for agriculture or industry. It is a more or less sporadic and accidental thing, both in its purposes and making; it lacks the logical development, the inevitable growth out of definite and plainly felt and generally understood needs of the national park or the city park.

> This need [in a state park] is the preservation of what might be called our representative scenery. The uncommon, the startling, or the sublime utters its message so clearly, affects the eye and the understanding even of explanation to induce him to vote to acquire and preserve the Yosemite, the Grand Canyon, or the Yellowstone. But these are not our characteristic American scenery. They are our natural wonders, our rarities, and stand in much the same relation to our average landscape that Lincoln, Shakespeare, or Beethoven stood to the average man.

> We have forty-eight states and many times forty-eight kinds of natural landscapes, all in their way interesting, and all, or nearly all, have this in common—they are continually and more and more being encroached on, exploited, diminished, or undermined or destroyed for economic

purposes, agriculture, or mining or industry. They may be used, or wasted, but always they are diminished.

In his relentless haste to subdue and plunder the earth, man not only wars on the vegetation with steel and fire, and utterly deranges the balance of the insect and bacterial world, good and bad, that lives on and by it, that fertilizes it like the bees and preys on it like the caterpillar and the innumerable scales and blights, and whose complex organism is so intricately and inextricably woven into it. For his protection or food or sport he kills all the game not small enough to escape him underground or overhead, so that all our wild animals seem doomed to inevitable extinction excepting those in artificial preserves.

If this goes on, as it inevitably must as population and its need of support increases, what will be left of our characteristic scenery and animals in a hundred years? What in a thousand?

Yet it is right that man should subdue and replenish the earth, that he should cut down its trees, till its prairies, and dig the metals out of its mines, for all these are necessary to his existence. But even at that, it is surely possible to leave enough of the streams and templed hills of New England, the mountain forests of the Alleghanies, the middle country below them, the vegetable seas of the prairies, the scenery of the coasts, of the Great Divide, and the Pacific Slope, for them to see and understand and enjoy somewhat of that which we still possess in such abundance. To those looking into the future it will be clear that, as time goes on, the surviving remnants of our scenery, and that inseparable part of it, the animals, will be in the parks, national, state, and private.

The only power that can create and maintain in perpetuity a nation-wide and complete system of such parks and preserves is the nation itself, acting through its state governments; and as the Federal Government has already preëmpted the scenic wonders for the national parks, and as the nation at large is not interested in the preservation of local scenery any more than in the details of local government of states or towns, it would seem logical for the several and separate states to take care of the preserving of their own local scenery and animals, of their own indigenous flora and fauna. And even as a number of separate and individual villages, towns, cities and states, each with its own governing machinery, local conditions, local ambitions, pride, and emulations, all contribute to the unity of a nation, so a great number of state parks, created by local enterprise and energy and under the stimulus of local zeal and pride, would become in reality a correlated system of national parks that would preserve a complete and representative body of actual true and authentic examples and records of our manifold types of scenery and wild animals for all time to come.

The city park might be said to supply the needs that artificial scenery and spaces can supply, but the state park would supply those of natural scenery, an epitome of what is commonly called the country. The city park is usually a conventionalizing of scenery natural or artificial; the state park would be a preservation or reproduction of one or both of them.

Probably no more interesting problems in landscape design than such state parks are likely to occur. They would require not only the preservation of natural scenery, the non-interference with it, the minimizing or rendering as subordinate as possible of artificial works, as in national parks; they would often demand the actual restoration of original conditions, and this would mean often what might be called the intensification, the encouragement of growth richer and more characteristic than the original, the reproduction not of what was actually once there, but what might have been under the most favoring conditions, the helping of nature to do her best.

Such a system of state parks might be created in two ways. After many years, when many states have acquired parks in the usual more or less accidental ways, they might be correlated as at least a part of a complete system. But a far better and quicker way would be by common agreement among the states, under which a general plan of procedure would be formulated and adopted. This might be accomplished by the creation of a central advisory body, which would devise a general scheme and policy with the aid of delegates from all the states, and to which each state would resort for guidance in matters concerning the common weal.

Caparn's pamphlet, "State Parks" (1921), was published by *The National Municipal Review* and printed separately by suggestion of the American Civic Association. In its Introduction he says:

First we began with city parks in the middle of the last century. Then certain men of vision saw that there was within our borders scenery so rare and so superb that it must not be destroyed, and existing on too great a scale to be owned and controlled by any power less than the United States. Thus we got the national parks. And now, some twenty-two states [at the time of writing--later in the article he gives twenty-six states] have discovered that the national parks are not so near home as they could wish them, and that they have, within their own borders, natural scenery so situated or so characteristic or of such historic interest that it ought not to be left to the vicissitudes of private ownership, but must be acquired for the use of the people at large, who alone can possess and protect it for the common good. Under private ownership it is never safe from injury for private advantage. It must be made safe for the common advantage by public ownership in perpetuity.

Reasons for this spreading public sentiment are not far to seek. No one who stops to think can avoid being deeply impressed by the enormous destruction of natural conditions that goes on in order that the earth may support its populations. But what seems almost appalling to those who are sensitive to natural beauty, to whom the unscarred face of the earth seems a thing to be treasured, is the wanton unnecessary waste and ruin too often wrought in converting the resources of the globe to man's uses.

The first great public parks of Europe were the demesnes of royalty or nobility, confiscated or otherwise converted to the common use. In our own country, when the city population grew thicker and unoccupied land within their limits scarcer and more difficult to protect, people found that the only way to solve the problem of public rights in open spaces was to acquire title to them and develop them systematically for the best uses of the greatest number. As city population increased still more, and city parks became less adequate to their needs, and as traveling facilities increased, it was found that parks further afield were getting out of the luxury class and into that of necessities. Now that visitors can easily reach them, we are beginning to find that we cannot well get along without them; and though the growth of state parks may not be altogether due to the growth of the automobile, they have followed it closely. Indeed, it seems doubtful whether state parks could ever become very popular without the motor car.

The reasons that the park promoters give (seemingly in their own defense, as though they had to defend themselves for defending the parks) are nearly always the same. (1) to preserve natural scenery for aesthetic and economic purposes; (2) to provide places for popular recreation; (3) to preserve places of historic interest.

Take, for instance, the account of the geologic history of Starved Rock Park, Illinois. It says that once upon a time the sea covered the interior of the continent and deposited shell material sufficient, aided by some precipitation of lime from the sea water, to give rise to the lower magnesium limestone 250 feet thick! Later, the St. Peter's sandstone was deposited on the limestone, and over this the silts, sands and vegetable matter which resulted in the formation known as the Coal Measures. Think of the unimaginable lapses of time necessary for all this (for we can merely talk about millions of years, not really imagine them), the passionless deliberation of the cosmic processes, relentless in creation and destruction alike!

And all these things, and many more just as grand and awe-inspiring had to happen before Illinois could rear Abraham Lincoln and the lesser men who have made the state of Illinois as we know it. Every state in the Union has a history no less ancient and impressive than this, and all are different. Surely a subject of the profoundest appeal to the imagination this history of the manifestation of the Cosmic will and brain before the ephemeral will and brain of man had appeared and struggled. And no place could be better to illustrate and preserve this history than a state park.

It seems to the writer that every state park ought to contain a museum, and this museum should contain whatever relics and memorials of the park's human history may be available and appropriate. It should also contain specimens of every kind of rock and other geologic stratum within the park limits. There would be a gallery of illustrations of the various ages of the park, labeled thus for instance; This is a probable view in the park in the Carboniferous Era; This in the Early Mesozoic; This in the Eocene; This just before the First Glacial; and These are the animals that certainly or probably roamed through the park in these several epochs, and These are the trees and plants through which they roamed. There should be as complete a collection of fossils and other remains to testify to all this.

Examples of more or less denuded land made into state parks are the Harriman-Palisades Park in New York and New Jersey, and the Metropolitan Park system of Boston. Much of the Bronx River reservation in New York was entirely despoiled. All these sites were worthwhile as parks because of their proximity to great cities.

To future generations it will surely be of the greatest interest to be able to wander among the New England hills, or the Illinois prairies or Pennsylvania pinewoods, substantially as they were when Columbus sailed from Genoa; to be able to see what America was, not only in her rare moments, but in her everyday garb. This is easy now, but will become more and more difficult as time goes on.

Palisades Interstate Park

Details of one park, which has been the subject of another article, will give some idea of the park descriptions. Palisades Interstate Park in New York and New Jersey was created in 1900 to stop the destruction of the palisades and preserve them as a park. It is controlled by an unpaid commission appointed by the governors of the two states and supported by appropriations from the states and by private contributions. To date, 1920, $13,119,419 has been put into the park in acquiring lands and general development work.

Much forestry work has been done, and more than 5,000,000 young trees and many native shrubs have been planted. One hundred and forty-nine kinds of flowers, 96 trees, 38 animals, 151 birds and 36 fish found in the park are listed. Lists of shrubs, butterflies, moths, reptiles, insects and geological specimens are not yet completed.

Every encouragement and facility is offered to camping. On the most picturesque lakes are standard mess and play pavilions all designed to harmonize with natural surroundings. Natural history exhibitions, musical and other entertainments are frequently arranged for visitors.

Anyone who travels in this park is likely to be struck by the fortunate survival of so much superb scenery so near a great city, if not uninjured, at any rate not destroyed, and easily capable of being restored in the course of time to its original condition.

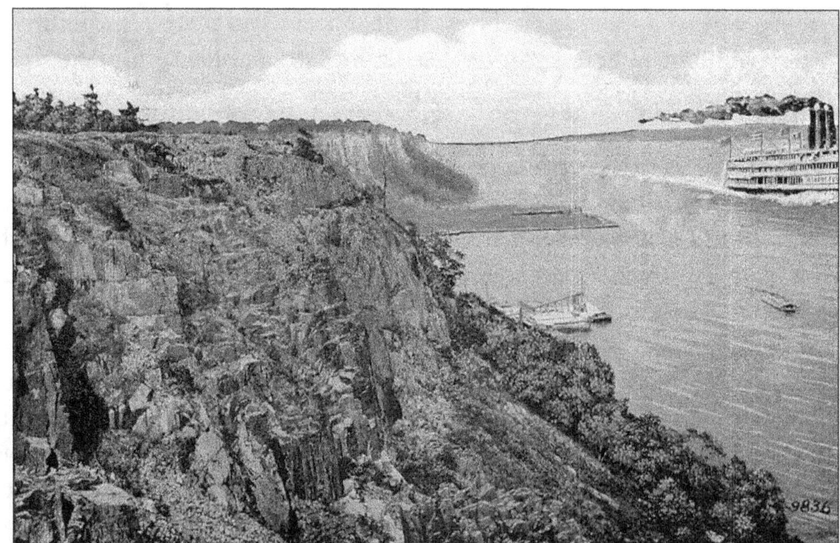

13.1 Part of Palisades Interstate Park on the Hudson River. The Robert Fulton, a Hudson River Day Line ship that plied the Hudson from New York to Albany, is seen, right, on its trip south.

In an article in *Parks & Recreation* (1922-March), he further describes the Palisades Park: This is the widest in scope and most costly of all State Park enterprises. It serves a greater population than any other, that of the communities of which New York City is the center (about 4-5 million inhabitants at the time). None is more important in preserving natural scenery, not even the Natural Parks and Saving the Redwoods projects in California, for the redwoods could be restored—in twenty or thirty centuries; but were the Palisades once destroyed, it would take a geologic epoch with such a terrestrial convulsion as created them to restore them.

The Palisades are a precipice of trap rock of generally vertical structure from 300 to 500 feet high extending some twelve miles north of Fort Lee, New Jersey (opposite 130th Street New York City) along the west bank of the Hudson River. Although New Jersey has the privilege of owning them, they really belong to New York, for New Jersey cannot see them, while they are in full view of the western edge of New York City.

Like many other great parks, this one was made possible by one man, George Waldbridge Perkins, who died June 18, 1920, and who raised the money for its acquisition and development. It was created in 1900 by the States of New York and New Jersey to stop the destruction of the Palisades by quarrying and to preserve them for a park. In 1906 the reservation was extended to take in Hook Mountain, and in 1910 again extended north to Newburgh and westward to include about 10,000 acres of the Ramapo Mountains, this last being the gift of Mrs. E. H. Harriman.

In February 1911, the writer, as one of a committee of the Municipal Art Society of New York, spent a Sunday in a tramping tour of inspection across the then recently acquired Harriman section to Tuxedo through a foot of snow. Much of the land was in cut-over woods, some of it in farms of a kind that made the visitors feel much relieved that the region was to become a park. The farms were owned by people who lived in much the way of paleolithic men excepting for the occasional use of canned food.

Caparn continues with discussion of the administration, as laid down by Perkins, and of the recreational and other offerings of the park, including camping, boating, hiking, police protection, religious services, camps for girls, Bear Mountain Inn and transportation to the park.[1]

As in his recommendations a few years later for Yellowstone, he notes: All buildings and other works of construction are designed to interfere with the natural conditions as little as possible. Considerable work in forestry, tree and shrub planting, etc., is carried on. A herd of elk has been established in the park.

His next foray into state park creation, development and management is his article "Need of Landscape and Architectural Experts in State Park Development" (1924): How do you make a state park? Make the park according to the suggestion of the site itself. Ask yourself the preliminary questions—What is the situation, the size, the present character, the surroundings, and –What are to be the uses of this piece of land? Then make the scheme to fit all these conditions, whatever they may be.

It is one of those problems that will solve itself, and the problem of the solver is not to invent a clever, striking and beautiful plan merely for its own sake, but to discern what is this solution that offers itself, to see the thing right in front of him, often the most difficult to do.

You may perhaps have noticed that so far, I have not used the word 'design' or 'designer.' This was done advisedly, for it seems somewhat futile and inappropriate to speak of 'designing' a thing that was chosen because it was done by the Great Designer, that is to be preserved as an example of His work whose value consists in its having been conceived and executed in a style and spirit and method and scale quite beyond our capacity.

Instead of using the word 'design' with regard to state parks, I would say that we should try to interpret and display them: we should try to understand what its creator was thinking of when he made it, and to do to it only such things as would help to make the thought clear to others: to make it approachable and usable and understandable by as many people of as many present and future generations as possible; to take out of it nothing that would be seriously missed, and to put into it nothing that would seem an intrusion; to do nothing, in fact, that would seem to mar the idea of its creation, and to do all we can to illuminate it.

This is obviously written of the ideal state park, but the ideal does not often exist, even in state parks. Mostly damage has been done to a greater or less extent by man for his own needs as he saw them, which seemed to him vastly more important than the destruction he wrought. Here it is that the Interpreter may find his difficulty and his opportunity.

Let us suppose the Interpreter is confronted with a State Park problem. How will he approach it? I suggest that he stay on the ground, travel in and through it long enough to feel that he has absorbed the spirit, not only of it, but of the surrounding country. That he study somewhat the geology and the flora and the two histories, the long one before man arrived, and the short one after his coming.

What I would call 'improvements' in a state park are first the encouragement and increase of such of the indigenous vegetation as we might consider most desirable. To what extent this should be done, must be left to our interpretive side; how it should be done, is merely a question for our farming or horticultural or plant fostering knowledge. And this suggests incidentally how valuable an agency the state parks may become in preserving our most attractive and characteristic plants which we all seem to conspire to destroy in proportion to the love we have for them. Concern is given to the pillage of our ericaceae, that wonderful botanical family that seems to contain only plants that both the florist and the landscape architect unite in considering desirable and 'choice' as the nursery catalogues call it. In this family are the laurel, the rhododendron and the azaleas, and for may years we have been wrenching them from their homes and shipping them somewhere else. I claim no exemption, for I have been helping; I have to, in self defense, and I fear we shall all have to until these, our most precious floral treasures are exhausted and survive wild only in state parks. Many other fascinating, but less popular plants belong to this family, as for instance, the andromeda, the bearberry and the trailing arbutus, and I suggest that whenever they are found wild in a state park, that park be regarded as a refuge for the ericaceae.

In another class of 'improvement' in state parks would be, for example, the creation of a lake where a basin already exists, but no barrier to impound the waters. Such a lake cannot usually be distinguished from a natural one, and the interpreter may well expend his skill and judgment in constructing a dam that will seem as much a part of the scenery as the lake itself.

An example of possible repair, though not of restoration, might be a disused stone quarry. It has been made by processes not so very dissimilar to those of Nature, who has always rent and destroyed her own rocks in every way and on a vast scale, and when they are exposed to the air, has proceeded to weather and decorate them after her own leisurely fashion. In the course of years, the raw stone of the quarry will weather and mellow, and completion of the work of reclamation may be greatly hastened by the filling of pockets and other places with soil for the growth of suitable trees, shrubs and plants. There are enormous and shocking scars of blasting in the Palisades Park on the west bank of the Hudson River; but these will gradually take on the color of the other rocks, and the appearance of a natural formation might be simulated by the removal of more rock, until shapes and proportions in harmony with those of geological action are attained.

The road question in parks seems to be taking on this peculiar aspect; though there is more wheeled traffic in parks than ever before, fewer roads are required in many parks. It is necessary in any class of parks to be careful not to put in roads [for the safety of pedestrians], unless really necessary or they may defeat the ends for which the park was created, which are those of a refuge, a place of safety and relief from the pressure of civilization.

It is not possible to say what state park buildings should be like, but it is easy to say that they should be in the state park picture. One way of accomplishing this is to build them of the local materials, for instance, boulders where they are available, wood where they are not. There will be cases where both wood and boulders are scarce as, for instance, by the seashore, but where however, sand is plentiful, and this seems to suggest concrete. But even here I hesitate to advise the use of concrete placed where it can be seen.

Since nothing could contribute more to a popular appreciation of and desire to protect state parks than a knowledge and understanding of them, it is suggested that there be pictures and descriptions, and perhaps mounted specimens of the birds, animals and fishes, of the plants, trees and bushes founding the park easily accessible to visitors. Records of historical events should be in plain view. And there should be some account of that geological history of the park, compared with which, the history since man's arrival is like that of yesterday, and it should be illustrated with such specimens of rocks and fossils as may be available, and models or pictures of extinct animals that certainly or probably in habited it.

To sum up: A park is either a work of art whose beauty is created by man, or it has another kind of beauty, the product of the harmonious forces of Nature. All its costly constructive works will not avail to make it what it should be unless they combine to give it that quality of charm which impresses everybody, but which can hardly be analyzed or described, which everybody wants but nobody really understands. Those who can do this are landscape architects. Those who can design buildings which seem an inseparable part of the scheme are architects.

14 The Small Place
His contribution to a book of designs...1918

Of particular interest to Caparn was the design of the yard or garden of a small property, on which he produced a number of articles and designs, including his last publication, in July 1945, on the "Layout of an American front yard." He provided early solutions to the problem as viewed by a landscape architect. The articles gave advice on placing the house on the property, the design of the lot, the selection of trees and shrubs, annuals and perennials, the need not to clutter the space, the careful selection and placement of anything growing or colored in unusual ways, the design of rose gardens, cutting gardens, of flower beds, walks, rock and water gardens and driveways. These subjects he wrote about in two series of articles, in *Countryside* (1917) and *Arts and Decoration* (1936-37).

But the small place looking onto the Premium River, an inlet of the Long Island Sound, in Larchmont, New York, held special affection for him, both because of the limitations it imposed on the landscape artist and the solutions he found to the creation of an effective informal design of the property. It was mentioned in two of his articles and formed a chapter in the book by Elsa Rehmann titled *The Small Place.*[1]

Augustus H. W. Johnson and his wife Louise were the original owners of the property on Woodbine Avenue in Larchmont, New York, and builders of the home about 1910 that they called "Thornledge" as it was built on a ledge of rock and had a profusion of thorn bushes around it. Mr. Johnson was the manufacturer of plumbing supplies. He was better known at the time, however, as a yachtsman. He was Secretary of the Larchmont Yacht Club and raced his thirty-foot sloop *Newasi* in ocean races out of the Club, as indicated in an article on Dec. 19, 1907 in *The New York Times.*

The Small Place (1918)

In the book by Rehmann, Caparn states in his chapter "Informal Arrangement of a Small Property":

> This oblong piece of land, less than an acre, lies between the street and a picturesque inlet of Long Island Sound. An outcrop of rock formed the highest part of the ground, which sloped first gently, then with an abrupt dip toward the water. The house stands very near the street boundary which is an advantage as it allows an uninterrupted use of the grounds.

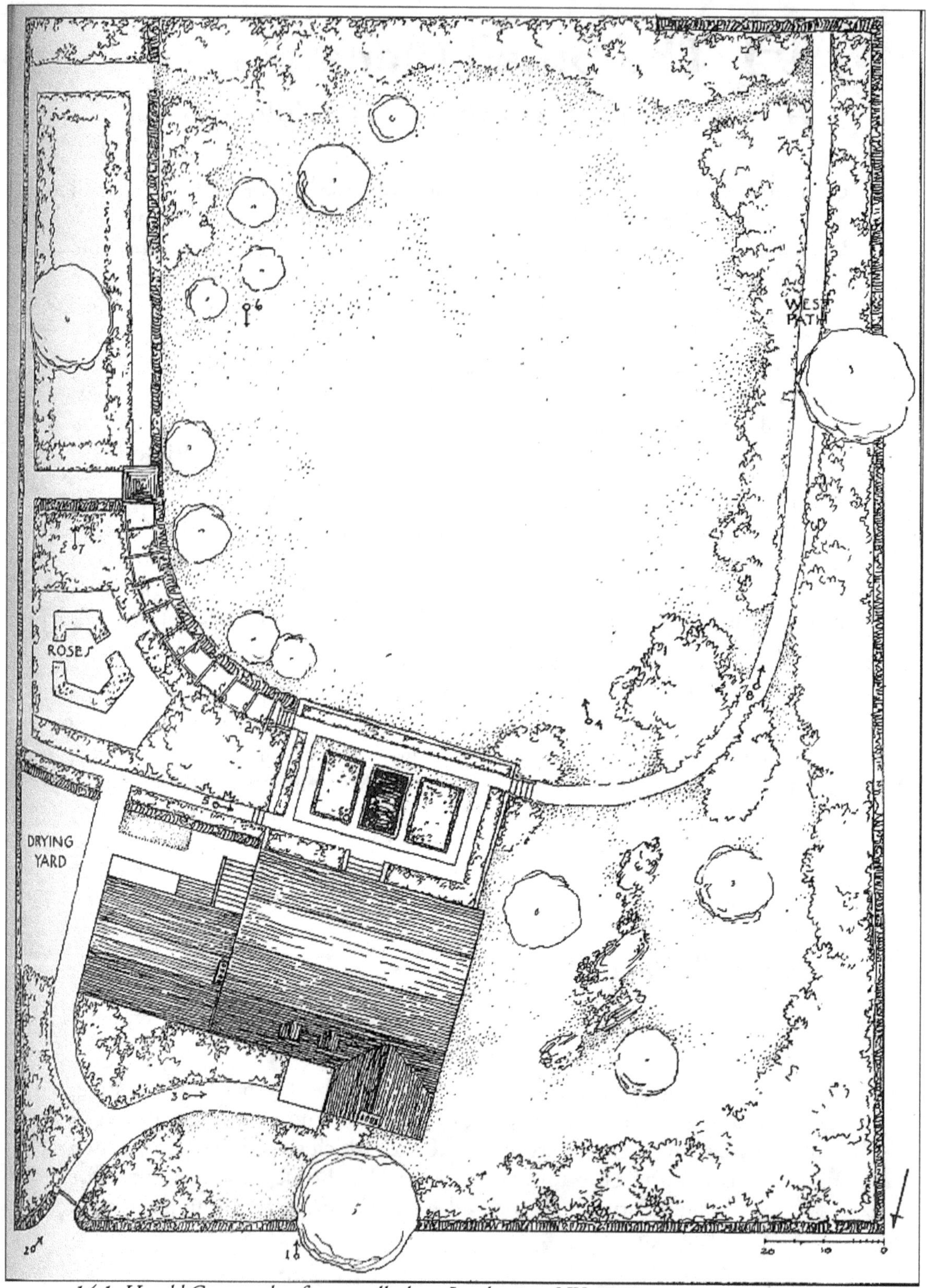

14.1 *Harold Caparn plan for a small place, Larchmont, NY, 1918*

On a small property this fact is particularly worthy of note as it was very desirable to get a big expanse of lawn as a foreground for the inlet view. As this is on the southern side of the house it was important, too, to place the main rooms upon it.

This same care is shown in placing the house parallel to the stream at the foot of the property and caused its unusual angle to the street which is not noticeable at all because of the ingenious arrangement of the entrance with the inset of the gate on the diagonal. Inside the gate, the shrubbery, the curve of the brick walk, and the tangle of Thorns hide the front door. The Carmine Pillar Roses and Clematis on the gate arch, the Rhododendrons along the house wall, the Laurels around the front porch, the Thorns along the walk, the Apple tree near the hedge, the shrubs grouped in a heavy mass along the side boundary combine in giving continuous interest and color to the entrance walk and emphasize the informal character of the house.

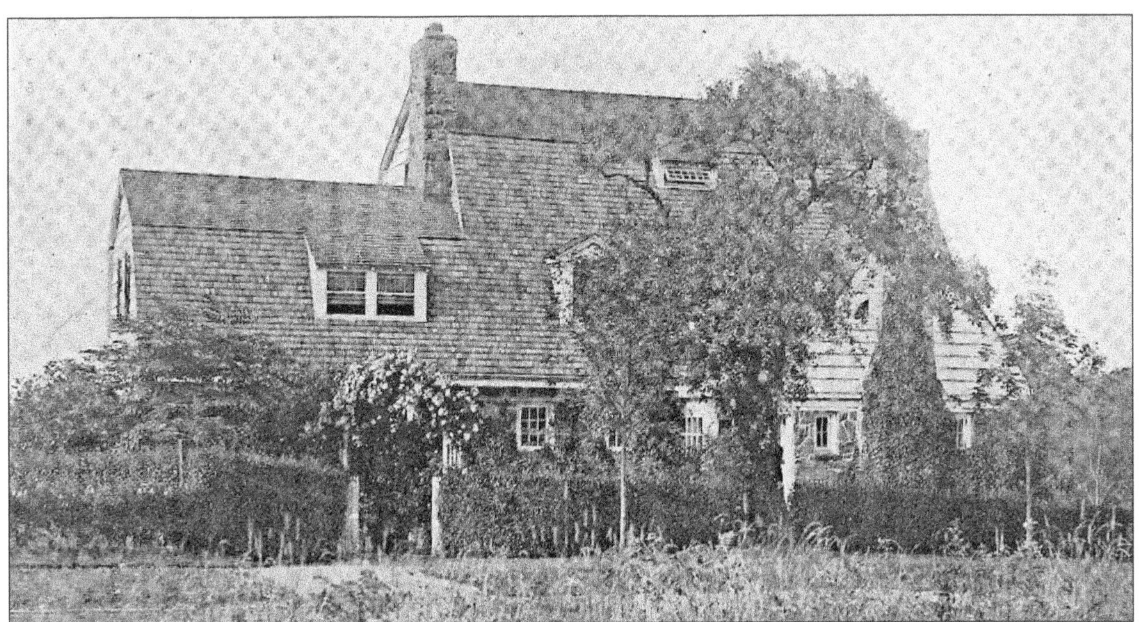

14.2 Harold Caparn design, view facing street in Larchmont. The house is set at an angle on the property so that it is parallel to the river on the other side of the home; an arched gateway is off-set from the front entrance creating an illusion of regularity as it meets the street.

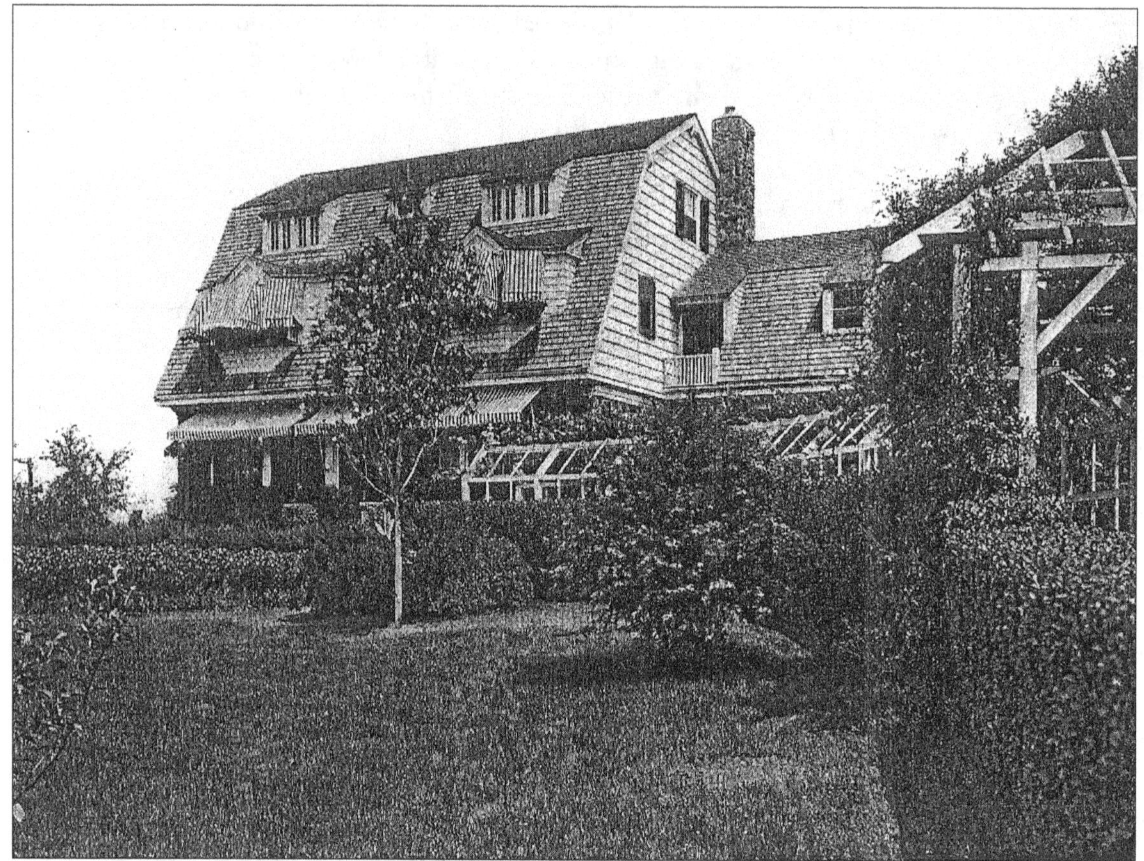

14.3 Harold Caparn design, house side facing the river, view of lawn and pergola.

Tree and shrub enclosures are absolute essentials in developing lawns. What they add to the lawn, in giving privacy and in creating general interest, is not generally appreciated nor understood by owners of small properties. For the complete and intensive use of a piece of ground, even of this size, more than a lawn is necessary.

A terrace is a means of transition between the house and lawn. Terraces are capable of many forms, shapes, and characters. They can be spacious, dignified, ornate, and formal to harmonize with the most elaborate house, they can be as small, simple, and informal as any suburban house may require. Here the small oblong grass plot is surrounded by narrow brick paths which are bounded on the outer side by unclipped Barberry hedging. This is the simplest form a terrace can take. It is particularly fortunate in winter to have such a sunny spot close to the house. The brick paths make it dry to walk on and the red Barberry berries look bright and cheery.

Steps from the terrace lead down to narrow strips of ground on the east and west sides of the lawn. The eastern side of the property was originally thought out as the service side of the garden but it is so full of color and flowers that it hardly gives any suggestion of the original intention. A path runs along the whole length to a tool house. It is shut off from the lawn by a hedge and for part of the way it is under the curving grape arbor. On the side of the arbor is an oddly shaped little piece of ground given to Roses and small fruits.

Every garden should have Roses for cutting and yet Hybrid Tea and Hybrid Perpetual Roses can hardly be associated with shrubbery [that is, they are not planted for their foliage, in Caparn's scheme]. Here, they have been planted in beds with the Gooseberries and Currants. This arrangement gives both Roses and small fruits the space they need for good development. To the south of the Roses is an oblong plot originally planned for the vegetable garden, but now a secluded little nook. The great old Apple tree makes it a nice shady little spot with the simple lawn space between yellow Iris that grow on one side and white and pink Peonies on the other.

The west side of the property was developed in a purely decorative way. The west path starts at the terrace and makes a big generous curve to the extreme western side of the grounds. It is an informal one passing through masses of shrubbery. Such paths, full of interest in growing and flowering things, are ways of making the grounds seem larger. The result is gained simply by engrossing one's interest in every step of the way so that one lingers longer upon it. A curved path is better for this than a straight one. The curved path gradually unfolds its varied pictures to the beholder as he passes. In such careful massing the shrubs can be used in small groups, sometimes only one of a kind, sometimes five or six plants used together. In this kind of grouping there is always something new and interesting, always something different on the path to attract attention, through the whole cycle of seasons. While the attention given to seasonal effects makes this path of continual interest, it is the consideration given to the foliage effect and to shrub habit which bonds the shrubs together into a unified border. It is the complexity of these varied considerations that makes border planting such a difficult problem, one which requires an artistic feeling to do it justice.

15 An Historic Village
Design as Symbol...1918

During WWI, Frederick Law Olmsted, Jr. was charged by the federal government with overseeing the layout and development of housing where workers were needed to support the war effort. He assigned Harold Caparn the planning of three villages in Alabama. Caparn drew on his earlier consideration of town planning of villages in Bridegport, Conneciticut, and his writing on the subject, in laying out the villages.

On his client list, as job number 603, Caparn gives the enigmatic entry "Housing Bureau." The clarification of that entry is found in *Transactions of the American Society of Landscape Architects, vol 2*:

> CAPARN, H. A. Landscape Architect and Town Planner, T. P. D., U. S. H. C. Projects at the Alabama Nitrate Towns of Florence, Sheffield and Tuscumbia from August 8 to November 12, 1918.[1]

The acronyms represent the Town Planning Division (TPD) of the United States Housing Corporation (USHC). The entry further notes that the USHC is the executive organization formed within the Bureau of Industrial Housing and Transportation of the Department of Labor. Caparn shortened "Bureau of Industrial Housing" simply to "Housing Bureau" for his client list. Caparn maintained his own office at 18 East 41st Street in Manhattan while carrying out the project in Alabama.

Located on the outskirts of Sheffield, in northwest Alabama close to the Tennessee River, the rural village was constructed to house military and civilian personnel who were engaged in a project there vital to winning World War I. President Woodrow Wilson selected Sheffield in September 1917 as the site for Nitrate Plant No. 1 as provided in the National Defense Act of the previous year. The American Cyanamid Company contracted in November 1917 to build and operate Nitrate Plant No. 2. The Federal Government looked to the time when one of these plants, each testing a different process, could make America independent of any foreign source of the needed ingredient for munitions to win the war. Work in the Tennessee River on the Wilson Dam named after the president, that was necessary to supply electricity to the plants, began in the next year.

Village No. 1 is significant for several reasons: it was connected with Nitrate Plant No. 1 in the effort to produce ammonium nitrate, an essential element in munitions; it included the home of the commanding officer of the US Army

Corps of Engineers in charge of the project; it was built by the Federal Government quickly during the war employing early mass design and production techniques. Its distinctive Mission-style houses and other buildings still all sit on their original sites, and the overall plan of the Village is a unique design. These attributes recommended it in 1984 to acceptance on the National Register of Historic Places.[2]

The historic district of Village No. 1 comprises the original 85 bungalows, a school/civic center, an unmarried-officers barracks, several parks and an expressive overall street design. The whole Village was built in just over seven months from mid-May 1918 to full completion by the end of that year.

Houses in Village No. 2, were associated with Nitrate Plant No. 2 at Tuscumbia. Houses in Village No. 3, at Florence, north of the river, were associated with the construction of the Wilson Dam. In the three villages a total of about 1,500 homes were built. Homes in Villages No. 2 and No. 3 were moved in 1950 to other locations in the area. Those villages therefore no longer exist. There is some discrepancy in sources as to the architects of the homes and other buildings in Village 1.[3] But only Village No. 1 remains as built in 1918.

After the signing of the Armistice with Germany on November 11, 1918, both President Wilson, who had provided direction, and Congress, which had provided funding, lost interest in the nitrate project and the plants were put on stand-by status in the summer of 1919. Workers living in the homes remained, now paying rent. But issues remained.

The New York Times noted excessive spending for housing for workers during the war; further it stated: "Without a dissenting vote the House passed and sent to the Senate today a bill ordering the sale of housing facilities erected by the Government during the war to relieve congestion in many industrial centres. The measure also abolishes the United States Housing Bureau, transferring the properties to the Treasury for sale to private persons."[4] The houses in Village No. 1 were taken over by the Tennessee Valley Authority (TVA) in 1933, then later sold to individuals at auction in 1949.

The map drawn for the TVA (15.1), based on Caparn's design of the Village, shows the contributing buildings to the historic district of Village No. 1— houses, school (right) and barracks (top). The buildings—houses (two far left, center and top) and another school (right)—were built later. Two of the original homes have since been demolished, one by fire, the other by termites, so 83 homes remain. The unmarried-officers barracks was later the site of a progressive school, still later it was remodeled into apartments.

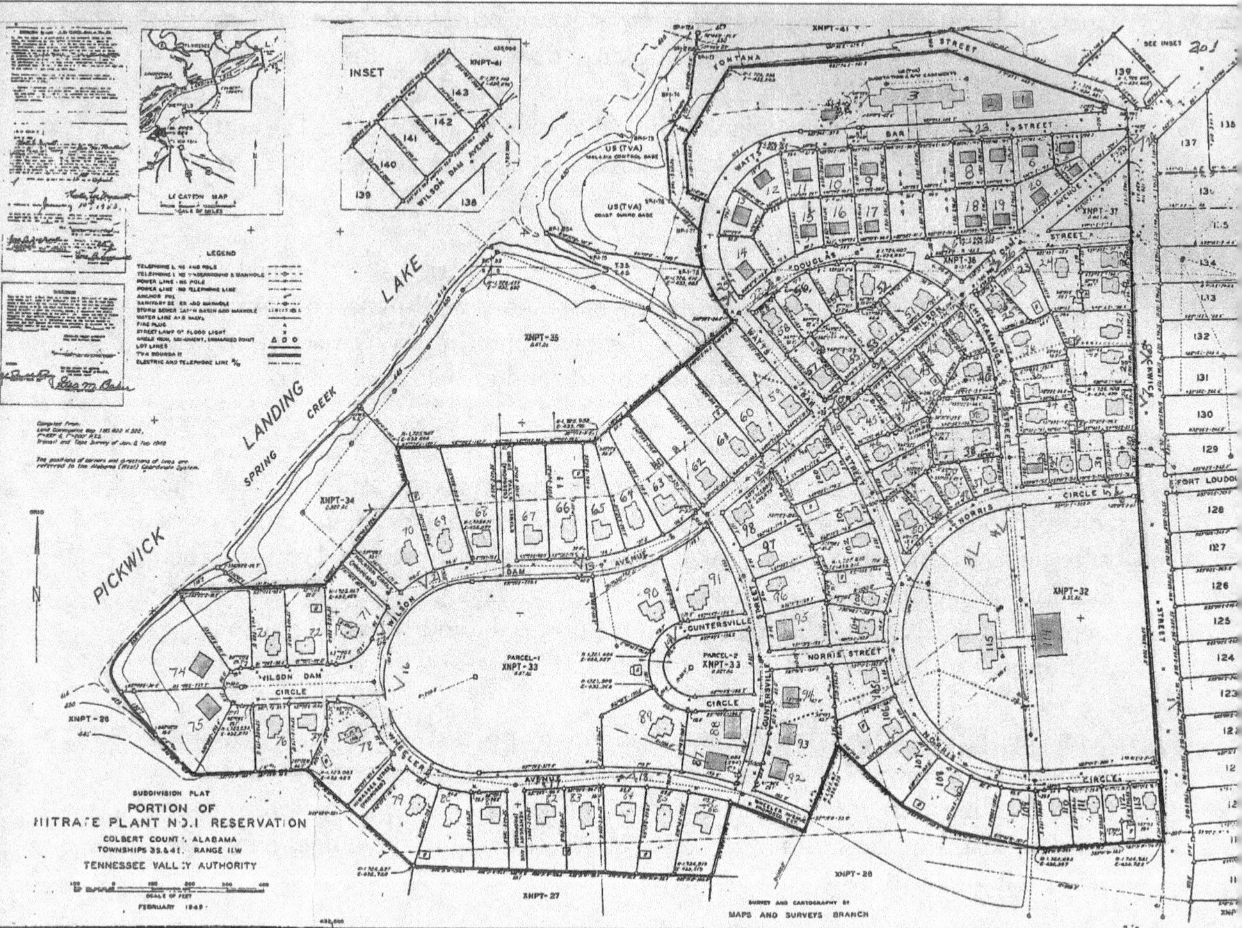

15.1 *Harold Caparn design as town planner of lots, streets and parks, Nitrate Plant No. 1 Reservation, outlining Village No. 1.*[5] *Darkened buildings are later additions.*

Caparn had previous experience working for the Housing Bureau on several industrial villages in Bridgeport, Connecticut. That work is given on his client list as entry number 586, for the Bridgeport Housing Co. The villages there are mentioned in an article in *The New York Times*: "Under the direction of the Bridgeport Chamber of Commerce, [city manufacturers] organized into a concern known as the Bridgeport Housing Company, each putting up a sum sufficient to insure the development of a large number of well-built apartment and unit houses."[6] The first four projects of apartments and houses provided for 250 families.

Village No. 1 in Sheffield, was built by The J. G. White Engineering Company, as mentioned in several sources. Their office was at 43 Exchange Place in lower Manhattan, as given on the plans for the commanding officer's home in the Village. They were a company of national reach, doing important projects from coast to coast. As seen in the early photos below, the company had work progressing simultaneously on many houses and the larger buildings in Village No. 1.

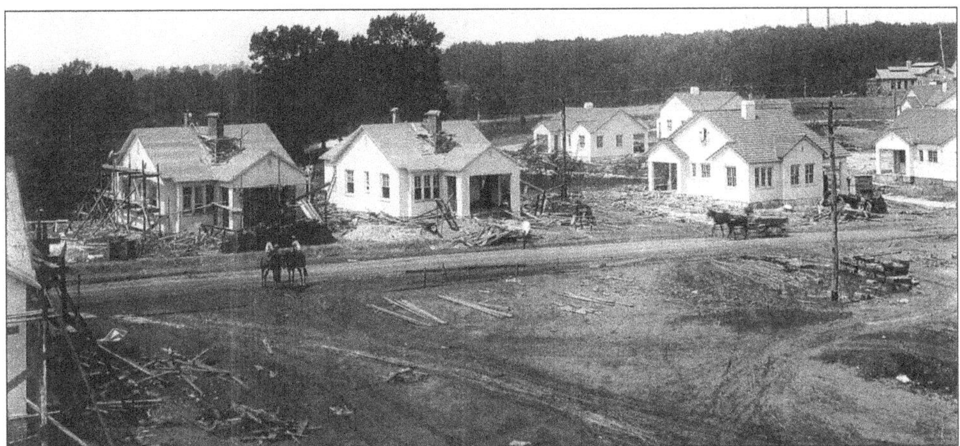

15.2 Harold Caparn design of street and lots, Village No. 1. Homes under construction. Photo, August 28, 1918. Note that on the two houses to the left, the porches face front, on the two to the right, the porches face to the side. Such variety of house design and placement is found throughout the village.

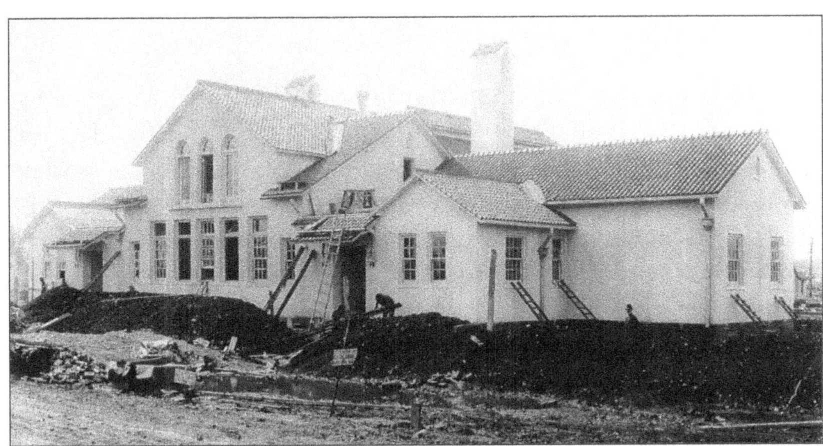

15.3 Harold Caparn design, placement of principal buildings, Village No. 1. Front view of the village school/civic center under construction. Caparn took the school/civic center as the central design element for the whole Village. The axis upon which the village design was formed runs from the rear of this most important building for the Village. Photo, October 31, 1918.

There were about half a dozen different house plans for the bungalows, all with stucco exteriors and red tile roofs. Characteristically they had central chimneys, porches and gables with rounded-arch vents. The houses were grouped so that the different sizes and designs were not all located together, but placed in varying harmonious arrangements. In addition, two officer's homes were slightly larger and the commanding officer's home still more expansive. As seen in the photograph of the school/civic center (15.3), some chimneys had an opening and cover reminiscent of a bell tower in California Mission-style churches, from which the overall style of the buildings was derived.

Although several architectural firms are mentioned in sources, the author posits that the likely architectural firm was that of Mann and MacNeille of New York City. Attribution is supported as stated in the report by the Chief of Ordinance: Mann and MacNeille "submitted the first sketches of five-room cottages on April 24, and on May 11 construction work was begun."

Even with Mann and MacNeille's experience in designing other industrial towns, it is most likely that some advance planning was necessary for Village No. 1, since it was distinct from other industrial villages of the time. Two and a half weeks from submitting the designs to the beginning of construction indicates some prior work by the architects and advance coordination between architects and builder. In addition, the general plan of the village streets, house lots and provisions for water and drainage would require that the landscape architect be brought into the advanced planning as well. Each of the three planning entities—architects, construction company and landscape architect—had offices in New York City.

Several assumptions can be made concerning the schedule to get housing for workers planned and built quickly for the war effort. Once the decisions were made in the Fall of 1917 to locate a nitrate plant in Sheffield, the design principals for Village No. 1 likely would have begun their planning no later than January 1918. That would have allowed a little more than three months for the landscape architect/town planner to lay out the village and for the architects to design the houses and other buildings and plan for purchase and shipping of materials by April. That would also have been in time for the presentation of designs to the Nitrate Division of the Army, and for construction to begin in mid-May.

These plans would have required some coordinating meetings, made easier because the principals were all in New York City. The general plan, presumably laid out and coordinated by Caparn from a topographical map of the area, would not have been difficult because the site of Village No. 1 was mostly level, on the plain of the Tennessee River. An engineer of the J. G. White Engineering Company, on site, could have staked out the design of the Village on Caparn's general plan, in order for work then to begin in May. Caparn had worked in such manner with a local civil engineer on a real estate project at the Village of Cayuga Heights at Ithaca, New York, before his work on Village No 1.

Construction techniques used in building Village No. 1 are of interest. Materials, fixtures and appliances were selected to fit all or most of the homes; some were prefabricated. The home designs were laid out for the sub-contractors and workmen not in full-scale drawings, but on letter-sized sheets with all the details of construction enumerated. That provided speed and accuracy in construction. The home designs were influenced by Craftsman and Mission styles, well known at the time and giving a simple, yet aesthetic coordination to the village as a whole. While having similarities to other industrial villages of the era, Village No. 1 remains of interest in part because of these design and construction elements and the coordinated Mission style of the buildings. The overall layout of Village No. 1 is of special interest. Before 1918 Caparn had written several articles that are relevant to his design of Village No. 1.[7]

> In "The Value of the Curve in Street Architecture" he said: Lines of beauty do, or ought to, move in every park road or garden path that is not straight. A mere street curb is able to express a sweep of line that is living and dignified and a real pleasure to every one who can see it."[7] His design of the Village streets, seen in the map, and the photo, illustrates the value he placed in their curving nature, both for the delight found as vistas opened around bends, but also for the beauty of the street found in the curves themselves.

Caparn's presence on site would have been needed from August through November 1918, to oversee the final landscape work on each of the three villages and to make certain that the workmen correctly brought his plans into realization for the curving streets of the Village No. 1. As he had said in his article, curving streets were more difficult to lay out and to convey to construction workers than the right-angle, grid-like streets of Paris or New York.

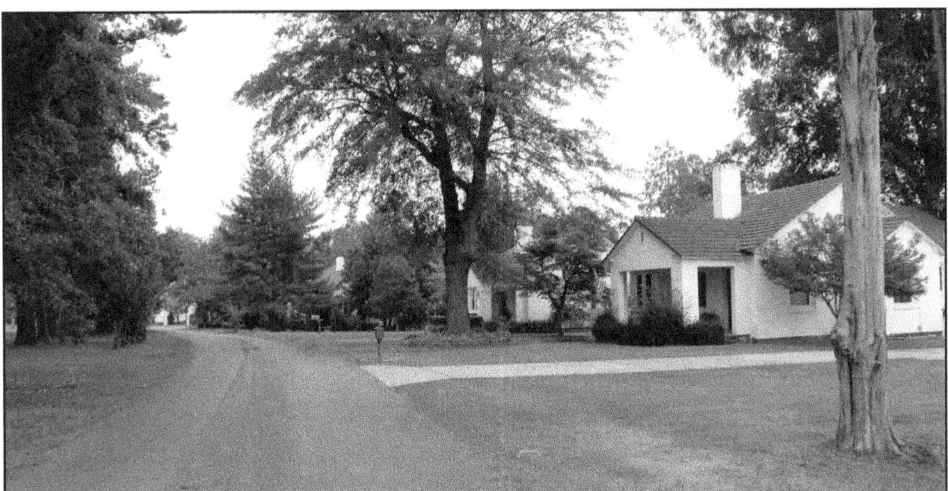

15.4 Harold Caparn design, Wilson Dam Avenue, illustrating the value and the grace of a curve in the design of a street where around the bend delightful new vistas may unfold— here a park.

In his 1907 article on "The Question of Civic Improvement," Caparn shows himself to be at the front of the movement for civic improvement, which is understood now as town planning. He says in that article:

> How would one make a town if one were able to start from the beginning? Continuing, he says: If, then, the town is the common home of all, it should be conceived and constructed for the greatest good to the greatest number. How is this to be achieved, and what would be the characteristics of the ideal home of the community?" He enumerates the requirements for the ideal community as "ease of going to and fro, for exchanging ideas and for all kinds of communication, every provision made for the general health, recreation and personal liberty, when light and air are free for all, and when all unnecessary noise, unsightly object, bad odors and other impediments to the peace and quietness and leisure that are the right of every man have been eliminated. They are such as no one through superior wealth, social position, opportunity, or other reason, should monopolize.

> Moreover, the ideal city would be devised as much for beauty as utility, because beauty is as practically useful as things purely utilitarian. Applied to a city or village, it really means the elimination of the unfit, the pretentious and the untrue. It does not necessarily mean the spending of much money, but it does mean the lavish spending of thought.

> To be more specific, it means the planning of the streets, so that they will develop as beautifully as their uses will allow, the provision of sites for public monuments, the proper distribution of parks and open spaces, the generous planting of trees, the establishment of 'civic centres,' and the designing and arrangement of public buildings so that they shall be worthy in themselves and shall each enhance the effort of the other. In proportion as these things are done well, light and air, convenience of traffic and business health and quiet will be assured to the community, and its prosperity and happiness will be increased.[8]

These ideal attributes are all seen in Caparn's layout of Village No. 1. They are reflected by the architects in the design of the more public buildings--school/civic center and the officers' barracks--in the same style as all the houses, and that each of these 'civic centre' buildings is enhanced by a spacious park. They can be found in the parks of the village that are open, with plenty of fresh air and light. They can also be found in the layout of the streets and the communication of a principal street, Wilson Dam Avenue, to the town of Sheffield.

Because of Caparn's early background in music, the model that he selected for the bell was that of an English handbell. The bell throughout history has participated in ceremony, often of a joyful or hopeful nature. The body of a handbell provided the shape of the outline of the principal streets surrounding the two central parks in Village No. 1. A handbell also has a leather handle that makes a loop at the top by which the player can grasp it. That loop was translated by Caparn into the street turned back upon itself at the top of the "body" of the bell-shaped streets. It is an early cul-de-sac, whose only purpose was to provide access to the homes there, not to connect to a further destination. Originally there were only four homes directly on the street and one each at the corners leading to the street. In a similar manner, a semi-circular street at the base of the bell was created by Caparn to provide private access to the three officer's homes. It encloses a small park on which the homes face. It represents the "clapper" of the bell.

The whole of the Village was laid out by Caparn on the formal design element of an axis running from the rear of the school/civic center at Norris Circle, with its surrounding park-like grounds. The axis runs up Norris Street--across from the school building--through the small park of about an acre formed by Guntersville Circle, the "clapper," through the larger park of about five acres, outlined by Wilson Dam Avenue to the north and Wheeler Avenue to the south, forming the "body" of the bell, to Wilson Dam Circle, which is the "handle" of the bell, seen in the village map and an early aerial photo of the village (15.5).

Caparn thereby makes the school building and surrounding large park, used as a community meeting-place, important to the village as its foundation. Next in importance come the officer's homes fronting on the small park, with street privacy of access and the enjoyment provided by their own park. That park moves directly to a small rise overlooking the larger park. It would be a natural and ideal place to view military or civilian events and celebrations in the large open park. It would also provide, as in Caparn's description in "Civic Improvement," a place of honor for a monument, for example, to those who had served in World War I, should that have been in the community's plans.

In an early photograph of the village (15.5), with the caption set by the printer of the postcard, the bell design was quickly associated with the "Liberty Bell" of Revolutionary America. Without further reflection or research, the name stuck.

There are physical differences, however, between the Liberty Bell, cast originally by the old and famous Whitechapel Bell Foundry in England in the eighteenth century, and an English handbell, many of which were also cast by Whitechapel. Handbells would have been known to Caparn through 19th-century models used widely in bell-choirs in English churches, such as St. Mary Magdalene in Newark on Trent where he attended and sang as a boy chorister. He was a bit later an

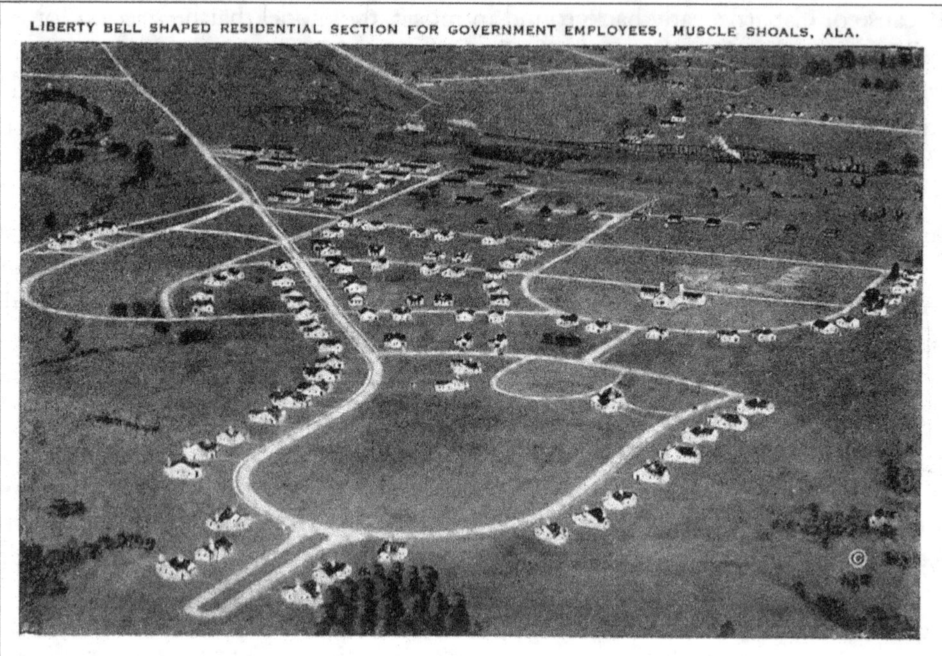

15.5 Harold Caparn design, 1918, Village No. 1, Sheffield, AL. Aerial photo, 1920s. The bell design and the axis from the school, upper right, through the large park, to the handle of the bell can be viewed.

instructor of choirboys at St. Edmunds School, associated with Canterbury Cathedral, where he also sang in the choir. His musical training and experience was reflected in several landscape designs where he included spaces for musical performances. From youth through adult, music, about which he had wide knowledge, was an integral part of his life.

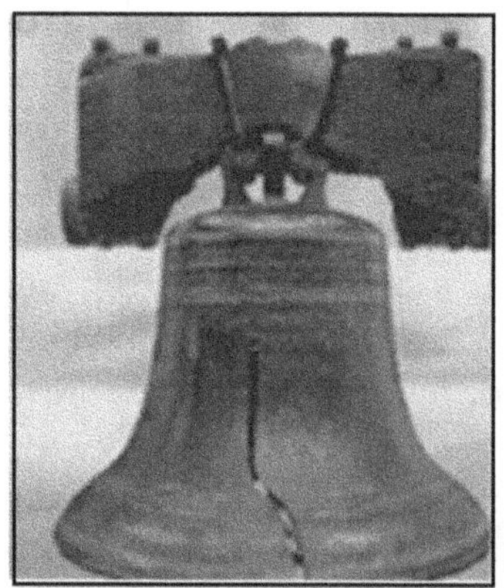

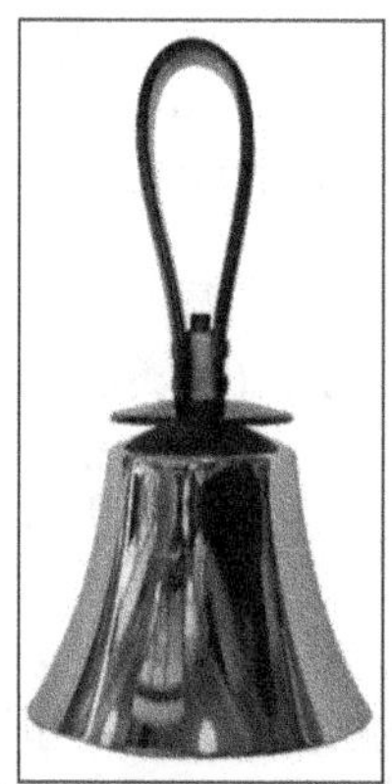

15.6 Liberty Bell
15.7 English handbell

The clearest difference between the Liberty Bell and an English handbell is that the Liberty Bell hangs from a heavy wooden support or yoke, rather than being held by a person by a handle, like a handbell. It's most famous characteristic is the crack running vertically from the lip up the body of the bell.

While there is a driveway from the rear of the commanding Lieutenant Colonel's home to the street, as seen in the aerial postcard photo (15.5, right center, near the bottom, or lip, of the bell), its placement does not reflect the upward direction of the crack in the Liberty Bell. This driveway provided service access for delivery of ice, food and other supplies to the rear of the commanding officer's home, as was considered appropriate at the time. A rear or side entrance was provided in better homes of the period, as here, for such purposes. No front driveway then interrupted the sweeping view of gracious lawn when arriving at the senior officer's home on Guntersville Circle for entertainments that would have been considered obligatory for the Colonel and his wife.

Neither are the wooden supporting yoke and its attachments to the Liberty Bell reflected in the cul-de-sac at the top of the bell design of Village No. 1. That boulevard-like street is modeled on the open-sided leather handle of a handbell. The single-lane street to these homes would have represented to Caparn such a bell handle and would have extended the length of the large park he designed, to which it is attached. It here provides a small park-like green for the six homes facing on this street, as partially seen in 15.8 and more clearly in 15.5. It is a balancing element to the street and small park for the three officer's homes facing Guntersville Circle.

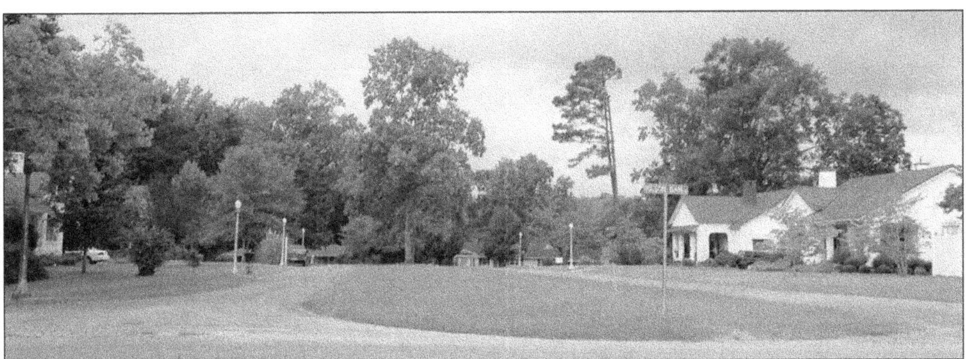

15.8 Harold Caparn design, Village No. 1. Cul-de-sac representing the handle of the bell. Two homes on either side of the street are original; those at the far end of the street are later additions. The street in the foreground, at the bottom of the photo above, defines the top of the body of the bell.

Caparn's inspiration for designing the streets in the shape of a bell was to express rejoicing known from his youth in the ringing of bells, especially relevant in 1918 to the hope for liberty in the outcome of the World War. As an immigrant (1889), then naturalized citizen (1900), he had worked successfully in America for many years; he had a strong desire not only for personal liberty, expressed in the open-air parks, but also for national liberty, expressed in the village bell design as a whole. He had fervent aspirations for success in the Great War both for England, his native country, and for America, his adopted land. Those sentiments he uniquely combined and expressed in the bell design of the Village. They illustrate his genius in bringing together these elements into the overall design of the Village. They provide a reason for its continued attraction to resident and visitor alike.

Because of its expanse, the bell design of the Village is not readily evident on the ground. Residents have said that they lived there for years before they knew of the design. But the design provided an order, spaciousness and beauty that are immediately apparent as one walks about the Village. Discovering its design through a map or aerial photo adds to the pleasure in the place.

The parks Caparn designed for Village No. 1--like Washington Park and Grant Park in Yonkers, New York--display simplicity of execution at the same time their use provided repose and recreation for the community. They reflect the informal approach to landscape design that he discussed in many of his articles. The parks in Village No. 1 were incorporated into the village design because Caparn saw they could easily and quickly be built on the topography that was mostly level. They would provide access to plenty of fresh air and light to enhance village living. As he said of Grant Park in Yonkers: "On large expanses of turf, undisfigured by roads or superfluous objects of any kind, depends the dignified and reposeful effect of park scenery."

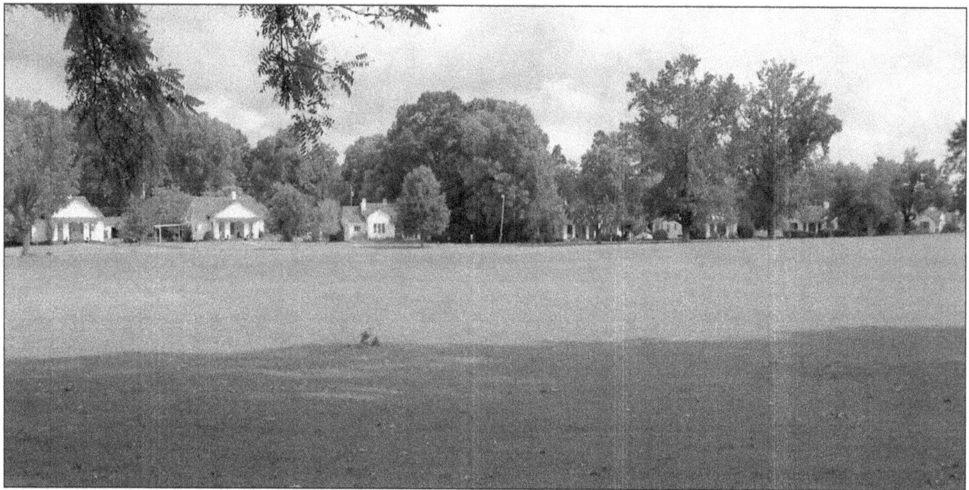

15.9 Harold Caparn design, large park, Village No. 1. Looking across the broad expanse of turf forming the body of the bell, to homes on Wilson Dam Avenue.

If we understand that Caparn's intent in the bell layout of Village No. 1 streets and parks was to bring into one design a symbol of liberty both for the United Kingdom and the United States, then this 1918 village may still appropriately be called "liberty bell village."

16 National Parks

Another voice for the wilderness...1922–1944

The National Parks were founded by an Act of Congress in August 1916. The effort at establishing the parks was led by John Muir, Stephen Mather, Horace Albright and many others who fought and won their battles for the national inheritance.

By the early 1920s Caparn felt the need to add his voice to those who promoted the establishment of national parks. In 1922 he wrote a plea that the charge to the National Parks Committee be of sufficient breadth to protect the scenic wonders and that we think about the harm we do in placing commercial interests over those of preservation and replenishment of our natural resources. He contributed that plea to the discussion on the scope of the Committee in a short paper titled "Do None Of Us Think?" In part:

> After no one knows how many hundreds of thousands or millions of years of evolution, the vertebrate animals and the pine, the sequoia and the hardwood tree and the scenery of this epoch have appeared. We found them in such abundance that, to the short sight and the dull imagination of most of those who saw them a few generations ago, they seemed inexhaustible. Those who cut down a sequoia probably never stop to think that it took two thousand years to grow and those who kill or encourage the wholesale killing of large game animals or commercially useful animals like seals, never seem to reflect on the miracle of the existence of these things, and that any one of them is an incomparably more wonderful and delicate machine than human ingenuity could ever construct.

> It is not that the earth must not be subdued to our uses. But in converting the earth to our uses we bid fair to destroy it for all uses. Of the coal and oil deposited we consume millions of tons in a day. Consume it we must, for we have built up our civilization on it. But is it not the very wantonness of haste, carelessness, stupidity and insolence to burn it up two or three times as fast as is needed, hardly even to study, much less enforce the means of utilizing it to the best advantage, so that the air we breathe is so polluted in the large cities that it will not support vegetation, yet is considered good enough to support us?

> Our lumbering and farming methods combined send millions of tons of the most fertile soil to silt up the Atlantic Ocean. It took an epoch to put

it there, and we get rid of it in part of a century. How long will the metals last at the present rate of consumption? What shall we, or, rather, our posterity, do when they are gone? As with our resources of coal, oil and lumber, so with our scenery. We are so possessed with the frenzy of commercial gain, we are so blind to the spiritual side of life, that only by the continual fighting of a tiny minority can the national parks, the rarest and most inspiring culmination of geologic processes be saved from the universal wreck.

The National Parks Committee was organized to defend the national parks, but these are only isolated jewels in the vast treasury of natural resources that we are hurrying to squander and ruin. The danger that threatens the national parks is the same that threatens the lives, the prosperity, the happiness, and even the decent existence, if not of ourselves, of our posterity. Nature has been prodigally generous to us, she has showered us with riches beyond the dreams of avarice. But if we do not learn how to use, how to conserve, how to invest them, so that they will increase instead of dwindling, she will deprive us of them with the same calm relentlessness with which she bestowed them, and leave us an earth which will be a fit theater for the painful and ignominious suicide of the human race.

He followed this plea for a wide-ranging scope to the National Parks Committee with several published defenses of a portion of the Yellowstone and stated that no effort was too great to save the beauty of the Falls at Niagara, the first reservation among State Parks. He supported Jackson Hole National Monument in the debate in Congress whether to override the President's order creating it, since "such scenery is a national, not an individual or local possession." While his full public professional standing in the ASLA came later than the beginnings of the National Park initiatives, once he was in a position to do so he added his voice in vigorous support of their ongoing preservation and protection.

Local considerations

Yellowstone National Park had been established in 1872. After the turn of the century, it and the other parks created in the interim were under the jurisdiction of the Secretaries of various Federal departments: War, Agriculture and Interior. Six years prior to Caparn's plea to the National Parks Committee, the National Park Service had been founded to collect together under one organization the management of the Parks.

Caparn personally knew leaders in the Park movement. He communicated with and published articles through Dr. J. Horace McFarland, who as president of the American Civic Association, which he founded, supported to the public the need for a Federal agency to administer the parks. Caparn was a member and officer of the American Civic Association from 1904 and continued with its later evolution into the American Planning and Civic Association. Stephen T. Mather, the parks great proponent and sometime donator, became the first Director of the National Park Service. Horace M. Albright, who had assisted Mather in so many details, succeeded him as Director, later becoming the Superintendent of Yellowstone National Park.

At the invitation of Superintendent Albright, during September 1926, Caparn made a horseback and overnight camping trip with Albright in Yellowstone National Park to make recommendations about a portion of the park. In particular he consulted on boundary issues along the Bechler River, where local farmers wanted the meadows there made into a reservoir to supply them with water.[1]

Caparn stated clearly the premise that without the meadows in the foreground the distant mountains beyond could not be seen to advantage: All the parts of the scene are interdependent. Anything that interferes with these processes, that injects any new and inconsistent element into their slow and orderly progress, will mar the perfection of the picture and interfere with the purpose for which the Park was created—the preservation of rare scenery in its natural state, as far as may be possible consistent with making it accessible.

He also suggested changes along the Grand Canyon of the Yellowstone; that wooden stairways, ramps and railings be replaced with more natural materials found in the vicinity. These recommendations were included in the 1932 master plan for the area, finally implemented in the mid-1930s.[2] They changed the future face of the park architecture.

An international consideration

In regard to the Niagara Reservation created in 1885 (Niagara Falls State Park), Caparn pointed out on several occasions in articles the problems of diverting water, jointly owned under treaty by the United States and Canada, from the Niagara Horseshoe Falls for purposes of electricity generation. At risk also was the continuing reduction of the Canadian Falls by means of the breaking off of about seven feet per year of the rock at the edge over which the water flowed. Engineering reports suggested diverting the flow of water from the front edge to the sides of the Horseshoe and to the American Falls. Recommendations were made of building small islands or a submerged weir above the Falls. In either case, Caparn says, "No price is too high to pay for the preservation of the beauty of Niagara, not even that of converting it, technically, into an artificial cateract."[3]

National Monument considerations

The Antiquities Act passed by Congress in 1906 allowed presidents to add lands and special sites to lists of national protection without Congressional approval. Between that date and about thirty-five years later, a few such sites, mostly in the unrepresented territories of Arizona and Alaska, were selected by presidents for special recognition. But when President Franklin D. Roosevelt proclaimed Jackson Hole National Monument in Wyoming on March 15, 1943, he faced stiff opposition from the congressman from Wyoming, Mr. Barrett. Barrett introduced H. R. 2241 to abolish the monument.

Caparn followed the argument, and the letters for it from residents, in the Congressional Record of June 7 and 9, 1944. He wrote to the *New York Herald Tribune* in support on June 23; his letter was published in the Sunday edition on July 9, under the headline: "Future of Jackson Hole: It Is Logically a Part of Grand Teton National Park, Says Harold Caparn." This letter, written in his late seventies, contains most of his argument for state and national parks, so it is quoted here *in toto*:

> It looks as though this dispute about Jackson's Hole could not be settled. Yet, those who have studied it most and longest are agreed that Jackson's Hole is indispensable to the Grand Teton National Park. Mr. John D. Rockefeller has given a large sum of money toward the purchase of the land, and the President of the United States has declared it a national monument, as he has a legal right to do, because he considered it to the advantage of the forty-eight states.

> Now a fact not yet appreciated by the average citizen is that a piece of scenery that is very rare and high class and irreplaceable is not merely so much real estate to be measured and recorded as the personal property of an individual to be disposed of as he please. In those tremendous cataclysms, millions of years apart, those geological epochs when the world was being made over by the upthrusting of mountain ranges and the submerging of forest (as, for instance, those from which coal was made), sublime scenery was created, great areas of it of little use for farming of any kind, but well worth traveling across a continent to look at.

> Now such scenery is a national, not an individual or local possession. In these United States such scenery in Idaho or California belongs as much to Florida or Connecticut as to the Mid-West. It is logically and should be legally, the property of the forty-eight states, not any one of them; a Federal, not a state possession. It might be compared to the City of Washington, which belongs to all the states, yet is in none of them.

Those who have looked at this subject from such a point of view are able to see clearly that the Jackson's Hole tract is, logically and scenically, part of the Grand Teton spectacle. If you want to see any large thing clearly, you instinctively stand away from it, and the larger it is, the farther away you must get. To appear to best advantage, the Grand Teton, must be seen from a distance; it must have a foreground proportioned in size and character to the magnificent background. And the foreground must be free from all structures or other objects that would mar the great spectacle.

So long as the Jackson's Hole lands or any part of them are in private hands, there will remain the danger of the introduction of features which, however unobjectionable they might be in other places and conditions, might seriously mar the great picture which millions of citizens and visitors from other countries who value such things would wish to retain in their original perfection.

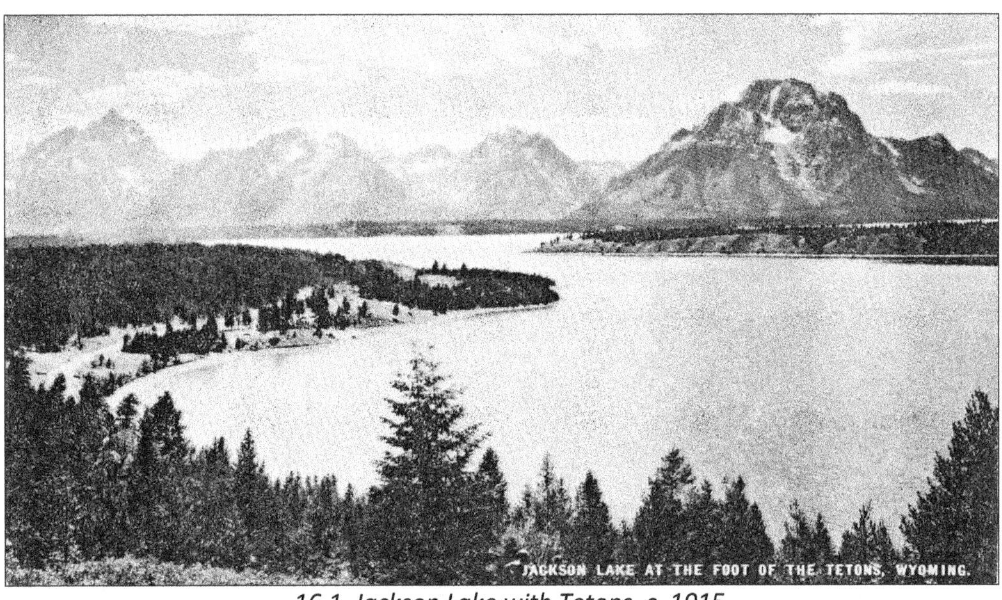

16.1 Jackson Lake with Tetons, c. 1915.

He sent this letter, before publication, to his friend Horace M. Albright, at 30 Rockefeller Plaza, NY. On June 27, Albright wrote Caparn from his office there: "It is fine to see your signature again and to know that you are still keeping closely in touch with conservation matters." Albright asked him to write his Congressman to oppose HR-2241, and to get his statement about the monument published. He also asked that a copy be sent to Newton B. Drury, Director of the National Park Service, in Chicago. Pressed for time, Caparn spoke by phone with Freeman Tilden at the NPS Office in Chicago on July 19. He added his voice, significant at the time, to the support for the park.

Congress voted on September 14, 1950, to enlarge Grand Teton National Park, established in 1929, to include Jackson Hole National Monument, Teton National Forest acreage and Jackson Lake with other federally-owned lands, and including 35,000 acres donated by John D. Rockefeller, Jr. The sometimes acrimonious rivalry among local farmers, landowners and their proponents, and the supporters of adding to a great natural wilderness, a twenty-some year saga, finally concluded successfully. Caparn's vision for the area, to the delight and use of many, came to fruition not long after his death.

17 College Campuses
A botanic garden and an arboretum...1930–1938

Before launching into the designs of college campuses that had specific educational purposes, we should note that Caparn also designed three other campuses, for health care facilities, that were of a more general nature intended to give pleasure and comfort to the residents. They were the Mountain Home for Disabled Volunteer Soldiers at Johnson City, Tennessee, the Masonic Home, at Utica, New York, a retirement home and health facility, and the Mt. McGregor Sanitorium at Wilton, New York, built by the Metropolitan Life Insurance Company to treat tuberculosis patients, especially those employed by the company. The Masonic Home, which continues to operate, received many complements on its landscape.

Caparn wrote four articles about the need, in the design of botanic gardens, for the intertwining considerations of botany, gardening and horticulture, the difference between a public garden and a private one and the educational value of presenting on the ground the theory of plant evolution. Two of these articles concern the Brooklyn Botanic Garden and will be found in that chapter.

Lebanon Valley College

We come then to Caparn's article about the botanic garden he designed for a professor of botany at Lebanon Valley College in Annville, PA, who wanted to take his students outdoors to study evolution in the plant world. This garden was limited by the extent of the quadrangle of the original buildings of the College. With some deletions over the Brooklyn Botanic Garden plan, it still gave a picture on the ground of the theory of the evolution of plants. Although buildings have been replaced and new structures added, some of the larger trees of that garden remain at the College.[1] Beside providing a lovely setting for the central quadrangle of the College and its buildings, the botanic garden also served classes as an outdoor laboratory.

An aerial view (17.1), shows the area designed and planted by Caparn. Bounded by White Oak St. (west), Lebanon Alley (south), College Ave (east), Sheridan Ave (north). Buildings fronting on the quad, seen above are the Administration (center right in trees) and North Hall (upper right).

> Caparn said that readers of his "Scientific and Decorative Principles in a Botanical Laboratory" (1930), will be familiar with the division and subdivision of plants; these are the classifications of the landscape architect, the gardener and nurseryman who makes them, as he must, for their value in artistic compositions.

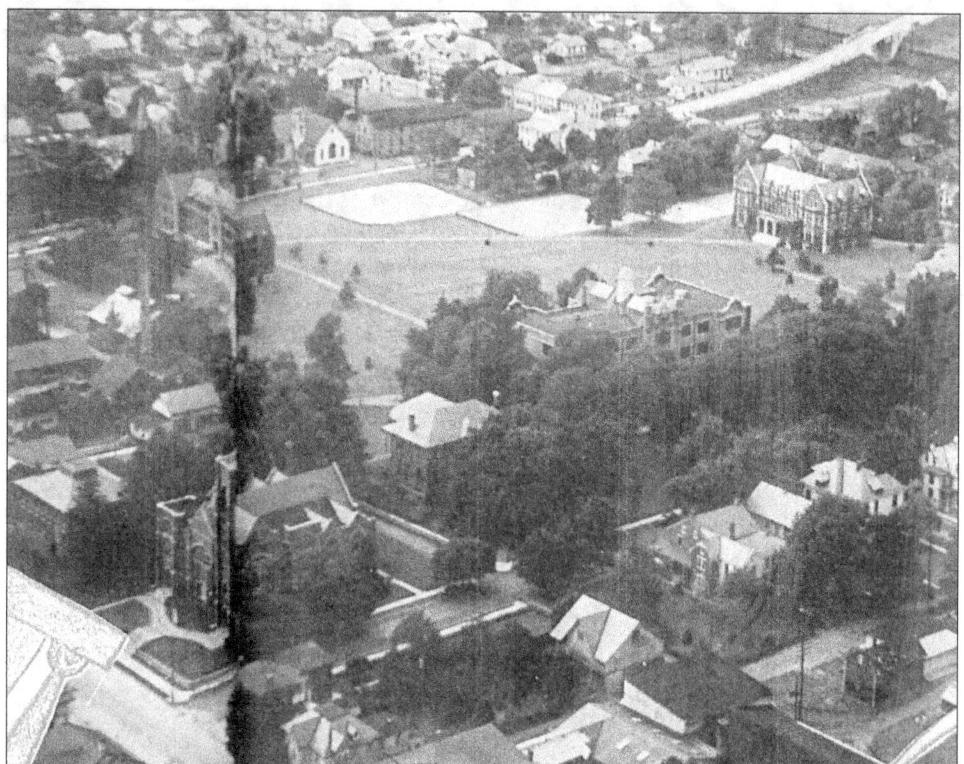

17.1 Harold Caparn landscape design, central quadangle. Lebanon Valley College.

The landscape architect is concerned with: (1) What do they look like and what is their form, habit, size, color and texture of foliage, or potentiality of flowering? (2) Are they evergreen or deciduous? (3) Will they grow in the climate? (4) Are they procurable? In fact, his knowledge of plant material will become systematic and intimate instead of casual and superficial—a subject discussed by Mariana Griswold Van Rensselaer in her 'Art Out of Doors.'

This last topic had been the subject of a series of seven articles Caparn published much earlier in *Countryside* (1917), on The House Outdoors. He clearly knew her book (1893); it was influential in the development of landscape design during the period under discussion.

Caparn continues, the question naturally arises: Can a scientific classification be harmonized with a decorative composition? The accompanying plan of the planting on the campus of Lebanon Valley College is an attempt to show that it can be done under certain circumstances. The method of accomplishment in the present case is simple. It consists in using only such plants to represent an order or family as lend themselves to the effect desired.

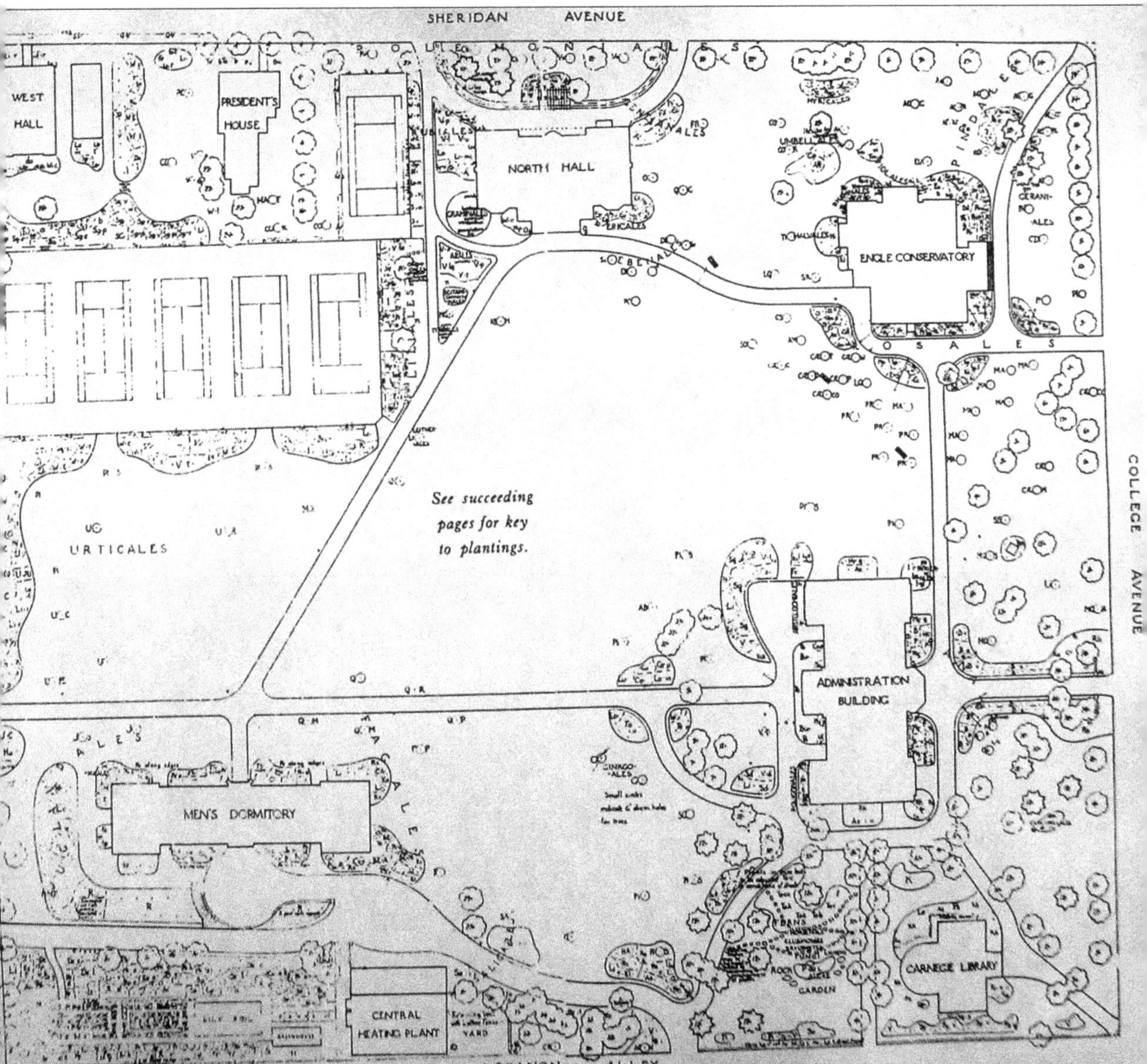

17.2 Harold Caparn landscape plan, central quadrangle, Lebanon Valley College.

The photographs of the College (17.3, 17.4) appeared in yearbooks of the 1940s. The photographs were taken by Luther Grant Harpel of the family of local photographers. Portions of Caparn's landscapes can be seen in the photographs.

His next article was on "Popular Botany and Botanic Gardens" (January 1932). Its purpose was to convince the lay person of the value of some knowledge of botany. Anyone who can do this, "can soon learn to find a strange plant in the woods or meadows, put it under a pocket microscope, and with the aid of the Flora (book) trace it through its division, order, family, genus, species, and variety."

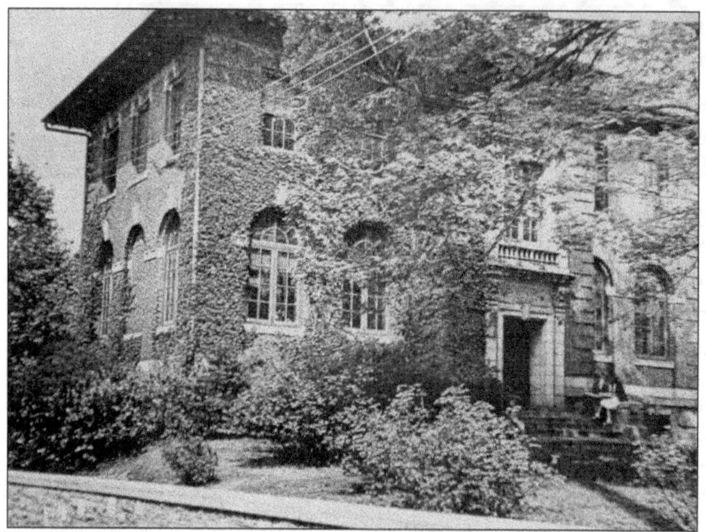

17.3 Harold Caparn landscape design, Lebanon Valley College, view of the Carnegie Library.

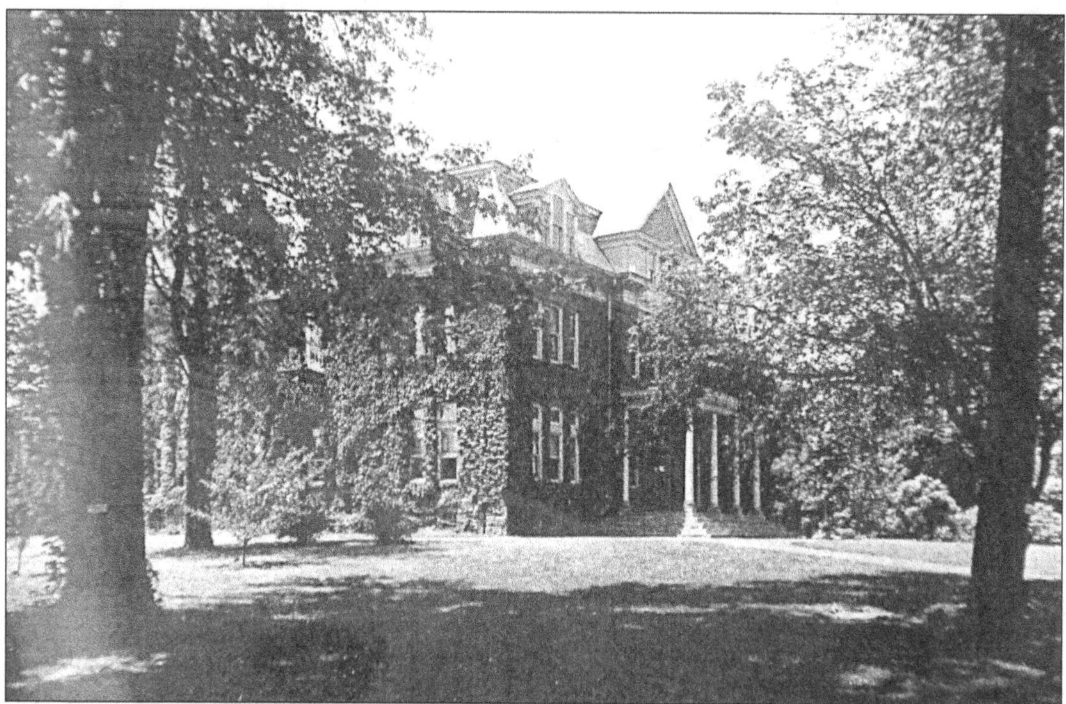

17.4 Harold Caparn landscape design, Lebanon Valley College, view of the Conservatory of Music.

He continues: A knowledge of the outward forms of plants, which is not only general but also particular, not only inclusive but also analytical, is of very great value, not alone to the ordinary plant lover, but especially to the landscape architect it gives a new key to and a new perception of that indispensable part of his equipment, a feeling for the *character*, textures, and quality of foliage, and its *expression* whether in small or large masses. (his italics)

The primary purpose of a botanic garden is not to create a work of art, but to convey as much information about as many kinds of plants—economic, horticultural, and purely scientific—as its plan and scope will permit. It should be a center to which one can go in search of plants, new and old, rare and common, where they can be seen in growth, and where the salient facts about them, cultural and otherwise, can be learned.

Nevertheless for all its scientific purpose and plan, the botanic garden must be made attractive to look at, or the public will not come to see it; and if they are not interested in it, they will be unwilling to pay taxes to support it, and private subscriptions will not be forthcoming…Yet the problem is not insoluble, and this abides in the fact that there is always an esthetic possibility somewhere in a well ordered and efficient thing.

In the last analysis, it is the spirit that counts in any garden composition. If the spirit of order, proportion, fitness of means to end, and joyousness illumines the whole, the dullish radiance of rules and conventions will be eclipsed and superseded.

Brooklyn College

Brooklyn College in Brooklyn, NY, although not given on Caparn's client list, is mentioned by his daughter Rhys in her summary of his work for the ASLA Council of Fellows. She is likely the source also of his obituary in *The New York Sun* newspaper (Tues, Sept. 25, 1945, 32) which states that he did work on the campus.

In the Brooklyn College archives there is a letter from Acting President of the College, Mario E. Cosenza, dated June 25, 1938 addressed to Professor Earl A. Martin, Chairman of the Building Committee of the College. It states that at the meeting of the Board of Higher Education held on June 6, 1938 the following resolution was adopted:

RE-APPOINTMENT OF HAROLD A. CAPARN, Consulting Landscape Architect.

WHEREAS, The Brooklyn College Administrative Committee on December 15th, 1937 approved the employment of Mr. Harold A. Caparn as consulting landscape architect for Brooklyn College for a period of six months, and

WHEREAS, Work on the landscaping project will not be completed before December 31, 1938; therefore be it

RESOLVED, That the Board of Higher Education approves the re-appointment of Mr. Harold A. Caparn as consulting landscape architect for Brooklyn College for the purpose of continuing supervising the landscaping work now in progress, for a period of six months, beginning July 1, 1938 to December 31, 1938.

The extent of the work evident at the College may not have been finished in the period of only one year; there may have been further extensions to the appointment that do not now survive. We shall explore first the development of the College, then look into Caparn's contributions to the campus.

Brooklyn College was founded in May 1930 from the conflation of Hunter College, for women, and New York City College, for men. A young architect, Randolph Evans, who worked for the Wood-Harmon Corporation, drew a plan in 1932 for a proposed college campus on a plot of land in Brooklyn owned by his employer. Evans envisioned a campus with a central quadrangle fronting a library with a tall clock tower.

On October 2, 1935, Mayor Fiorella La Guardia broke ground for the new campus. In the next year President Franklin D. Roosevelt laid the cornerstone of the new gymnasium. In 1938 Harry Gideonse, at age 39, became president of the College and led it for the next twenty-seven years, including the college acceptance, in 1961, as part of the City University of New York. It is now known as CUNY Brooklyn.

On a plot of twenty-six acres in the midst of tightly spaced housing on the surrounding grid of streets, the campus, in its layout and landscape enhancement, provided an oasis that became known for its beauty. The chief planner and architect of the campus, Randolph Evans, was given, appropriately, full credit. He proposed the site and laid out the basic design with a library building centered on a quadrangle bounded by two significant academic buildings. He provided the style for the campus in brick buildings modeled after the campus of the University of Virginia. He gave the site good structure in placing the Library on the controlling axis and facing an expanse of lawn framed by trees. He continued to be involved with the building of the campus, which, at first comprised what became known as the East Quad. Later the campus was expanded to include a complementary West Quad.

Evans, together with landscape architect Richard C. Murdock planned the campus, especially the East Quad. Evans designed the buildings, established the style and the general plan for the College and its future development. Together they laid out the East Quad central lawn, the walks, drainage system and other details. The College then turned for expert advice on developing a campus planting plan to Harold Caparn, the consulting landscape architect for more than the previous twenty-five years at the neighboring Brooklyn Botanic Garden. Almost ten years prior to his engagement by Brooklyn College, Caparn had laid out the landscape of the central quad of Lebanon Valley College as a botanic garden with emphasis on the evolution of trees and shrubs. At Brooklyn College, however, Caparn pursued a different direction, designing a campus landscape that displayed a broad collection of shrubs and trees in the manner of an arboretum.

The extent to which his planting efforts proved to be successful can be found in descriptions of the early campus and the survey, less than a decade later, entitled *Many a Tree Grows in Brooklyn* (Brooklyn College, 1946). The survey identifies and places each tree on the campus. Its listing gives twenty-one families of trees with forty-four genera. It does not include the many shrubs that were also planted at the time. Some can be discerned in a later survey of 1987; many were no doubt replaced, and some added, as the maintenance of the beauty of the campus was carried forward.

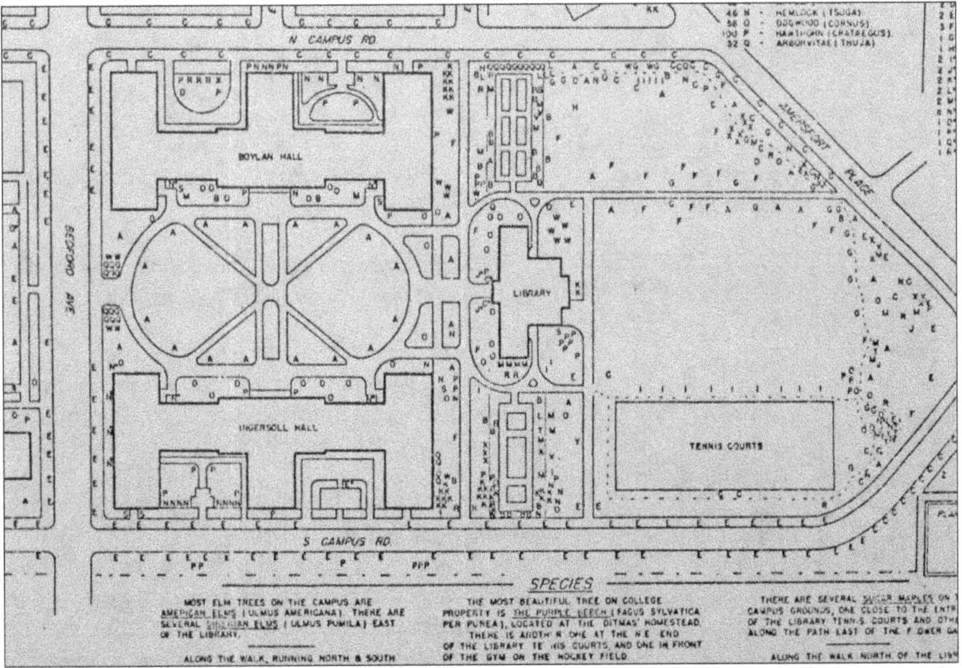

17.5 Harold Caparn design. A portion of 1946 survey of trees on campus, focusing on the East Quad and Library. Number and genus of trees is keyed in the following.

The map gives a view of the compact nature of the campus as it has grown, with West Quad, now built up beyond Bedford Avenue (defined by buildings 5, 10, 7). Note the central location of the Library with the tall clock tower; to that original building has been added a large expansion (13) bringing the Library and its amenities to modern usage. Note to the left of the Library the Lily Pond (in small letters), a feature designed by Caparn and still a focal point of the surrounding area. The East Quad between Boylan Hall (4) and Ingersoll Hall (11) still presents, from the principal entrance on Bedford Avenue, a beautiful and imposing view across the long green, framed by trees.

— GENUS —

LETTER		GENERA	LETTER		GENERA
40 A	-	ELM (ULMUS)	19 R	-	PINE (PINUS)
60 B	-	CHERRY (PRUNUS)	8 S	-	JUDAS OR REDBUD (CERCIS)
129 C	-	MAPLE (ACER)	8 T	-	HERCULES CLUB (ARALIA)
3 D	-	INDIAN BEAN (CATALPA)	2 U	-	WILLOW (SALIX)
109 E	-	OAK (QUERCUS)	4 V	-	ASH (FRAXINUS)
30 F	-	LINDEN (TILIA)	32 W	-	IRON WOOD (CARPINUS)
50 G	-	MAIDEN HAIR (GINKGO)	25 X	-	SILVERBELL (HALESIA)
8 H	-	HONEY LOCUST (GLEDITSIA)	1 Y	-	SYCAMORE (PLATANUS)
20 I	-	YELLOW WOOD (CLADRASTIS)	4 Z	-	SPRUCE (PICEA)
8 J	-	BEECH (FAGUS)	2 A*	-	CEDAR (CEDRUS)
51 K	-	POPLAR (POPULUS)	2 B*	-	FIR (ABIES)
14 L	-	BIRCH (BETULA)	2 C*	-	CYPRESS (CUPRESSUS)
88 M	-	APPLE (MALUS)	2 D*	-	CORK TREE (PHELLODENDRON)
46 N	-	HEMLOCK (TSUGA)	2 E*	-	SASSAFRAS (SASSAFRAS)
58 O	-	DOGWOOD (CORNUS)	3 F*	-	PEAR (PYRUS)
100 P	-	HAWTHORN (CRATAEGUS)	1 G*	-	PEACH (PRUNUS)
32 Q	-	ARBORVITAE (THUJA)	1 H*	-	TREE OF HEAVEN (AILANTHUS)
			2 I*	-	CRYPTOMERIA (CRYPTOMERIA)
			2 J*	-	DOUGLAS FIR (PSEUDOTSUGA)
			2 K*	-	MOUNTAIN ASH (SORBUS)
			2 L*	-	RED CEDAR (JUNIPERUS)
			2 M*	-	BALD CYPRESS (TAXODIUM)
			8 N*	-	YEW (TAXUS)
			1 O*	-	KATSURA TREE (CERCIDIPHYLLUM)
			1 P*	-	MULBERRY (BROUSSONETIA)
			1 Q*	-	MAGNOLIA (MAGNOLIA)
			1 R*	-	CHESTNUT (CASTANEA)

17.6 Harold Caparn key to planting plan, above. Note the elms (A) ringing East Quad in front of the Library in illustration 17.5. From the 1946 survey.

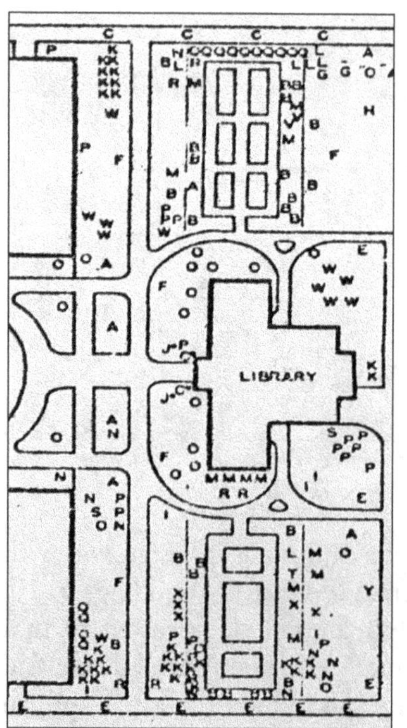

17.7 Harold Caparn design, shows the Library and to the north side (top) the sunken Perennial Garden,

17.8. The garden no longer exists; it has been replaced by the Whitehead building and the adjacent outdoor Library Café plaza. To the south of the Library is the still extant Lily Pond Garden,

17.9. It is also a sunken garden, with plantings at both ends and a pool at the center.
The embankments are thickly planted and the benches surrounding the pool provide a quiet respite site for students, faculty and visitors to enjoy the surrounding beauty of the garden. Its value to the campus can be seen in its daily use and the fact that it has continued to survive in the face of growing demand for building space as the College has flourished. The general campus map still shows its location to the southwest of the Library. Beside the many trees and shrubs, it is a focal point of the enhancement of the campus.

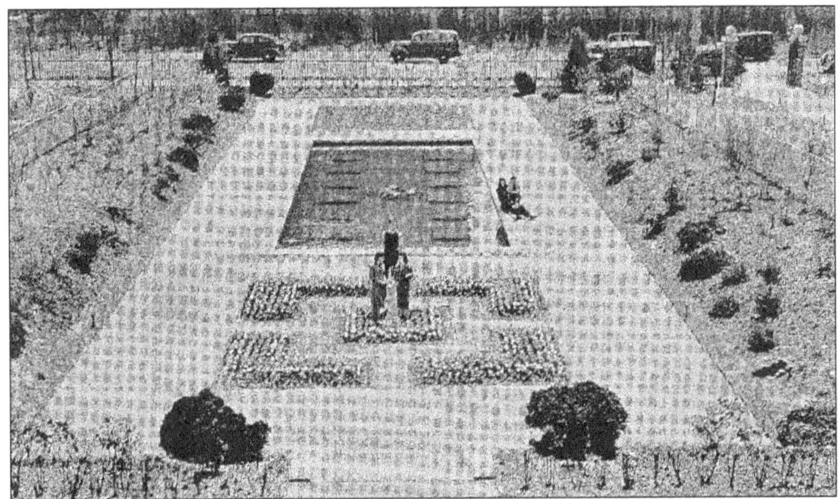

17.8 Harold Caparn design, Perennial Garden (also known as the tulip garden), north side of Library. This garden no longer exists.

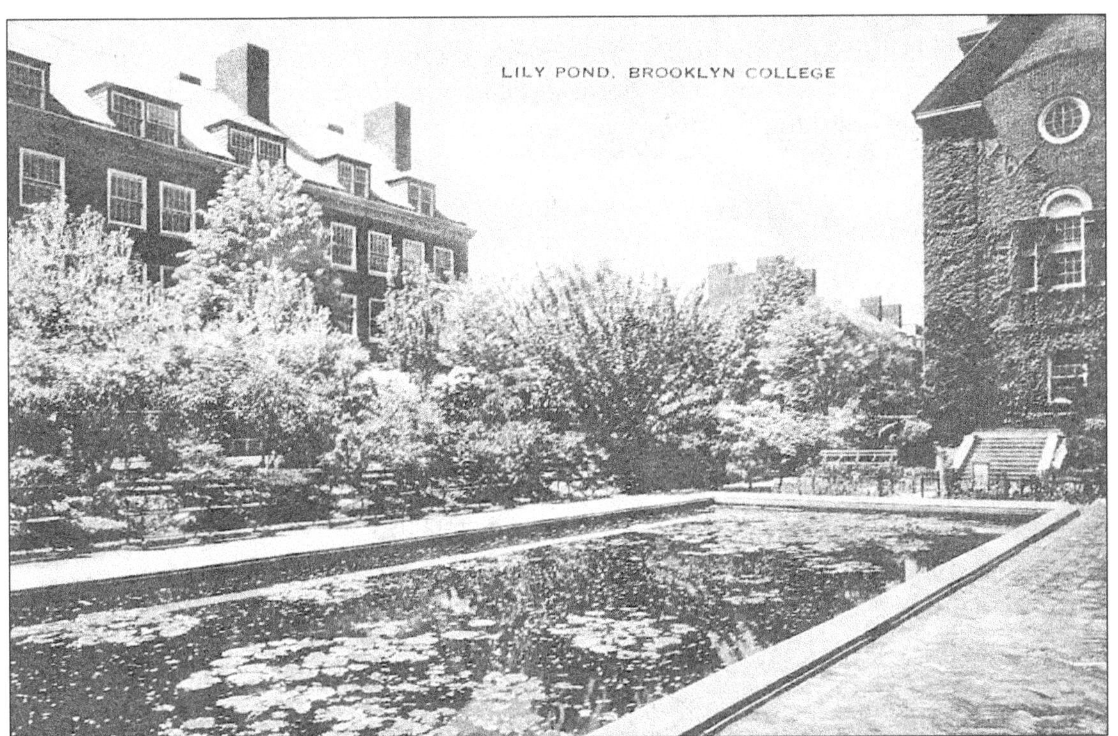

17.9 Harold Caparn design, Lily Pond Garden, south side of Library (the original Library building is to the right) Photos c.1945.

A campus tour guide begins with a description of the Lily Pond Garden, which was shown under construction in 1938 on the cover of the book.[2] The description here is edited for a brief presentation:

"With about one-fourth of the woody plant species on campus, the Lily Pond Garden is a botanic garden in its own right. Starting at the northeastern corner are two wintergreen barberries, one of the most spinescent shrubs on campus. Walking toward the stairs down into the garden is a rosebud cherry, with pendulous branches and small flowers that bloom in April. Down the steps and to the left is a star magnolia, with slightly cone-shaped leaves and white flowers. Ahead are several Oregon grapes; these shrubs, related to the wintergreen barberries, differ in two ways: they are spineless, and their leaves are compound. The blue violet berries of these plants look somewhat like grapes—hence the name." The full list of trees around the Lily Pond Garden can be seen below.

Almost fifty years after Caparn began work on the campus, there was still pride in its beauty. It generated a book describing the trees and shrubs at the time. Some of the original plantings have been replaced. The point illustrated is that the College has maintained and extended the plantings and beauty created by Caparn. The full list of trees, from the earlier survey, surrounding the Lily Pond Garden follows.

Lily Pond Garden, full tree list, in two sections, reading L to R, top to bottom around the garden, starting in the northwest corner, 17.9. Survey, 1946. Letters below are keyed to the plan for the Library area, seen above.

Section 1	Section 2
1 yellow Wood (I)	
3 Cherry (B)	1 Cherry (B)
3 Silverbell (X)	1 Elm (A)
2 Hawthorn (P)	1 Birch (L)
6 Poplar (K)	1 Apple (M)
1 Indian Bean (Catalpa) (D)	1 Dogwood (O)
2 Hawthorn (P)	1 Hemculis Club (T)
2 Pine (R)	1 Apple (M)
2 Poplar (K)	1 Sycamore (Y)
	2 Silverbell (X)
across bottom	1 Apple (M)
4 Cherry (B)	1 Yellow Wood (I)
2 Hemlock (N)	1 Hawthorn (P)
	3 Hemlock (N)
	5 Poplar (K)
	1 Cherry (B)
	1 Dogwood (O)
	1 Oak (E)

Framing the East Quad facing the Library, Caparn planted elms. They are seen as they grew, in the following two photographs. As they have aged, the College has considered removing or replacing them. Since their original planting, they have enhanced the campus for about seventy-five years.

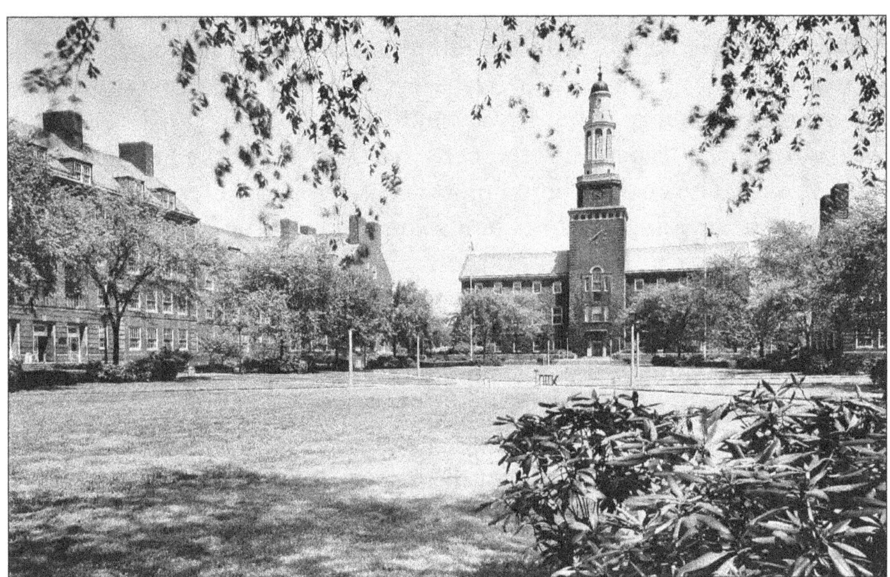

17.10 Harold Caparn design, East Quad, looking down the long green to the Library with clock tower. Boylan Hall is to the left. July 1956. Note the relative growth state of the elm trees around the green.

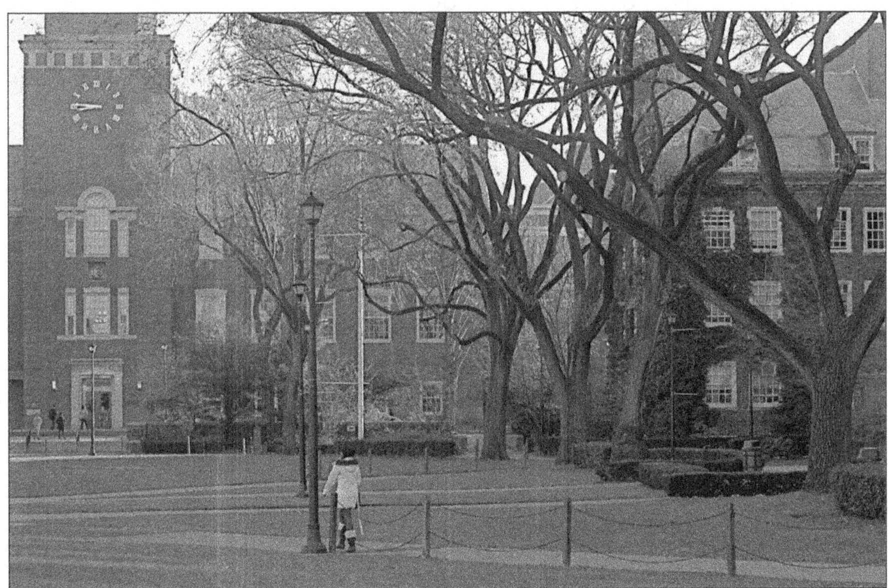

17.11 Harold Caparn design. Remaining elms in East Quad, before Ingersoll Hall, December 2011. The plantings in one of the small gardens in front of the Library and original design of walks can be seen. The elms still provide a magnificent stately frame for the green, as Caparn envisioned.

18 Founding

American Society of Landscape Architects...1931

This important statement, on the founding of the American Society of Landscape Architects, was researched by Caparn in the documents of the founders and reviewed by several of them. It was published in January 1931 in *American Landscape Architect*. Caparn saw the need, before more of the founders passed, to summarize what he knew to be an important event in the life of the profession. Along the way he reveals something of his knowledge of the history of landscape architecture. He states its place as a fine art, his admiration for the work of Frederick Law Olmsted, Sr., the efforts that led up to the founding of the Society and the identification of the first officers and charter members. The essential information on the founding of the Society is given here. Additional relevant information can be found in the original article.

Caparn begins with a survey of the history of landscape architecture: For a few thousand years gardens were made, as a matter of course, by architects, or by those who followed their lines. Then, in the High Renaissance, architects began to specialize in gardens, pleasure grounds and forests designed in an architectural manner. Their climax was reached in LeNôtre, who was a gardener's son with a gardener's training. Then came the long interval of naturalistic design which seems to have been pervaded by the idea, more or less distinct or hazy as the case might be, that the two styles or manners were inconsistent, even hostile, and could not be harmonized.

<u>Early Landscape Architects</u> For two centuries or so previous to about 1890, the art of landscape design was perhaps unique in that there was during most of the time, one outstanding practitioner with a crowd of followers, most of them at such a distance that they are hardly perceptible today. Names of such exceptional prominence are LeNôtre, Kent, "Capability" Brown, Repton, Alphand, André, Downing, Olmsted, and Vaux. All were men of conspicuous individuality and achievement, each working in his own style or manner.

In America the first distinguished name was that of no less a personage than George Washington who, like Thomas Jefferson, and many other country gentlemen of his time, laid out the grounds of his own home with a vision, simplicity and grasp of fundamental principles that have remained worthy of study to this day.

In fact, for about a century, the growth of landscape design was along the amateur rather than the professional line, as is shown by the number of works which by their at least partial survival have proved that they are worthy to survive; for, barring accidents, survival is probably the acid test of a work of art. And it is not unlikely that American professional landscape design, which might be said to have begun with Andrew Jackson Downing, owes its sudden efflorescence in his works and in those of Olmsted and Vaux to the generations of cultivated amateurs who prepared the way by laying out their own country places with the aid of such advice as they were able to secure.

<u>A Fine Art</u> Like other arts, landscape design requires peace and plenty for its development. It seems somewhat incongruous that, although its purpose and tendency to an eminent degree are to produce a feeling of peace, and considering its scale and its influence on the lives of those who see it, it is the least costly of all arts. It seems inconsistent, too, that, although landscape design is one of the most widely practiced of the arts (for there must be at least the rudiments of it wherever there is a building that can be called a home with some free space around it), yet it is the art which less often than any other is produced by adequate and ordered thought and technical skill.

People of sufficient means began to acquire and develop large country estates on the banks of the Hudson river. They used whatever traditions of planning there were; they had excellent libraries and the culture to use them, and some imported skilled gardeners or architects from England or France to assist them.

<u>In the United States</u> It was in this way that Andre Michaux came to the United States, and the movement resulted in the career of Andrew Jackson Downing (1815-1852), who saw the opening for a specialist and became the first professional landscape architect in this country. Since Downing the succession has been unbroken. Professionally speaking, Olmsted and Vaux were the direct descendants of Downing and it was their work and influence, especially that of F. L. Olmsted, the elder, that produced the practitioners who came together in the American Society of Landscape Architects just in time to open the present century with the advent of the new profession among the other fine arts.

<u>Tribute to Olmsted</u> There seems to be no doubt that the contributions of the landscape architects to the Chicago World's Fair of 1893 not only added much to its unity, impressiveness and charm but also probably paved the way for the advent of the American Society of Landscape Architects six years later. The work of the elder Olmsted, especially his

famous lagoon bordered in part, unless I mistake, with salix discolor and other native trees and shrubs, his success not alone of harmonizing a conception of this kind with its surroundings, but in getting it executed and winning the approval of a group of architects of European training and convincing them of its rightness, elicited from D. H. Burnham, the guiding spirit of the great project, this encomium: 'Each of you know the name and genius of him who stands first in the heart and confidence of American artists, the creator of your own parks and many other city parks. He it is who has been our best adviser and common mentor. In the highest sense he is the planner of the Exposition—Frederick Law Olmsted. No word of his has fallen to the ground among us since first he joined us some thirty months ago. An artist, he paints with lakes and wooded slopes; with lawns and banks and forest-covered hills, with mountain sides and ocean views. He should stand where I do tonight, not for his deeds of later years alone, but for what his brain has wrought and his pen has taught for half a century.

<u>Professional Status</u> This is a cursory sketch of the causes and events that made it possible in 1899, despite the unfortunate loss of Henry Sargent Codman and Charles Eliot, to assemble not less than eleven practitioners calling themselves landscape architects, most of them in well established practice under standards such as those of the doctor, the lawyer and other professional people. These might be said to consist in taking remuneration for services not in the form of unknown profits on the sale of merchandise, but as fees for the special skill and knowledge of what construction should be undertaken and why, and what materials should be bought and what should be done with them to solve the problem in question. This is a charge for advice whether verbal or written or in the form of plans and specifications, all being methods of informing the client what, in the opinion of his professional adviser, he should do, and how he should spend his money. Thus it appeared that 'the art of arranging land and landscape for use and enjoyment' as Charles Eliot (quoted in the Constitutions of 1902 and 1909) put it, had come of age; that the inevitable trend of civilization and accumulation of wealth in times of peace had produced a new calling, not of specialized architects nor nurserymen nor gardeners, but experts in what the architect and the gardener had been doing or attempting to do for so many centuries. The American Society of Landscape Architects, then, is one of the results of modern specialization; for as knowledge and skill increase, the followers of an art, a craft, a business or profession, find that its complexity or ramifications are beyond the capacity of one person, and so concentrate on one branch of it.

<u>The Repton Club</u> The earliest attempt of landscape designers to fraternize and join their forces in a common cause is best described in the words of F. L. Olmsted. He says: 'There was in existence for some years in Boston a very informal organization (if it could be called an organization, having no bylaw and no written records) known as the 'Repton Club.' It included Manning, Ernest Bowditch, Aspinwall and Lincoln (engineers who did a good deal of landscape work), my brother, John, and me, and I think Joseph Curtis (formerly associated with Copeland) and probably some others. I was made secretary as being the youngest member. And, informal as it all was, the 'Repton Club' was certainly a forerunner of the Boston Chapter of the American Society of Landscape Architects.

<u>Beginnings of A. S. L. A.</u> In 1897 Mr. Warren H. Manning of Boston attempted to get the Boston men to form a society; but the time was felt to be hardly ripe, and the movement that resulted in the founding of the American Society of Landscape Architects was started by Mr. Samuel Parsons, Jr., then landscape architect of the city of New York. There had been a reorganization of the park department due to the incorporation of the boroughs of Manhattan, Bronx, Brooklyn, Queens and Richmond into the city of Greater New York, and Mr. Parsons was conceded the privilege of undertaking private work on condition of giving one-half of his time to the park department. Though so busy a man, he was yet able to find time for efforts to unite the landscape architects of New York City into a body.

The first documentary evidence of this is a letter from Samuel Parsons, Jr., of Parsons and Pentecost, St. James Building, Broadway and 26th Street, NYC, to Charles Lowrie on February 24, 1898 inviting him to a meeting at 10 AM 'for a gathering of about four people who have mutual interests in landscape architecture.' During 1898 there appear to have been several meetings at which Mr. Lowrie urged the inclusion of members of the profession outside of New York. The Boston contingent hesitated for some time, fearing that there were not enough members available to form a national body; but by December 21, the opinion of both New Yorkers and others had crystallized sufficiently to elicit a letter from Samuel Parsons to Charles Lowrie: 'I have your letter and recognize the force of your arguments. Mr. Barrett, Mr. Manning, and Mr. D. Vaux and ourselves discussed the matter at length last Saturday evening. It was the sense of the meeting that Mr. Manning be asked to correspond with several Boston landscape architects to see if they would not come in with us. When Mr. Manning has received answers, we will have another meeting, between Christmas and New Year's. We will notify you.'

<u>Charter Members</u> The meeting at which the American Society of Landscape Architects was organized was held at the office of Parsons and Pentecost, New York, on January 4, 1899. There followed a letter from Daniel W. Langton, 115 East 23rd Street, NYC to Charles Lowrie on May 8, 1899: 'I too am sorry you could not have come the other night and feared you were ill. The executive committee decided that J. C. Olmsted and F. L. Olmsted, Jr., Brookline, Mass., Warren Manning, Boston, Samuel Parsons, Jr., George Pentecost, Jr., Downing Vaux, Charles N. Lowrie, Nathan F. Barrett, Daniel W. Langton, and Miss Beatrix Jones, all of New York, and O. C. Simonds, Chicago, were the original fellows and liable to the $10 fine.'

<u>The First Officers</u> The first president was John C. Olmsted; vice president, Samuel Parsons, Jr.; secretary, Daniel W. Langton, and treasurer Charles N. Lowrie. The constitution and by-laws were drawn up by Daniel W. Langton and Charles N. Lowrie, and adopted with slight revisions at a meeting on March 27, 1899. There were present John C. Olmsted, Ossian C. Simonds, Daniel W. Langton, Downing Vaux, Samuel Parsons, Jr., George F. Pentecost, Jr., Charles N. Lowrie.

Caparn continues: A letter from Daniel W. Langton, secretary, dated December 23, 1899, records that Miss Elizabeth Bullard of Bridgeport, Conn., had been duly elected a fellow, and that Arthur Shurtleff of Brookline, Mass., and E. Maitland Armstrong and Albert B. Russell of NYC were duly elected juniors. They might be described as the charter juniors. Miss Bullard was the first professional woman landscape architect of whom the writer is aware.

The surprising thing about the list of charter members is not its shortness, but its length, and the fact that, for the first time in history so many qualified practitioners successfully conducting their work on professional lines should have appeared at one time, instead of the succession of one-man reigns of the previous two centuries. No less than five of them—Mrs. Farrand (then Miss Beatrix Jones), F. L. Olmsted (Jr.), Warren H. Manning, Ossian C. Simonds, Charles N. Lowrie—are still in active practice.

Of those who have gone before, Downing Vaux (son of Calvert Vaux, one of the designers of Central Park, NY) was secretary for ten years (1900-1909) with a thorough devotion to his job, and was at least as indispensable to the keeping of his struggling organization together as secretaries usually are. Nathan Barrett was a bluff and genial idealist with a strong tendency towards formal designs on a large scale. John C. Olmsted, with a wider and longer experience than any, and with the reputation of a very able designer among those who knew him best (his staff), was yet one of the most modest of men, and ready with patient consideration of the views of others. Daniel W. Langton, with the social qualities of the southerner, was a good artist with the kind of temperament that often goes therewith. He died early, but not before he was threatened with blindness, that immeasurable calamity for a landscape architect. Samuel Parsons, too, an idealist in a different way, filled for many years a difficult and often thankless position in the New York park department, and was a staunch defender of the integrity of the original design of Central Park. The writer remembers them all, with a keen appreciation of their diverse personalities, their single-minded devotion to their calling, and a sense of the privilege of having known them.

Caparn appended this note: The author wishes to acknowledge his indebtedness to the following for their reading of, and suggestions to, the manuscript: Mrs. Beatrix Farrand, Charles N. Lowrie, Warren H. Manning, Frederick Law Olmsted and Ossian C. Simonds, charter members and fellows of the A. S. L. A.; Richard Schermerhorn, F. A. S. L. A., and Miss Margaret Parsons. The letters quoted are from the records of Mr. Lowrie.

19 A Woodland Garden

Beauty at the New York World's Fair...1936--1940

The New York World's Fair officially opened on April 30, 1939. President Franklin D. Roosevelt declared it so over radio and the new communications medium of television. It was located along the Flushing River in Queens in what would become, when the Fair closed after two seasons, Flushing Meadow Park. The Horticultural Exhibition--Gardens on Parade--laid out by William A. Delano, opened on May 18, 1939. Charles Downing Lay, landscape architect for the City of New York, was the consulting landscape architect.

The Exhibition Buildings were designed and decorated by the important New York architectural firm of Delano & Aldrich. On opening day of the Parade of Gardens, Robert Moses, Park Commissioner of the City of New York, accepted the future donation of trees and shrubs from the exhibitors at the Fair to enhance the Park that would remain after the Fair was over. The theme of the Fair, "The World of Tomorrow," was an opportunity for the exhibitors, struggling with the effects of the Great Depression, to show innovative and desirable products that gave hope for a brighter future. War in Europe, however, would overcome some of the countries with exhibition halls at the Fair and some of their workers who could not return home when the two seasons--it was open April to October-- each year of 1939 and 1940, finally ended. When it closed, at noon on October 27, a commemorative postal cover was issued proclaiming it "The Greatest Show of Your Lifetime."

Preparations on the site for the Fair had begun three years before the opening. During that time, Harold Caparn wrote several letters regarding the Fair. To Olin Downes, music critic of *The New York Times* (March 3, 1936), in support of a concert hall:

> The reference of Mr. George McAneny [president of the Fair at the time] in his address at the luncheon of the Municipal Art Society last Saturday to a World's Fair concert hall with 'the largest organ in the world' suggested to me that here, at last, might be the opportunity for really great performances of those few choral works that stand on solitary and apparently unattainable eminences. I am thinking especially of Bach's Mass in B minor and Handel's Messiah and Israel [in Egypt].

> He goes on: I was greatly intrigued by your idea of presenting every phase of notable musical art. When I admit being a classicist I really mean that I have not much interest except in the best of all types of art. Thus I

expect that the best of jazz, Stephen C. Foster and negro spirituals will become classic if they are not so already.

Downes responds (March 24, 1936) agreeing and suggesting works before and after those referred to: "I only hope there will be the slightest hope of undertaking such a really broad and representative program at the World's Fair as the one which I attempted briefly to outline. The event would then be something absolutely epochal in the history of this country."
Caparn writes back to Downes in more detail, concluding: I think your great concert hall might do much to put community or co-operative [choral] music where, in view of its importance, it belongs, side by side with that of our great orchestras.

Caparn's training and choir participation as a youth is no doubt reflected in the enthusiasm of this statement. The large concert hall was built at the Fair. The programming for the 2,500 seat hall stands outside the present study.

To George McAneny, as president of the Fair, Caparn wrote directly (May 7, 1936) to protest the concept that had been put forward (*New York Herald Tribune*, May 5) of holding the Fair in "One Big Building."

He says: Instead of being 'new,' it is the oldest of all, that of the Crystal Palace Exhibition of 1851 [in Hyde Park, London]. It is the principle of the museum, excepting that a museum contains exhibits of related things, while a modern Fair is likely to be made up of the products of art, science, and industry to say nothing of things that would hardly come under any of these. The separate buildings of a Fair make possible that scenic interest and variety do much to make the attraction of the whole. I would think that these intervals in the open air are very valuable to the visitor in giving a rest from the contemplation of one subject and a period of mental adjustment to the next.

The debate raged briefly, but industries, interests and countries eventually each had their own buildings. Caparn was satisfied with the interval from building to building; he felt it would give the visitor opportunity for rest and time for adjustment.

One of the respites, for the over 45 million visitors that walked the grounds of the Fair, was the horticultural display of Gardens on Parade, located in the Government Zone across the Lagoon of Nations from the Town of Tomorrow. The Gardens occupied five and one-half acres, divided by architect William A. Delano into twenty-five gardens. The central circle in the plan, 19.1, was the garden dedicated to the memory of the president of the New York Horticultural Society, a sponsoring organization. The gardens in the Parade ranged from

Formal to Informal, from an Old New England to French and English gardens, and through gardens of Yesterday, Today and Tomorrow.

One garden included 125 varieties of irises from the Brooklyn Botanic Garden collection, a site designed by Caparn, that included intermediate bearded iries, bred by his cousin, iris propagator William John Caparne, of the isle of Guernsey. The Herb and Knot Gardens, presented by the Brooklyn Botanic Garden, were on old English designs interpreted at that Garden by Caparn. The Jackson & Perkins Company presented an International Rose Garden of about 8,000 plants in 250 varieties from 18 different countries consisting particularly of Climbing, Polyantha, Floribunda and Hybrid Tea roses; as they said: "Greatest emphasis has been placed on demonstration plantings of the new Floribunda group and the more recent introductions in the Hybrid Tea class." The garden drew much attention and admiration from rose lovers.

Beside the contributions to the gardens by the exhibitors, the Parade of Gardens was the work of the Garden Club of America and Federated Garden Clubs from twenty-five states and Bermuda. Member organizations built several of the gardens. They also provided a regular schedule of exhibits of flower arrangements and extensive educational exhibits in the adjoining Exhibition Hall and Exhibition Arcade. Sponsoring organizations included The Horticultural Society of New York, the New York Florists Club, the Society of American Florists, The New York Botanical Garden, and the Brooklyn Botanic Garden.

Contributions of plant material and other assistance came from many other organizations and estate owners and their gardeners, especially William R. Coe of "Planting Fields," Oyster Bay, Long Island and his superintendent W. G. Carter; Andrew Fullerton, of the Nemour Estate, Wilmington, Delaware; Garden in the Woods, of South Sudbury, Massachusetts; Mrs. Harold Irving Pratt of "Wilwyn," Glen Cove, Long Island; H. McK. Twombly of "Florham," Convent Station, New Jersey and his superintendent Robert Tyson, among others.

The Parade of Gardens was operated by Hortus, Inc., a non-profit organization of which Mrs. Harold Irving Pratt, herself a gardener of note with a large estate, was president. A. M. Dauernheim was executive vice-president and general manager, and Dr. C. Stuart Gager, director of the Brooklyn Botanic Garden, was a vice-president. As Dauernheim acknowledged in commending the contributors, "Gardens on Parade was the outstanding horticultural display of the century."

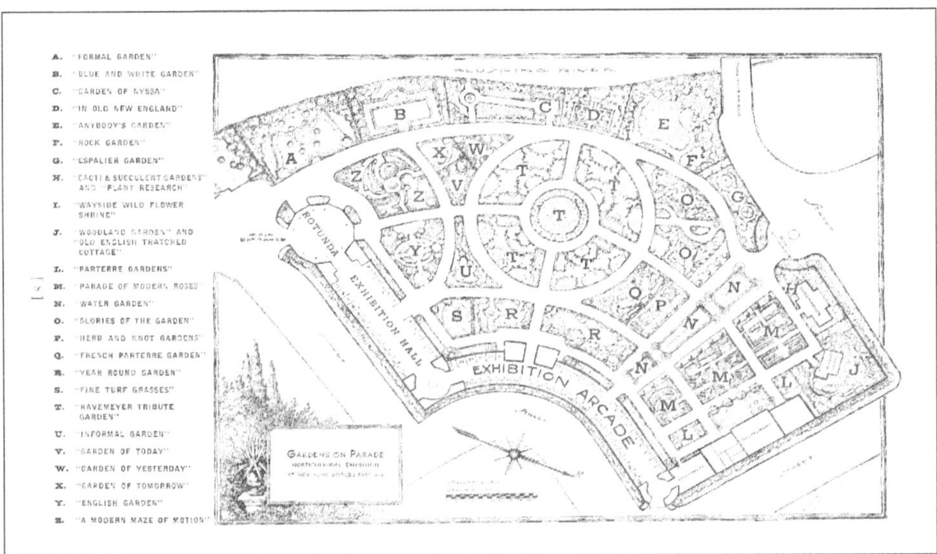

19.1 Layout of Gardens on Parade.

The Woodland Garden, designed by Harold A. Caparn, was located in the northwest corner of the Gardens, at "J" in 19.1. Next to it to the west, at "H", was the Lord and Burnham greenhouse with a Plant Research exhibit by the Department of Floriculture and Ornamental Horticulture at Cornell University, sponsored by the New York Florists Club. On the other side, to the east was the restaurant for the area, before which were formed, at "L", two Parterre Gardens. They were designed by graduates of the Lowthorpe School of Landscape Architecture, Groton, Massachusetts, in honor of the school and the Horticultural Society of New York. The plant material was donated by Mrs. Harold Irving Pratt. At "M", was the extensive rose display of Jackson and Perkins.

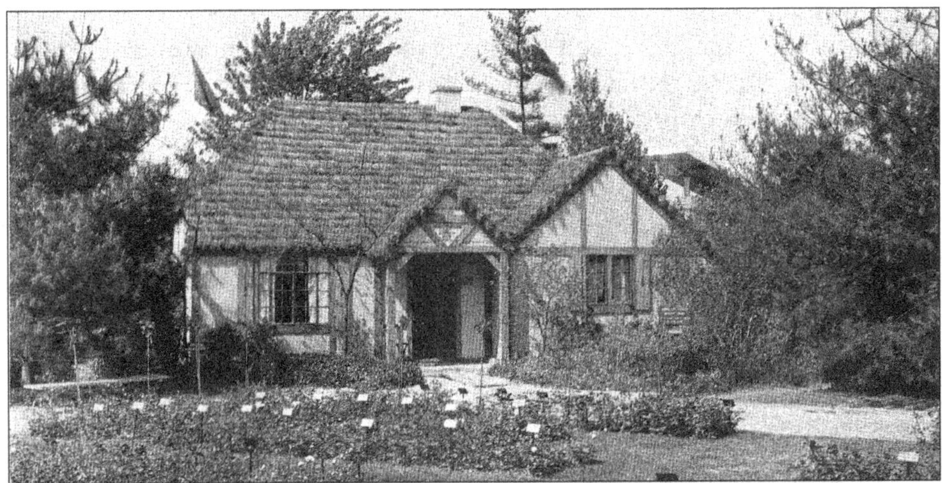

19.2 Harold Caparn landscape, setting for the Thatched Cottage in the Woodland Garden. Rose display in foreground is by Jackson and Perkins.

Thus framed at a corner of the Gardens, the Woodland Garden comprised one-sixth of an acre, or a little more than 6,500 square feet. The location allowed it to be enclosed at the outside by white pines, red cedars, hemlocks and white birches, giving it a peaceful, contemplative aspect, set off from the rest of the Fair. At the front center of the Woodland Garden was a thatched cottage similar to those found in villages in England. It was constructed by the Old English Thatch Company of Stamford, Connecticut. It was a focal point used for meetings of the Garden Clubs.

The Woodland Garden as an exhibit was presented by the Garden Clubs of America on Long Island, particularly those of the North Country, East Hampton, Southampton, Suffolk, Lawrence and the South Side Garden Clubs. Most of the plant material came from Long Island. Beside his connection to a Parade of Gardens sponsor, as consulting landscape architect at the Brooklyn Botanic Garden, Caparn had also designed several estates on Long Island. He was the senior landscape architect whose design was seen at the Parade of Gardens. The Woodland Garden was a gem of his later years.

The description of the Woodland Garden in the horticulture exhibition souvenir book states: "Foliage of the strongly contrasted forms, textures and greens of pines, cedars, rhododendrons, mountain laurel, andromedas, leucothoe, azaleas, clethra, hawthorne, dogwoods, red maple, a wild apple tree, viburnums and ferns accentuate this beautiful setting. The leafage of deciduous shrubs and trees provide for varied natural colors in the changing seasons. A small stream winds through the garden, fringed with marsh marigold, trillium, jack-in-the-pulpit, violets, lobelias and baneberry."

Planting of the brook and spring was done by Marcel LePiniec and his assistant James Aitcheson. LePiniec was a nurseryman, horticulturist and rock garden expert after whom several species and a prize have more recently been named. A path wound through the trees next to the brook. The Woodland Garden, with the brook and spring that were made to mechanically recycle from waters provided by the nearby river to a holding tank, may be seen as a further refinement of Caparn's Wild Garden at Onteora Park of seventeen years earlier.

Several newspaper articles further described the Woodland Garden. C. F. Greeves-Carpenter writing in *The New York Times* (July 30, 1939), said: One of the most original and intriguing gardens is that surrounding the old English thatched cottage. This planting, designed by Harold A. Caparn and Marcel LePiniec, differs from all the other exhibits, as White Pines and Red Cedars have been arranged so cleverly as to enclose the garden without giving the appearance of forming a hedge or fence.

Interspersed with the pines and cedars are a number of dogwoods, Scarlet Maples, rhododendrons and Mountain Laurel as well as a large variety of berry-bearing plants and innumerable native perennials. Through this planting a winding brook meanders in such a natural manner as to create the impression that the woodland, like Topsy, "jist growed" there.

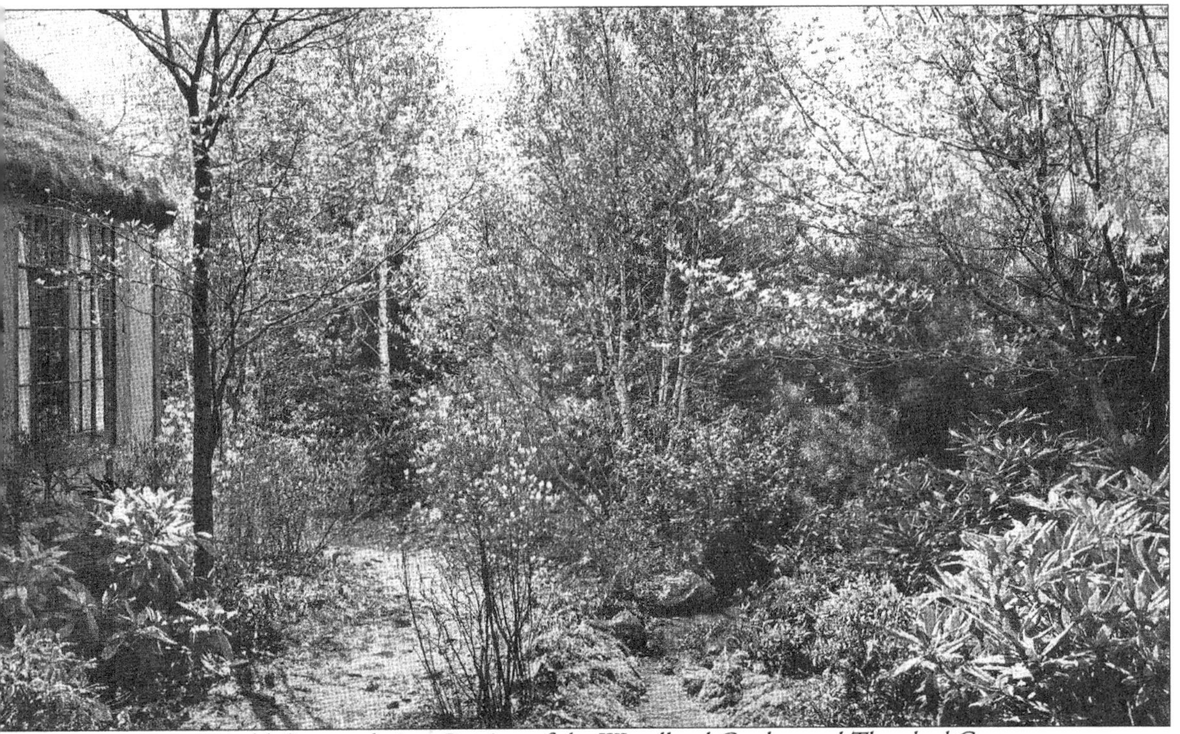

19.3 Harold Caparn design. Portion of the Woodland Garden and Thatched Cottage.

The water for the exhibit emanates from an underground tank from which it is pumped to the "source" of the stream: an artificial "sand spring" which flows over to form the brook. The water, disappearing at the front of the cottage, is returned to the tank. Thus a continuously flowing brook is simulated.

The bed of the stream is of well-packed clay to keep the water from seeping through and covered, of course, with soil in which at intervals protruding bedded stones vary the width of the stream and create an impression of a water-worn channel. Aquatic plants, especially watercress, further help to substantiate the desired illusion of an age-old brook. The walk alongside, covered with pine needles and having no definite boundary lines, further heightens the effectiveness of this naturalistic woodland miniature.

Caparn's naturalistic and informal approach to garden design were well evident. Alice L. Dustan, later author of *Landscaping Your Own Home* (1955), writing in *The New York Times* (May 26, 1940), provides a full and poetic rendering under the heading "A Restful Woodland Garden Created for the World's Fair." Her very complete description is worth quoting quite fully.

> A Spring morning following a gentle rain is one of the pleasantest times to visit the Woodland Garden at Gardens on Parade at the New York World's Fair. The voluble refrain of a song sparrow and the softer undertone of the brook winding beneath hemlocks and birches make traffic noises on the near-by highway seem remote and inconsequential. Smell of moist earth, glow of petals opening in patchy sunlight, green freshness of unfurling leaves, all add their spell in transferring the visitor's thoughts from the wonders of the World of Tomorrow to the restfulness of a small piece of natural beauty.

> On first approach, the Woodland Garden is seen as a charming setting for the "Old English Thatched Cottage," headquarters for garden club members. Background trees of sufficient height and density have been chosen so they entirely close out view of the road beyond and give scale to the little bungalow which nestles below them. Gardeners who have the idea that grass is the only suitable ground-cover foreground to a house will be pleasantly surprised by the door-yard planting of the Thatched Cottage. A large bed of blue violets makes a uniform flower-bedecked carpet to the left of the walk. On the other side, where the public path turns and gives more space, two types of blueberry have been used, Low-bush (Vaccinium pennsylvanicum) as a ground cover and Highbush as a medium-sized shrub. Another worthwhile woody plant of two to two-and-a-half foot height, which could be more often used as a ground cover, is Yellow-root (Zanthorhiza apiifolia). Flourishing here in a sunny spot, it is also valuable for shady locations where it will form a light growth with brownish purple flowers.

> Other native shrubs which have been nicely incorporated into the cottage's foundation planting are Sweetfern (Comptonia asplenifolia) and Bayberry, both of which flourish in sunny places with light soils. Bayberry makes a dense rounded growth somewhat resembling boxwood, and bearing waxy gray berries in the Fall. Though not evergreen, it holds its leaves late in Autumn. A few sumacs give height and Fall color to the planting. A shapely native hawthorn accents the door and gray birches are used against the house corner.

> A small brook provides the theme for the garden as it flows smoothly past a miniature meadow, widens out into a pool beneath an over-arching

shadbush, or veers around a boulder. The path, which often skirts the brook, affords an opportunity to see at close range the golden-cupped marsh marigold, white woods violets, porcelain-blue Houstonia flowers and the nodding bellworts. Later in the season color along the brook will be picked up by various gentians, lobelias, rhododendrons and the fragrant sweet pepperbush (Clethra alnifolia).

All man-made, including the brook, which is supplied by an automatic pump, the woodland garden has the ring of true naturalness. Harold Caparn of New York, landscape architect who designed the garden, and Marcel LePiniec of Bergenfield, New Jersey, who supervised the choice and planting of the perennials, ground covers and ferns, have not imitated an actual piece of woodland. Rather, they have simulated some of nature's most attractive details even to the well-worn rocks in the streambed.

In the scant sunlight and thick mat of needles beneath White Pines few plants flourish naturally. Only an occasional fern or flowering plant, such as ladyslipper, Bunchberry and Partridgeberry really enjoys such a situation. So the designers of the Woodland Garden have wisely left sparsely planted the area beneath the large White Pine to one side of the cottage.

Planting has been kept low in the Gray Birch "meadows" to create a feeling of spaciousness, even through the thickly planted background is only a few feet distant. The blue and white underplanting of Virginia Bluebell and Poets' Narcissus in early Spring is later replaced by drifts of Blue Phlox and trilliums, with unfurling fern fronds. In another corner of the garden a low group of rhododendrons has been planted beside the brook so that one can look over it into a lush marshy spot where a corky-branched Sweet Gum shelters ferns, meadowrues and snakeroots.

Architectural notes of interest are a mellow-toned wooden bench and foot bridges across the stream. A little two-foot lead figure of St. Francis serves the useful purpose of a bird feeder. It contains an inner seed-compartment and gravity-feed tray at the foot of the figure. Designed by E. H. Low, the statue is part of an exhibit of garden sculpture on view in Gardens on Parade. Birds which have been attracted to the garden include songsparrows, robins, catbirds, warblers and other Spring transients.

The element of surprise is a factor which has been employed to good advantage in the Woodland Garden. Rounding a bend, one may come on the pleasing combination of pink Azalea nudiflora and low blue Iris cristata and Jacob's Ladder. Or it may be the gray-green of White Pine, with bold rhododendron foliage, below which are a crowd of umbrella Mayapples and several different species of trillium, including the white crimson-marked Painted Trillium. Not all the plants included, it will be noted, are native to this section of the State. The Crested Iris is indigenous in Maryland, south to Georgia, and Painted Trillium likes the cooler atmosphere of mountain sections. But all plants used are of the informal shade-loving type which fit into a woodland setting.

Dustan's article, a contemporary description by a knowledgeable observer, clearly shows what Caparn had stated in various of his own articles: that curves in paths and roads provided pleasing and unexpected views to the attentive and that the natural, informal approach to making a garden was a delight both to the eye and mind. Caparn's vision for this garden led to many delights among the garden clubs who found it a pleasant setting for their meetings in the thatched cottage and the visitors and critics who reported on the beautiful Woodland Garden.

Postlude

Harold Caparn, over his career in Pittsburgh (1890-97), Yonkers (1898-1902) and Manhattan (1902-45), made contributions to the ongoing development of landscape architecture in three principal areas:

As a designer and writer about botanic gardens. His botanic garden plan for the central quad of Lebanon Valley College can be seen in the college Library. The Brooklyn Botanic Garden continues as a major public entity for display, education and research on plant life.

As a designer and writer about parks. Several of his city parks continue to provide public enjoyment. His writing and public support furthered the development of state parks. He had influence on the design and scope of several national parks.

As a teacher and writer about landscape architecture. His writing and teaching on the informal style of design influenced amateur and professional alike. What he taught of that approach to design had gone through the filter of this own considerable thought and applied experience. He continually shared his knowledge and insights through advice sought and consultations given, in his many published letters and articles, his presentations at public and professional meetings and in his teaching on the informal style in the first course offered on landscape architecture by Columbia University.

Caparn's article, on the founding of the American Society of Landscape Architects in 1899, preserved the essential documents and gave the growing organization a clear view of its roots. He was elected an early Fellow in 1905 by the founding charter members. He was named an editor of the first ASLA *Transactions* (1899-1908) together with James Sturgis Pray, chair of the department at Harvard University and Downing Vaux, son of one of the designers of Central Park and a founding member. Charles Downing Lay, landscape architect for the City of New York, noted that Caparn served the ASLA as a Regional Trustee in 1907-1908.

In ASLA *Transactions* II (1909-1921/22), we see him recorded as an active participant on the Board of Trustees (1909-1919), as Treasurer (1909-1912), President (1911-1912), Vice-President (1915-1919); member of committees on Education (1912-13), Professional Practice and Ethics (1915-1917), Publicity (1915-1919 and 1921-1923) and Exhibitions (1920-21). Caparn was elected president of the ASLA New York Chapter during 1920-1923, in order to extend his campaign in support of New York's city parks and particularly Central Park. From

1929, he chaired both the Policies and the Frederick Law Olmsted Memorial Committees. In each position in the Society he worked toward advancing the greater good for the profession and the public face of the organization. His membership and service in the ASLA spanned more than thirty-five years.

He used his membership in the organizations to which he belonged to further his goals of supporting, expanding, beautifying and bringing to public attention large and small parks, those which existed and those that would come into being with help from his writing and influence. He held membership in the New York City Club and on its parks committee, the City Gardens Club where he was vice president and chair of its parks committee. As a member of the Municipal Art Society, he participated in exhibitions and helped make determinations about the placement of public art. With other members of the Municipal Art Society he tramped the snowed grounds of Palisades Interstate Park to help determine how that Park could best be preserved and used. He had a wide and active role in promoting city and state parks.

He was a member of the Architectural League of New York City at the same time as Joseph H. Freedlander, also a Beaux-Arts graduate. For Leon Gillette, a fellow Beaux-Arts graduate and designer of an estate at Tuxedo Park, he provided a design consultation. Caparn, drawing on his architectural training at the Ecole des Beaux-Arts, early in his New York career wrote several articles critiquing the new architectural designs of early sky-scrapers. In 1907, he served on the Architectural League's Committee on Annual Exhibition in the Sub-Committee on Architecture with Freedlander, whose office was up Fifth Avenue from Caparn's own (Nos. 156 & 244).

At the same time, his colleague Charles Wellford Leavitt, Jr., was Secretary of the ASLA Exhibition Committee, his friend, the artist John White Alexander, was chairman of the Sub-Committee on Decoration and sculptor Isidore Konti, creator of the memorial at the edge of Caparn-designed Washington Park in Yonkers, was on the Sub-Committee on Sculpture. Caparn's interests, acquaintances and influence extended beyond his professional work on landscapes.

In the nation's capital, on December 12, 1912, Harold Caparn was the featured speaker on "The Relation of Landscape to Architecture" at the concluding banquet of the annual convention of the American Institute of Architects. With his training and writing on architecture and his professional work and standing in the field of landscape architecture, he was the ideal person to discuss such relationships to a significant meeting of professional artists.

He was a charter member of the American Civic Association when it was organized in the merger of 1904 with the American League for Civic Improvement. On November 16, 1909, for a meeting of the American Civic Association, he gave a talk on "Waterfronts" in Cincinnati, Ohio. He had reference to his proposal for a great water park in Jamaica Bay and his article on that subject in 1907. He was noted in 1911 as state park chairman for New York of the American Civic Association, a step on the way to his influential writings on the development of state parks. His two articles and a talk, "State Parks" (1921), were published by *The National Municipal Review.* The three pieces were considered of sufficient import that they were printed separately as a pamphlet by suggestion of the American Civic Association. In the initial issue in 1929 of the *American Civic Annual* he authored an article on safeguarding Central Park. He was a member of the Civic Association Board and Advisory Council, including the 1935 merger when the National Conference on City Planning joined with the Civic Association to become the American Planning and Civic Association. His service to this evolving organization spanned forty years.

Through his writing, talks and work with such organizations, his public image was often as a leader in **saving the built environment**—Central Park from commercialization and mismanagement and its trees from destruction by tunneling for a subway. As **preserving the natural environment**—Niagara Falls and the Canadian Falls when commercial water diversion could damage them, and Palisades Interstate Park when quarrying could forever reduce them to rubble. As **creating new liveable environments**—Village 1 is a distinctive design to comfortably house federal workers. The Bronx Zoo is an oasis for both animals and people. Cayuga Heights, with a welcoming entrance, has well-placed lots and gracious curving tree-lined streets. It was described as an elite, desireable residential addition to the city of Ithaca.

The author of his obituary for the American Planning and Civic Association called him a "gentle, gracious man." He stood five feet ten inches tall, of lean build, with brown hair and blue eyes. A well-traveled Englishman, his demeanor was reserved, direct and respectful of all whom he met. His friends and colleagues regularly sought him out for his valued advice. He held truth and beauty in highest regard in his personal and professional work. As he said, "a garden is not beautiful unless it is also useful, meaning true to its purpose, and not useful unless it is beautiful, therefore providing pleasure and reposeful access to the viewer."

Harold ap Rhys Caparn died on Monday, September 24, 1945, at age 80 years and 9 months, two months after retiring as consulting landscape architect for the Brooklyn Botanic Garden. His obituary appeared the next day in *The New York Times.* Some of the esteem in which he was held and the level of his public image may be seen in the *Times,* which devoted ten column inches and a photograph of him at the top of that page.

H. A. CAPARN DEAD; LANDSCAPE EXPERT

Consultant to Botanic Garden, Brooklyn, 1912-45, Designed Many of Its Features

Harold ap Rhys Caparn, consulting landscape architect to the Brooklyn Botanic Gardens from 1932 until early this year, died yesterday in the Manhattan General Hospital after a brief illness. He resided at 230 West Fifty-ninth Street and had an office at 144 East Thirtieth Street. His age was 81.

Born in Newark-on-Trent, England, of Welsh and English descent, he was a master at the Cathedral School, Canterbury, and then studied at the Ecole des Beaux Arts, Paris, before coming to New York more than forty-five years ago.

His work with the Brooklyn Botanic Garden began in January, 1912, when the Garden was in its preliminary stages. The design of the walks had been done by Olmsted brothers, but from then on nearly all of the Garden's features, including the Rose Garden, the Water Gardens, the Horticultural Sections and the Systematic Section, with its plant families in botanical sequence, were designed by Mr. Caparn.

He was also the designer of the campus of Brooklyn College, and did landscape work for the New York Zoological Park in the Bronx, the House Office Building in Washington, D. C., and Lincoln Park in Newark, N. J.

Mr. Caparn designed many gardens on private estates in Long Island, Westchester County and Connecticut. One of his best pieces of work was done at Tannersville, N. Y., for Mrs. Ben Ali Haggin.

He was long a crusader against encroachments on Central Park and other parks in the city. Mr. Caparn protested against proposed exhibits of sculpture in Central Park, denounced suggestions of swimming pools, a wading pool, a stadium and other features as a memorial to the dead of the first World War and opposed ripping up a border of the park for subway construction. Parks, he maintained, were things of beauty and not playgrounds or places for commercial activities.

Mr. Caparn was a former president of the New York Chapter of the American Society of Landscape Architects, had been vice president of the City Gardens Club and chairman of its committee on parks and was a member of the Architectural League of New York. He had served on the City Club's park committee.

At one time he taught landscape architecture at Columbia University.

He leaves a widow, Mrs. Clara Jones Caparn; two daughters, Mrs. Johannes Steel of New York, wife of the radio commentator and writer, and Mrs. Robert M. Moore Jr. of New York; a brother, Arthur Caparn, and a sister, Mrs. Annie Shackleton of Short Hills, N. J., and two granddaughters.

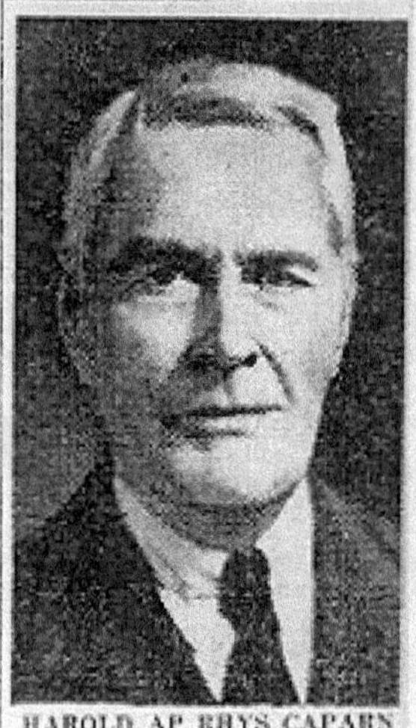

20.1 The New York Times, Tues., September 25, 1945 Obituary of Harold ap Rhys Caparn
Photo: Blank & Stolier Studio, New York, 1941

Correction:

Harold ap Rhys Caparn, former President of the ASLA, consulting landscape architect to the Brooklyn Botanic Garden from January 1912, where he designed architectural features and notable gardens for over 32 years until his retirement in July of this year, died yesterday in Manhattan General Hospital after a brief illness. His age was 80 years, 9 months.

The New York Herald Tribune also ran his obituary, adding information to the one in the *Times*. It states that it was he, as a member of the parks committee of the City Club in 1931, who suggested the development of Jacob Riis Park in the Rockaways on Long Island, now part of the Gateway National Recreation Area. Jamaica Bay, its islands and environs, of which that shore of Long Island is a part, was an area in which Caparn long had an interest, beginning with a talk on it in 1906. Caparn's talk, writing and support may have saved the area from commercial development for wharves and shipping, which plan was on the minds of local politicians.

This obituary also mentions his work at the Brooklyn Botanic Garden, especially his design of the compass on the floor of the Laboratory [Administration] Plaza, composed of different color stones brought from all parts of the world. It notes that the center of the Plaza is set off by a compass with a sundial [armillary sphere] with design both by Harold and his sculptor daughter Rhys, on a black marble pedestal. It acknowledges as well his design of the fountain [funded by Albert Jenkins] between the lily pools. A porcelain plate made by Wedgwood in 1955 commemorates The Lily Pool, a gift of Alfred Treadway White, and identifies the landscape designer in 1919 as Harold A. Caparn.

Charles Downing Lay, whose office of landscape architecture (1902-1948) in New York City paralleled Caparn's in time, and who, as editor and publisher of *Landscape Architecture,* had published Caparn's articles, wrote a necrology for the American Society of Landscape Architects, saying of Caparn: "In all his associations as in his writings and many activities, he was distinguished by his probity. He expressed his ideas well and always with firmness and conviction, which was the result of his belief in the artistic and social value of the profession he had chosen."

Harlean James, Executive Secretary of the American Planning and Civic Association, said, "Our policies were frequently formed in the light of his advice. He has left a mark upon land planning in this country."

Horace Albright, President of the American Planning and Civic Association, said, "He was not only an extremely able landscape artist but was a man of broad interests, not only in his professional field but in the entire range of conservation and urban redevelopment. His great talents added to his high public spirit and unselfish devotion to enterprises benefitting our nation and its citizens."

Appendices

Endnotes

1.1 = chapter number 1, endnote number 1

1.1 Guy Hemingway, *The Caparn Family of Newark & Some of Their Descendants*, 1979, typescript, Newark Library, Newark on Trent, Nottinghamshire, U.K., 54: "born Sunday December 18th, 1864, 9-10 p.m. at Newark on Trent, Notts. HAROLD AP-PRECE CAPARN, son of the above Thomas John and Anne Elizabeth Caparn. Birth registered on January 17th, 1865. Baptised July 11, 1865 at St. Mary's Church, Newark, [Church of St. Mary Magdalene] by The Rev. Robert F. Wheeler, Incumbent of Cullersgate, Northants." [Northamptonshire] The Rev. Wheeler, a cousin of Ann Elizabeth, was later to become Dean of Durham Cathedral.

1.2 Harold's middle name was variously spelled Ap-Prece (family bible), Apreece (1871 Newark Census, 1886 University of London certificate) and ap Rhys (American naturalization papers). The patronymic "ap Rhys" became in English, "ap Price" (ap Preece), eventually, just Price as a surname. Harold's family used "ap Rhys" to signify "son of Price," his mother's paternal lineage. His mother's maternal relation to George Villiers, first Duke of Buckingham, is stated in a nineteenth-century inventory of Ann Elizabeth Price's family furniture, art works and other belongings. Since he signed his U.S. naturalization papers in 1900 as "Harold ap Rhys Caparn," this form of his name, in his own hand, is taken as authoritative.

1.3 N. G. Jackson, *Newark Magnus – The Story of a Gift* (Nottingham: J. and H. Bell Ltd., 1964), passim. The book details the history of the gift in 1530/31 by Thomas Magnus, priest, supporter and ambassador of Henry VIII, the purposes of which were (1) the establishment and endowment of a free grammar school, (2) the provision and endowment of a song (choir) school to ensure the maintenance of a high standard of worship in the parish church, (3) a sufficient sum to guarantee efficient administration of the bequest, and (4) occasional sums to be used for the general well-being of the church or town.

1.4 Robin A. Fenner, *A Genius Undeclared--William John Caparne F.R.H.S.* (Tavistock, Devon: Stannery Gallery, 1994), (hereafter Fenner 1-*Genius*) "The Family Caparn," 19-23, 26. Harold's cousin William John was at Magnus Grammar School from 1865 to 1874; he studied art at the École des Beaux-Arts in Paris in 1875, transferring to the Académie Julian in 1876. Positing Harold for a similar period of schooling, he would have attended Magnus Grammar School from the fall of 1873 through the spring of 1882, that is, from age 9 to 18.

1.5 N. G. Jackson, op. cit., 161. Wm. H. Caparn, Jr. is referred to as "Choragus," i.e., leader of a choir or choral performance. Hemingway, op. cit., 49, re Caparn as conductor of the Musical Society; the *Newark Advertiser* of February 17, 1864, advertised his concert "when a portion of the [G. F. Handel] Messiah recently performed with such success will be repeated." Hemingway, *The Caparn Family*, 50: "William Horner Caparn Jr. no doubt found his nephew Harold a good match with an eager mind and was happy to supply lessons in piano and organ in easy exchange for his father's mentoring his son William in horticulture and art." Fenner 1-Genius, 25:

"The Fussell brothers (artists) were friends and visitors to the home of the Caparn family, renowned locally for their musical entertainment evenings."

1.6 Robin A. Fenner, *Guernsey—My Heaven on Earth, William John Caparne F.R.H.S.* (Tavistock, Devon: Stannery Gallery, 1998), (hereafter Fenner II-Guernsey) "Furthering the History of the Family Caparn," 22: "The two brothers, William Horner, Jr. and Thomas John and their families were close, providing help in gardening and music for each other and for their children." A similar approach by Thomas John Caparn in providing instruction for his son, Harold, outside of his work at the Magnus School, seems most likely in the areas of art and horticulture. William John Caparne may have added the "e" to his last name to differentiate himself as an artist from his uncle, also an artist. Caparne painted many flower and marine works and propagated irises. See the website dedicated to him for more on his art and horticulture.

1.7 Robert Beverly Hale. *Rhys Caparn.* (Danbury, CT: Retrospective Press, 1972), 1, Harold's daughter Rhys mentions Darwin and Locke; a set of the works of Dickens come from Thomas John Caparn. Collection of the author.

1.8 Rhys Caparn Steel, *Biographical Data Sheets*, Council of Fellows, ASLA, July 8, 1977 (hereafter Rhys *Data Sheets*). She mentions Canterbury School, without making clear whether that was the name of the school, or rather, that she is referring to St. Edmund's School, the choir school for boys, connected with Canterbury Cathedral. The latter is presumed based on the author's communication with an incumbent of the Choir School position at St. Mary Magdalene, himself a former student at St. Edmund's School. Being a tutor at St. Edmund's School and singing in the Canterbury Cathedral Choir would only have been possible for a good scholar who had been trained in a foundation (i.e., endowed) song school, such as that at St. Mary Magdalene. That training would have included reading music, writing music, music theory, vocal technique for good singing and knowledge of the repertoire needed to perform for a regular full schedule of Church of England services, such as sung portions of the Eucharist (Mass), Evensong, Compline and occasional services such as burials, installations, and festivals as well as psalms, canticles, hymns and anthems in regular use.

1.9 The certificate may mean only that he was accepted and enrolled; it does not necessarily mean that he took a degree. After graduation from the Magnus Grammar School his position at St. Edmund's School accounts for the interval of about four years before applying to University. Caparn archive.

1.10 Several sources, including Rhys *Data Sheets*, state that he studied at the Ecole des Beaux-Arts. None give dates. The author poses the dates of Caparn's study at the Ecole as about 1887-1889; he could also have continued his studies during summers. *Country Life in America* (1920), 49, gives also that he studied architecture at Columbia University and in Buray's Atelier in Paris. See his 1905 article, "A Visit to Paris," on the gardens in Paris.

1.11 Caparn's application for a replacement naturalization paper states: "My certificate of naturalization was issued to me at New York on Sep (very faint) 1890." The same naturalization document states that he arrived in the United States on September 23, 1889. The photograph of Caparn was by the D'Ana Studio, New York, also used by other members of his family. It confirms his arrival, relative age and likely interaction with his family in Short Hills, New Jersey.

1.12 Hemingway, *The Caparn Family of Newark*, 1-3. Guy Hemingway, *Caparn Entries in the Newark Parish Church Register*, typescript, Newark Library, nd., 1-7. From 1613 when Daniel Capon (b. 1584) was married through 1759 when Ann Capon was baptized, the name was spelled variously Capon, Caperne, Capporne, Capperne, Caper, Capern, Caporne, Capron, Capren, Caporn, Capurn, Capane, Caperon, Cappern. From a 1763 entry on May 5, for the baptism of John Caparn, son of William and Ann, through the 19th century the spelling becomes regularly Caparn. [modern pronunciation: Capárn--kuh-parn (vowel sounds like barn)]

1.13 Hemingway, op. cit., 35. Fenner I – *Genius*, 20: "By 1860, the firm of W. H. Caparn and Son, Nurserymen and Seedsmen, had become one of the major horticultural firms in the Midlands, their King's Road Nurseries covering an area of some nineteen acres. The firm's order books record requirements from all over the country and seeds were to be supplied to the titled gentry in various parts of Great Britain." Re Auditor, Actuary and Bank Secretary: Fenner 1-Genius, 20; later dates: *Accounts and Papers of the House of Commons*, 1865, Newark upon Trent Savings Bank, shows William Horner Caparn as Secretary and Thomas John Caparn as Actuary. The same records show Officers of Savings Banks for 1877, giving Thomas John Caparn as Secretary.

1.14 A sketchbook belonging to Thomas John Caparn, contains the date, 1853, on a sketch, signed when Thomas was age nineteen or twenty. Thomas would have been age 21 when his nephew William was born (Nov. 8, 1855) and age 30 when his son Harold was born (Dec. 18, 1864). Thomas owned his own nursery and was supporting himself at age 20; he was therefore a mature young man when he later began mentoring his nephew and his son in horticulture and in art.

1.15 Family bible gives information on the marriage of Ann Elizabeth and Thomas John Caparn and the births of another son, Arthur Tom (m. Emily Aurelie Charon), and three daughters, Margaret Jane (Caparn) English (m. Dr. David Eugene English), Annie Smith (Caparn) Shackleton (m. photographer James Shackleton) and Ethel Rose Caroline (Caparn) Hall (m. John Edward Hall). A genealogy, by Kathleen Caparn, begun in 1924, gives the marriages.

1.16 Hemingway, op. cit., 55, cited from advertisement in the *Newark Advertiser* of January 20, 1864.

1.17 Ibid., 56. Garden design prize also mentioned in the *Newark Advertiser* in November 1869.

1.18 Hemingway, op. cit., 57 - 58. Fenner 1-Genius, 21-22. Fenner II-Guernsey, 22. He is noted as having continued his former nursery business while opening the new business in accountancy and liquidation. Opening this office and his later move to America may have been influenced by a downturn in British agricultural investments from those based on land toward those based on machines. Products, production, transport, financing and labor followed this trend during the last quarter of the nineteenth century. On his move to America: Fenner 1-*Genius*, 22; Fenner 11-*Guernsey*, 22. Any question of why he moved in Fenner 1 was dispelled in Fenner 11. A 1906 map at the Millburn-Short Hills Historical Society Museum in New Jersey identifies property of about nine acres on White Oak Ridge Road in Short Hills as belonging to T. J. Caparn.

1.19 Advertisement in *The Budget*, June 16, 1886, p. 5; held by the Millburn Free Public Library, in the Millburn Township Historical Archives.

1.20 Envelopes with imprinted return address, postmarked 1899 through 1903. Collection of the author.

1.21 Short Hills, New Jersey, *The Item*, June 25, 1925.

1.22 Caparn was not recorded in Pittsburgh in 1890. Elliott says in his book *Adventures of a Horticulturist* (self-published, 1935), 95, "a young architect, a Beaux-Arts man, came to Pittsburg, and his first work was for a Standard Oil man." Elliott talks about that event as of fifty years ago, i.e., 1885, which is most likely a "rounding" of his memory of the time and date. While Elliott would have valued Caparn's education at L'Ecole des Beaux-Arts, the date given is earlier than his confirmed arrival in the US in 1889. Mention of it in his book, however, shows Elliott perhaps later claiming credit for hiring Caparn as a young man while knowing of Caparn's later professional accomplishments.

1.23 Rhys Caparn's ASLA data sheets (1977) state "1894-99 worked in office and field for J. Wilkinson Elliott of Pittsburgh." C. D. Lay's necrology *in Landscape Architecture* (1945) states 1894-99, probably following Rhys for this information, which seems a "rounding" of dates/duration of information not known first hand. Caparn, however, signs "Composition in Landscape-art," his first article in *Garden and Forest*, as from Pittsburgh in 1893. It seems unlikely that Caparn would have published such a bold article in the first year or two of his first employment in his new country. The same and other issues of *Garden and Forest* carry advertisements by J. Wilkinson Elliott that show him as a nurseryman; they also give him as a "landscape architect." Elliott preferred the title "landscape gardener," admitting that he was not a draughtsman. The latter role was likely filled at the Elliott Nursery by Caparn. Caparn's letter to the editor of *Garden and Forest* in 1896 and his other articles in that journal, further attest to his residence in Pittsburgh and his confidence in publishing in a respected journal.

1.24 During the time Caparn worked for him, J. Wilkinson Elliott gave a lecture for the Massachusetts Horticultural Society. The talk, "A Plea for Hardy plants," is found in the 1895 *Transactions of the Society*. The talk was influenced by his father's earlier discussion of the same topic.

1.25 Elliott's book *A Plea for Hardy Plants,* is an expansion of his talk to the Society. It was published in 1902 by Doubleday, Page & Co. New York. Caparn's plan, published in 1902, can be seen here on p.12, illustration 1.5.

4.1 G(eorge) A(rthur) Yarwood, FASLA, appended a note to a copy of Lay's necrology: "report on Prof. Practice and Charges, Caparn, H. A., 5th Ave., NYC, writes that he has for some time past been practicing professionally; that he had training in the practice of landscape architecture received in the office of J. W. Elliott, Pittsburg and started in business for himself in 1899." As regards this date, he may have been pointing out to a colleague that his practice was newly engaged in a large work, the Bronx Zoo, in 1899. His letter to the editor of *The New York Times*, however, signed as from Yonkers in the year earlier, places him already at Yonkers. Rhys says in the *Data Sheets* (1977) that he opened his New York office in 1902, as does C. D. Lay in his necrology. These references are to New York City, i.e., Manhattan, where his office was at 156 Fifth Avenue.

4.2 Caparn is shown among James L. Greenleaf, Ferruccio Vitale, Charles Wellford Leavitt, Jr., Albert D. Taylor, Arthur R. Nichols, George E. Kessler and Frederick

Law Olmsted, Jr. with his associates in the Olmsted Brothers firm, James Frederick Dawson and Percival Gallagher.

5.1   Caparn published a letter in *The New York Times* on February 21, 1898 and signed it as from Yonkers. He shows knowledge of Samuel Parsons, requesting that he return as superintendent of Central Park. This is a foreshadowing of his concern about New York parks that he writes about in 1912 and following, towards his writing about Central Park during the 1920s.

5.2   A period map shows T. R. Almond properties in Dunwoodie Heights with frontages of 450 feet on Hayward Street, of 350 feet on Seminary Avenue and a third property of 150 by 125 feet. The Almond residence is pictured in *Yonkers Illustrated* (1902).

5.3   See online information by the New York City Department of Parks and Recreation, and others, including photographs of Inwood Hill Park as it exists.

5.4   See online information regarding the history and development of Battery Park City.

6.1   The Zoo states that it opened to the public on November 8, 1899, with 22 exhibits and 843 animals. The history of the Zoo is contained in New York Zoological Society Reports and in recent histories online.

6.2   Letters and other documents preserved in the archives of the Zoological Society (since 1993 the Wildlife Conservation Society) from November 1899 through December 1904, give a glimpse of negotiations among Caparn, Director Hornaday and the Board of Managers overseeing the work as the Zoological Park was built in its earliest stages.

6.3   Caparn had studied architecture at the Ecole des Beaux Arts prior to his work at the Zoo and was able to communicate directly with Heinz and LaFarge on design considerations.

6.4   A letter of July 28, 1902, from Hornaday to Caparn requests that he plan for the fountain. Barely less than a week later Caparn responds protesting its placement in Baird Court. Correspondence dragged on between the Zoo and the Municipal Art Society, which had to approve public art installations. Neither side appeared happy with the placement of the fountain, nor the construction of its base.

6.5   One such letter came from J. C. Willever, an officer of Western Union Telegraph Company and friend of Caparn. *New York Times*, May 1, 1904.

7.1   A watercolor of the interior of St. Stephan's Church, Millburn, NJ, by Thomas J. Caparn, hangs in the entrance to the Church. The Willever home required custom-made decorative tiles produced by the Moravian Pottery and Tile Works of Doylestown, Pennsylvania. Caparn appears in the company records as the landscape architect for the Willever estate.

7.2   Jerome B. Pound, *Memoirs of Jerome B. Pound* (self-published, printed in The United States of America, 1949), 152-53. Photograph from which the post card view was made, p. 154.

7.3   On the owners and estates see *Tuxedo Park – The Historic Houses*, ed. by Christian R. Sonne & Chiu yin Hemple, with photographs by James Bleecker (Tuxedo Park, NY: Tuxedo Historical Society, 2007). Trask house, 194-99. Scofield house, 222-225.

7.4 James Ben Ali Haggin, Sr. died in 1914. James Ben Ali Haggin Jr. had died in 1891. Lee Wood Haggin, his widow, referred to herself as Mrs. Ben Ali Haggin, but occasionally as Lee Wood Haggin. Her son, (James) Ben Ali Haggin III, was a painter and designer in New York. Her other son, Louis Lee Haggin, inherited his grandfather's horse farm near Lexington, Kentucky. Caparn did landscape design also for Louis Lee Haggin, Client List no. 593.

7.5 Charles Henry Door, "The Possibilities of Colour in the Open," *The International Studio* vol. 53 (July 1914), xviii. In part: "There stands the coloured figure of Saint Rose of Lima, in foliated ornamentation of roses and branching vines. This ornamentation makes a pattern of green, purple and rose on a background of gold. The shrine is placed in a niche of the stone wall, the entire garden being composed to afford a vista of the picture. To the right and left are climbing roses and forget-me-nots, and roses form a carpet after the manner of the foregrounds of the pictures of Fra Angelico. Saint Rose is portrayed in the garb of a Dominican nun, in the attitude of blessing the garden."

7.6 "Taming Wildmuir," by Tovah Martin, photos by Mick Hales (*Old House Journal*, June 2018) on the new approach to planting the Cloister Garden.

7.7 In 2001-02, Candace Wheeler's work in wallpaper, textiles, interior design and in these businesses and in association with Louis Comfort Tiffany, was recognized by an exhibit at the Metropolitan Museum of Art, New York City.

7.8 Information on Onteora Park is found in documents in the Onteora Library, together with the plan for the Wild Garden and the blueprint for the surrounds of the Club House and Theatre.

7.9 Frederick Augustus Dwight (1873-1958) married Elizabeth King Wakeman (1871-1921). Mary Elizabeth Davis (1875-1943) married George Monod (1865-1921) of Paris. After the deaths of their spouses, Frederick married (Mary) Elizabeth in 1922, who then gave her name as Elizabeth D[avis] Dwight. See ref. online to genealogy of Jean Monod and information by historian, Seth Kaller. Retrieved 8/19

8.1 Robert Beverly Hale, *Rhys Caparn* (Danbury, CT: Retrospective Press, 1972), 2, Rhys states the property was acquired in her birth year, 1909, but an entry in *The New York Times* gives the date as June 1911.

8.2 Ibid., 2; letter from Rhys to her father, Collection of the author.

8.3 Caparn offices:
    156 Fifth Avenue (ASLA *Transactions*, 1899-1908)
    220 West 42nd Street, (*Municipal Journal*, vol. XLV, no. 7 Aug. 17, 1918)
    18 East 41st Street (*Transactions*, 1909-1921, *NYTimes*, 1925-1926)
    285 Madison Avenue (*Transactions*, (1922-1926)
    144 East 30th Street (letters, *New York Times*, obituary))
    residences:
    208 East 39th Street, 1910
    Fernie Farm, retreat, c.1912, *NY Social Register*, 1918ff
    221 East 68th Street (*NY Social Register*, 1920)
    472 Park Place, c. 1925
    133 East 40th Street (*NY Social Blue Book*, 1930)
    20 Gramercy Park (*NY Social Register*, 1936; daughter Anne's wedding

announcement, *Social Register,* 1938)

230 West 59ᵗʰ Street (*New York Times,* obituary, 1945)

8.4   Rhys states that he immediately set about landscaping the property. Caparn's archive supplied photographs of the home with a recital-sized music studio on the upper floor as a large open space with a grand piano, and several photos of the landscaping, including that with Rhys about age 12, taken by Harold, using her to give scale to the shrubs and trees.

10.1 Correspondence and plans from 1910 through 1919 between the Olmsted Brothers firm and Caparn can be found in the archives of the Frederick Law Olmsted National Historic Site, Brookline, MA; also, Library of Congress, Olmsted Associates, Brooklyn Institute-Botanic Garden, Job File 3960, folders 1-4. On McKim Mead and White see the nomination paper on the laboratory (administration) building by the Landmarks Preservation Commission (March 13, 2007). The General Plan by the Olmsted Brothers firm is in *Landscape Architecture,* vol. V, no. 4 (July 1915), 160.

10.2 The letter of Caparn's appointment, from authority of the Trustees, for the "instruction in Architecture during the Summer Session of 1911"; a separate schedule of office and consultation hours shows him at 609 Havemeyer, and gives his area as "landscape and design"; also available, a letter to Caparn as a "Lecturer in Landscape Architecture" the appointment extending "from July 1, 1912 to June 30, 1913" by authority of the President. Caparn archive. Harold A. Caparn, "The Course in Landscape Architecture at Columbia University" *Landscape Architecture* (Jan. 1912), 59-61, identifies the instructors, describes the material, 61. The course is mentioned also in Harold A. Caparn, "Landscape Design and the Designer of Landscape," *Architectural Record* 31-5 (May 1912), 539.

10.3 *Brooklyn Botanic Garden Record,* 1-2 (April 1912), 32, gives Caparn's appointment, stating: "The appointment was made with the hearty approval of the landscape architects" [the Olmsted Brothers]. See also Harold A. Caparn, "Planting a Botanic Garden," *Landscape Architecture* 5 (July 1915), 158.

10.4 *Landscape Architecture* 5 (July 1915), 160-161. For a detailed diagram of the Systematic Section, see Harold A. Caparn, "The Planning of a Botanic Garden," *Landscape Architecture* 22 (July 1932), 261-269. (Illustration 10.21) See especially the "Additional Note," p. 269, on the changes over time to the Systematic Section to bring it "up to date" as the knowledge of botany advanced. Photographs of Brooklyn Botanic Garden plans and scenes, Caparn archive.

10.5 *Brooklyn Botanic Garden Record* 7, No. 2, (April, 1918), 57. "Special beds and borders have been prepared for Japanese Iris, German Iris, Intermediate Iris, and other groups. There are now in the collection over 90 horticultural varieties and about 15 species." The Intermediate Iris mentioned may well have included examples bred by William John Caparne and sent to his cousin. See Fenner II, 45, where he states that Caparne originated the Intermediate Bearded Iris.

10.6 Brooklyn Botanic Garden illustration by Rodica Prato, map of the Garden.

10.7 Rhys Caparn stated to the writer that she had made the figures for the armillary sphere, which the writer saw in 1995 in the Magnolia Plaza, and again in 2006 in the renovated Plaza to wonderful effect; an acquisition list at the Garden shows that it was erected in 1933 and that Harold designed it and Rhys contributed to the design. It was funded by a bequest of Alfred W. Jenkins. More on the compass and granite base in *Brooklyn Botanic Garden Record* 22 (1933), 207; a drawing of the design on the front cover of BBG *Record* 23 (1934) and description, 40. Rhys Caparn's donation of her sculpture, "Moonrise," is pictured in the *Brooklyn Botanic Garden Report*, 1980-1982. Photo of "Moonrise," Hale, op. cit., 65, and dust jacket outside back cover.

11.1 University of the Pacific Library, Holt-Atherton Special Collections. Letter, April 4, 1912, from Harold Caparn to John Muir.

12.1 Details of Newman and Blood, their families, homes and the development of Cayuga Heights in Carol U. Sisler, *Enterprising Families, Ithaca, New York: Their Houses and Businesses* (Ithaca: Enterprise publishing, 1986), 105-114.

12.2 Elizabeth L. Watson, *Houses for Science – A pictorial History of Cold Spring Spring Harbor* (Cold Spring Harbor Laboratory Press, 1991) and Elizabeth L. Watson, *Grounds for Knowledge – A Guide to Cold Spring Harbor Laboratory's Landscapes & Buildings* (Cold Spring Harbor Laboratory Press, 2008).

12.3 H. A. Caparn, plan for lots and streets for the Long Island Biological Association, 1926. Additional notes on the location of buildings by the author. The plan is held in the archives of the Cold Spring Harbor Biological Laboratory. The letter from Caparn to Harris is in the Caparn archive.

13.1 Further information on the history and development of Palisades Interstate Park may be found online under The Palisades and Palisades Interstate Park. accessed 8/30/19.

14.1 Elsa Rehmann, *The Small Place*, G. P. Putnam's Sons, New York, 1918.

15.1 American Society of Landscape Architects, *Transactions of the American Society of Landscape Architects 1909 – 1921*, vol. 2, 1922, 75. The entry is under the heading "War Records of Those Who Were Fellows and Members During the Years 1917 and 1918." Caparn's leave-taking from the Brooklyn Botanic Garden to Alabama in connection with town planning of three "nitrate towns" in Florence, Sheffield and Tuscumbia, is noted in *Brooklyn Botanic Garden Record*, vol. VII, no. 4 (Oct. 1918), 121.

15.2 United States Department of the Interior, National Park Service, National Register of Historic Places, *Nomination papers for Nitrate Village No. 1 Historic District* (1984). The papers provide information on the village, the houses and the approach to building the houses.

15.3 The architectural firm was identified as Ewing and Allen in Ralph F. Warner, "Muscle Shoals—A New Industrial Town in Alabama," *Architectural Review* vol. VIII, No. 1 (January 1919), 18. This reference is to Village No.2. That attribution was relied upon in the nomination of Village No. 1 to the National Register. The Muscle Shoals area includes Florence, Tuscumbia, Sheffield and Muscle Shoals.

Announcement was made in *Municipal Journal*, vol. XLV, no. 7 (Aug. 17, 1918), 137, for the towns of Florence, Sheffield and Tuscumbia, that Architects and Engineers for new U. S. Housing Plans were Warren & Knight, Birmingham, Town Planner was Harold A. Caparn, 220 W. 42nd St., NYC, and Engineer was Julian Kindrick,

Birmingham, AL. This announcement was also carried in *The American Contractor*, vol. 39 (Aug. 17, 1918), 22; and in *Heating & Ventilating Magazine*, vol. 15 (Oct. 1918), 56.

An alternate attribution to the architectural firm of Mann and MacNeille was made in United States Government, War Department, Ordnance Office Nitrate Division and Department of Agriculture, Fixed Nitrogen Research Laboratory, "Report on the Fixation and Utilization of Nitrogen," (March 29, 1922), by Major General C. C. Williams, Chief of Ordinance.

While the Warner attribution is clearly not related to Village No. 1, as the plan and the homes were not of the stated design, it could apply to Village No. 2. Regarding the work of Warren & Knight, announcements in several magazines might have picked up earlier information that was later changed, was incorrect, or applied to Village No. 3.

The attribution by Maj. General Williams, coming after the completion of Village No. 1, in a review of the overall process where previous reports and plans were available, seems to the writer to favor Mann and MacNeille as architects of Village No. 1. The following information on Mann and MacNeille and their relation to Caparn and the J. G. White Construction Co. appears also to support their attribution for the architectural work on Village No. 1.

Horace B. Mann (1868-1937), architect, a native of Orange, New Jersey, is identified in a University of Chicago *Alumni Directory* (1919) as one of the principals of Mann, MacNeille & Lindberg. He studied architecture at Columbia University and won a traveling scholarship to France and Italy. He was the brother-in-law of Perry R. MacNeille; together they had a successful practice in New York City from 1902 until 1931 at the death of MacNeille.

Perry R. MacNeille (1872-1931), architect, was a resident of Summit, New Jersey. He published "The Architect's Relationship to an Industrial Housing Development" in *Architectural Forum* (April 1918) and on related issues in The Town of Perry Point, MD, A Development of the U. S. Ordinance Department, Mann and MacNeille Architects" in *Architectural Review* (January 1919). MacNeille died at Summit where he had been President of the City Planning Commission; he was on the City Planning Committee of the American Civic Association and during WWI was director of the housing branch of the Army Ordnance Department. Caparn was treasurer of the American Civic Association. Caparn's family lived in Short Hills and Summit; he may have known MacNeille prior to work on Village No. 1. With town planner, architects and construction company all having offices in New York City, it would have been an easy task to coordinate planning there prior to work on site. MacNeille's publications, their dates, his connections to the ACA and his work as housing director for the Army Ordnance Department favor attribution of Village One houses and buildings to the firm.

15.4 *The New York Times*, "Votes to Abolish Housing Bureau," (December 18, 1919), 16.

15.5 *Nomination papers*, National Register of Historic Places, 1984, 16.

15.6 *The New York Times* (August 17, 1919) 71.

15.7 Harold A. Caparn, "The Value of the Curve in Street Architecture," *Architectural Record* (March 1905), reprinted in *The Origins of Modern Architecture*, selected essays from *Architectural Record*, ed. Eric Uhfelder, (Dover Publications, Inc., 1998), 152.

15.8 Harold A. Caparn, "The Question of Civic Improvement," *The Sewanee Revue Quarterly* (University of the South, Sewanee, Tennessee, October 1907), 498.

16.1 Caparn started his campaign to save the meadows with two articles in January 1927. "The Preservation of Bechler Meadows," *Parks & Recreation* 10 (Jan. 1927), 212-215, illus., and "Preserving the Unity of Yellowstone Park Scenery," *Landscape Architecture* 17 (Jan. 1927), 77-81, illus., quote on 79-80. An editorial appeared in the same issue, 126-27, against "the attempted grab—by local interests for local profit—of the Bechler Meadows." Caparn followed up with a letter in February to Hon. Addison T. Smith, House of Representatives, in part, "If Congress should relax its vigilance and let the local people into the Bechler Meadows...for a few years increased prosperity...then the old process would go on again: new settlers would come in...again there would not be enough water to go round, and the raid on the Bechler Meadows would be followed by one on some other part of the Park...and Idaho and the neighboring states would lose not only this unparalleled scenic wonder, but one of their best business assets." This letter continued the campaign, being printed also in *Landscape Architecture 27-4* (July 1927), 300-301. The Meadows remain in the southwest corner of Yellowstone National Park along the Bechler River a place for hiking and scenic beauty.

16.2 Rydell, Kiki Leigh and Mary Shivers Culpin, *Managing the Matchless Wonders—A History of Administrative Development in Yellowstone National Park, 1872-1965* (National Park Service: Yellowstone Center for Resources, 2006), 96. "He used the visit to make suggestions for improving the landscape character of the ...observation decks along the Grand Canyon of the Yellowstone. Caparn urged that the wooden stairways, ramps and railings that had been installed about 1920 be replaced with earthen paths and masonry parapets of native stone." Park historian Linda Flint McClelland stated that the plans for these replacements were the "first consideration of the area from a landscape standpoint."

16.3 Harold A. Caparn, "The Present Status of Niagara Falls." *Landscape Architecture 4-3* (April 1914), 81-88. In sum, p. 87: "So the most wonderful spectacle of its kind in the civilized world, this great revenue-producing work of nature, and all this vast commerce of the Lakes, are to be impaired or destroyed for the advantage of a few private promoters." Also, H. A. Caparn, "Present Status of Water Diversions from Niagara Falls" *Parks and Recreation 10* (Jan. 1927), 290.

17.1 Susan Verhoek, PhD, Professor Emerita, Department of Biology, Lebanon Valley College, found the Caparn plan in the College archives and identified the remaining trees on campus.

17.2 *Touring the Brooklyn College Landscape—A Guide to the shrubs and Trees on the Brooklyn College Campus*, by Maurice Bolaski '87, with Dr. Roy E. McGowan, Faculty Advisor (Brooklyn College, 1987).

Illustrations

Frontispiece

Harold ap Rhys Caparn. Photograph by Associated News Graphic Service, Inc. West 57th Street, New York City. c. 1935. Caparn archive.

Chapter number. Illustration number (1.1)

1.1   Harold Caparn. Photo: D'Ana Studio, New York. c. 1889. Collection of the author.

1.2   Thomas John Caparn. c. 1909. Collection of the author. Likely by his son-in-law, photographer James Shackleton, husband of Annie Smith (Caparn) Shackleton.

1.3   *The Budget, vol. 1, no. 24, Millburn, NJ, advertisement, Wednesday, June 16, 1886, 5.* Courtesy The Millburn Free Public Library, held in the Millburn Township Historical Archives. Ref. by Lynne Ranieri, curator, Millburn-Short Hills Historical Society Museum. In the ad, London (sic) is John Claudius Loudon, Scottish garden designer and writer; like Uvedale Price and Humphry Repton, his works were known by the Caparns.

1.4   Harold Caparn, c. 1897, age 33. Photo: Zuven Studio, Pittsburgh. Collection of the author.

1.5   Harold Caparn, Plan for a Large City Place, J. Wilkinson Elliott, *A Plea for Hardy Plants,* 1902, 67.

4.1   Harold Caparn. *Country Life in America* 38, 1920, 49.

5.1   Map, portion of Yonkers with Washington Park. *Yonkers,* G. W. Bromley & Co., 34 Pine Street, NY, 1914, p. 8. David Rumsey Map Collection, Stanford University Library.

5.2   Washington Park, Yonkers, NY. Photo on a postcard publ. by Valentine & Sons, New York, c. 1907.

5.3   Grant Park, Yonkers, NY. Central lawn, grove and boulders. photo, H. A. Caparn, c. 1905. Caparn archive.

5.4   Grant Park central lawn, grove and boulders. photo O. Chamberlain, 2007.

5.5   Grant Park, Yonkers, NY, area of rock garden. photo H. A. Caparn. c. 1905. Caparn archive.

5.6   Harold Caparn, "Rest House in Columbus Park, Yonkers, N. Y.," *The Architectural Record,* vol. 36, no. 2, August, 1914, 164, general plan, 165, also sketch. Cf. Caparn, "An Unusual Park Construction Problem," in *Park and Cemetery,* 1914, 122; shows addition of some walks, right side of plan. Plan with article by Caparn, "Columbus Park at Yonkers, N.Y.," *Parks & Recreation* 12, Nov.-Dec. 1928, 77-80, gives photos after construction.

6.1   Plan for Baird Court. *Fifth Annual Report* of the New York Zoological Society, for the year 1900 (published June 1, 1901). Used with permission, Wildlife Conservation Society.

6.2   New York Zoological Park, Approach to Rockefeller Fountain, The Great Steps, Italianate Garden and Baird Court. Postcard pub. New York Zoological Society, c. 1910, printed by Quadri-Color Co., Jamaica, NY.

11.1   Harold Caparn photograph, c. 1910, Central Park Mall. Caparn archive.

12.1   Illustration showing homes at the entrance to Cayuga Heights. Carol Sisler, *Enterprising Families, Ithaca, New York: Their Houses and Businesses,* Ithaca: Enterprise Publishing, 1986, 109.

12.2   Harold Caparn, plan of Cayuga Heights. Map, 1921, by Carl Crandall, CE, who staked out the lots according to Caparn's general plan of 1914. "White Park" [bounded east and west by Triphammer and Highland and south by Kline Road/grounds of the Country Club of Ithaca and north by Iroquois Road].

12.3   Harold Caparn, plan for lots and streets for the Long Island Biological Association, 1926. Additional notes on the location of the buildings by the author. The Caparn plan is reproduced in *Houses for Science,* by Elizabeth L. Watson (Cold Spring Harbor Laboratory Press, 1991).

13.1   Part of Palisades Interstate Park on the Hudson River. pub. Manhattan Post Card Co., NY, c. 1920. The Robert Fulton day liner was put in service in 1909.

14.1   Harold Caparn, "An Informal Arrangement of a Small Property," in Elsa Rehmann, *The Small Place,* G. P. Putnam's Sons, New York, 1918, facing p. 74.

14.2   Harold Caparn design, house toward street. ibid., facing 75.

14.3   Harold Caparn design, view of lawn and pergola. ibid., facing 79.

15.1   Harold Caparn layout of lots, streets, parks. TVA map. Portion of Nitrate Plant No. 1 Reservation, Feb. 1949.

15.2   Harold Caparn design, streets and lots under construction, Village No. 1 homes. Photographer unknown, dated Aug. 28, 1918.

15.3   Harold Caparn design of placement school/civic center, under construction. Village No. 1. Photographer unknown, dated Oct. 31, 1918. Photographs courtesy Richard Sheridan, historian, Sheffield, AL

15.4   Harold Caparn curved street design, Village No. 1, Wilson Dam Ave. Photo, O. Chamberlain, 2008.

15.5   Harold Caparn design, lots, streets, parks. Village No. 1, Aerial view, Photo by Benjamin West, 200 Broadway, New York; published by Frank E. Cooper, 253 Broadway, NY. Caption, top of card, by the publisher. Card Courtesy Robert Ekiss, Historic Commission member.

15.6   Liberty Bell. NB: yoke, shape, direction of crack.

15.7   English handbell. NB: handle, shape, continuous surface.

15.8   Harold Caparn design, Village No. 1, an early cul-de-sac. Photo, O. Chamberlain, 2008.

15.9   Harold Caparn design of principle park as body of handbell, Village No. 1, view across park to homes on Wilson Dam Ave. Photo, O. Chamberlain, 2008

16.1   Jackson Lake. a real photo postcard, pub. Conoco, c. 1915.

17.1   Harold Caparn design, Lebanon Valley College, aerial view of central quadrangle. Photo by Ted Gress, c. 1942.

Harold A. Caparn, Client List
category of work, job number, annotation

Work categorized:
- A. Public Parks, Gardens, Memorials and Country Clubs
- B. Churches, Cemeteries and Cemetery Lots
- C. Businesses
- D. Real Estate Projects
- E. Colleges, Schools and Institutions
- F. Private Estates and Homes
    + indicates a work that is added to the client list from other sources
    - indicates a work the nature of which is not known
    ? indicates a work tentatively identified

Caparn extant public and private works
   Public – accessible
488 Bronx Zoo (New York Zoological Park)
491 Grant Park, Yonkers
522 Denison Park, Corning
573 Cayuga Heights, Ithaca
575 Brooklyn Botanic Garden
584 Madison Square Park, NYC
597 Law Memorial Park, Briarcliff Manor
603 Village No. 1, Sheffield
647 J. Gordon Edwards mausoleum, Kensico Cemetery
653 Lebanon Valley College, central quad
  +Brooklyn College (CUNYBrooklyn), east quad, lily pond

   Private – not open to public
507 Willever estate, Millburn
524 Webb Horton house, Middletown
538 Johnson property, Larchmont
551 Hungerford estate, Briarcliff Manor
568 Eaton property, Norwich
574 Tanner property, Ithaca
585 Haggin estate, garden, Onteora Park
587 Tully home, Locust Valley
617 Masonic Home, Utica
622 Wild Garden, Library, Onteora Park
623 Griggs estate, Ardsley on Hudson
624 Caparn retreat, Briarcliff Manor
633 Mairs estate, Briarcliff Manor
638 Dwight property, Onteora Park

(A) Public Parks, Gardens, Memorials and Country Clubs

488. N. Y. Zoological Park--The Bronx Zoo; The Bronx, NY. Work in 1899 as consultant, 1900-1904 as principal landscape architect of the formal grand entrance concourse and central Baird court; roads and walkways, and the planned natural look of the rest of the Zoo. Baird Court with surrounding buildings and stairs has been identified by the New York City Landmarks Commission as significant for its relation to the City Beautiful movement and for the influence on it from the court at the Chicago World's Fair in the layout of buildings of similar height and design around an open court. A major park, still showing Caparn's landscape designs, the entrance concourse, great steps and gardens and central court have been recently restored. Accessible.

491. Yonkers Parks. Yonkers, NY. Caparn won a competition to design two parks in 1900. Washington Park, in the center of town and also of government, is now filled with buildings; Grant Park, in a neighborhood, is extant and accessible. It is mentioned in the announcement of his appointment at Brooklyn Botanic Garden.

522. Corning Park – Corning, N.Y., also mentioned in the announcement of his appointment as consulting landscape architect in the BBG *Record*, v. 2 (1913), p. 32. Identified as Denison Park by the Corning Painted-Post Historical Society. When Caparn did the design in 1906 it was of thirty-three acres, which he laid out in an informal manner. See *Historic Landscape Report Canfield Park & Denison Park, Corning, New York* (State University of New York, Syracuse, NY, September 1994). Plans not available. Later another seven acres, with swimming pool and pavilion were added.

526. Rorick's Glen. Elmira, NY. Park and Theatre grounds. Designed c. 1900-1902. No plans available. Can be seen on postcards of the time.

531. Elizabeth Park – Elizabeth, NJ (?) --

547. Hackensack Parks – Hackensack, NJ. --

560. Montclair Golf Club. West Orange, NJ. Likely the grounds for the clubhouse; the four nine-hole golf courses were laid out by known designers. Founded c. 1893; it is one of the largest and oldest in the US. Caparn work would have been c. 1900. No plans.

562. Telawana Park, Competition. Queens, NY. In 1914 renamed Jacob Riis Park. Olmsted Brothers firm lists job 534 also as Telawana Park, with no plans. Caparn article (1907); Letters NYTimes (1931-8), (1932-5), other articles of the period about the park also name Caparn. Listed, National Register of Historic Places, 1981.

564. Hiker Monument – to Spanish-American war veterans. Utica (?)

565. Burnham Park Competition – in honor of Daniel Burnham, Chicago (?)

571. Richmond Canal Competition – Richmond County (?)

575. Brooklyn Botanic Garden. Brooklyn, NY. Caparn was officially appointed consulting landscape architect to the Garden Jan. 1, 1912; he retired, July 1945. He worked independently, in consultation with the Olmsted Brothers, 1911-1919 as they laid out the overall design and prepared the ground. Caparn consultant work 1911 on the Native Flora Garden. From 1912 on he designed the Systematic Section-renamed Plant Family Collection, Water Lily Terrace and fountain, Cranford Rose Garden, pavilion, and Rose Arc, pool, Magnolia Plaza, armillary sphere and compass, Osborne Garden, fountains, benches, columns, and other areas. Articles (1915-7), (1932-7), (1942). Accessible. Caparn's best-known work, done for the Garden, (1911) 1912-1945.

576. John Jay Park. -- Manhattan, NY. Named after the first Chief Justice of the Supreme Court. Caparn likely did work on or designed the park for C. D. Lay, the landscape architect of New York City. Upper west side of Manhattan. Extant. Now a neighborhood park, with recreational equipment.

577. Harlem Speedway. Retaining Wall. Along Harlem River, Queens, NY. c. 1900.

578. Newark Park Board. Newark, NJ. Lincoln Park, a small memorial park with statue of Abraham Lincoln. An illustration of a proposed fountain for Lincoln Park was entered by Caparn in an exhibit by the Chicago Architectural Club at the Art Institute of Chicago in 1914. Milford Park, a triangular park between Milford and Elizabeth Aves. c. 1925. Article (1925-7).

584. C. D. Lay, Madison Square Plan. Manhattan, NY. Park between Fifth and Madison Aves. Article (1896-4). This entry is likely for later work than the article. Again, design alterations for C. D. Lay, Landscape Architect of NYC.

590. Briarcliff Manor Pumping Station. Briarcliff Manor, NY. Park surrounding the village wells. c. 1925. Article (1925-11) Design not implemented; now overgrown.

597. Briarcliff Park. Briarcliff Manor, NY. Now Law Memorial Park, named after the Village's founder, Walter W. Law; 6-7 acre park located in the center of the Village of Briarcliff Manor. Areas with old trees, a small walled pool; later added swimming pool and tennis courts, new pavilion. Accessible.

606. The Grove, Stockwell, Ind –

607. Hayes Park, (Newark Memorial Centre) –

620. Elpico Country Club – Poughkeepsie, NY --

621. Newark War Memorial –

622. Onteora Garden Club. Onteora Park, NY. Designed a Wild Garden for the Onteora Garden Club, Mrs. Ben Ali Haggin, president, to the rear of the Onteora Library, in honor of the founder of Onteora, Candace Wheeler. 1922. Ground plan in the Onteora Library. Extant in part.

625. Doane Memorial. -- Newark, NJ. Statue with surrounding area. c. 1908.

626. Rutherford Station Park &c -- Rutherford, NJ. Described in newspaper article of the time. Beautification of commuter rail stations popular, with small parks.

627. Central Park -- Manhattan, NY. May refer to his many articles and letters on the park. No known work on the park.

641. Ivanhoe Park. -- Summit, NJ. c. 1920.

655. H. R. Office Bldg. -- Washington, D.C. Planting of the Cannon Office Building for the House of Representatives; perhaps a subcontract for the Olmsted Brothers. Photograph, no plan.

664. Woodland Garden, World's Fair. Queens, NY. A featured garden in the Parade of Gardens at the World's Fair, 1939-1940. Letters unpub. (1935-3), (1936-5). *NY Times* articles acclaim the Garden.

+ Columbus Park, Yonkers. Yonkers, NY., c. 1914. Article (1928-11).

+ Treat Memorial, Landing Park, Newark, NJ. Planting plan. Likely done as subcontract for the Olmsted Brothers. 1916. Plan in files, Olmsted NHS, Brookline, MA.

+ Onteora Park, NY. Plan for landscape design for the Club House (golf club/dining facility) and the 250 seat Theatre next to the Club House. Sketch and blueprint, with planting plan and plant list, 1926. The plan was not implemented, likely because by the time agreement had been reached as to its undertaking, the Depression struck. Sketch and blueprint, Onteora Park Library. Rare to have both Caparn sketch and blueprint.

(B) Churches, Cemeteries and Cemetery Lots

510. St. Philip in the Highlands. -- Garrison, NY. Listed, National Register of Historic Places (October 1995). No plan available. The church records do not detail his work.

519. Pinelawn Cemetery – Pinelawn Road, Farmingdale, Suffolk Co., Long Island, NY. Cemetery & Memorial Park. (?) No plan available.

536. Christ Church, New Brighton. Staten Island, NY. No plan available. The church is now a listed New York City Landmark. Although the architects are known, no mention is made of the landscape architect. No church records detail his work.

545. L. C. Smith Cemetery Lot – Lyman Cornelius Smith (1850-1910) (?), businessman, donor. Oakwood Cemetery, Syracuse, NY. Mausoleum, landscaped. Smith Hall, College of Visual and Performing Arts, Syracuse University. see Rhys Caparn Papers, Syracuse University Library.

552. St. Mary's Cemetery – Yonkers, NY, Sprain Road (?)

554. Lakeview Cemetery, Ithaca. Ithaca, NY. Overlooking Cayuga Lake. Not far from his design for a portion of the Village of Cayuga Heights. No plan available. Exists in part.

555. W. H. Miller, Cemetery Lot --

581. Goodwin Brown Cemetery Lot – Brown was attorney in NYC, lobbyist at state and national levels for mental health issues. Location of lot (?)

647. J. G. Edwards-Kensico. J. Gordon Edwards (1867-1925), Canadian actor, film director, producer. Kensico Cemetery, mausoleum with free-standing minarets. Valhalla, Westchester County, NY. Photo of the mausoleum available online.

(C) Businesses

521. H. P. Sinclaire & Co. Corning, NY. Cut glass company. Caparn also did work for the president of Corning Glass, Client list number 523, Houghton. One client may have recommended Caparn to the other. No plans available. The Sinclaire Co. is described by Estelle Sinclaire Farrar, in her book on Sinclaire (Garden City, NY, 1974), 14-15, in the spring of 1905: "When the factory reopened (after a fire), landscaping was still incomplete. Rare shrubs arrived from New England and the Middle Atlantic states in the spring to circle and shade the deep front lawn. Sinclaire had built Corning's only garden factory. The cost of his landscaping equaled the price of the big plot. Engravers worked on the first floor, cutters on the second; Sinclaire had the cutting frames installed so that

each man could look out a window at the shady grounds. The arrangement was unique in Corning."

556. Elliott Nursery Co. Pittsburgh, PA. Work for J. Wilkinson Elliott, from c. 1890 to 1897, when he left for Yonkers, N.Y. to set up his own solo office. He was noted by Elliott as capable of drawing designs for the nursery landscape work.

602. Outdoor Theatre, Briarcliff Manor, NY. Not built due to WWI. Article (1918-6). Illus. plans. Caparn designed a theatre that was flexible to produce modern, classic and Greek theatre.

635. Thayer Hotel Corporation. -- A Thayer Hotel at West Point, NY, is known from 1926. The successor hotel group is still active. No plans available.

656. Brooklyn Boro Gas Co. --

+ McKesson and Robbins (see client list 644, F. D. Coster). McKesson Corp. is still active. No plans available. Unpub. Letter (1928-11 from Caparn's attorney to Coster regarding non-payment). Coster's misdirection of funds while president of McKesson and Robbins created a major 20th century scandal resulting in changes in professional accounting procedures.

(D) Real Estate Projects

515. East Orange Park. East Orange, NJ. Layout of lots for development. c. 1921.

543. Glen Ridge Realty Co. – in the borough of Glen Ridge, Essex County, NJ. (?)

553. Great Neck Improvement Co. – Great Neck Estates, about 100 lots. Now in the Village of Great Neck Estates on the peninsula of Great Neck, in the Town of North Hempstead, on the North Shore of Long Island, in Nassau County; the Village of Great Neck Estates was incorporated as one of nine villages in Great Neck in 1911. No plan available.

573. Jared T. Newman. Ithaca, NY. Newman engaged Caparn to lay out "White Park," Cayuga Heights, described in articles in the local newspaper from 1914. Newman named a section of the development "Caparn," calling him "a very capable landscape architect." WWI intervened to inhibit selling lots and building homes; continued after the war. Article online "Cayuga Heights, New York," mentions Caparn. accessed 8/30/19. Site extant, accessible.

586. Bridgeport Housing Co. Bridgeport, CT. About WWI, Caparn laid out industrial villages for the Bridgeport Housing Co. and the Federal Government. c. 1917.

589. Putnam Valley, Property Owners. – Town of Putnam Valley, in Putnam County, NY, in the Hudson Highlands. No plan available.

603. Housing Bureau [Village No. 1, Sheffield, Alabama]. Reference from ASLA *Transactions*, vol. 2. Caparn was assigned by Frederick Law Olmsted, Jr., to lay out three industrial villages in NW Alabama. Village No. 1 of 1918 in Sheffield, is extant, accessible. Caparn's symbolic design hoping for victory for England and America in WWI resulted in principal streets and park areas in the shape of an English handbell looking forward to ring in celebration. On National Register of Historic Places (1984).

612. Hasbrouck Heights. – A borough in Bergen County, NJ, within easy commuting distance from Manhattan. No plan available.

640. L. I. Biol Assn [Long Island Biological Association] later Cold Spring Harbor Laboratory, Cold Spring Harbor/Laurel Hollow, Long Island, NY. 1926. Extant; developed along the line of Caparn's plan, but not directly on it, due to exigencies in opportunities for construction of laboratories and other buildings. On the National Register of Historic Places. See books by Elizabeth L. Watson. Article, photos online. Accessed 8/29/19.

(E) Colleges, Schools and Institutions

490. Washington -- 1903 article on design of central Federal Government portion of city, including Washington Memorial, Lincoln Memorial, Executive Mansion, Mall. Article presented an ideal proposal; was not implemented.

542. Farm Colony – Staten Island, NY. When Staten Island became a borough of New York City in 1898, the city renamed what had been the Richmond County Poor Farm as the New York City Farm Colony [also known as the Staten Island Farm Colony]. In 1915 its administration was merged with that of Sea View Hospital.

548. Arnot Art Gallery. Elmira, NY. Home of Matthias Arnot, who collected art works housed in his home, later gallery, now museum. Museum extant, landscape changed.

561. Board of Education, Peekskill. NY. --

563. Coles Memorial Fountain (Columbia University). Manhattan, NY. Design for the area surrounding the fountain. Stanford White, architect, likely designed the fountain. No plan or planting by Caparn extant.

566. Newark Board of Education --

569. Mt. McGregor Sanitorium. Wilton, NY. Built for the Metropolitan Life Insurance Company, c. 1912, a first for employee care. Extensive campus, landscape, buildings. Extant. Now used for other purposes.

617. Masonic Home, Utica. Utica, NY. Retirement home, health care facility, c. 1902. Extant. No plan. At the time, the landscape was very favorably reviewed.

637. Home for Seamen's Children – St. Georges, Staten Island, NY. Orphan, health care campus. Across from no. 542, above. Listed for preservation.

653. Lebanon Valley College. Annville, PA. Caparn designed the central quadrangle as a botanic lab in an evolutionary scheme like the Brooklyn Botanic Garden. c. 1930. Article (1930-12). Extant. New buildings have replaced much of the original landscape design; a few old trees remain. Caparn plan in the College Library.

654. Manhasset Grade School – Manhasset, Long Island, NY. --

+ Mountain Home for Disabled Volunteer Soldiers, Johnson City, TN. Built c. 1901. Caparn designed a landscape plan for the 447-acre campus. Plan extant in a photograph. Caparn archive.

+ Brooklyn College. Brooklyn, NY. Now CUNY Brooklyn. Caparn was engaged in 1937 for the planting of the campus in the following year(s). No Caparn plan available. Plantings illustrated in two books on the campus trees and shrubs. Some old elms on East Quad, planted under Caparn, extant. Lily Pond Garden at south side of Library, extant.

(F) Private Estates and Homes

489. Mrs. A. B. Blodgett. -- Wife of Superintendent of Schools, Syracuse, NY.

492. D. A. Bullard. President, Schuylerville National Bank, Schuylerville, NY. Caparn estate ground plan included an early garden for only roses and a garden in Japanese style.

493. J(oseph) E(dward) Willard. Fairfax, VA. Lt. Governor of Virginia, 1902-1906, Ambassador to Spain. Estate ground plan, photo.

494. R. Tompkins. – Yale graduate; wife donated 700 acres to Yale, 1923.

495. R. H. Curtis. --

496. E(dward). L. Fuller. Scranton, PA president of International Salt Co. --

497. Austin Lathrop. -- Superintendent of NY State Prisons, c. 1900.

498. A. E. Nettleton &

H. S. Wilkinson -- Nettleton founded high quality shoe company, Syracuse; Wilkinson owned a clothing company. See also Client List No. 595.

499. T. S. Williams. President, Brooklyn Rapid Transit Company; on the Board of the Brooklyn Institute of Arts and Sciences; from knowing Caparn's work at the Brooklyn Botanic Garden, recommended him to the director of the Long Island Biological Association for design work. Both these organizations were under the umbrella of the Brooklyn Institute of Arts and Sciences, as was Brooklyn Academy of Music, Brooklyn Museum of Art and Brooklyn Children's Museum. See NYTimes (Jan. 3, 1915). Possibly work also for his estate.

500. T. R. Ball. --

501. John A. Dix. -- Governor, State of New York 1911-13. Designed his estate (Albany); Dix was on the board of the bank headed by Bullard, no. 492, above.

502. F. T. King. --

503. J. R. McComb. --

504. Frank Bergen. -- Chief Counsel, Public Service Corporation of New Jersey; Elizabeth, NJ.

505. Mrs. A. B. Abbott & -- A. M. Spier

506. A. F. Riach. – officer of Produce Bank, NYC (?) --

507. J. C. Willever. Vice President, Western Union. Caparn designed his estate at Millburn, NJ., c. 1910. A gate with waterfall is extant, as is the home. Friend of Caparn; supported his work at the Bronx Zoo.

508. Frank D. Kingsbury. Chairman of the Legislative Committee of the New York State League of Savings and Loan Associations. President of Savings & Loan, Corning, NY. Article (1917-2). Caparn ground plan. c. 1910; photo, rear grounds, in ASLA *Illustrations of Work of Members* (1931), plate 17.

509. G. S. Knowlton. – Incorporator, Raquette Foundry, Waterford, CT

511. G. W. Valentine. --

512. A. M. Dulles. – Allen Macy Dulles, Pastor, 1897-1904, First Presbyterian Church, Watertown, NY. Father of John Foster Dulles, U.S. Sec. of State and Allen Dulles, Director, Central Intelligence Agency. No plan.

513. F. W. Kelsey. – Park Commissioner of Essex County, NJ, member of the Committee on Parks of the Municipal Art Society, on which Caparn also served. Frederick W. Kelsey wrote a detailed book on *The First County Park System – A complete history of the inception and development of the Essex County Parks*

of New Jersey (Washington, D.C.: McGrath Publishing Co. & National Recreation and Park Association, 1905); he was Vice President of the Commission that worked with Frederick Law Olmsted on Essex County Parks. Caparn, personal work for Kelsey estate (?).

514. Mrs. T. R. Almond. -- Yonkers, NY. Wife of owner of a tool manufacturing company, Brooklyn; member, Chamber of Commerce, Yonkers. an early work. Home pictured in *Yonkers Illustrated*, 1902.

516. A. H. Vesey. – author of books, c. 1905.

517. B. W. Wellington. -- Secretary, State Bankers' Association of New York. Vice President of Q. W. Wellington & Co Bank, Corning, NY. Benjamin W. was the son of Q. W. Wellington, q.v. client list number 527.

518. Marvin Olcott. – Incorporator, Corning Brake Shoe Company, Corning, NY. Partner of Olcott & Drake, General Insurance Agents, formed in Corning, October 1890.

520. W. E. Gorton. --

523. Alan[son] Houghton. -- President, Corning Glass; member of Congress, Ambassador to Germany and England. Vestryman of Christ Church, Corning, next to the property of Frank Kingsbury, No. 508. Amo Houghton, grandson: "no information on landscaping available" (his letter to the author, 2010). Alanson Houghton married Adelaide, the daughter of Quincy W. Wellington, president of Wellington Bank.

524. Eugene Horton. – Heir of oil and textile magnate Webb Horton. Horton House is on the National Register of Historic Places. Middletown, NY.

525. William B. Howland. – President, The Independent Corporation, publisher *The Independent* and *Countryside Magazine*; his country home, "Seven Chimneys," Washington Township, Bergen County, northern NJ, for which it is likely Caparn did landscape design; Howland lived in NYC at the Hotel Chelsea, W. 23rd St. "Seven Chimneys" is now on the National Register of Historic Places. Caparn published articles in *The Independent*. J. Horace McFarland, President of the American Civic Association, of which Howland was Treasurer, presided at his memorial held at the National Arts Club, 14 Grammercy Park, NYC. Howland was also President of the Commissioners of the State Reservation at Niagara, NY, on which Caparn wrote. (*NY Times*, Feb. 28, 1917). Spencer Trask (see no. 532, below) and Wm. B. Howland were among charter members of the American Institute of Social Service granted by the Regents of the University of the State of New York (*NY Times*, Dec. 22, 1902).

527. Q. W. Wellington &

Callaway – Wellington was Bank President, Corning, NY. See client list no. 517. The Q. W. Wellington & Co. Bank was organized in 1862. The daughter of Q. W. Wellington married Alanson Houghton. Q. W. Wellington was a member of Christ Church, Corning. Wellington died May 3, 1920 at age 88. On Monday, May 12, 1920, the Wellington Bank was transferred to the Corning Trust Company.

529. Miss Grace Scofield. Tuxedo Park, NY. Wife of painter, school headmaster at Tuxedo Park, Leon D. Bonnet. Home, designed by Leon Gillette for mother, Mary Scofield with Japanese styling; Caparn may have recommended the designer of BBG Japanese Hill and Pond Garden to Gillette. Client List note: "no plan". Caparn may also have advised Gillette on design of gardens on the estate.

530. L. M. Brown. Glens Falls, NY. ground plan. Sec., Finch, Pruyn & Co., lumber and paper products.

532. J. T. Tower. Tuxedo, NY. Heir, with his brother, of Poughkeepsie Iron Works fortune, from his father. Purchased the Spencer Trask home at Tuxedo Park.

533. J. Liebman –

534. D. O'Day --

535. H. J. Park. Purchase, NY. Hobart J. Park estate of 2000 acres, mansion, Westchester County. Country estate, Long Island. Caparn work c. 1910, a year or two after the house was built. Park was mentioned by Caparn in *Country Life in America* (1920). The house owner is not identified in a plan by Caparn in his 1917 series of articles. Information retrieved *The New York Times* 5/16/2012.

537. L. S. Sadler --

538. A. H. W. Johnson. Larchmont, NY. Yatchsman. The plan and photographs of the home can be found in a chapter in Elsa Rehmann's book, *The Small Place.* Caparn's plan is illustrated and described in the chapter.

539. Leon Gillette, NYC. Partner, Walker & Gillette, architects. Designed home, Mary Scofield, mother of client list no. 529, Tuxedo Park, NY. Caparn consultation (no plan).

540. C. Pinkerton --

541. H. A. Sill &
    C. W. Young. Sill was Professor of Ancient History, Cornell, Ithaca, NY.

544. B. L. Kennelly. -- NYC. Real estate owner, broker.

546. Voorhis --

549. Walker Pettyjohn – businessman, Mayor, Rotarian, president, Chamber of Commerce, Lynchburg, VA.

551. U(ri). T. Hungerford. -- NYC. Owner, Hungerford Brass and Copper Co. Resident of Briarcliff Manor, NY, where he built an estate high above the Hudson River.

557. Bertram H. Borden. -- Rumson, NJ. Philanthropist. Caparn estate design (?).

558. John A. Hoagland. -- Brooklyn and Long Island. Son of founder, Royal Baking Powder Co. Caparn work, c. 1910.

559. Mrs. P. Lavigne --

567. Frank Lyman. -- NYC. Attorney. Caparn work c. 1910. Estate in Northampton, MA. Member of a well-known Northampton family. Merchant interests in Brooklyn, probably in trade with the Far East. Home, gardens pictured.

568. R. D. Eaton – Norwich, NY. House designed by Gaggin and Gaggin Architects of Syracuse, NY, in 1914 as the home of Robert D. and Maria Smith Eaton at 72 S. Broad St.; Eaton was president, then chairman of Norwich Pharmacal Company. Caparn designed the estate grounds; a sunken garden led from the rear of the Eaton home to the offices of the Norwich Pharmacal Co. On New York and National Registers of Historic Places.

570. Carl Bannwart. -- Newark, NJ. Superintendent, Shade Tree Bureau, Newark. Work with parks in Newark. Caparn work at Bannwart home (?).

572. Lowell H. Brown. -- Riverdale, Bronx, NY. Engineer, politician.

573. Jared T. Newman. Ithaca, NY. Engaged Caparn to lay out "White Park," c. 1914, which later became part of the Village of Cayuga Heights. Named a section of the Village "Caparn." Personal work on Newman home landscape (?).

574. J. H. Tanner. Ithaca, NY. Son-in-law of Jared T. Newman. Professor, Cornell. Ground plan, photo of home.

579. Henry T. Lumb – NYC. Attended ecclesiastical event, Cathedral of St. John the Devine, of the Episcopal Diocese of New York, 1910. Trustee Duchess County Historical Society. No plan available.

580. Melville Clark. DeKalb, IL. Story & Clark Piano Co., Owner, Melville Clark Piano Co., pianos, reed organs, player pianos. No plan available.

582. J. F. Eagleson --

583. H. W. Chapin – general manager, treasurer, Brown-Lipe Gear Co., Syracuse, NY. (?)

585. Mrs. (James) Ben Ali Haggin (Jr), NYC and Onteora Park, NY. Commissioned design of estate (c.1914) and work at the Onteora Library (c. 1922). Article (1914-4), Illus. Outstanding example of Caparn's design of estate and garden. Private. Extant. Recreated.

587. W. J. Tully. Married Clara Houghton of Corning. Country estate at Locust Valley, Long Island. Caparn designed rose garden for the estate (1917) that served as the model for the Cranford Rose Garden, BBG. Articles (1918), (1921-11), illus.

588. Thomas L. Raymond. -- Newark, NJ. Mayor of Newark.

591. N. W. Walker, Wyndover --

592. Julius Boehm --

593. Louis Lee Haggin. -- Lexington, KY. Son of (Lee Wood Haggin)-Mrs. Ben Ali Haggin, Jr.

594. Charles Lane Poor. -- NYC. Professor, astronomy, Columbia University.

595. H. S. Wilkinson. -- Chairman, Crucible Steel, President, Toledo Shipbuilding, Great Lakes shipping operator, other. (d. Chicago, Apr 11, 1937) home, Greenwich, CT. c. 1920.

596. A. H. Ball -- cf. no. 500.

598. J. W. Harriman. Brookville, L.I., President, Harriman National Bank. Photos of estate available. No plan.

599. H. H. Deloss. -- Bridgeport, CT. President, Bridgeport Housing Co. (cf. no. 586).

600. B. Ris --

601. Miss A. H. Williams – (cf. 499)

604. Mrs. M. J. Fox – Mortimer J. Fox, architect, NY, Foxden, Peekskill, NY. Mrs. Fox, gardener, member, New York Botanical Garden, director, North American Lily Society. --

605. W. P. Hardenbergh. -- Bernardsville, NJ. Fellow, American Geographical Society.

608. Miss Betsey B. Davis. -- NYC. President of the Alumni Assoc., 1877-78. Hunter College, Manhattan.

609. E. P. Morse --

610. T. A. Ball – (cf. 500, 596)

611. Robert Reichman --

613. A. W. Miles --

614. Walter E. Kelley – lawyer, Columbia University, A.B. 07, LL.B 10. NYC & Yonkers --

615. Mrs. W. J. Knapp. -- Rye, NY. Husband member of Apawamis Club, well-known golf, squash and tennis club.

616. F. W. Hills --

618. Hugh J. Chisholm. -- NYC. Glens Falls, NY, estate. Founder, International Paper Co., other companies. Member, board of New York Zoological Park. Philanthropist.

619. Seelye Benedict. -- Rye, NY, Southampton, L.I., Member, Apawamis Club.

623. Maitland F. Griggs. "Barberries," home, Ardsley on Hudson, NY. Attorney, art donor to the Metropolitan Museum and Yale University. Caparn design for the estate, c. 1910. Pictured.

624. H. A. Caparn. Possibly his work landscaping his country retreat at Briarcliff Manor, NY.

628. J. N. Leyne --

629. Caldwell --

630. J. B. Pound. -- Lookout Mountain, TN. President, owner, J. B. Pound Hotels. c. 1920s – 30s. Seventeen-acre estate on the east brow of Lookout Mountain. House built 1928, designed by Chattanooga architect Clarence T. Jones, in Mediterranean style, with extensive tile interior. Good description of Caparn landscaping of estate in Pound's *Memoirs* self-published, 1949.

631. W. B. Miller --

632. W. K. Rohrbach --

633. Olney B. Mairs. -- NYC. lawyer, resident, "Greylock," Briarcliff Manor, NY. Illus.

634. Fred Marks --

636. Edward L. Tilton. -- NYC. Architect, known for Carnegie Libraries

638. Eliz. D. Dwight – Caparn work for home in Onteora Park, NY. Detailed plan, illus.

639. Frederich C. Walker --

642. Henry Walter --

643. J. M. Morehead. – John Motley Morehead--Engineering executive, Part-owner, Union Carbide Corporation (later a subsidiary of The Dow Chemical Co.); Mayor, Rye, NY 1925-1930; Pres. Herbert Hoover appointed him Minister to Sweden, 1930-1934. Pledged $500,000 in 1962 (age 92) to build new city hall for Rye.

644. F. D. Coster. NYC, Bridgeport, CT. -- President, McKesson & Robbins Co. Caparn work for both company and estate. Company financial management precipitated a major 20th century scandal.

645. Mrs. Emily Lefferts Jones. – Wife of atty Dwight A. Jones, Yale grad., corporate attorney.

646. Simon Ollinger --

647. J. G. Edwards-Kensico J. Gordon Edwards (1867-1925), Canadian actor, film director, producer Fox film Corp. spectacles, Theda Bara productions. Kensico Cemetery, mausoleum with free-standing minarets. Valhalla, Westchester County, NY. photo online, accessed September 2019

648. H. A. Bvaelors --

649. T. J. Valentine --

650. Mason Day --

651. Washburne --

652. Sterrett --

657. F. W. Collins --

658. [J. D.] Maguire. -- NYC. Official, American Steam Pump Co.

659. John S. Roberts --

660. Mrs. Gertrude Adams --

661. Mrs. E. A. Baily --

662. Schiedung --

663. Lourie –

665. Moore --

666. Lamb. -- Charles R. (?) artist, designer, Dewey Arch, Madison Square Park, Fifth Avenue, NYC. Caparn articles regarding the Arch and NYC failure to build permanent arch.

667. Misc. H.A.C. – Possibly consultations with various clients, landscape architects, architects

+ home, informal garden 2-3 acres – Owner not known. Article (1904-5) illus.

Harold A. Caparn: A Timeline of selected events

On home and locations see endnote 8.3; landscape design dates are an approximation based on references to the work

1864	Dec. 18 - Harold ap Rhys, first born son of Thomas John & Ann Elizabeth (Price) Caparn, Newark on Trent, Nottinghamshire, U.K.
1872	grandfather Wm. H. Caparn dies; Thomas John Caparn consolidates his father's nursery with his own
1873 – 1882	scholar at Thomas Magnus Grammar School, Newark on Trent choirster, St. Mary Magdalene, Newark
1882	fall - tutor, St. Edmund's School, Canterbury, cathedral choir school
1884	father, mother, brother, three sisters immigrate to America, settle in Short Hills, NJ
1886	June - matriculates, University of London, placed in First Division
1886	father, brother form nursery/landscape design partnership, NJ
1887	fall - studies architecture at Ecole des Beaux-Arts, Paris
1889	Sept. 23 - Harold immigrates to America, arrives in New York
1890	employed by J. Wilkinson Elliott Nursery, Pittsburgh, PA (date?)
1893	brother Arthur, employed by Pitcher & Manda, U.S. Nurseries
1893	Dec - publishes first article, "Composition in Landscape-art," on informal style, in *Garden & Forest,* signed, Pittsburgh, PA
1894	Dec. 19 - Thomas J. Caparn, "landscape architect," *NY Times*
1894	article, "The Aesthetic Value of Roads and Walks," *Garden & Forest*
1895	J. Wilkinson Elliott, employer, talk, "A Plea for Hardy Plants, "Massachusetts Horticulture Society, Boston
1896	Apr - first published ground plan, "Madison Square Again," *Gar & For*
1897	Aug - article, "Planting for the Future," signed, Pittsburgh, *Gar & For*
1898	Feb - first letter to *NY Times,* "Wants Parsons Back," signed, Yonkers, NY
1898	office as landscape architect, 46 Warburton Ave., Yonkers
1898	summer tours France, Italy, studies gardens
1899	Wm. Caparne, cousin, elected Fellow, Royal Horticulture Society
1899	Thomas John Caparn, father, office as landscape architect, 925 Broad St., Newark, NJ
1899	Oct 11 - first letter re Dewey Naval Arch, *The New York Times*
1899	Nov. - consulting Landscape Architect, New York Zoological Park
1900 - 1904	Landscape Architect to New York Zoological Park, Bronx, NY, designs Entrance Concourse, Baird Court, a New York City Landmark
1900	designs grounds, Mrs. T. R. Almond, Yonkers, NY
1900	article, "An Ideal Cemetery" *Park & Cemetery*

1900	Mar. 3 - naturalized U. S. citizen, US District Court, NY
1900	Mar. - wins competition to design Grant, Washington Parks, Yonkers
1900	designs Matthew Arnot grounds, home/art gallery, Elmira, NY
1900 - 1902	designs Rorick's Glen Park & Theatre grounds, Elmira, NY
1901	ground plan, Mountain Home for Disabled Volunteer Soldiers, Johnson City, TN
1902	moves office to 156 Fifth Ave, Manhattan, NYC
1902	second published plan, "Plan for a Large City Place," in Elliott book *A Plea for Hardy Plants*
1902	designs Masonic Home landscape, Utica, NY
1903	Mar - article, "Informal Outdoor Art," *Architectural Record*
1903	article, "Development of Washington," *Am Arch & Bldr News*
1903	Nov. - article, "An Unfinished Piece of New York," *Arch & Bldrs Mag*
1903	estate plan, Hon. J. E. Willard, Fairfax, Lt. Gov., VA., his first design exhibited, Chicago Architectural Club at Art Institute of Chicago
1904	studies architecture at Columbia University, NY
1904	charter member, American Civic and Planning Association
1904	letter defends animal preservation at the Bronx Zoo, *The NY Times*
1904	Aug - letter, NYTimes, "Monotony of Right Angles, and Central Park"
1905	estate plan D. A. Bullard, Schuylerville, NY; plan exhibited, 1906, Chicago Architectural Club at Art Institute of Chicago
1905	designs factory garden, H. P. Sinclaire Cut Glass Co., Corning, NY
1905	studies architecture in Atelier Buray, Paris, France
1905	article, "The making of a small garden" *House Beautiful*
1905	March - article, "The Value of the Curve in Street Architecture," *Arch. Rec.*
1905	Nov. 14 - elected Fellow, paper read, "A Visit to Paris," at NY meeting, American Society of Landscape Architects (ASLA), pub. *Trans I*
1906	designs Denison Park, Corning, NY
1906	designs estate grounds of Joseph T. Tower, Tuxedo Park, NY
1906	Jul - article, "The riddle of the tall building," *The Craftsman*
1906	Sept. - article, "Parallelogram Park," *The Craftsman*
1906	Oct. 12 -marriage to Clara Howard (Jones) Royall in NYC
1907	elected Regional Trustee, ASLA
1907	exhibited as member Municipal Art Soc., at NY Architectural League
1907	Aug. 16 - born, daughter Anne Howard
1907	talk (1906), article, "A Great Water Park, Jamaica Bay," ASLA *Trans. I*
1907	Oct. - article, "The Question of Civic Improvement," *Sewanee Review*
1908	June article, "Treating the Grounds About the House," ArchRec
1908	designs estate, for Eugene Horton, the Webb Horton mansion, NRHP
1909 - 1912	elected Treasurer, ASLA; member Board of Trustees, 1909-1919
1909	Apr. - letter, NYTimes "Choose Delegates to Fight Park Grab"
1909	Jul. 28 - born, daughter Rhys, Onteora Park, NY
1909	Nov. 16 -speaker, "Waterfronts" Amer Civic Assoc, Cincinnati, OH

1910	Maitland F. Griggs estate design, Ardsley on Hudson, NY, illustrated in ASLA *Work of Members* (1931)
1910	Oct. - article, "Statuary in informal settings," *Landscape Architecture* 1
1910 - 1912	estate designs: J. A. Dix, Gov., Albany, NY; J. C. Willever, Millburn, NJ; Frank Lyman, Northampton, MA; Frank Kingsbury, Corning, NY; Hobart J. Park, Purchase, NY, U.T. Hungerford, Briarcliff Manor, NY.
1911 - 1912	elected President, American Society of Landscape Architects, member, Standing Committee on Education, preps curriculum Columbia Univ.
1911	consulting, Brooklyn Botanic Garden, re Native Plant Garden
1911	Jun. - purchases Fernie Farm, Briarcliff Manor, NY, as country retreat
1911	summer, teaches Columbia University's first course on landscape architecture
1911	Jul. - article, "Modern meditations among the tombs," *Land Arch*
1912	Jan. 1 - appointed consulting landscape architect, Brooklyn Botanic Garden (BBG) holds position until retirement 1945; begins work on Systematic Section (now Plant Family Collection)
1912	editor, ASLA *Transactions I*, with J. S. Pray and D. Vaux
1912 - 1914	design, Mt. McGregor Sanitorium, Wilton, NY, for Met Life Ins. Co.
1912	May - article, "Landscape Design and the Designer of Landscape," *ArchRec*
1912	Jul - article, "Central Park, a work of art," *Landscape Architecture* 2
1912	consulting on Grace Scofield estate, Tuxedo Park, NY
1912	Dec. - judge, garden competition, Montclair, NJ, article, *House & Garden*
1912	Dec. 12 - speaker, "The Relation of Landscape to Architecture" AIA convention concluding banquet, Washington, D.C.
1913	Wm. J. Caparne, cousin, sends irises for Brooklyn Botanic Garden
1914	design of Columbus Park, Yonkers; article, plan
1914	Apr. - article on Caparn design, cloister garden, Onteora Park, NY, *Crafts*
1914—1920s	work on estate, garden for Mrs. Ben Ali Haggin, Onteora Park; drawing, cloister garden, exhibited Architectural League of New York and Architectural Club of Chicago at Art Institute of Chicago
1914ff	laid out streets, lots, "White Park," Cayuga Heights, Ithaca, NY
1915 – 1919	elected Vice President, ASLA (James S. Pray, Pres.) on Standing Comm., Professional Practice & Ethics (1915-1917)
1915	article, "Planting a botanic garden," at BBG, LA 5
1915	design, Lake View Cemetery, Ithaca, NY
1915	estate plan, Olney Mairs, Briarcliff Manor, NY
1915	estate plan, L. M. Brown, Glens Falls, NY
1915	designs estate, Robt & Maria Eaton, Norwich, NY (NY, NRHP)
1915	designs grounds, Wm. B. Howland "Seven Chimneys" (NRHP}
1916	plan, grounds of Prof. J. H. Tanner of Cornell, Ithaca, NY

1916	Apr - plan, Treat Memorial, Landing Park, Newark, NJ (for Olmsted Brothers firm)
1916	designs estate of Joseph W. Harriman, Brookville, L.I., NY
1917	Jan. - article, "Some Reasons for a System of State Parks," *Land. Arch*
1917	Jan.-Jul. - seven-article series, "The House Outdoors" *The Countryside* includes ground plans: Kingsbury, Tanner, Brown, Park
1917	laid out industrial villages, Bridgeport CT, for Bridgeport Housing Co.
1917	plan, grounds of A. H. W. Johnson, Larchmont, NY
1917	designs estate, rose garden, W. J. Tully, Locust Valley, L.I., NY
1917	Dec. - review, book by Prof. F. Waugh, *Outdoor Theatres, Intl Gar Cl*
1918	book chapter, "Informal Arrangement of a Small Property," of A. H. W. Johnson, Larchmont, NY, in Rehmann, *The Small Place*
1918	article, "A Rose-Garden with a Reason" *Amer. Rose Annual* on estate of Wm. J. Tully, model for Cranford Rose Garden, BBG
1918	Mar. - review, book by F. Waugh, *The Natural Style in Landscape Gardening,* in *Journal of the International Garden Club*
1918	Mar. 9 - talk, article, "Sculpture & Statuary," Metropolitan Museum, NY
1918	June - article, design, "An Outdoor Theatre," for Briarcliff Manor, NY
1918	Aug-Nov - Landscape Architect & Town Planner, three wartime industrial villages in Alabama, especially Village No. 1, Sheffield, Al. (NRHP)
1919	designs Water Gardens and Fountain, Brooklyn Botanic Garden
1919	first design of rose garden, BBG
1919	Jan. - article, "A billboard catechism" begins campaign against billboards
1920	elected President, NY Chapter, ASLA, fights to preserve Central Park, Manhattan. On Standing Comm., Exhibitions, 1920-1921.
1920	Harold and Clara listed in New York Social Blue Book
1920	Jun. - pictured, "Landscape Architects Who Have Designed Gardens for Some of Our Great Country Estates," *Country Life in America*
1920	plan, "Wild Garden," Library, Onteora Park, NY
1920	designs estate of H. S. Wilkinson, Greenwich, CT
1921	article, "The Working Out of a Real Rose-Garden" *Am Rose Ann.* rationale for rose-garden of Wm. J. Tully, model for Rose Garden, BBG
1921	laid out streets and lots East Orange Park, NJ
1921	Apr. - letter, "The New York Post Office Blight," *The New York Times,* pub. as article, *Civic Comment* 6 (Oct.)
1921	Jul. - talk, "Wild Gardening," Library, Onteora Park
1921	Sept. 7 - Dedication, Wild Garden to Candace Wheeler, Onteora Park
1921	Nov. - "State Parks" printed as supplement, *National Municipal Review*
1922	Jan 16 - letter, *New York Times,* "Park Administration," begins his long fight to get New York parks under a rotating volunteer board overseeing professional park management—in opposition to the political spoils system of arbitrarily appointed superintendents
1922	Mar. - article, "Palisades Interstate Park," *Parks & Recreation*
1922	Apr. 7 - "Do None of Us Think?" re scope of National Parks Committee

1923   Nov. 5 - letter, "Cost of a Park Subway," *The New York Times,* re Central Park trees

1925   Jan. 4 - article, "Suggests Changes for Central Park" *The New York Times*

1925   design of Law Memorial Park, Briarcliff Manor, for founder

1925   plan, larger Rose Garden, Brooklyn Botanic Garden

1925   designs estate grounds J. M. Morehead, III, Rye, NY

1925   May 27 - HAC focus of article "Would Take Parks Out of Politics" *NY Times*

1925   article, "About Municipal Rose-Gardens," *Amer. Rose Annual*

1925   Jun. 23 - death of father, Thomas John Caparn

1925   Jul., Nov. - articles: "Milford Park," Newark; "Law Memorial Park," Briarcliff Manor, on his designs for these parks

1926   review of final report, Bronx Parkway Commission, *Nat Mun Rev*

1926   Jan 1 - article, "Milestones in the Progress of Outdoor Advertising Regulation – The Present Stage" *City Planning*

1926   Mar 22 - *NY Times* article, Caparn office 18 East 41ˢᵗ St. Manhattan

1926   Mar. 26 - letter "For A Park Board" *The New York Times*

1926   Sept. - consulting trip, Yellowstone Nat'l Park, with Supt. Horace Albright

1926   ground plan for Club House, Theatre, Onteora Park (not implemented)

1926   laid out streets, lots, Cold Spring Harbor Bio. Laboratory, L.I., NY

1927   Jan. - article, "Preserving Yellowstone scenery" *Landscape Architecture*

1927   Jan. - article, "The Status of Niagara Falls" *Parks & Recreation*

1927   Jan. - detailed ground plan, for Elizabeth D. Dwight, Onteora Park, NY

1927   Feb. 2 - article, "Wants City Parks Under New Control" *The NY Times*

1927   designs estate of J. B. Pound, "Stonedge" Lookout Mtn., TN

1927   work begun on the Cranford Rose Garden, BBG

1928   designs grounds, home and business, F. Donald Coster, McKesson & Robbins, Inc.; letter from Caparn atty. to Coster

1928   Apr. - review, book by F. L. Olmsted, Jr. & Theodora Kimball, "Central Park, as a work of art" *Landscape Architecture*

1929   chair, Frederick Law Olmsted (Sr.) Memorial Committee, ASLA

1929   article, "Restoration of Central Park," *Amer. Civic Annual* 1

1929   Apr. - article, "Thoughts on planting composition," *Land. Architecture*

1929   Jun. - article, "Scapa helps scrap billboards," *National Municipal Review*

1930   three articles on state parks reprinted for conference, Wash. D.C. "A State Park Anthology"

1930   Jul. - article, "The Preservation of Landscape Park Scenery Under City Conditions," *Landscape Architecture.* begins campaign against coal smoke pollution; includes letters to Mayor F. LaGuardia

1930   Dec. - article, "Scientific & decorative principles," design, central quadrangle, Lebanon Valley College, Annville, PA. *Am. L. Arch.*

Timeline

1931	Jan. - article, "The Founding of the American Society of Landscape Architects" *American Landscape Architect*
1931	Jan. - article, "Informal Design," *Landscape Architecture*
1931	Mar. 24 - letter, "Central Park Plans" *The New York Times*
1931	Jul. - letter, "Keep Inwood Park, Manhattan, Natural" *NY Times*
1932	Jan. - article, "Popular Botany and Botanic Gardens" *Land. Architecture*
1932	spring - "Magnolia Plaza" planted, BBG
1932	Jul - article, "The Planning of a Botanic Garden," *Land. Architecture*
1933	Jul. – BBG Armillary Sphere designed Harold, astrological band designed Rhys; installed, Magnolia Plaza, *BBG Report*
1934	Oct. - letter, *New York Herald Tribune*, "Our Vanishing Farm Land," re mismanagement, erosion of farm land
1935	Apr. 9 - letter to Serge Koussevitzky, conductor, Boston Symphony, critiques work just performed in NY, "Lulu Suite" by Alban Berg
1935	designs grounds of F. G. Frost, Jr., architect, New Rochelle, NY
1935	Oct. - letter to Mayor F. LaGuardia, protesting smoke pollution
1935	elevation, North Addition, planted, BBG, "Osborne Garden" ded. 1939
1935	Dec. 13 - letter to Leopold Stokowski, conductor, Philadelphia Orchestra re performance in NY of G. F. Handel's "Water Music Suite"
1936	Apr - fourteen-article series, "Garden Decoration," *Arts & Dec.* begins
1936	May - letter to Pres., World's Fair, objects to one large bldg. concept
1936	elevation, Cranford Rose Arc, Brooklyn Botanic Garden
1937	Sept. - fourteen-article series "Garden Decoration" ends
1938	designs planting for Brooklyn College, East campus
1939	article, "Roses in the Landscape," *Amer. Rose Annual*
1939	Mar. - letter, "Adding to Battery Park" *The New York Times*,
1939	designs "Woodland Garden" New York World's Fair, reviewed with acclaim in *The New York Times* (7/30/1939 & 5/26/1940)
1940	article, "Ground forms in Landscape Composition," *Land. Arch.*
1940 – 1941	articles, "What Rose Bushes to Use," "Making a Municipal Rose-Garden," *Amer. Rose Annual*
1941	Apr. - letter, "Battery Park Plan Proposed" *The New York Times*
1942	article, "The Brooklyn Rose-Garden" *American Rose Annual*
1943	Feb. - letter, re mixed use for skyscrapers, *New York Herald Tribune*
1944	Jun. 23 - letter, "Future of Jackson Hole" *New York Herald Tribune*
1945	Jul. - plan, "Layout of an American front yard," *BBG Record*
1945	Jul. - retires as consulting Landscape Architect, Brooklyn Botanic Garden
1945	Sept. 24 - death of Harold ap Rhys Caparn, age 80 years, 9 months, NYC

1946   Jan. - reprint in book, *A Garden for You*, of thirteen of the fourteen-
              article series, pub. in *Arts and Decoration*, 1936-1937

Bibliography

Harold A. Caparn articles

Column one, date of publication, 1893-12 indicates 1893-December

Column two, abbreviations for the various journals cited:

AmArBN	American Architect and Building News
AmCvAn	American Civic Annual
AmCvAssn	American Civic Association
AmLArch	American Landscape Architect
AmRAn	American Rose Annual
Ar&CR	Architect and Contract Reporter
Ar&BldM	Architect's and Builder's Magazine
ArchRec	Architectural Record
Archit	Architecture
A&Dec	Arts and Decoration
BBGRec	Brooklyn Botanic Garden Record
CGCBul	City Gardens Club Bulletin
CLife	Country Life In America
CtyPlan	City Planning
Countrys	Countryside
Crafts	Craftsman
CvCom	Civic Comment
Gar&For	Garden and Forest
HsBeau	House Beautiful
Hs&Gar	House and Garden
Indepndt	The Independent
JnlGarClb	Journal of the International Garden Club
LA	Landscape Architecture
NConfSPk	National Conference on State Parks
NMunRev	National Municipal Review
NPFFG	National Plant, Flower, and Fruit Guild Magazine
P&Cem	Park and Cemetery and Landscape Gardening
P&Rec	Parks and Recreation
PenPts	Pencil Points
PCvCom	Planning and Civic Comment
Pl&Gar	Plants and Garden
RlGar	Real Gardening
SewanRev	Sewanee Review
Touchst	Touchstone
Trans 1	Transactions of the ASLA vol. 1, 1899-1908

Column three, author, (Caparn, Harold) indicates about the subject

Column four, title and pages, words may be omitted to fit the space

Harold A. Caparn Articles

date	source	author (about)	title	pages
1893-12	Gar&For 6	Caparn, Harold A.	Composition in Landscape-art. 522-23	
1894-7	Gar&For 7	Caparn, Harold A.	The Aesthetic Value of Roads and Walks. 272-73	
1894-9	Gar&For 7	Caparn, Harold A.	Carpet Bedding. 382-83	
1896-4	Gar&For 9	Caparn, Harold A.	Madison Square Again. 178	
1897-8	Gar&For 10	Caparn, Harold A.	Planting for the Future. 312-13	
1900-3	P&Cem 10	Caparn, Harold A.	An Ideal Cemetery. 8-9	
1903	AmArBN 79	Caparn, Harold A.	The development of Washington. 4-6	
1903-3	ArchRec 13	Caparn, Harold A.	Informal Outdoor Art. 259-69	
1903-11	Ar&BldM 5	Caparn, Harold A.	An unfinished piece of New York. 47-57	
1904-5	HsBeau 15	Caparn, Harold A. 337-41	An informal garden of 2 or 3 acres.	
1905	Trans 1	Caparn, Harold A.	A visit to Paris. 65-8	
1905-3	ArchRec	Caparn, Harold A.	The Value of the Curve in Street Architecture.	
1905-4	HsBeau 17	Caparn, Harold A.	The making of a small garden. 16-18	
1905-4	Ar&CR 73	Caparn, Harold A.	The curve in street architecture. 277-78	
1906-7	Crafts 10	Caparn, Harold A.	The riddle of the tall building. 477-88	
1906-9	Crafts 10	Caparn, Harold A.	Parallelogram Park-Sub.Life..Sq. Mile. 767-74	
1907	Trans 1	Caparn, Harold A.	A great water park in Jamaica Bay. 92-6	
1907-10	SewanRev	Caparn, Harold A.	The Question of Civic Improvement. 497-502	
1908-6	ArchRec 23	Caparn, Harold A.	Treating the ground…suburban house. 433-43	
1910-10	LA 1	Caparn, Harold A.	Statuary in informal settings. 22-30	
1911-7	LA 1	Caparn, Harold A.	Modern meditations among the tombs. 172-80	
1912	Trans 1	(Caparn, Harold)	appointed. ed. with James S. Pray, Downing Vaux	
1912-1	LA 2	Caparn, Harold A.	The course in landscape architecture. 59-61	
1912-1	LA 2	(Caparn, Harold)	editorial, 88. On recently instituted instruction	
1912-4	BBG Rec	(Caparn, Harold) Gager, Dir.	HAC listed with BBG staff, Stuart	
1912-5	ArchRec 31	Caparn, Harold A.	Landscape Design & the Designer of Landscape	
1912-7	LA 2	Caparn, Harold A. art. 167-76	Central Park, New York: a work of	
1912-12	Hs&Gar 22	Caparn, Harold A. 370-3, 396-8	Garden Contest, What Developed.	

1913-4	BBG Rec	(Caparn, Harold)	Vol II. No. 2, 32; HAC appointment as LA.
1914-4	LA 4	Caparn, Harold A. 81-8	The present status of Niagara Falls.
1914-4	Crafts 26	Caparn, Harold A.	drawing, Haggin cloister garden; about the garden
1915-7	LA 5	Caparn, Harold A.	Planting a botanic garden (BBG). 157-162, with Norman Taylor.
1917-1	LA 7	Caparn, Harold A.	Some reasons for a system of state parks. 65-72
1917-1	Countrys	Caparn, Harold A.	The house outdoors. 24. Introduc tion to series
1917-2	Countrys	Caparn, Harold A.	Placing the House on the Lot. 64-6
1917-3	Countrys	Caparn, Harold A.	The General Plan. 128-9, 161
1917-4	Countrys	Caparn, Harold A.	The House Outdoors-Don't Clutter It. 196-7
1917-5	Countrys	Caparn, Harold A.	Furnishing the House Outdoors. 263-5, 292-3
1917-6	Countrys	Caparn, Harold A.	Shrubs for the house outdoors. 334-5, 340
1917-7	Countrys	Caparn, Harold A.	Freak vegetation. 385, 396
1917-7	LA 7	Caparn, Harold A.	Advice. 193-4
1917-7	Indepndt	Caparn, Harold A.	The Plan of Your Place. 178
1917-12	JInGarClb	Caparn, Harold A.	Bk. Rev.: F. A. Waugh, Outdoor Theatres. 546-9
1918	Rehmann	Caparn, Harold A. 73-82	Informal Arr. Of a Small Property.
1918-1	Indepndt	Caparn, Harold A.	Your Place in Your Town. 32
1918-2	Indepndt	Caparn, Harold A.	Getting the Right Fence. 192
1918-3	Indepndt	Caparn, Harold A.	Making the Soil Produce. 358
1918-3	JInGarClb	Caparn, Harold A.	Bk. Rev.: F.A. Waugh, Natural Style...Gar. 143
1918-4	LA 8	Caparn, Harold A.	Public regulation of private build ings. 133-40
1918-5	Indepndt	Caparn, Harold A.	City Lawns. 212, 224-5
1918-6	Touchst 3	Caparn, Harold A.	Landscape architects and better crops. 282, 84
1918-6	JInGarClb	Caparn, Harold A.	A Design for an Outdoor Theatre. 252-55
1919	ArchRec	(Caparn, Harold) in parks	Talk to ASLA on public memorials
1919-1	LA 9	Caparn, Harold A.	A billboard catechism. 76-8
1919-2	Archit 39	Caparn, Harold A. 34-8	Garden architecture and sculpture.
1919-6	Archit 39	Caparn, Harold A.	Architecture and the greenhouse. 153-6
1920-4	LA 10	Caparn, Harold A.	Economizing on trained brains. 137-41

1920-6	P&Rec 3	Caparn, Harold A.	The impending epidemic (mem. sculp). 3-6
1920-6	Hs&Gar 37	Caparn, Harold A.	Statuary in the small garden. 27-9, 88
1920-6	CLife 38	(Caparn, Harold)	Land. Arch..Who Have Designed..C. Estates. 49
1920-9	Indepndt	Caparn, Harold A.	Use Your Garbage (recycling). 386
1921-4	R&Rec 4	Caparn, Harold A.	Increasing a community's park as sets. 195-7
1921-10	CvCom 6	Caparn, Harold A. (let. NYTimes)	The New York post office blight. 4
1921-11	AmRAn 6	Caparn, Harold A.	The Working Out of a Real Rose-Garden. 72-4
1921-11	NMunR 10	Caparn, Harold A.	State Parks. 581-600. Printed as supplement
1922-3	P&Rec 5	Caparn, Harold A.	The Palisades Interstate Park. 355-6
1922-4	AmCvAssn	Caparn, Harold A.	Do None of Us Think? (Nat'l Parks Committee)
1922-12	NMunR 11	Caparn, Harold A.	Ze ceety pays. 403
1923-11	P&Rec 7	Caparn, Harold A.	The Colleoni statue. 147-8
1924-6	LMvCmFr 1	Caparn, Harold A.	C'est la ville qui paie! reprint, Fr. Journal, 1922-12
1924-7	P&Rec 7	Caparn, Harold A.	Defends Central Park. 658-9 (let. to ed.)
1924-9	P&Rec 8	Caparn, Harold A.	Need of experts in state park dev. 36-7
1924-10	LA 15	Caparn, Harold A.	Comments on conference, state parks. 30-2
1925	AmRAn 10	Caparn, Harold A.	About Municipal Rose-Gardens. 35-42
1925	AmRAn 10	Caparn, Harold A.	Designing a small rose garden. 43-9
1925-5	P&Rec 8	Caparn, Harold A.	What and why is a park? 441, 443
1925-5	reprint	Caparn, Harold A. InstParkExec	What and Why is a Park? 4pp Nat-InstParkExec
1925-7	P&Rec 8	Caparn, Harold A.	How often does one see..good park? 513-15
1925-7	P&Rec 8	Caparn, Harold A.	Milford Park in Newark, NJ. 521-2
1925-10	P&Rec 8	Caparn, Harold A.	Some principles of park gov. (ref. NYC) 15-20
1925-11	P&Rec 9	Caparn, Harold A. 157-9	Law Mem. Park, Briarcliff Manor.
1926	NMunR 15	Caparn, Harold A.	Rev. Bronx Parkway Commission Reports. 608
1926-1	CtyPlan 2	Caparn, Harold A.	Milestone..progress of outdoor adv. regs. 164-74
1927-1	P&Rec 10	Caparn, Harold A.	The irritating billboard. 290-2
1927-1	P&Rec 10	Caparn, Harold A.	Present..water diversions..Niagara Falls. 288-90
1927-1	LA 17	Caparn, Harold A.	Preserving..Yellowstone Park scenery. 77-82
1927-1	LA 17	Caparn, Harold A.	editorial, against taking Bechler Meadows

1927-1	P&Rec 10	Caparn, Harold A.	The Preservation of Bechler Mead ows. 212-15
1927-5	NPFFG 16	Caparn, Harold A.	Some thoughts..planting..church grounds. 6-8, 29
1927-7	LA 17	Caparn, Harold A.	Economic pressure and national parks. 300-1
1928-4	LA 18	Caparn, Harold A.	Bk. Rev.: Central Park, as a work of art
1928-7	LA 18	Caparn, Harold A.	The billboard dilemma. 298-303
1928-11	P&Rec 12	Caparn, Harold A.	Columbus Park at Yonkers, N.Y. 77-80
1929	AmCvAn 1	Caparn, Harold A.	The restoration of Central Park. 200-2
1929-4	LA 19	Caparn, Harold A.	Thoughts on planting composition. 141-56
1929-5	BBGRec	(Caparn, Harold)	Vo. 18, No. 3, 188. schematic, sys tematic section
1929-6	NMunRev 18	Caparn, Harold A.	Scapa helps scrap billboards. 366-69
1930	NConfSPk	Caparn, Harold A.	State Park Anthology. (reprnt 1921-11) 583-89
1930	NConfSPk	HAC & J. Downer	Planning a State Park. 96-104
1930	NConfSPk	Caparn, Harold A.	State Park Anthology. (reprnt 1924-10) 30-2
1930-2	CGCBul	Caparn, Harold A.	Broadleaf evergreens for city plant ing. 6-7
1930-7	LA 20	Caparn, Harold A.	The preservation of park scen ery..city cond. 327-32
1930-12	AmLArch 3	Caparn, Harold A.	Sci & dec. principles. (Leb Val Coll) 12-16, 38-9
1931-1	LA 21	Caparn, Harold A.	informal design. 105-9
1931-1	AmLArch 4	Caparn, Harold A.	Founding of American Society of Land. Arch.
1931-10	P&Rec 15	Caparn, Harold A.	Park contraptions. 50-1
1932-1	LA 22	Caparn, Harold A.	Popular botany and botanic gardens. 81-8
1932-6	AmLArch 6	Caparn, Harold A.	Professional charges. 6
1932-7	LA 22	Caparn, Harold A.	The planning of a botanic garden. 261-69
1933-3	P&Rec 16	Caparn, Harold A.	Park damage. 314-15, 376, 411
1933-7	BBGRec	(Caparn, Harold)	Armillary Sphere at BBG. 207
1933-9	P&Rec 16	Caparn, Harold A.	Park policing. 9-10, 450-1, 492-3
1934-4	BBGRec	(Caparn, Harold)	Armillary Sphere, by Harold & Rhys, Cover, 40
1936	Harp&Row	Caparn, Harold A.	articles in The Garden Dict., N. Taylor, ed.
1936-4	A&Dec 44	Caparn, Harold A.	Study..if planning a perennial bor der. 29, 45
1936-4	A&Dec 44	Caparn, Harold A.	Making your own rock garden. 35, 43, 48
1936-5	A&Dec 44	Caparn, Harold A.	Through one summer..annual gar den. 38, 46
1936-5	A&Dec 44	Caparn, Harold A.	The essential shrubbery border. 39, 46

1936-6	A&Dec 44	Caparn, Harold A.	A foundation for water gardens. 32-3
1936-8	A&Dec 44	Caparn, Harold A.	Hot weather gardens. 33-4, 47
1936-9	A&Dec 45	Caparn, Harold A.	The massing and grouping of ever greens. 36-7
1936-10	A&Dec 45	Caparn, Harold A.	Planting bulbs..next spring's gar dens. 40-2, 55
1937-1	A&Dec 45	Caparn, Harold A.	Garden decoration..modern house. 34-5, 44
1937-3	A&Dec 46	Caparn, Harold A.	If you love roses. 28-30, 39
1937-3	A&Dec 46	Caparn, Harold A.	The average yard. 42-3, 53
1937-4	A&Dec 46	Caparn, Harold A.	Garden paths..how to make them. 27-9, 45, 55
1937-5	A&Dec 46	Caparn, Harold A.	What and why is a cutting garden? 37, 40
1937-9	A&Dec 47	Caparn, Harold A.	A red spring garden. 28-30, 39
1938-12	RlGar 1	Caparn, Harold A.	Thoughts on relating.house. grounds. 13-17
1939	AmRAn 24	Caparn, Harold A.	Roses in the Landscape. 129-31
1940-10	LA 31	Caparn, Harold A.	Ground forms in landsc. comp. 19-20 re Cntrl Pk
1941	AmRAn 26	Caparn, Harold A.	What Rose bushes to Use, and Where. 49-53
1941	AmRAn 26	Caparn, Harold A.	Making a Municipal Rose-Garden. 59-60
1941-2	PenPts 22	Caparn, Harold A.	Notes re LA retention..three years. 10
1942	AmRAn 27	Caparn, Harold A.	The Brooklyn Rose-Garden. 112-14
1944-3	unpub	Caparn, Harold A.	Glacial Boulders in Gardens. 2+p. typescript
1945-7	Pl&Gar 1	Caparn, Harold A.	Layout of an American front yard. 68-9
1945-12	LA 36	(Caparn, Harold)	C. D. Lay, a biographical minute. 22-3
1946-1	McBride pub	Caparn, Harold A.	O'Donnell, ed. A Garden for You. Reprint 1937-3/1
1946-1	McBride	Caparn, Harold A.	A Garden for You. Reprint 1937/4
1946-1	McBride	Caparn, Harold A.	A Garden for You. Reprint 1936-5/1
1946-1	McBride	Caparn, Harold A.	A Garden for You. Reprint 1936-4/1
1946-1	McBride	Caparn, Harold A.	A Garden for You. Reprint 1936-10
1946-1	McBride	Caparn, Harold A.	A Garden for You. Reprint 1936-5/2
1946-1	McBride	Caparn, Harold A.	A Garden for You. Reprint 1936-4/2
1946-1	McBride	Caparn, Harold A.	A Garden for You. Reprint 1937-3/2
1946-1	McBride	Caparn, Harold A.	A Garden for You. Reprint 1936-8
1946-1	McBride	Caparn, Harold A.	A Garden for You. Reprint 1937-9
1946-1	McBride	Caparn, Harold A.	A Garden for You. Reprint 1937-5
1946-1	McBride	Caparn, Harold A.	A Garden for You. Reprint 1936-9

Harold A. Caparn
Letters published

Date	To	From	Title, subject
1894-12	NYTimes	(Caparn, Thos. J)	article: Does Not Agree with Mr. Olmsted
1898-2	NYTimes	Caparn, Harold A.	to Ed. Wants Mr. Parson Back (signed, Yonkers)
1899-3	NYTimes	Caparn, Harold A.	to Ed. In Defense of the Bushes (signed, Yonkers)
1899-10	NYTimes	Caparn, Harold A. (7th Ave/110 St)	to Ed. Site for the Dewey Arch (7th
1899-10	NYTimes	Caparn, Harold A.	to Ed. No Objection to Ellipse re Dewey Arch
1900-11	NYTimes	Caparn, Harold A.	to Ed. The Oratorio Society
1901-1	NYTimes	Caparn, Harold A.	to Ed. The Naval Arch, Dewey Cel ebrations
1902-2	NYTimes	Caparn, Harold A.	to Ed. The Artist and the Artisan
1903-7	NYTimes	Caparn, Harold A.	to Ed. Reclamation of Swamp Lands
1903-8	NYTimes	Caparn, Harold A.	to Ed. Plans for Repression of the Mosquito
1904-4	NYTimes	Caparn, Harold A.	to Ed. Value of the [Bronx] "Zoo"
1904-4	NYTimes	E. H. N.	to Ed. A Good Word for the "Zoo"
1904-5	NYTimes	Willever, J. C.	to Ed. Interest in the "Zoo"
1904-8	NYTimes	Caparn, Harold A.	to Ed. Monotony of Right Angles re Central Park
1908-2	NYTimes	Caparn, Harold A.	to Ed. The Poor Do Use the Small Parks
1909-2	NYTimes	(Caparn, Harold) talk by Caparn	article Bacchante Parade to Dance,
1909-4	NYTimes	Caparn, Harold A.	to Ed. Park Area: Encroachments Bad
1909-4	NYTimes	(Caparn, Harold)	article Choose Delegates to Fight Park Grab
1911-2	NYTimes	(Caparn, Harold)	article Develop Fifth Ave on Lines of Beauty
1911-3	NYTimes	(Caparn, Harold)	editorial Merchants Ask City Repave Fifth Ave
1911-3	NYTimes	(Caparn, Harold) of Streets	article Fight Bill Changing Control
1911-3	NYTimes	Caparn, Harold A.	to Ed. The Parks in Spring
1911-6	NYTimes	(Caparn, Harold) arcliff Manor	article purchase of Fernie Farm, Bri
1911-8	NYTimes	Caparn, Harold A.	to Ed. New York's Parks: Liberty Allowed In
1912-3	NYTimes	Caparn, Harold A.	to Ed. New Central Park Lawns
1912-5	NYTimes	Caparn, Harold A.	to Ed. Building Sites in Central Park: Lenox Lib.

1912-6	NYTimes	(Caparn, Harold)	article Who Picked Park for Lenox Library?
1912-6	NYTimes	Caparn, Harold A.	to Ed. American Parks vs European Parks
1912-6	NYTimes	(Caparn, Harold)	article Noted Men to Lead Park Defense Fight
1912-7	NYTimes	(Caparn, Harold)	article: Garden Beautiful Contest Winners
1913-12	NYTimes	Caparn, Harold A.	to Ed. Good Landscape Design: co-operation
1913-12	NYTimes	Caparn, Harold A.	to Ed. Landscape Designs
1913-12	NYTimes	Ebel, M. C.	to Ed. Landscape Designs (Nat. Ass. Gardener)
1914-2	NYTimes	Caparn, Harold A.	to Ed. Central Park a Playground
1914-3	NYTimes	Caparn, Harold A.	to Ed. Its Lawns and Scenery Offer Recreation
1914-5	NYTimes	Caparn, Harold A.	to Ed. St. John's Church Worth Saving
1916-3	NYTimes	Caparn, Harold A.	to Ed. Modest Appeal: Park in Winter-Cntrl Pk
1916-9	NYTimes	Caparn, Harold A.	to Ed. Open Spaces More..Than Stadium
1916-12	NYTimes	Caparn, Harold A.	to Ed. High Bridge, Harlem River
1918-3	NYTimes	(Caparn, Harold)	article City Brevities: Caparn talk Met Museum
1921-8	NYTimes	Caparn, Harold A.	to Ed. Money for the Parks (Samuel Parsons)
1921-10	NYTimes	Caparn, Harold A.	to Ed. Post Office Blight: City Hall Park
1922-1	NYTimes	Caparn, Harold A.	to Ed. Park Administration
1922-4	NYTimes	(Caparn, Harold)	article Landscape Society Joins Park Protest
1922-6	NYTimes	Caparn, Harold A.	to Ed. Protests Park as Dumping Ground
1922-7	NYTimes	Caparn, Harold A.	to Ed. Central Park Memorial re reservoir
1922-7	NYTimes	Caparn, Harold A.	to Ed. Forty Elms in the Mall
1922-8	NYTimes	(Caparn, Harold) Pushcarts	to Ed. Policy in Park Mgmt: City's
1923-11	NYTimes	Caparn, Harold A.	to Ed. Cost of a Park Subway: fifty years
1923-11	NYTimes	Caparn, Harold A.	article Call Subway Plan A Threat to Parks
1923-12	NYTimes	Caparn, Harold A.	to Ed. Starving the Parks: deterioration
1924-3	NYTimes	(Caparn, Harold)	to Ed. Repelling Park Attacks
1924-3	NYTimes	(Caparn, Harold)	to Ed. Latest Raid Must be Defeated
1924-3	NYTimes	(Caparn, Harold)	article Block Park Site Seizure Art Center

1924-3	NYTimes	(Caparn, Harold)	article Park Invasion Fight is Taken to Albany
1924-4	NYTimes	Caparn, Harold A.	article Plan Mass Meeting on Park Invasions
1924-4	NYTimes	Caparn, Harold A.	article Home rule Bill May Protect Park
1924-6	NYTimes	Caparn, Harold A.	to Ed. Enright's Memorial Plan
1924-7	P&Rec	(Caparn, Harold)	to Ed. Defends Central Park
1924-8	NYTimes	Caparn, Harold A.	to Ed. Parks or Playgrounds?
1924-8	NYTimes	Caparn, Harold A.	editorial Topics of the Times: Ca parn re Parks
1924-10	NYTimes	Caparn, Harold A.	to Ed. The Cost of Our Parks: more money
1924-12	NYTimes	Caparn, Harold A.	to Ed. Would Bar Politics from Park System
1924-12	NYTimes	Caparn, Harold A.	to Ed. Closing Central Park to Autos
1925-1	NYTimes	Caparn, Harold A.	to Ed. Suggests Changes to Central Park
1925-4	NYTimes	(Caparn, Harold)	to Ed. Protecting the Parks: Central Park
1925-5	NYTimes	Caparn, Harold A.	article Park Playgrounds Draw Di vers Views
1925-5	NYTimes	Caparn, Harold A.	to Ed. Would Take Parks Out of Politics
1925-8	NYTimes	(Caparn, Harold) nuity needed	to Ed. The Parks and Politics: conti
1925-10	NYTimes	(Caparn, Harold)	to Ed. Women and the Parks
1925-11	NYTimes	(Caparn, Harold)	article Hylan Loses Fight for Park Memorial
1925-12	NYTimes	(Caparn, Harold)	article Organize to Help Save Cen tral Park
1925-12	NYTimes	(Caparn, Harold) Defense	article Eleven Sign Papers for Park
1925-12	NYTimes	Caparn, Harold A.	article Park Defenders Will Incorpo rate
1926-1	NYTimes	Caparn, Harold A.	article Walker Opposes Invasion of Parks
1926-3	NYTimes	(Caparn, Harold) Urged	to Ed. One-Man Control for Parks
1926-3	NYTimes	Caparn, Harold A.	to Ed. For A Park Board
1926-3	NYTimes	Caparn, Harold A.	article Mrs. Pratt Submits Park Re form Bill
1926-6	NYTimes	Caparn, Biarold A.	to Ed. Objectors to Mrs. Pratt's Bill: Park Admin.
1926-11	NYTimes	Caparn, Harold A.	to Ed. Despoliation is Feared of Na tional Parks
1926-12	NYTimes	(Caparn, Harold)	to Ed. Concerning Bechler Meadows

1927-2	NYTimes	Caparn, Harold A.	to Ed. Wants City Parks Under New Control
1927-6	NYTimes	(Caparn, Harold)	article Progress of City Gardens Club
1927-12	NYTimes	(Caparn, Harold)	to Ed. Bechler Meadows No En croachment
1928-5	NYTimes	Caparn, Harold A.	article Park Bodies Merge in New Association
1929-3	NYTimes	Caparn, Harold A.	article Straus Urges Veto of Con course Bill
1929-12	NYTimes	Caparn, Harold A.	to Ed. A Plea for Sidewalks re Saw Mill Riv Prkwy
1930-6	NYTimes	Caparn, Harold A.	to Ed. Dangerous Fallacy
1930-8	NYTimes	(Caparn, Harold)	article Playgrounds Not Perfect
1931-3	NYTimes	Caparn, Harold A.	to Ed. Central Park Plans
1931-6	NYTimes	Caparn, Harold A.	article New Riis Park Plan Includes Golf Area
1931-7	NYTimes	Caparn, Harold A.	to Ed. Inwood Park: Develop on Natural Lines
1931-8	NYTimes	Caparn, Harold A.	to Ed. The Riis Park Golf Course
1931-8	NYTimes	(Caparn, Harold)	article Competition Urged for Riis Park Plan
1931-8	NYTimes	(Caparn, Harold)	article To Weigh Riis Park Plans
1931-8	NYTimes	(Caparn, Harold)	article Benninger to Back Riis Park Golf Plan
1931-10	NYTimes	Caparn, Harold A.	to Ed. Air Pollution: Plant Life Not Only Affected
1932-5	NYTimes	(Caparn, Harold)	article Scope of Riis Park Broadened in Plan
1932-5	NYTimes	Caparn, Harold A.	to Ed. Golf in Jacob Riis Park
1932-5	NYTimes	HAC "Bystander"	to Ed. Golf as a Fad
1932-10	NYTimes	Caparn, Harold A.	to Ed. Amendment No. 1 re State Forests
1933-5	NYTimes	Caparn, Harold A.	to Ed. Those Who Need The Park
1933-5	NYTimes	(Caparn, Harold)	article Central Park Carried to Mayor
1934-3	NYTimes	(Caparn, Harold)	article Landscape Plans Put on Exhi bition
1934-5	NYTimes	(Caparn, Harold)	article Hodson and Moses Clash on Uniforms
1934-10	NYHerTri	Caparn, Harold A.	article Our Vanishing Farm Land
1934-10	NYTimes	Caparn, Harold A.	to Ed. Regulating Use of Land re soil erosion
1935-2	NYTimes	Caparn, Harold A.	to Ed. suggests Water Music per formance
1935-5	NYHerTri	Caparn, Harold A.	to L. Gilman, comments on perfor mances
1937-8	NYHerTri	Caparn, Harold A.	to Ed. Children at Play

1939-3	NYTimes	Caparn, Harold A.	to Ed. Battery Bridge Opposed
1939-3	NYHerTri	Caparn, Harold A.	to Ed. Proposed Battery Park bridge and park
1939-3	NYTimes	Caparn, Harold A.	to Ed. Adding to Battery Park
1939-7	NYTimes	(Caparn, Harold)	article Design for Outdoor Living, World's Fair
1940-8	NYTimes	(Caparn, Harold)	article A Wildwood Path at World's Fair
1941-3	NYTimes	Caparn, Harold A.	to Ed. Battery Park Plan Proposed
1941-4	NYTimes	Caparn, Harold A. for area	to Ed. Battery Park Plan Proposed,
1941-9	NYHerTri	HAC "Bystander"	to Ed. Chance of Invasion Seen, His tory invoked
1943-11	NYHerTri	HAC "Bystander"	to Ed. Germ of Big Business
1944-3	NYHerTri	HAC "Bystander"	to Ed. Wilkie, Then Dewey
1944-6	NYHerTri	Caparn, Harold A. ism	Various Preventives Against Vandal
1944-7	NYHerTri	Caparn, Harold A.	to Ed. Future of Jackson Hole
1944-9	NYHerTri	HAC "Bystander" WWII	to Ed. Would Hang Ringleaders of
1944-9	NYHerTri	HAC "Bystander"	to Ed. Scientific Approach Needed re STD
1945-1	NYHerTri	Caparn, Harold A.	to Ed. Choking on Smoke

Harold A. Caparn
Obituaries and related material

Date	source	writer	
1945-9	NYTimes	Caparn, Rhys	H. A. Caparn Dead; Landscape Ex pert; photo
1945-9	NYHerTri	Caparn, Rhys	Harold Caparn obituary
1945	NYSun	Caparn, Rhys	notice of death
1945-10	LA 36	Lay, Ch. Downing	Harold Caparn necrology, for the ASLA. 22-3
1945-10	P&CC 10	editor	Obituary, 45. Charter member, AmCvAssn 1904
1945-10	Clara Caparn	Albright, Horace	letter of condolence to Mrs. Caparn
1945-11	Rhys Steel	Lawton, Elizabeth	letter of condolence, Nat'l Roadside Council
1946-2	Clara Caparn	James, Harlean	resolution of sorrow by Board AmCvAssn

Harold A. Caparn Photographs

List No.	number	photographer	subject
491	3 photos	attr. H. A. Caparn	Grant Park, Yonkers, NY
492	1 photo	unknown	Estate Plan, D.A. Bullard, Schuylerville, NY
493	5 photos	attr. H. A. Caparn	Estate of Hon. Jos. E. Willard, Fairfax, VA
507	3 photos	attr. H. A. Caparn	Estate of J. C. Willever, Millburn, NJ
574	1 photo	Sheldon	Home, J. H. Tanner, Ithaca, NY
575	2 photos	attr. H. A. Caparn	BBG, Magnolia plaza with armillary sphere by HAC
575	1 photo	attr. H. A. Caparn	Jenkins Bridge, sketch for design
575	1 photo	L. Buhle	Jenkins Bridge, as built
575	2 photos	attr. H. A. Caparn	2 bridges/marsh; 1 bridge/gully; early site
575	3 photos	attr. H. A. Caparn	three views, armillary sphere, c. 1933
575	1 photo	Caparn, Harold A.	Jenkins Fountain "HAC LA" on reverse
575	1 photo	Caparn, Harold A.	Systematic Section: beds of campanules
575	1 photo	Caparn, Harold A.	Design, Rose Garden, Dec. 7, 1925
575	5 photos	attr. H. A. Caparn	five views on the lake, c. 1938
575	1 photo	attr. H. A. Caparn	view from Overlook, Cranford Rose Garden
575	1 photo	attr. H. A. Caparn	Willows along the brook
587	5 photos	attr. H. A. Caparn	Views of home, rose garden, Tully estate, LI, NY
623	3 photos	Smutny, R. V.	Estate, Maitland F. Griggs, Ardsley on Hudson, NY
624	5 photos	attr. H. A. Caparn	Caparn country retreat, Briarcliff Manor, NY
624	7 photos	attr. H. A. Caparn	Caparn retreat, home/studio, interior, exterior
624	6 photos	attr. H. A. Caparn	Caparn retreat, views of landscaping
1903	9 photos	attr. H. A. Caparn	illus. article "An Unfinished Piece of New York"
1904	5 photos	attr. H. A. Caparn	article "An Informal Garden"
1906	1 photo	Caparn, Harold A.	Central Park, The Mall at its prime
1907	2 photos	attr. H. A. Caparn	article "A Great Water Park in Jamaica Bay"
1910	18 photos	attr. H. A. Caparn	article "Statuary in Informal Settings"
1911	4 photos	attr. H. A. Caparn	article "Modern Meditations"
1912	6 photos	attr. H. A. Caparn	article "Central Park NY: A Work of Art"
c. 1915	1 photo	attr. H. A. Caparn	Clara Caparn seated in her music studio
1917	1 photo	attr. H. A. Caparn	article "The House Outdoors"
1918	8 photos	attr. H. A. Caparn	chapter "Informal Arrangement of a Small Place"
1925	2 photos	attr. H. A. Caparn	article "Milford Park in Newark, NJ"
1928	4 photos	attr. H. A. Caparn	article "Columbus Park at Yonkers, NY"
1930	3 photos	Caparn, Harold A.	article "Preservation of Landscape Scenery"
1940	2 photos	Caparn, Harold A.	article "Ground Forms in Landscape Composition"

Bibliography

Authors

Bridges, William. A Gathering of Animals. New York: Harper & Row, 1966. Information on the early history of the New York Zoological Park.

Elliott, James Wilkinson. A Plea for Hardy Plants, New York: Doubleday, Page & Co., 1902. 96 pp. with photographs and garden plans. Reprinted and expanded from his lecture for the Massachusetts Horticultural Society, 1895, that was published in the Society Transactions of that year. Includes a Caparn ground plan, plant list and description that Elliott endorsed as "very good."

Elliott, J. Wilkinson. Adventures of a Horticulturist, published by the author in limited edition, Point Loma, CA, 1935; printed by Mount Pleasant Press, J. Horace McFarland Co., Harrisburg, PA. Preface by J. Horace McFarland. Elliott's views on gardens, his entrepreneurship as an importer of plant material, his speculation in various business ventures and his knowledge of important people, for some of whom he did garden and estate designs.

Fenner, Robin A. A Genius Undeclared--The life, works and times of William John Caparne F. R. H. S. Tavistock, Devon: Stannery Gallery, 1994. Information also on Harold Caparn's father, Thomas John Caparn, and others in the family.

Fenner, Robin A. Guernsey—My Heaven on Earth, William John Caparne F. R. H. S. His adopted island, Iris and other flowers. Tavistock, Devon: Stannery Gallery, 1998. Both volumes add to information on Harold Caparn's family, on Harold's cousin William and his horticultural and artistic interests.

Gilmartin, Gregory F. Shaping the City: New York and the Municipal Art Society. New York: Clarkson Potter Publishers, 1995. Caparn and the small parks movement in NYC.

Grese, Robert. Jens Jensen: Maker of Natural Parks and Gardens. The Johns Hopkins University Press, 1998. Quotes Caparn, "Thoughts on Planting Composition" as a context for Jensen's work.

Hale, Robert Beverly. Rhys Caparn. Danbury, CT: Retrospective Press, 1972. Briefly mentions her father. On her work as a sculptor.

Hemingway, Guy. "The Caparn Family of Newark & Some of Their Descendants," typescript, 1979. Newark Library, Nottinghamshire, U. K. Entries on family members cited, especially Thomas John Caparn and his work.

Hemingway, Guy. "Caparn Entries in the Newark Parish Church Register," typescript, n.d., Newark Library, Nottinghamshire, U.K.

Hubbard, Henry Vincent and Theodora Kimball, An Introduction to the Study of Landscape Design (1917), rev. and reprinted Boston: Hubbard Educational Trust, 1967. Cites Caparn articles on composition, planting design, structures (statuary), cemeteries and parks. Used as text for course study in landscape architecture.

Jackson, Noel George. Newark Magnus: The Story of a Gift. Nottingham: J. and H. Bell, Ltd., 1964. The gift from Thomas Magnus, the emissary of Henry VIII, that founded the Magnus Grammar School and the Song School at St. Mary Magdalene, with some history of the Song School Masters and the Music Masters at the Grammar

School, especially Samuel Reay and William H. Caparn, Jr., Harold's uncle and music tutor during his youth.

McCullough, David. The Greater Journey – Americans in Paris. New York: Simon & Schuster, 2011. On the attraction of Paris as a destination for medical students, visual artists, writers, architects and musicians.

Miller, Sara Cedar. Seeing Central Park – The Official Guide to the World's Greatest Urban Park. New York: Harry N. Abrams, Inc., 2009. Illustrations, Map.

O'Donnell, Thomas C. A Garden for You. New York: Robert M. McBride & Company, 1946. Reprints thirteen of the fourteen Caparn articles from the series in Arts & Decoration, 1936-37.

Pound, Jerome Balaam. Memoirs of Jerome B. Pound. Privately published by the author in limited edition, 1949. Although he mentions the architect Clarence T. Jones, he does not mention Caparn as landscape architect. There is a short description of the estate "Stonedge," on Lookout Mountain, TN, and a photo of the entrance to the estate, 152-54. The photo was made into a postcard. J. B. Pound is given as no. 630 on Caparn's client list.

Rehmann, Elsa. The Small Place: Its Landscape Architecture. New York: G. P. Putnam, 1918. Contains Caparn's chapter on his design of a landscape for a home in Larchmont, New York.

Rydell, Kiki Leigh and Mary Shivers Culpin, Managing the Matchless Wonders, A History of Administrative Development in Yellowstone National Park, 1872-1965. National Park Service, Yellowstone Center for Resources, 2006. Mentions Caparn's contribution to the design of walks, walls and other natural elements.

Schroeder, Fred E. H. Front Yard America. Madison, WI: University of Wisconsin Press, 1993, 2001.

Sisler, Carol U. Enterprising Families, Ithaca, New York, Their Houses and Businesses. Ithaca, New York: Enterprise Publishing, 1986. Information on Cayuga Heights.

Sonne, Christian R. and Chiu yin Hempel, with photographs by James Bleecker. Tuxedo Park: The Historic Houses. Tuxedo Park, New York: Tuxedo Historical Society, 2007. Background on two estates on which Caparn did landscape designs.

Steel, Rhys Caparn. Biographical Data sheets, Council of Fellows, American Society of Landscape Architects, July 8, 1977. Reference on his life and work. Collection of the writer; also filed in H. A. Caparn, ASLA.

Stilgoe, John R. Borderland: Origins of the American Suburb, 1820-1939. Princeton University Press, 1990.

Tankard, Judith B. Beatrix Farrand. New York: The Monacelli Press, 2009. Reference to Caparn's article on the founding of the ASLA, of which Farrand was a reader prior to publication.

Taylor, Norman, ed. The Garden Dictionary. New York: Harper & Row, 1936. Some entries by Caparn. Taylor assisted with the 1915 article by Caparn on planting the Brooklyn Botanic Garden.

Uhlfelder, Eric. The Origins of Modern Architecture. Courier Dover Pub., 1998; reprints H. A. Caparn, "The Value of the Curve in Street Architecture," Architectural Record, April 1905. Illus.

Van Rensselaer, Mariana Griswold. Art out-of-doors: Hints on Good Taste in Gardening. New York: Charles Scribner's Sons, 1893. 1911 ed. Reprinted 2009; other reprints available. 1925 ed. Gives changes between the first edition and to date. Caparn cites Art out of doors in his article on Lebanon Valley College grounds (1930) on the knowledge needed for a landscape designer.

Maurice Volaski '87, with Dr. Roy E. McGowan, Faculty Advisor. Touring the Brooklyn College Landscape – A Guide to the Shrubs and Trees on the Brooklyn College Campus. Brooklyn College, 1987.

Watson, Elizabeth L. Grounds for Knowledge: A Guide to Cold Spring Harbor Laboratory's Landscapes & Buildings. New York: Cold Spring Harbor Laboratory Press, 2008. Gives the development of the grounds, buildings and arboretum.

Watson, Elizabeth L. Houses for Science. New York: Cold spring Harbor Laboratory Press, 1991. Gives the plan (1926) by Caparn for the layout of the campus at the time.

Wilson, William H. The City Beautiful Movement. Baltimore: The Johns Hopkins University Press, 1989. Gives the historical context to Caparn's writing relative to the idea, which he does not name.

Sources

Art Institute of Chicago, Ryerson and Burnham Libraries. Exhibition Catalogues of the Chicago Architectural Club, 1903, 1906, 1907, 1914, listing Harold Caparn entries to exhibits. (retrieved 2/7/2010)

Briarcliff Manor—Scarborough Historical Society Museum. Maps, information and photographs of the environs of estates and the Caparn retreat.

Cold Spring Harbor, Long Island, New York, Cold Spring Harbor Biological Laboratory, Archive. Plot plan (1926) by Harold Caparn of the design for the 32 acres. Correspondence between the Laboratory Director and Caparn.

Cornell University, Ithaca, NY, Carl A. Kroch Library, Division of Rare and Manuscript Collections. Guide to the Harold Caparn Collection. Charles Downing Lay papers, re Madison Square Plan, The Future of Jamaica Bay, NY World's Fair Gardens on Parade; Papers of the American Planning and Civic Association; Harlean James correspondence; a copy of the separately reprinted article "What and Why is a Park." Jared T. Newman Papers on the real estate development at Cayuga Heights, Ithaca, laid out by Caparn.

Frederick Law Olmsted National Historical Site, Brookline, MA. Planting plan for Treat Memorial, Landing Park, Newark, NJ; photograph by Caparn of Central Park; listing of Olmsted Brothers work on Brooklyn Botanic Garden (1910-1919), Caparn involvement cited.

Georgetown University Library, Washington DC. Lawrence Gilman papers, Box: 1, Fold: 50, correspondence from Harold Caparn, 5/25/1935. Gilman was music critic for the New York Herald Tribune, radio commentator of broadcasts of the NY Philharmonic concerts. Typed letter signed.

Gustav Stickley, The Craftsman (December 1906), "Soldiers' Home in Tennessee: A Noteworthy Example of a Group of Institutional Buildings Planned as a Whole." Discusses the careful and beautiful relation of buildings and grounds. (April 1914, 35) Caparn drawing of the Cloister Garden, on Wildmuir estate, Onteora Park, NY, 48, about the Cloister Garden.

Harvard University, Arnold Arboretum Research Library, Jamaica Plain, MA. Various journals and A Cumulative Index to Arnoldia, 1970-2000, vols. 30-60: (60) [3] 5; and "Correspondence: Madison Square Again" [1896] (60) [3] 19. (the article in Garden and Forest).

Harvard University, Graduate School of Design, Frances Loeb Library/Library of Congress. American Landscape and Architectural Design 1850-1920. Slide, "Caparn Home, front yard, Briar Cliff (sic) Manor, NY." Shows mature landscaping done by Caparn at his country retreat with his daughter Rhys, about age 12, for scale, c. 1921. Original photo in collection of the author, now in Caparn Collection, Cornell. Early journals in which Caparn published articles.

Kathleen LaFrank, nomination papers, Eaton Family Residence/Jewish Center of Norwich (NY), at 75 S. Broad St., to the State and National Registers of Historic Places, 2009.

Library of Congress, five items, letters to Caparn from the Olmsted firm.

Bibliography

Minnesota Historical Society, Quetico-Superior Council, Inventory of Records. Correspondence, 1928-1932, between Ernest C. Oberholtzer, outdoorsman and conservationist and Harold Caparn for the latter to serve on a national advisory board; endorsement of the Quetico-Superior program by the ASLA; Caparn's support of the Shipstead-Nolan bill

Moravian Pottery and Tile Works, a National Historic Landmark. Museum, Bucks County, Doylestown, PA. Order for Willever estate, Millburn, NJ, Caparn recorded as landscape architect. Founder H. C. Mercer was a supporter of the Arts and Crafts movement.

National Archives, Washington, DC. Informal notes, from Caparn to National Park Service Superintendent Albright, in 1926, regarding a portion of Yellowstone National Park, in Record Group 79.

National Register of Historic Places. Nomination papers for Nitrate Village No. 1, Sheffield, Alabama (1984). see Endnote 15.3, later research and attribution of the houses to the New York firm of Mann and MacNeille. reference to Harold Caparn as Landscape Architect and Town Planner, p. 154. Mann and MacNeille, Harold Caparn and The White Construction Co. had offices in New York City.

New York Public Library. Rare books and Manuscripts Division. Richard Rogers Bowker Papers. Correspondence with Caparn re National Council for the Protection of Roadside Beauty.

Onteora Library, Onteora Park, Tannersville, New York. Planting plan for "Wild Garden"; journal of Mrs. Ben Ali Haggin (Jr.) recording plant gifts to garden dedicated to Candace Wheeler; plan, supervision of garden by Harold A. Caparn. Program for the Dedication of the Wheeler Wild Garden. Caparn plan (not implemented) for the Fieldhouse and Theatre at Onteora Park, 1926.

Pennsylvania State Archives, Harrisburg, Manuscript Group 85. J. Horace McFarland Papers, American Civic Association, Caparn: writing on billboards, 1918; correspondence, 1916, 1920, 1922; Yellowstone National Park Boundary Commission- Bechler River Basin, 1930; article, 1922, "Do None of Us Think?" National Parks Addresses and Articles, on the scope under discussion, of the National Parks Commission.

University of North Carolina, Chapel Hill, Wilson Library, Manuscripts Department. Materials concerning Clara Howard (Jones) Caparn.

University of the Pacific Library, Holt-Atherton Special Collections. Image of letter, April 4, 1912, from Harold Caparn to John Muir. (retrieved 5/2/10).

Westchester County Archives, Historic American Engineering Record (HAER), Bronx River Parkway Reservation. History, summary and photographs of the project, encompassing 1896 -1961. (retrieved 2/9/2010) Caparn wrote a review of this work.

Wildlife Conservation Society Archives, Bronx Zoo, The Bronx, NY. Correspondence between Caparn and Zoo. Annual Reports on progress of Caparn re landscape design for the Zoo. Report, Landmarks Preservation Commission (June 20, 2000) on designating Baird Court (Astor Court) and surrounding buildings and landscape as an Individual Landmark, City of New York, especially for its representation of the "City Beautiful" movement.

Acknowledgments

To the many librarians and archivists who have collected, catalogued, filed and have retrieved for me journals, books, plans, photographs and other materials that have been essential to the preparation of this work.

To the compliers of The New York Times Archive who have made available many informative articles that reveal insight to Caparn's works, clients and his own thoughts.

To the following people, and some not named, who I owe many thanks for their own research and their help with mine.

Barbara Allier, Librarian, Brooklyn College Library Archives and Special Collections, for providing the letter confirming Caparn's appointment at the College.

Annette Brown for granting permission to photograph the Griggs estate, Ardsley on Hudson, NY.

Arthur L. Caparn, Jr., of Virginia, Charles E. Caparn and Barbara (Caparn) Nitzberg, of New Jersey, for information on Arthur Tom Caparn and viewing of paintings by Thomas John Caparn.

James T. Chamberlain of Westford, MA, for the map of waterfront development on Jamaica Bay and Jacob Riis Park, Brooklyn and Queens, NY, subjects of Caparn's interest and proposals.

Caryl Clark, Professor of Music History and Culture, Faculty of Music at the University of Toronto, for providing access to documents and photographs at the Onteora Park Library and for calling attention to the Wheeler Dedication Program.

T. Michele Clark, Archivist, Frederick Law Olmsted National Historic Site, National Park Service, Brookline, MA, for assistance with reviewing and photographing holdings relative to Caparn.

Sheila Connor, Horticultural Research Archivist, The Arnold Arboretum, Harvard University, for viewing the Caparn archive materials and suggesting that they become a book.

Jo Cormier, of Stonedge Village, Lookout Mountain, TN, for description of the original estate "Stonedge" of Mr. and Mrs. J. B. Pound and her memories of the estate.

Lynne Crowley, archivist of the Larchmont Historical Society, for the identification of the home on Woodbine Avenue overlooking the Premium River, an inlet of the Long Island Sound, the subject of Caparn's chapter in Elsa Rehmann's book of landscape design solutions The Small Place (1918).

Robert Ekiss, a Village No. 1 resident, Sheffield, AL and Historic Commission member, for the sharing of his research, calling attention to the report by General Williams and providing the postcard view of Village No. 1.

Marlea Graham, for her generous sharing of research on J. Wilkinson Elliott, Caparn's employer in Pittsburgh where he began his career in landscape architecture.

Acknowledgements

M. Lee Griggs, III, for reference to the photos in the portfolio of the Roman Landscape Contracting Company of the property of Maitland F. Griggs, also the property of Frank Lyman.

Richmond "Duke" Hubbard, M.D. and his wife, Jeanne, of Bethel, CT, for preserving an essential portion of the Caparn archive, given into their possession, then placing it into mine.

Patricia Jonas, Director of Library Services, and Mae Pan, Archivist, Brooklyn Botanic Garden, for making available the Garden's holdings on Caparn.

Dan Kyte, Chief, Domiciliary Operations and Historian, James H. Quillen Veterans Administration Medical Center, Mountain Home, for information on the home and access to a thesis about the site.

Marianne LaBatto, archivist, Brooklyn College Library, for enthusiastic assistance with information and documents held by the Library.

Kathleen LaFrank, New York Historic Preservation Office, for identification of the home of Robert D. and Maria Smith Eaton, Norwich, NY, and her nomination of it to the State and National Registers of Historic Places (2009).

R. Lawrence (Larry) McCaffrey, New York and Onteora Park, for his generous sharing of information on the Park and the Wheeler-Haggin estate, reconstruction of the Caparn-designed cloister garden and introduction to other contributors of information on the Park.

Joseph and Shari Monasebian for gracious introduction to Caparn work in Briarcliff Manor.

Alexandra (Hallowell) Moore, Harold Caparn's granddaughter, for information and insight on Harold, Clara, Anne and Rhys.

Keith N. Morgan, of Boston University, for his early suggestions for the book.

Timothy D. O'Neil, of Cranston, RI, for calling attention to the ASLA – Illustrations of Work of Members, and photos of work by Caparn.

Philip (Pete) Palmer, for calling to the author's attention the previously unknown blueprint and sketch of the Onteora Park Clubhouse and Theatre.

Edwin Payne, for his generous introduction to work of Caparn in Briarcliff Manor.

Don Penny and Paige Siempelkamp for a warm welcome and house tour in Briarcliff Manor.

Elizabeth Macy Petty of Newburyport, MA and an Onteora Park family for graciously sharing her photos and information on Caparn, the Park and her connections to people there.

Damian Ridealgh, New York and Onteora Park, for preserving and sharing significant Caparn information.

Lynne K. Ranieri, curator of the Millburn-Short Hills Historical Society Museum for access to a map of Short Hills, NJ, including White Oak Ridge Road; especially for bringing to the writer's attention the advertisements by Thomas John and Arthur T. Caparn in The Budget of 1886; for her identification of the East Gate of the J. C. Willever estate, extant in Millburn, NJ.

Richard Sheridan, past president of the Tennessee Valley Historical Society, City Historian of Sheffield, TN, Historic Commission member, editor and contributor to Sheffield History and Recollections, Journal of Muscle Shoals History, Vol. XVIII, for the generous sharing of his research in providing insight to the three villages and the dam, together with early photographs of Village No. 1.

Karen K. Smith, Executive Director, Briarcliff Manor-Scarborough Historical Society for her knowledgeable introduction to the information, places and people that bring life to Briarcliff Manor.

Christian R. Sonne, resident and historian of Tuxedo Park, who shared his affectionate insights on the Park, its people and its architecture, editor of a book on the historic houses of Tuxedo Park.

Madeleine Thompson, Librarian and Archivist, Wildlife Conservation Society, Bronx, NY, for help with questions and documents in the Library.

Cathy Weisman Topol, Author, Research Associate, Department of Education and Child Study, Smith College, for information on the Frank Lyman home; also for directing the author to information on the Lyman estate courtesy the Northampton Historical Society.

Susan Verhoek, Emerita Biology Professor, Lebanon Valley College, Annville, PA, for identification of the plan in the College archive and information on the grounds, including identification of remaining trees in the plan.

David Wakeman, for information on Elizabeth Davis Monod and Frederick Augustus Dwight of Onteora Park.

Michelle Wallach, for identification of the W. J. Tully home and the contribution of a photograph of the rose garden and plaque related to it identifying Caparn as the landscape architect.

Betsy Griggs Wilson for her help and information on the estate of Maitland F. Griggs, Ardsley on Hudson, NY.

Index

About the Author

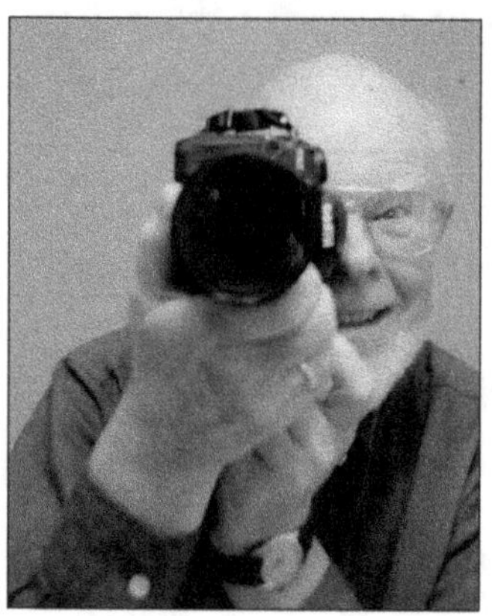

Oliver Chamberlain has published articles on Harold Caparn and on his early employer, J. Wilkinson Elliott and has provided articles and photographs on Caparn and Elliott for "Pioneers," online for The Cultural Landscape Foundation. His entry on Caparn in *Shaping the American Landscape*, University of Virginia Press, provides a basic overview. His book, *Landscapes and Writings of Harold Caparn, 1890-1945*, Infinity Publications, gives a comprehensive view of Caparn's family and his work.

Chamberlain has been a professor and for ten years chair of music history in the Department of Composition and History, College of Musical Arts, Bowling Green State University, Ohio. He was for a decade executive director of the Center for the Arts at the University of Massachusetts Lowell. He is the fifth generation of the Caparn/Chamberlain family to have interest in the art of landscape design and other visual and performing arts. He and his family live on a plot he has designed near Providence, R.I.